Retire Secure

for

Professors

and

TIAA Participants

James Lange
CPA/Attorney

Foreword by:
Burton Malkiel

Professor Emeritus, Princeton University
Author, *A Random Walk Down Wall Street*

Book Cover & Interior by Abrams Design, Pittsburgh, PA

Cartoons by Randy Bish and Michael McParlane

Cover Photo: University of Pittsburgh's Cathedral of Learning, Pittsburgh, PA

Additional Disclaimer Regarding TIAA

TIAA is a registered trademark of Teachers Insurance and Annuity Association of America. This book is not prepared, endorsed, sponsored, or approved by Teachers Insurance and Annuity Association of America.

The author is not and never has been affiliated with, endorsed or sponsored by, or licensed by Teachers Insurance and Annuity Association of America.

Teachers Insurance and Annuity Association of America is not the source or origin of any of the strategies or recommendations described in this book.

The author disclaims any right, title, or interest in the use of any Teachers Insurance and Annuity Association of America trademark or other intellectual property right.

Additional Disclaimer Regarding Lange Financial Group, LLC

Lange Financial Group, LLC is a registered investment advisory firm registered with the Commonwealth of Pennsylvania Department of banking, Harrisburg, Pennsylvania. In addition, the firm is registered as a registered investment advisory firm in the states of Arizona, Florida, New York, Ohio, and Virginia.

Lange Financial Group may not provide investment advisory services to any residents of states in which the firm does not maintain an investment advisory registration. This does not in any way imply that Lange Financial Group is failing to preserve its rights under the respective states' de minimis rule.

The presence of this book shall not in any direct or indirect fashion, be construed or interpreted to suggest that the firm is offering to sell or soliciting to provide investment advisory services to residents of any state or states in which the firm is not maintaining an investment advisory registration.

Again Lange Financial Group preserves all rights under each state's de minimis rule, but wishes to emphasize that it is not directly or indirectly soliciting investment advisory clients in states where it has no legal right to do.

"James Lange has long been my 'go to' for help in understanding the complexities of retirement accounts and explaining them to our viewers. I can't imagine anybody better able to guide professors as they do their retirement planning."

> — **Bill Flanagan**,
> Producer and Host, *Our Region's Business*, WPXI-TV

"Professors need to understand the options as Lange presents them in Chapter 4. Don't leave this analysis up to an advisor since their interests may not match yours."

> — **Dan Keppel**,
> Author of *The New American Retirement System: A $2,000,000 Tax-Free Wealth Reserve*

"The **Retire Secure for Professors** chapter on gifting and spending strategies is an area many investors get wrong—Jim's ideas in this chapter are great advice that I practice in my own life."

> — **Taylor Larimore**,
> Author of *The Bogleheads' Guide to the Three-Fund Portfolio*

"Jim Lange is a master of the subject and has helped thousands of people reach retirement with more money as a result of his sage advice. Jim is my go-to when I have a question regarding complex retirement questions."

> — **John D. Bledsoe, CFP, CLU, ChFC, MSFS, AEP, EIEIO**

"In a world where facts and data are assaulted, **Retire Secure for Professors** is a trusted source of information on which professors can rely. Jim's analysis is like Moneyball for professors' retirement and estate planning."

> — **Nicole L. Maholtz**,
> President and CEO, **Brentmark, Inc.** *(Financial Software)*

"Jim Lange's remarkable and unique book dives right into what retired professors need to know about their finances. He does a very thorough job of making clear the recent changes in tax laws to anyone whose eyes glaze over when hearing elsewhere about the IRS' requirements. He offers straightforward advice about how to preserve your assets for as long as possible, and how to avoid a huge tax burden for your heirs. This is an invaluable tool to educate any academic professional as well as their families."

> — **Carolyn L. Rosenblatt**, Attorney
> Author of *Hidden Truths About Retirement and Long-Term Care*

"Lange Financial Group (and Jim Lange) offers solutions to those professors who've diligently saved their entire careers, all the while unaware of the potential tax bombs they and their heirs may be facing."

— **Adam Yofan**, Wealth Advisor, **Buckingham Strategic Wealth**

"As a former Assistant Professor of Biology in higher education, the approach of *Retire Secure for Professors* who have TIAA and CREF will be warmly welcomed by those in the profession. James Lange provides a roadmap for making the most of your retirement."

— **Jan Cullinane**, Author of *The New Retirement,*
The Single Woman's Guide to Retirement, and *Retire Happy*

"Knowledge is power and the specialized knowledge you acquire when you read and internalize the information in this book can save you a fortune. Get this book, read it, and put these ideas to work. They will save or give you thousands of dollars!"

— **Brian Tracy**, Speaker; Consultant; Author *(80 books in 51 languages)*

"Nationally known IRA expert James Lange presents many little-known income tax and estate planning tips and traps for college and university professors (or anyone else) having a substantial portion of their assets in retirement benefits in an easy-to-understand way."

— **Bruce D. Steiner, Esq.**, Co-Author, CCH's *The Roth Answer Book*

"As a physician, I'm jealous that there is a *Retire Secure* specifically designed for professors but not one for doctors. The entire *Retire Secure* series is the perfect nuts and bolts guide not only to saving for retirement but also to spending from that nest egg in retirement."

— **James M. Dahle, MD**, Founder of **The White Coat Investor**

"Few in the legal or accounting profession have the technical grasp on the complexities of the tax laws as Jim Lange. Fewer still have Jim's ability to distill that labyrinth and morass of information into an intelligible format that is also 'actionable,' i.e., simplified to the point where it is both understandable and can be put to immediate use. As a retired tax law professor, I appreciate, applaud, and highly recommend *Retire Secure for Professors*. This may be the finest investment in your financial future you will ever make!"

— **Stephan R. Leimberg, Esq.**,
Publisher, **Leimberg Information Services, Inc. (LISI)**

"James Lange's book, *Retire Secure for Professors*, is not only relevant to professors but is applicable to a broad audience of IRA and retirement plan owners. Jim's insight and wisdom will be incredibly helpful in understanding the tax law regarding IRAs and retirement planning and is a must for investors and advisors."

— **Robert S. Keebler, CPA/PFS, MST, AEP** *(Distinguished)*

"James Lange's book, *Retire Secure for Professors*, is a must-read for academics and other professionals approaching retirement who have diligently used tax-deferred investment plans to accumulate wealth. The SECURE Act, which went into effect in January 2020, has drastically affected the ability to pass this wealth on to heirs, and limited the benefits of retirement accounts. Mr. Lange points out the pitfalls of the retirement savings options available to employees of educational institutions, and suggests strategies to avoid unexpected tax burdens, achieve a comfortable retirement, mitigate inflation risk, and make sure your beneficiaries receive the fruits of your labor."

— **Martha Maeda,**
Author of *Retire Rich with Your Roth IRA, Roth 401k, and Roth 403b: Investment Strategies for Your Roth IRA*

Table of Contents

Foreword
by Burton G. Malkiel*
Professor Emeritus of Economics, Princeton University

Academics saving for retirement and living off their accumulated savings are urgently in need of sound, unconflicted advice in negotiating the complex set of investment and tax issues that can make the difference between a comfortable and stress-free retirement and a difficult one.

Investment and tax *"experts"* have always been active in offering their services, but their advice has often been designed to maximize their fees rather than to optimize results for their clients. Conflicted and misleading information existed long before the Internet, but social media has vastly increased the scale, severity, and impact of misinformation as digital platforms have extended their reach and become more central to our lives.

Educators have characteristically gravitated to peer reviewed, empirically based material to get information they can trust. But how does one find a trusted source? As a retired college professor, let me assure you that if you follow the sound advice provided by Jim Lange in this book, you will be sure to know that you are taking the right financial steps to increase your and your family's financial security. This book provides exactly the information you can trust.

In my own publications designed for a wide audience, I have tried to distill decades of historical evidence on financial markets to facilitate practical, evidence-based investment decisions. These include broad diversification to contain risk, strategies to minimize costs, and the use of index funds as the primary investment vehicles. Jim Lange builds on these investment concepts to provide serviceable rules for optimal retirement planning and minimization of taxes.

While his advice is applicable for all individuals, the recommendations in this book are specifically tailored for educators who have saved through investment vehicles such as TIAA and CREF. TIAA, a fixed income investment vehicle, has been offered to educators for a century. CREF, a provider of equity funds, has been serving the educational community since 1952. Vanguard funds have more recently become available for academics.

---

* Author of **A Random Walk Down Wall Street**, 50th anniversary edition, 2022. *Note: prior editions sold 1.5 million copies.* Professor Emeritus of Economics, Princeton University.

Chapter 8 provides specific guidance on how to select the best distribution options from TIAA, CREF, and other investment accounts so as to get the most out of the assets you have. In Chapter 9, advice is presented on when allocating a portion of your retirement money to an annuity is appropriate. The pros and cons of alternative strategies are clearly presented, and illustrations from Lange's over 30 years of experience will help readers identify elements that resonate with their own personal situations.

The book is completely up to date. It chronicles the potentially disastrous consequences of the 2020 SECURE Act for owners of well-funded TIAA, IRAs, and other retirement plans. This section of the book should spur action to protect your heirs from the onerous tax consequences that could seriously undermine your efforts to leave your family a bit of a financial legacy. And excellent advice is delivered in Chapter 14 on *The Best Estate Plan for Most Married University Faculty Members and TIAA Investors After the Secure Act*.

Some of the most useful material in the book concerns Roth IRA conversions. I have not seen a better discussion of the advantages and potential pitfalls of converting your IRA into a Roth. In general, there can be enormous value in conversions for both retirement plan owners and their heirs, but the book is very clear on the caution such decisions deserve.

There are many more gems in this book. Guidance is given on charitable giving, family gifting, life insurance, and estate planning strategies. The practical and tested advice that is offered will serve college professors and other educators extremely well. No one does it better and explains it more clearly than Jim Lange.

Introduction

by Larry Swedroe

Author and Chief Research Officer, Buckingham Strategic Wealth

Wouldn't it be good to know you were taking the right financial steps to increase your and your family's financial security? But as a person who believes in science, math, and peer-reviewed materials, where do you go to get information you know you can trust? Not only would the right information apply to large retirement plans of any type, but it would also have to cover the singularities of professors' finances, including knowing and understanding the nuances of TIAA distribution rules to optimize your strategies.

A good and trusted source is in your hands. Reading this book and acting on the recommendations will change your family's financial future by potentially hundreds of thousands of dollars. If you have any doubt about the value of the information, or the credibility of the source, read the testimonials from some of the top trusted experts in the field, including many professors.

Thinking about financial planning might be low on your to-do list. But you still must make critical decisions about your family's finances, and your short- and long-term retirement and estate planning strategies. Your own financial security and that of your spouse and your family are too important to jeopardize.

This book offers professors, and everyone else with a retirement plan, excellent guidance, recommendations, and answers to help you make the most of what you have. In particular, Chapter 8 stands out by offering answers to *One of the Great Mysteries of Life—How Should Professors Access and TIAA Investors Access Their TIAA and CREF Accounts after Retirement?* The chapter spells out the specific distribution options for both TIAA and CREF, and offers options if you are not satisfied with the choices you have already made.

Annuities can be confusing for people to understand. What does the word mean? How does it apply to TIAA and CREF holdings? Should you annuitize? Among other valuable discussions in Chapter 9, Jim offers two mini case studies that illustrate when annuitizing might be a good option and when allocating a portion of your retirement money toward an annuity is appropriate.

One of Jim's strengths is describing the pros and cons of any strategy. His clear narrative, with many examples illustrated through stories drawn from his experience of more than 30 years in the field, allows readers to quickly identify elements that resonate with their own experiences and situations. Jim is a good storyteller, and it elevates this book's readability on topics that can sometimes seem a bit dry.

Jim and his team of respected CPAs and lawyers have devoted countless hours and resources to unearthing and exposing the negative consequences of the 2020 SECURE Act for owners of well-funded TIAA, IRAs, and other retirement plans. This section of the book should spur action to protect your heirs from the onerous taxes that will likely hit them when they are at the peak of their profession and in the highest tax bracket. The tax consequences will seriously undermine your efforts to leave your family a legacy. Jim offers multiple solutions to mitigate the damage.

Some of Jim's excellent advice is delivered in Chapter 14 on *The Best Estate Plan for Most Married University Faculty Members and TIAA Investors After the Secure Act*. When the bulk of your assets are in retirement plans, it is critical to have well-drafted beneficiary designations. His clear-eyed assessment of one of the biggest challenges of estate planning for owners of well-funded retirement plans—the uncertainty inherent in trying to predict the future—offers a clear and compelling argument for the flexibility he has built into what he refers to as Lange's Cascading Beneficiary Plan.

Jim's discussion on Roth IRA conversions is not to be overlooked. He has probably done more research—quantitative and qualitative—on this topic than most professionals in the field. His full dissection of Roth IRA conversions is in another of his books, **The Roth Revolution**, but his abbreviated treatment in this book is illuminating, particularly his strong recommendation to approach Roth IRA conversions with a full understanding of a complete financial masterplan in conjunction with a qualified advisor. Jim sees enormous value in Roth IRA conversions for both retirement plan owners and their heirs, but he approaches them with the caution they deserve.

There are many more important topics in this book—guidance on charitable giving, family gifting, a thorough discussion of asset allocation, life insurance, and more. You will be surprised and inspired by Jim's excellent advice on how *Money Can Buy Happiness*. He obviously puts his clients' best interests first, and he is candid in discussing how he tries to live by the advice he offers.

Jim's practical advice makes this book required reading for professors. Tens or hundreds of thousands of dollars could hang in the balance for you and your family. For anyone approaching retirement or in retirement, you would be wise to take Jim's recommendations to heart and, most importantly, to take action.

How to Read this Book

We do not expect or for that matter even recommend that you read every page of this book unless you have a serious sleep problem. Instead, we would encourage you to look at the detailed Table of Contents (TOC) and read the chapters or even portions of each chapter that grab your attention. We have spent many hours fine tuning the TOC, and we think you will find it an excellent starting point to search for a topic or topics of interest.

Obviously, you will benefit greatly if you read all sections of the book that apply to your situation, and then, either on your own or with some help, act on some of the appropriate recommendations for you and your family.

Be warned, however, that many important decisions are multi-faceted and sometimes an incomplete reading or interpretation of a particular point may lead you to action that you would not take with a full understanding of the topic.

The TOC does a great job of helping you find the information you want. That said, here are few tips that could also save you time and reduce frustration.

Chapter 1 presents an overview of important concepts and a summary of the best order to accumulate money for retirement and the best order to spend money once you are retired. This chapter summarizes much of the content in the book. We highly recommend that as a minimum you read this chapter and the chapters that interest you.

Virtually every chapter contains proof that my recommendations have been mathematically tested and proven worthy. You may want to skip over portions of the proof and just read the advice. Sometimes, when I am looking for information or advice, I want to scream, *"Don't tell me why, just tell me what to do."* If you feel similarly, or you find yourself moving in that direction after realizing there is enormous support for virtually every recommendation I make, the book's sidebars and summaries at the end of the chapters will serve you well.

In addition, we have included many *"war stories"* to illustrate a concept. We know some readers like reading the stories more than the text describing the concepts and the math because it is more interesting and fun. For many of us, reading these war stories is the best way to learn and remember some of the concepts. Others will prefer to skip the stories. We have tried to graphically distinguish the concepts and math from the stories to make it easier for you to read what you like.

I would also encourage you to note separately any thoughts or concepts that you think might be important to your own planning. Then, either on your own or with the help of the appropriate financial professional, take action to improve your and your family's financial position.

If you are a financial professional, I encourage you to make a list of all your professor clients or for that matter all your clients who have substantial IRAs and retirement plans, even before you begin reading the book. As you read and reflect on the various strategies and hypothetical scenarios, you will likely get ideas for ways to personalize those strategies for specific clients. Then you can review the client files for the professors and IRA owners you identified during your reading to get an even better idea of whether those strategies might be beneficial for them. After that, you can schedule meetings with the clients for whom the strategies may be appropriate to discuss incorporating them into their retirement and estate plans.

I have tried to spice up the content by including some true stories (modified for confidentiality), a more than occasional sarcastic comment, at least one witty quote per chapter, and perhaps the most fun, the cartoons. I hope you enjoy them.

I also hope this book inspires you to take action on your retirement planning and that you and your family, and even potentially the charities that you support, will derive enormous benefits from this information. If you are interested in additional information, updates, and other valuable information, please go to **https://Faculty-Advisor.com** and sign up to receive a lot of valuable free information. If you or are interested in working with our firm, please see the section called *Save More, Have More, Leave More! The Lange Edge: A Truly Integrated Long-Term Financial Masterplan* in the back of the book.

Acknowledgments

Though I am listed as the author, the truth is that this book is the product of a monumental team effort. I and the readers who find value in these pages are indebted to a team of the best CPAs, and other professionals I could possibly hope to work with.

This is the finest book my team and I have ever written. Starting with the highly acclaimed third edition of **Retire Secure!** as a base, we made enormous improvements as well as updating much of the analysis.

I have been avoiding updating the third edition of **Retire Secure!** that was published in 2015 because it was so much work. Fortunately, I now have a much stronger and bigger staff of CPAs than I did in 2015. This book is the result of a massive collaboration that I could never have done on my own.

Special thanks to **Larry Swedroe, Chief Research Officer** of **Buckingham Wealth Partners**, for writing the Introduction, and joining my virtual events to answer investment questions.

Jennifer Hall, CPA, CMA, CFP, CRPC, helped by providing many important ideas as well as copy editing. Jen is a real tax nerd, and she added a lot of ideas acquired through a lifetime in the field and her extensive financial education. She also updated many of the calculations that **Shirl Trefelner** and **Steve Kohman** made for prior editions as well as working on new calculations and figures.

Liz Farr, CPA and writer, made extremely valuable contributions and edits. It is rare to find a CPA who can understand complicated tax concepts, let alone write articulately about them. Liz updated many of the seven-year-old chapters of the third edition of **Retire Secure!** which was technically quite difficult. In addition, she made valuable contributions on chapters specifically regarding TIAA.

Matt Schwartz, Esq. worked through some of the fine legal points of the law with me and reviewed the book for technical accuracy.

Shirl Trefelner, CPA, CSRP made major contributions to the *"number crunching"* effort by preparing many of the original graphs and charts in the chapters as well as updating a couple of the figures. She showed a lot of patience working on the book, especially the chapter regarding charitable remainder trusts, while handling her other responsibilities.

Steve Kohman, CPA, CSRP, CSEP and our veteran number cruncher made multiple contributions in the Roth IRA conversion chapter, the IRMAA chapter, and he was the primary author of the qualified charitable distribution chapter.

Special thanks to **Glenn Venturino, CPA** for not only great tax information but also for 35 wonderful years of service that unfortunately just ended when he retired last year.

Diane Markel, CPA, MBA and **BASW** reviewed this book for its technical accuracy.

Karen Mathias, Esq., our in-house Social Security expert, has provided excellent analysis on ways to optimize Social Security and on the advantages of combining Social Security strategies with Roth IRA conversions.

John Montoya, Esq. helped by updating the Inherited IRA minimum distribution chapter (which was a bear) as well as researching and adding valuable contributions to the section on beneficiaries with a disability.

Dominic Bonaccorsi, CPA also reviewed the book for technical accuracy.

Robert Hodson made valuable contributions in terms of content and improved clarity throughout.

Cynthia Nelson, our senior editor for 26 years, is not only a great editor, but her edits don't drown my voice, so my unique personality (and humor, where appropriate) is left intact after her edits. The book is more clear and easier to read in large part due to her valuable editing. Truthfully, she adds much more than an editor and is somewhere between a writer and an editor.

Special thanks go to **Randy Bish** and **Michael McParlane** for the cartoons throughout the book.

Carol Palmer also helped with some of the writing and was the inspiration for many of the cartoons.

Sandy Proto both contributed to the editing and was largely responsible for doing much of the behind the scenes work to make the book a success.

Erika Hubbard helped coordinate and direct the expert consultants and editors who worked on the book, served as a copy editor, and contributed to the content in several sections of the book.

Bryan Tann led the social media coverage of the book.

Eric Emerson led the marketing team efforts of the book.

Susan Abrams of **Abrams Design**, who has been working with us for over 35 years, designed the book's cover and interior and made the figures easier to understand.

Other team members, though not directly involved with the book, allowed me and other team members the luxury of working on the book, and frankly we would not have a company without them. Special thanks to **Alice Davis, Rhonda Round, Daryl Ross, Donna Master, Erin Einwag, Justin Pape, Mary Naeser, Rachael Waltonbaugh**, and **Sue Jeffries** for all your contributions.

Finally, though many of the team members mentioned above have been with me for almost 20 years, special recognition goes to **Glenn Venturino, CPA, Sandy Proto, Project Manager**, and **Steve Kohman, CPA, CSRP, CSEP**, who have been working with me for close to 30 years or more.

To matters of the heart, a special thanks to my wife and best friend, **Cindy**, and my daughter, **Erica**. Cindy is probably the only woman alive who could put up with being married to me. She made major edits in previous editions and edits in this edition also. Erica gave me permission to share that she has a disability and how we provided for her in the hope that this book will help readers better provide for their children with a disability. This book would never have happened without Cindy's and Erica's love and support.

Thank you all.

Special Note from the Author Regarding Client Confidentiality

I am the son of a journalism professor who had high journalistic integrity. She was a great fan of Walter Cronkite and before that Ed Murrow. I would love to say that all the client stories I include in the book are completely accurate. Unfortunately, if I reported actual client situations, it would be a violation of confidentiality which I place even above journalistic accuracy. Therefore, though the stories included were all inspired by actual events, I attempted to change the details enough to make them unidentifiable from the actual clients and events that inspired the stories.

SECURE Act 2.0

As we go to press, SECURE Act 2.0 has passed. The 90 provisions included in the bill provide incentives for both employees and employers.

In March, the House of Representatives passed a version of the bill, known as the SECURE Act 2.0. The Senate Finance Committee proposed a more expansive version later in 2022, known as the EARN Act. While neither bill passed, SECURE 2.0 reflects what was agreed to by both parties in December 2022.

The bi-partisan goal of the bill was to increase retirement savings through employer-sponsored plans and IRAs.

There are notable changes included in SECURE Act 2.0 which encompass 4,100 pages. Below is a snapshot of the "key" highlights that may impact your future retirement. Note: We have not included all the provisions of the bill—rather, we only included those provisions that we feel will have the most impact on our clients and their future retirement. These changes will affect your overall retirement planning.

We were surprised the legislation did not include any provisions to eliminate back-door Roth conversions and mega back-door Roth conversions, nor did it place more restrictive limits on Roth contributions. Earlier in the year, we were led to believe these Roth conversion/contribution strategies would be restricted.

It is also important to note that many of the provisions outlined below will require the employer to make plan amendments and/or modify their procedures to accommodate these changes. Therefore, it may be a while before some of these changes are implemented. The effective dates of the provisions vary between the passage of the SECURE Act 2.0 up to year 2028.

Please see the provisions below we thought were most important to our readers.

Employer Matching Contributions

Optional Roth Treatment vs. Pre-Tax Treatment: This is an important change and not thoroughly covered in this book. Effective in 2023, employers can now allow the employer match to go into a Roth account for 401(k)/403(b)/457(b) plans. The employee will be taxed on the contribution, and the match will be immediately vested.

This is an optional provision, and the employer plan must be amended to allow these types of contributions.

Required Minimum Distributions (RMDs)

Increased Age for RMDs: Currently, the age for RMDs is 72 (previously, the RMD age was 70½ before the SECURE Act was passed). Now, beginning on January 1, 2023, the age is 73, and by year 2033, the RMD is increased to age 75. We will now have an extra three years for additional planning considerations, including accelerating more Roth conversions and/or smoothing out Roth conversions over a period of time to lower IRMAA charges, net investment income taxes, and possibly, capital gains tax brackets.

Surviving Spouse: In 2024, a surviving spouse inheriting a retirement account will be treated as the deceased account holder for RMD purposes. If the surviving spouse is younger than their deceased spouse, they may be able to delay RMDs.

RMDs on Roth 401(k)s Eliminated: While you do not have to take RMDs on a Roth IRA, before SECURE Act 2.0, you had to take a RMD on a Roth employer plan. With SECURE Act 2.0, you no longer must take an RMD beginning in years 2024. Prior to SECURE Act 2.0, employees would roll their Roth 401(k) into a Roth IRA to avoid the RMD rules. With the passage of SECURE Act 2.0, they no longer must employ this strategy. By keeping their money in the 401(k)/403(b) Plan, the employee is provided with greater asset protection, as the employer sponsored plans are subject to ERISA rules and provide the best asset protection.

Increased Roth Contribution Opportunities

Roth SIMPLE and SEP IRAs: Roth contributions to SIMPLE and SEP IRAs are now permitted beginning in year 2023.

Catch-Up Contributions for High Income Earners: For employees earning $145,000 or more, their catch-up contributions will no longer be allowed to be tax-deferred. Instead, they will have to be in the form of Roth contributions beginning in 2024. This means these contributions will not be in the form of pre-tax dollars and will be subject to income taxes. Note: This does not affect catch-up contributions to IRAs (including SIMPLE IRAs). If the employer does not have a *"Roth"* feature in their employer-sponsored plan, then no employees will be permitted to make catch-up contributions.

Transfers from 529 Plans to Roth IRAs: Effective in 2024, a tax and penalty-free rollover from a 529 plan to Roth IRAs will be permitted under certain circumstances. Beneficiaries of 529 plans will be permitted to roll over up to $35,000 over the course of their lifetime from their 529 plan account in their name to their Roth IRA. The rollovers are subject to Roth IRA annual contributions limits, and the 529 plan account must have been established for more than 15 years. Note: The rollover contribution from the 529 plan to the Roth IRA replaces the Roth IRA contribution. It is not an addition to the Roth IRA contribution.

Increase in Catch-Up Limits

The retirement plan contribution limit is increased for those age 50 or older. For 2023, the catch-up contribution limit amount is limited to $7,500 and is indexed for inflation.

SECURE Act 2.0 provides a second layer increase in the contribution amount for those age 60, 61, 62, or 63, effective in tax years 2025. The *"second"* catch-up limitation is $10,000 for 401(k)/403(b) plans, and $5,000 for SIMPLE plans. These limits are also subject to inflation adjustments. This provision will dovetail with the provision above for employees earning more than $145,000 wherein the catch-up contribution will need to be in the form of a Roth contribution providing greater opportunity to contribute to their Roth 401(k)/403(b) account.

For participants of IRAs age 50 and older, the catch-up limit is $1,000. Under current law, the catch-up limit is not subject to increases for inflation. The current bill makes the IRA catch-up amount adjusted annually for inflation adjustments for years 2024 and thereafter.

Modification of Age Requirement for Qualified ABLE Plans

Previously, the disabled person had to be disabled before age 26 to have an ABLE account established; now, the disability must have begun before age 46 to qualify for an ABLE account effective in year 2026.

Disabled Beneficiaries and Special Needs Trusts

Charity as Remainder Beneficiary: Effective in 2023, a Special Needs Trust can now name a charity as the remainder beneficiary of the Special Needs Trust.

Penalty Reductions

RMD Penalty: The RMD penalty was 50% of what you should have withdrawn but did not prior to SECURE Act 2.0. Now, the penalty is reduced to 25% starting in 2023. Also, if you correct your distribution in a timely manner, the penalty is reduced to 10%.

Corrective Distributions of Excess IRA Contributions: No longer subject to the 10% excise penalty on excess contributions and the earnings on the contributions.

Statute of Limitations for Excise Tax on Excess Contributions and Accumulations: The statute of limitations for assessing the penalty for a missed or reduced RMD is three years. The statute of limitations for assessing the penalty for excess contributions is six years.

Penalty-free Distributions: Penalty-free distributions are permitted for *"unforeseeable or immediate financial needs relating to necessary personal or family emergency expenses"* up to $1,000. However, only one distribution may be made every three years or one per year if the distribution is repaid within three years. This provision is effective for distributions made in 2024 or later.

Withdrawals for Domestic Abuse: Effective after the passing of the SECURE Act 2.0 allows retirement plans to permit participants that self-certify that they have experienced domestic abuse to withdraw 50% of the account balance up to $10,000, indexed for inflation.

A distribution made under this section is not subject to the 10% excise penalty tax on early withdrawal distributions. Also, the participant has the opportunity to repay the withdrawn money over a period of three years and will be refunded the income taxes on the money that is repaid. This section is effective for distributions made in 2024.

Withdrawals for Terminal Illness: Effective after the passing of the SECURE Act 2.0, those individuals with a terminal illness will no longer be subject to the 10% early withdrawal penalty rules. The employee is considered terminally ill if they have been certified by a physician as having an illness or physical condition which can be reasonably be expected to result in death within 84 months. The distributions can be repaid within three years.

Withdrawals for Qualified Federally Declared Disasters: One can withdraw up to $22,000 from their retirement plan penalty-free in the event of a federal disaster. Taxes on the withdrawal can be spread over three years. The money can also be repaid into the retirement plan account. This change is retroactive to 1/26/21.

Withdrawals to Purchase Long-Term Care Contracts: Effective in years 2026, one can withdraw the lesser of 10% of their vested account balance up to $2,500/year to pay for long-term care premiums without paying the 10% early withdrawal penalty.

Age 50 Exception Expanded to Include Firefighters, Correction Officers, and Public Safety Workers with 25 or More Years of Service: Allows these employee groups to take penalty-free distributions at age 50.

Withdrawals for Hardship Distributions: Employers may rely on employee certifying that the hardship distributions conditions have been met.

Mandatory Automatic Enrollment

Effective in 2025, new 401(k) and 403(b) plans must automatically enroll eligible employees. Automatic deferrals start between 3% and 10% of compensation, increasing by 1% per year, to a maximum of at least 10% (no more than 15% of compensation). Note: This provision does not apply to current 401(k) and 401(b) plans.

Savers Credit: The Savers Credit is now a Savers Match into the retirement account *vs.* a deduction. It can be as much as a 50% match on the first $2,000 contributed. It is for low-income earners and begins in 2027.

Emergency Savings: Employers can add an emergency savings account that is a designated Roth account eligible to accept participant contributions beginning in 2024. Contributions are limited to $2,500/year and the first four withdrawals per year would be tax and penalty-free. Contributions may be eligible for an employer match as defined by the plan rules. The purpose of the emergency savings fund is to encourage employees to save for short-term and unexpected expenses.

Qualified Charitable Distributions (QCDs): The previous limit for QCDs was $100,000, but now with SECURE Act 2.0, they are indexed for inflation. In addition, you can make a one-time charitable distribution of $50,000 to a Charitable Remainder Trust (CRAT/CRUT) or a charitable gift annuity beginning in 2023 if you are age 70½ or older. This is an expansion of the type of charity that can receive a QCD.

Qualifying Longevity Annuity Contracts (QLACs): Effective for contracts purchased or exchanged in 2023 or later, up to $200,000 can be placed into a QLAC. Previously, only 25% of the qualified plan up to $145,000 could be placed into a QLAC. Also, there is a 90-day *"free look"* period that may be offered.

Employer Matching of Student Loan Repayments: Effective in 2024, employers have the option to match student loan repayments as if the student loan repayments were employee deferrals. This applies to 401(k)s, 403(b)s, SIMPLE, and 457(b)s.

Improving Coverage for Part-Time Workers: Prior to SECURE Act 2.0, part-time works needed to have at least 1,000 hours of service in a 12-month period or 500 service hours in a three consecutive year period to participate in the employer's qualified retirement plan. SECURE 2.0 reduces the three-year period to two years for plan years beginning in 2025.

De Minimus Incentives for Participation are Permitted: Employers may offer de minimus financial incentives to increase participation in retirement plans, such as gift cards. The financial incentives cannot be purchased with plan assets, however.

Creation of National Online Searchable Database: SECURE Act 2.0 creates a national database to assist employees to locate missing retirement plan assets. The database must be established within two years of the passing the SECURE Act 2.0.

A Note to TIAA Participants
Who Are Not Professors

Throughout the book, when I refer to the retirement plan owner, I usually use the word *"professor"* rather than *"professor and/or TIAA participants and/or IRA owners."* That is partially a matter of convenience and brevity but also because I wrote the original material specifically for professors. But as the book evolved, it became clear that our recommendations would be advantageous for the much broader audience of all TIAA participants. Our recommendations for the distribution options of your TIAA alone in Chapter 8 could make an enormous difference in the lives of TIAA participants from the *"financially comfortable but concerned"* column to the *"comfortable and secure"* column! So, as you are reading, please make the simple mental substitution of *"TIAA participant"* or *"IRA owner"* for *"professors."*

I believe this is my best material and extremely valuable for not only professors, but also TIAA participants. I also think most of it is valuable for all IRA and retirement plan owners.

I think there might be a psychological affinity among TIAA participants that I am acutely familiar with through my client work with professors and because both my mother and brother were professors. For example, most TIAA participants are working for a nonprofit—even doctors and most people didn't enter the nonprofit world to make the most money. So, in that respect, many TIAA participants are similar to professors—they are following their hearts while still trying to earn a decent living. It is hardly like they don't care about money—that is probably why you picked up this book—managing your retirement investments wisely will allow you to continue to do what you love to do with the confidence that once you retire, you will still be able to do the things you love.

There might be at least one other similarity. Many professors do not enjoy thinking about managing money and investments. It takes valuable time away from what they want to be doing. So, getting help and devising a long-term plan that can run on autopilot (with annual or biannual meetings) can seem appealing. This book offers detailed and critical guidance on many of the issues and concerns that you should be thinking about. For the *"died in the wool"* do-it-yourselfers, we hope this book is a great resource for you.

For a reader who can picture some of the enormous benefits of getting these strategies right and for someone who is happy to delegate that as well as investment services, this book can give you a cheat sheet for the qualities you should be looking for in an advisor and/or money manager. It can help you cull the not-so-good advisors (think selling products that they profit from) from true fiduciaries who put your best interests ahead of theirs. Needless to say, my team of professionals fall into the true fiduciary category, and you will find many references to our services throughout the book. There is more information on how you could potentially work with us at the back of the book.

I hope this book helps you find your path to a secure retirement.

With your best interests at heart,

James Lange
CPA/Attorney

Preamble:

My Journey to Working So Extensively with University Faculty—*632 of You to Be Exact!*

I didn't set out to become an expert in helping professors get the most out of their TIAA and CREF accounts, IRAs, and other retirement assets. Although my mother, brother, and many friends were university faculty members, I didn't make a conscious decision to orient my business toward providing guidance for professor's retirement and estate planning.

What actually happened was a bit more Mr. Magoo-like (for those who might not remember, he was the near-sighted cartoon character who bumbled and stumbled his way to success). Or, to put a more generous spin on my career path, I made some key decisions at opportune times that worked out well.

My Early Beginnings with Professors

In 1982, I was working my way through law school as a CPA working for Arthur Anderson, then a top national CPA firm, and also preparing tax returns *"on the side"*. I was talking to a fellow table tennis player named Art Tuden. Art taught anthropology at the University of Pittsburgh. He was complaining that he and his wife Agnes could not find a CPA who understood the tax complications of a university faculty lifestyle—sabbaticals, conference travel, consulting, professional associations, professional libraries, home offices, etc.

Anyway, I told him I would be happy to meet with his wife, Agnes (she handled the finances). To make a long story short, she was extremely pleased with how I handled all the complications on their tax return. Luckily for me, Art was a gregarious fellow, and within a year many of the members of the Anthropology Department of University of Pittsburgh became income-tax preparation clients. Of course, the more returns I did, the more of a tax expert I became in areas unique to faculty members. The word spread, and it wasn't too long before I found myself with hundreds of university faculty income-tax preparation clients.

While working my way through the evening division of Duquesne University School of Law while working as a CPA during the day. I took as many tax and estate planning courses as I could fit in my schedule.

In addition to my side CPA income tax preparation business, I worked in Arthur Andersen's tax department. Later, I joined the tax department of a top law firm in Pittsburgh, Buchanan Ingersoll, now Buchanan Ingersoll & Rooney. All the while, my tax preparation *"on-the-side"* business kept growing. After I graduated from law school, I knew I didn't want to become a corporate lawyer.

As a seasoned CPA who loved saving people money on taxes and a new attorney, I decided to expand my on-the-side CPA practice and establish my own estate planning law firm.

For most professors, particularly the older ones, their retirement plans, typically invested with TIAA and CREF were the largest assets in their estate. Money held in retirement accounts is known as *"qualified money,"* i.e., money in a retirement account that is protected from creditors by the Employee Retirement Income Security Act (ERISA).

By far, most qualified money is contributed on a pre-tax basis, rather than after-tax basis. But unless it is left to charity, eventually, someday, someone will pay income tax on that money. So now that I had all these *"retirement plan heavy"* university faculty income-tax-preparation clients, the next issue was, how could I develop the expertise to properly prepare their estate plans? How could I provide them pro-active strategic advice that CPAs don't typically provide?

In the beginning, while I certainly had clients from Carnegie Mellon University and other universities in the Pittsburgh area, the majority of my professor clients were from the University of Pittsburgh. The University of Pittsburgh has a generous matching system. Subject to exceptions and starting periods, if you contribute 8% of your salary to your retirement plan, the university contributes 12%. Even with a relatively modest salary, if 20% of your pay grows income-tax deferred for 20, 30, or 40 years, which leads to a significant accumulation.

The good news was that there were a lot of faculty members with very significant retirement plans. The bad news was a lot of faculty members and their families were going to be saddled with enormous tax liabilities, both while they were alive and after they were gone, unless they planned appropriately. That's where I came in.

By necessity, to provide the highest value to my professor clients, I had to become an expert in two areas: (1) planning for individuals with significant assets in retirement plans and (2) understanding the unique nuances of TIAA and CREF.

The best technical book on IRAs and retirement plans at the time was, and probably still is Natalie Choate's, *Life and Death Planning for Retirement Benefits*. Many practitioners use it as a reference manual. Since I was interested in really understanding the concepts and minutiae, I read the book cover to cover.

I read much of the existing IRA and retirement plan literature. Most of it was too general for me. I wanted specific strategies that given certain assumptions would produce more money and less taxes for IRA and retirement plan owners. I wanted to make data driven recommendations based on hard, reproducible calculations. So, I started "running the numbers" which is our shorthand for mathematically comparing the long-term results of different retirement and estate planning strategies for TIAA-CREF, IRAs, and other retirement plan assets.

What intrigued me the most were the dramatic differences in results among the different strategies I was testing. Examples of these dramatic differences between particular strategies appear throughout the book. We even include the assumptions for anyone who wants to attempt to reproduce the results.

As I began to understand the implications of the best ways to plan for individuals with substantial IRAs and retirement plans, I began to formulate what I call *"the bedrock principles"* which are summarized in Chapter 1. In the 1990s, I started publishing articles in peer-reviewed retirement and estate planning journals for IRAs and retirement plan owners and advisors. I also began presenting workshops for IRA and retirement plan owners and specialized workshops for university faculty.

Then in 1998, I published the first peer-reviewed article on Roth IRA conversions in the country which won article of the year in *The Tax Adviser*. *The Tax Adviser* is a monthly publication produced by the American Institute of CPAs, providing tax practitioners with comprehensive information on current planning, trends, and techniques. My plans and my involvement with university faculty have grown over the years. Today, we have 632 university faculty members as clients.

Why I Value Working with University Professors

I feel a certain affinity for the *"intellectual crowd,"* since I come from a family of faculty members (my mother and my brother).

Furthermore, many professors recognize the advantages of working with a financial team consisting of number-crunching CPAs, and money managers who are all familiar with TIAA. They recognize they have unique financial planning opportunities and pitfalls—even if they do not know what they are—and that it makes sense to seek out an experienced team to help them with their planning.

But there are other significant non-tangible factors to weigh when advising faculty members on their retirement planning. Something I have learned over the years is that professors frequently bring a different set of values to their thinking about retirement, especially when it comes to determining how long to keep working. Many professors retire *"when it is time for them to go,"* or at a logical time in the arc of their career without considering finances.

Professors speak to me about feeling useful, whether they believe they are still actively contributing to their field of study, whether they still have graduate students to shepherd through the PhD program—frequently, money isn't the primary focus. In one case, a professor wasn't enjoying his work anymore and had more than enough money to retire. His wife desperately wanted him to retire. But he wouldn't retire until that last graduate student he took on achieved his PhD. When I mention that to other professors, they took his dedication to his last graduate student as standard saying, *"Of course, you can't leave your graduate student hanging."*

Another professor could have taken an early retirement, but he didn't know what was going to happen to his professional library. It was his life's work. If he took an early retirement, he would have to move his library, and he didn't have a place to put it, and he could not find a place for it, at least in the short run. In the middle of dealing with Covid, the University didn't have time to plan for his library. For this professor, the future of his library had to be determined before he could retire, so he kept working.

I believe one of the most significant contributions I provide for my faculty clients is letting them know exactly where they stand with their finances. I like to give people options. For example, if you're happy spending $70,000 per year and have three million bucks in your retirement plan, then it may be obvious that continuing to work is optional. But usually, it is less clear. The other detail I like to work out is how much a professor can safely spend in retirement and never run out of money.

Another client comes to mind. We went over the numbers, and she learned that she could retire tomorrow and live quite comfortably for the rest of her life. Of course, this was great news. But her response, which I loved, was, *"I'm not going to quit tomorrow, but I'm not going to take any s*** from the chair anymore."* She's still working, but on her own terms.

Sometimes professors have no idea where they stand financially. It was liberating for this client to learn that her ability to live comfortably for the rest of her life was not dependent on continuing to work. So, work became optional, and she turned her job into something she enjoyed even more. Decisions about retiring early or continuing to work—assuming money is not an issue—are highly personal. And it's good to give professors options.

Another story involves a professor who was working hard, doing okay financially, but nowhere near having the finances to retire. His parents died, and he came into a large inheritance. He made the offhand comment, "What I'd really like to do is retire and live by the beach." I naively said, "Well, why don't you just do that?" He said, "No, because, well, I could not work down there, and I could never afford to buy a place on the beach and retire." And I was like, "Yeah, you can." He didn't believe me. So, we went through the numbers. I proved to him that, yes, you can retire.

I'm not going to tell you that I don't get excited about optimizing a series of Roth IRA conversions, developing a great estate plan, coming up with the best plan for distributing TIAA and CREF plans or saving a family several hundred thousand dollars in taxes. All of that is fun, satisfying and intellectually rewarding. But when you really change somebody's life—going from unhappy teaching to happy looking out on the ocean every day—that provides a different type of satisfaction.

It is especially gratifying in helping provide for their family and the obvious relief they get knowing that have taken the appropriate steps to provide for their family. For parents of a child with a disability like me, our almost consuming worry is providing and caring for our child both while we are alive and after we are gone. Helping parents of children with a disability is also quite meaningful.

Appreciating the Value of Data

Another trait that professors display is being data driven. If I show a professor on a spreadsheet, how and why what I'm suggesting is significantly better than the status quo, most, even the more stubborn *"know-it-all"* professors will consider the data. Professors are more open-minded than the general population to ideas that are not originally theirs. (Though I know some of you are thinking about some of your colleagues and questioning how I could possibly think that!)

But being data-driven is a very good trait. It also makes my life a lot more pleasant because in our *"what if"* scenarios, when our CPAs *"run the numbers"* (which is our shorthand term for completely analyzing finances over the long-term), we frequently see how different decisions can lead to monumentally different outcomes. Not just from a tax standpoint, but on how long you work, the way you think about work, how much you can afford to spend, how much you can afford to travel, buying a second home, etc. Then we combine different strategies like Roth IRA conversions, gifting, and optimizing Social Security, etc. to develop a unique long-term Financial Masterplan.

A secondary goal in writing this book is to increase your happiness by showing you that you likely can afford to spend more money than you currently spend, and that certain expenditures can dramatically increase happiness levels. I recognize most professors' reaction to a suggestion that they should consider increasing their spending with an emphatic *"No,"* but I urge you to keep an open mind and hear me out when you get to those chapters.

I was meeting with a professor who had a number of significant health problems that required a number of specialists. He expressed dissatisfaction with his medical treatment and how little time his PCP, presumably the doctor managing the team of specialists, could spend with him. I dared to suggest he consider joining a concierge medical practice. He immediately said, *"No way!"* as he was holding his back grimacing in pain. I don't know if it was back pain caused by his condition or the pain of thinking about spending more money.

Changing Retirement Plan Options

When my mother was forced to retire 35 years ago at age 70, there were very few options for accessing her retirement funds within TIAA and CREF. To oversimplify, the only real option for her was, *"Which type of a lifetime annuity would you like, Dr. Lange?"* There certainly may have been other options for other TIAA-CREF participants at the time, but not with her university. Well, since she had basically no choice, she accepted the income stream. She didn't have a lot of money, but her annuity, combined with Social Security, and with the payments that she received from me because I bought our family home, granted comfortable financial independence for her until her death at age 95.

Times have changed. There are so many more options today. It is also preferable to develop a plan and make these decisions before you decide to retire. On the other hand, most of us are in a *"clean up"* mode meaning however we got here, including having made a number of big mistakes, we are here now, and the question is *"What should I do now?"*

My Evolving Businesses

Establishing Lange Financial Group, LLC, and moving into money management was the next step in my evolution. We work with money managers, each with their own unique value-added services, and they oversee and manage the actual investing. We split the fees with them. Clients get the benefit of our strategies, which are updated on an annual basis, and a great money manager who adds their own value-added services. We also have a pure fee for service model, though as we get busier and busier, we may have to phase that service out.

Some professors handle a few functions themselves, such as preparing their own tax returns. That's fine with us. Many manage their own finances, or they work with an advisor who may not know the nuances of TIAA or many of the other strategies we recommend. Some even do their own wills. But many of them also realize that just like it's not wise to pack your own parachute, there are certain situations in which it pays to find and hire the appropriate experts to give you guidance. We find that professors who didn't pay a lot of attention to their finances during their careers don't magically change after retirement.

This is particularly true of professors who find better uses for their time than worrying about the nuances of managing their money and all the accompanying strategic decisions that have enormous opportunities. like Roth IRA conversions and appropriate estate planning as well as wanting to avoid the many pitfalls pertaining to retirement and estate planning.

My favorite clients were, and still are, university faculty members. But early on it was hard to write materials and be published if my sole focus was on university faculty. There was a huge demand for the kind of information that I had, not just for university faculty members, but for a more encompassing audience of IRA and retirement owners—and the myriad plans available to them.

My Publishing History

So, to make a long story short, I've written eight best-selling books covering many aspects of retirement and estate planning—everything from IRAs and retirement plans to Roth IRAs and Social Security, but not written specifically for university faculty. I have also been quoted 36 times in The Wall Street Journal.

I wrote three editions of a book called **Retire Secure!** The first two editions were published by Wiley, and I self-published the third edition in 2015. Though this book is called **Retire Secure for Professors**, there are major differences between the last edition of **Retire Secure!** The most obvious is the intended audience. This book is intended for professors and those in academia, even thought it would be of great value to any IRA or retirement plan owner.

Many professors have a different mindset regarding money and career than those outside academia. In addition, there are significant and unique aspects of TIAA that apply to many, if not most professors. In addition, there have been massive tax changes since the prior version of **Retire Secure!** and this book covers those changes in detail.

Finally, we have added two specialty chapters. One new chapter to the **Retire Secure!** series covers how to protect a beneficiary with a disability or chronic illness. This area has a special place in my heart because my daughter has a disability. As a parent with a child with a disability and someone who implemented a plan that will allow our daughter to be $1.8 million dollars in today's dollars than if we didn't do an appropriate plan, this is obviously a passion for me.

If you have or know of someone with a child with a disability, that is a critical chapter. A second new chapter is on point for unmarried partners, gay or straight.

That said, non-professors could easily skip certain chapters and still get enormous value from the book. For example, I will send a printed copy of this book to all my assets under management clients whether they are professors or not.

My most recent book before this book, **The IRA and Retirement Plan Owner's Guide to Beating the New Death Tax**, was specifically geared towards IRA and retirement plan owners who, like you, have been targeted by Congress to pay an outrageous amount of taxes after you die.

I believe it is essential that you develop an estate plan to dramatically reduce your taxes. That book was a smashing success. It ranked number one in multiple categories on Amazon when it was released.

Why I Wrote This Book

One of my long-term goals has been to write the best book on retirement and estate planning for university faculty. This book is the culmination of that goal. It combines some of the unique aspects of being a university professor with specific consideration of TIAA and CREF and a lot of the cutting-edge techniques that I developed for IRA and retirement plan owners.

One of my editors commented, *"Gee, Jim. There's a bunch of chapters in this book that look very much like your previous book that was written for a general IRA and retirement plan audience, not just college professors."* And I said, *"That's right, because those chapters are also extremely important for professors."*

In this book, I've also included chapters that are unique to professors. I also tried to write in *"professor-ese."* Everybody else talks about IRAs and 401(k)s. I talk to professors about 403(b)s, TIAA, and CREF.

But I've tried to address the common concerns of all IRA and retirement plan owners, as well as offering unique ideas and information specifically geared towards professors.

I'll freely admit that as much as I want to help professors get the most out of their TIAA and CREF accounts and other retirement plans, both while they're alive and after they're gone, I also have a business motivation to write the book. There are professors out there looking in vain for the types of integrated and specialized services we offer.

Many professors now attempt to deal with complex financial issues on their own or try to explain to their existing advisor some of the unique features that I address in this book. They deal with separate CPAs and financial advisors none of whom talk with each other. Frankly, for many professors it makes a lot more sense to do business with the person who wrote the book, and whose office includes number-crunching CPAs concentrating in qualified retirement plans including TIAA. We also work hand in hand with investment experts who provide their own value-added benefits.

Therefore, I will apologize in advance if you're turned off by some of the obvious self-serving plugs for service offers made throughout the book.

The letter at the end of the book called *Save More, Have More, Leave More! The Lange Edge: A Truly Integrated Long Term Financial Masterplan* discusses the possibility of working with some combination of our accounting firm, our investment advisory firm, and our affiliated investment firms. I am not reluctant to market the value I can bring to professors and their families. If you are interested in pursuing the possibility of working with me and/or our firm, please read that section to learn more about the services we offer and how you could potentially take advantage of a free consultation with me.

I'll also say that there is an ulterior motive in wanting more college/university professors as clients. I like professors. They seem to like working with me and our team. We have an affinity. Selfishly, I enjoy meeting and talking with my professor clients—they are generally an interesting group, even after they retire. I prefer spending my time serving people I like and for whom I believe our strategies and services can provide the most benefit. So, there are multiple pitches for doing business with our firm in this book.

But I believe our model is a win-win-win. Meaning, it is a win for our affiliated money managers, a win for me and my firm, and the biggest winner is the professors and their families we serve.

We bought and distributed 50,000 KN-95 masks to different charities and non-profits, family, friends, clients, and employees.

I hope you find this book helpful and instructional. As always, if you want help in getting the most out of what you've got, please see a description of our services in the back of the book. I also highly encourage you to go to **https://Faculty-Advisor.com** for valuable additional information, the upcoming schedule for new webinars, as well as viewing a video of a presentation I made for professors.

Then, whether it is with us, other trusted advisors, or on your own, please take action on what you learn to protect yourself and your family from massive taxation.

Respectfully submitted,

James Lange
CPA/Attorney

1

The Bedrock Principles of Retirement and Estate Planning

"Anyone may arrange his affairs so that his taxes shall be as low as possible; he is not bound to choose that pattern which best pays the treasury. There is not even a patriotic duty to increase one's taxes."

— Judge Learned Hand

We know that many readers don't make it past the first chapter, so we loaded this chapter with some of our most important recommendations for both workers and retirees. If you don't read anything else in this book, please read this chapter. We also encourage you to scan our detailed table of contents and read other relevant chapters or sections. Spending a little time learning the bedrock principles of retirement and estate planning is critical. You will understand the reasoning behind our recommendations and are more likely to implement changes. The difference between the status quo and implementation of optimal strategies could be life changing for you and your family.

Pay Taxes Later—Except for Roths

Don't pay taxes now; pay taxes later, except for the Roth IRA. These words, subject to exceptions, represent the *bedrock* principles of tax planning for accumulating and distributing wealth. It is critical in the accumulation stage when you are saving for retirement. It is essential in the distribution stage when you are withdrawing money from your portfolio after you retire. And in the estate-planning stage, it can dramatically improve the financial lives of your heirs.

The SECURE Act radically modified Required Minimum Distribution (RMD) rules for Inherited IRAs, inherited TIAA-CREF accounts and other retirement accounts. The new rules force your heirs to pay taxes at a significantly accelerated rate (in contrast to the previous *"stretch IRA"* rules). In other words, the new rules require your heirs to pay taxes sooner. That is a major problem for professors.

For many faculty members, your IRAs, TIAA, and other retirement accounts hold the bulk of your wealth, so planning for the distribution of your retirement accounts, both while you are alive and after you are gone, is critically important.

1

In addition, you likely have additional complications if those funds are held in Traditional TIAA accounts.

I did say *"Pay Taxes Later, except for a Roth IRA and by extension Roth retirement plan options and Roth conversions."* We devote four entire chapters to address Roth IRA conversions in this book. In addition, Roth IRA conversion strategies are mentioned many times throughout the book. It is one of the best defenses that a university faculty member can use to combat the devastation of the SECURE Act. For more on this, please see Chapters 15 and 16.

This book likely has all the information about Roth IRAs and Roth IRA conversions that you will ever want. That said, there is additional information comparing Roth IRAs, Roth 401(k)s, and Roth 403(b)s to Traditional retirement accounts, and the related issues of Roth IRA conversions.

If interested, please go to **https://PayTaxesLater.com/Books/**. There, you can download a free copy of one of our best-selling books, ***The Roth Revolution: Pay Taxes Once and Never Again***. If you are interested in Roth IRAs and Roth IRA conversions—and you probably should be—please read at least the Roth IRA chapters in this book. If you want to take it a step further, please read at least Chapter 1 of ***The Roth Revolution***. You can also get a printed copy by requesting it from our office (contact information is included in the back of the book) or by purchasing a copy from your favorite book seller.

In this chapter, I'll give you an overview of the principles of ensuring a secure retirement, which I will elaborate on in following chapters. For those of you who want to delve into more detail will find the full story in other chapters.

The Accumulation Years: Saving for Retirement While Working

First the conclusion, then the analysis.

Let's assume you have a certain amount of money that you can afford to contribute for your retirement. What is the best hierarchy for contributing to the different types of retirement plans available to you?

Subject to exception:

1. Take advantage of any employer match.
2. Take advantage of a Health Savings Account (HSAs), if available to you.
3. Contribute to Roth IRAs and back-door Roth IRAs.
4. Contribute to Traditional retirement plans or IRAs.
5. Contribute to nondeductible IRAs or nondeductible contributions to a retirement plan.

6. Save money in a plain old after-tax brokerage account.

Make no bones about it: the cardinal rule of saving for retirement is taking advantage of employer-matching contributions to any retirement plan. Most universities and many hospitals, non-profits, governments and museums offer matching contributions, but some offer a percentage of your salary regardless of whether you contribute to the plan. So, if your employer has a retirement plan and an employer match is available to you, make sure you are (1) participating in that plan and (2) contributing at least enough to take full advantage of the match. It's like free money!

For example, after a three-year waiting period, if a University of Pittsburgh faculty member contributes 8% of their salary to their retirement plan, the university adds another 12%. That's a 150% return on your money on day one, and that doesn't include the enormous tax benefits. Even if your employer matches "only" on a dollar-for-dollar basis, it is the same as a *100% return on your investment in one day.*

The money in your retirement plan grows either tax-deferred, as in a traditional IRA or 403(b), or tax-free in a Roth IRA or Roth 403(b). Most universities allow you the option to direct your own contributions to a Traditional or Roth account. However, even if you direct your own contributions to a Roth account, your employer's matching contribution used to always go into a Traditional account. Recent legislation has changed this and allows you to direct an employer's contribution to a Roth assuming your plan at work permits.

Health Savings Accounts

After taking advantage of your university's matching contribution, the next thing you should consider is making contributions to a Health Savings Account (HSA). HSAs are only available to those who choose a health insurance plan with a high deductible. HSAs have more tax benefits than a Roth IRA.

With an HSA you get a tax deduction for your contribution, the money grows tax-free, and the distribution is entirely tax-free, assuming you withdraw it to pay for qualified medical expenses. With a Roth IRA, you do not get a deduction up front. With a Traditional IRA, you do not enjoy tax-free treatment when you make a distribution.

With an HSA, there are no income-based contribution limits to qualify for the deduction. In addition, you do not have to wait until retirement or age 72 for tax-free and penalty-free withdrawals of contributions and earnings as long as the withdrawals are for qualified expenses.

A deduction for contributions to an HSA can reduce any type of taxable income, while deductions for contributions to a Traditional retirement plan require service-related income in order to receive a deduction. HSAs do not have any Required Minimum Distributions (RMDs) at a certain age as is required with Traditional retirement plans.

HSAs are the only area in the IRS tax code where you receive a deduction for a contribution and tax-free distributions for withdrawals. In addition, HSAs do not have a *"use it or lose it"* provision like flexible spending accounts, so they are a great way to sock away money for the increased medical expenses you will likely have in retirement.

Plus, under the current tax rules, there are no requirements to take the distribution in the year the qualified medical expense is incurred. This means you can save your receipts, allow your HSA account to grow, and take the distributions later tax-free. A solid tax strategy is to pay medical expenses from non-HSA funds, retain the expense documentation and defer taking the distribution until a time when you need to take a distribution. This strategy, however, assumes you can afford to pay the medical expenses from sources outside of your HSA. While keeping tax optimization in mind, it is advisable to spend the HSA before both spouses pass away since the HSA is subject to lump sum taxation when paid to a non-spousal beneficiary at death.

Unfortunately, under current law, anyone on Medicare is not permitted to contribute to an HSA. There is a proposed bill to make HSA contributions available to those individuals covered under Medicare since senior citizens are the group of individuals with the highest medical expenses. I will not provide any further coverage regarding HSAs in this book, but since this section is on the optimal way to save for retirement, I would be remiss to not mention them.

After contributing enough to get the full match from your employer's retirement plan and to your HSA (if you have access to an HSA), the next priority during the accumulation stage (subject to exceptions determined by personal circumstances) is to direct maximum contributions to your Roth 403(b)s or 401(k)s, and Roth IRAs through TIAA or Vanguard, or VALIC, or whichever provider your employer uses. Of course, with a plain old Roth IRA not associated with your employment, you have an enormous array of options.

Then, if you're eligible to participate, consider contributing the maximum to the Roth account in your university's 457(b) plan.

Many professors—and even some benefits administrators—are unaware that they may have access to a 457(b). Often faculty members can contribute to both 457(b) and 403(b) plans. That second contribution essentially allows you to double your retirement plan contributions. Please see the 457(b) section in Chapter 2 for important additional details about 457 plans.

Since combining a 457(b) plan with your Traditional retirement plan can double your retirement plan contributions, it will pay to find out if you have access to a 457(b) plan and consider whether you can afford additional contributions, even if it doesn't have a matching feature which it probably will not.

Finally, if you meet the income guidelines, contribute to a Roth IRA. If you do not meet the Roth income guidelines but you meet other requirements, contribute to a Traditional IRA, and use a technique called a *"back-door Roth IRA"* to immediately convert the Traditional IRA to a Roth. As we go to press, the back-door Roth IRA is still allowed, but we fear it will be eliminated sometime in the future. We cover the back-door Roth IRA conversion in Chapter 7.

Why Roth? Because the math proves that, subject to exception, you will have more purchasing power in the long run if you contribute to a Roth account than to a Traditional retirement account. Please see Chapter 4.

In my experience, the matching contributions offered to university faculty are extremely generous, sometimes exceeding 100%. By law, your employer's matching contributions used to have to go to the Traditional account in your retirement plan. Recent legislation gives employers the option to give you the option of whether the employer's contribution of your retirement plan is directed to a Traditional or Roth retirement plan (of course if the employer Roth contribution was selected, it would be included in your taxable income). Plans may need to be rewritten to include this option.

So, if you direct all of your own contributions to the Traditional account as well, every withdrawal that you take after you retire will be taxable. Most professors would be well served to have a diversity of Roth and Traditional accounts. I'll talk more about Roth IRA conversions in Chapter 7. Subject to exceptions, after the matching portion I generally recommend Roth IRAs and Roth 403(b)s.

Many professors, and even some benefits administrators, are unaware that they may have access to a 457(b). Often faculty members can contribute to both 457(b) and 403(b) plans. That second contribution essentially allows you to double your retirement plan contributions.

If your emloyer doesn't offer a Roth account in their retirement plan offerings, and you don't qualify for a Roth IRA contribution because your income is too high, and you don't qualify for a back-door Roth IRA conversion, or if you have exhausted those possibilities, the next best option would be to save inside a Traditional 403(b), 401(k), or even an IRA. Even though it's not tax-free, it is still preferable to saving in a taxable brokerage account. I cover this topic in greater depth in Chapter 2.

So, for the sake of simplicity, I offer this figure as proof of the value of saving in retirement accounts as opposed to a regular investment account (labeled after-tax funds). The figure that follows shows the difference in savings over a lifetime.

In the following figure, two professors with the same tax rates, investments, etc. invest in their retirement differently. The professor represented in the solid black line took advantage of his employer's retirement, even disregarding the match. The professor represented in the dashed line did not take advantage of his employer's retirement plan.

Figure 1.1

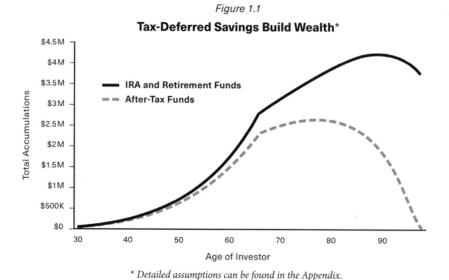

* *Detailed assumptions can be found in the Appendix.*

The professor who made Traditional (meaning, non-Roth) contributions to his employer's retirement plan enjoyed immediate tax savings and enjoyed tax-deferred growth during the accumulation years. That professor is represented by the solid black line. Ultimately, however, he had to pay taxes when he began taking distributions.

The professor who saved outside of his employer's retirement plan, didn't invest in a Roth, didn't get a tax break up front, and had to pay taxes on the interest, dividends, and realized capital gains every year. That professor is represented in the figure by the dashed line.

The professor who used his employer's plan had $1,118,724 more at age 80 than the professor who did not invest in his employer's plan, even though the amount of money he saved on a tax-adjusted basis was the same and there was no employer match. This figure reflects our basic premise that **paying taxes later** while you are in the accumulation stage means you can retire richer instead of *"broker."*

We have also analyzed the issue of saving in Roth 403(b)s and Roth IRAs versus Traditional 403(b)s and IRAs. Though the difference is not nearly as dramatic, subject to exceptions, workers contributing to Roth 403(b)s and Roth IRAs will usually be much better off in the long run than workers contributing to Traditional 403(b)s and IRAs. Please see Chapter 4.

Roth IRAs and Roth 403(b)s are wonderful because they can grow income tax-free for your life, your spouse's life, and for as many as 10 years after you and your spouse are gone. If your beneficiary qualifies under one of the exceptions, the Roth IRA to some extent can be invested tax-free for the life of your beneficiary. Additionally, for you and your spouse, there are no Required Minimum Distributions (RMD) for Roth IRAs. Roth 403(b)s no longer have RMD requirements.

Having the ability to access tax-free money during your retirement years can provide useful options. But since the passage of the SECURE Act, there is an even greater incentive for university faculty members to contribute to Roth 403(b)s and Roth IRAs instead of Traditional 403(b)s and IRAs.

The SECURE Act mandates that, subject to exceptions, your retirement plans must be fully distributed within 10 years of your and your spouse's death. That could be brutal if all inherited retirement money is subject to income tax. Your contributions to a Roth account and Roth conversions can provide you with much-needed flexibility during retirement and will be an even more valuable asset to leave behind.

Planning for Retirement Before You Retire

Advance planning for retirement and for your estate is always a good idea. First, you must make sure you have sufficient resources to afford the life you want to live after you retire. Unfortunately, more than one client has come to see me after they signed their retirement papers, and they will not be able to confidently afford the life they pictured. Had they come to me beforehand, I would have either counseled them to plan on spending less in retirement or to keep working. Working part time or teaching a course or two rarely has anywhere near the financial impact of just working longer.

Second, whether you understand the nuances of all your options or not, making the wrong choices can negatively impact your financial position and that of your family. We have seen many clients come through our doors over the years and for a multitude of reasons comment, *"I wish I would have met you five years ago."*

It is extremely profitable to do appropriate planning while you are still working. You and your family might profit in ways you could not have imagined. And there may be advantages that are not available if you wait until after retirement. I try to counsel all my clients to talk to me or someone on our team before announcing their retirement.

I would offer the same advice to you. Please see someone you trust that can provide good advice before you announce your retirement or sign any retirement papers. The same holds true with phased retirement.

Roth IRA Conversions

Please see Chapter 4 regarding Roth IRA and Roth 403(b) conversions. This is a critical topic for professors. This is also an area that most professors fail to *optimize*, and the result is a dramatic and unnecessary tax burden for themselves and their families.

The Distribution Years: Spend the Right Money First When You Retire
(including a New Wrinkle in our Bedrock Principle)

Again, we start with the conclusion and then move to the explanation. Assume you are retired, are receiving some income that you must pay taxes on (like Social Security, RMDs, interest and dividends, and capital gains), and you also have investments in Traditional retirement plans, Roth retirement plans, and plain old after-tax dollars. Subject to exception, we recommend you spend money in the following order:

1. **Spend your income first.**
2. **Spend your after-tax dollars that do not have any or much appreciation.**
3. **Spend your highly appreciated after-tax dollars.**

4. **Spend your Traditional retirement assets like IRAs and 403(b)s.**

5. **Spend your Roth dollars last.**

The following figure supports the premise that, subject to exception, you should spend your after-tax dollars before your retirement plan or IRA dollars.

In Figure 1.2, both professors start with the same amount of money in a regular brokerage account—which I refer to as after-tax dollars—and in their Traditional retirement plans which could be IRAs or 403(b)s and/or TIAA.

The figure indicates, subject to exceptions, that most readers should spend their after-tax dollars first and then IRA and retirement plan dollars. The solid line shows what happens to the first professor who spends after-tax dollars first and withdraws only the minimum from the IRA when required to (more on RMDs in the next section). *He paid-taxes-later.* The dashed line shows what happens to the second professor who spends his IRA before his after-tax dollars. *He paid-taxes-now.*

Figure 1.2
Spend the Right Money First*

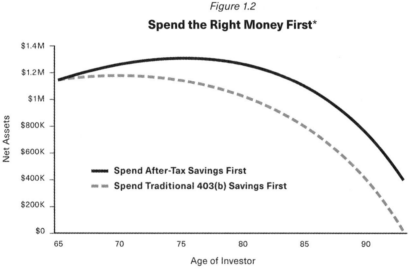

* Detailed assumptions can be found in the Appendix.

The only difference between the dashed line and the solid line in this figure is that the first professor retained more money in the tax-deferred IRA for a longer period. Even starting at age 65, the decision to defer income taxes for as long as possible gives the first professor an extra $340,199 if he or his spouse lives to age 89. If one of them lives longer, paying taxes later will be even more valuable to them.

Subject to exception, I generally prefer you not spend your Roth IRA dollars unless there is a good reason. The Roth IRA grows income tax-free for the rest of your life, your spouse's life and for 10 years after you and your spouse are gone. In addition, there is no Required Minimum Distribution for you or your spouse with a Roth IRA.

So, in general, the last dollars you want to spend are your Roth IRA dollars. Of course, there may be time when it makes sense to spend your Roth dollars before other retirement plan dollars if it keeps you in a lower tax bracket because the alternative would be making taxable withdrawals that would push you into a higher tax bracket.

That said, subject to exceptions, you and your spouse will realize a benefit by deferring the income taxes due on your retirement plans for as long as possible and generally hold off on spending your Roth IRA. And with the SECURE Act now part of the law, your children, and grandchildren (subject to some important exceptions, which I will cover in Chapter 12) will have to pay income taxes on the Inherited Traditional IRA within 10 years of your death.

A New Wrinkle in our Bedrock Principle

Since the passage of the SECURE Act, which will be explained in Chapter 12, adhering to the pay-taxes-later rule in the distribution stage might not always be the best advice. With income tax rates likely on the rise, for some professors it might make more sense to plan for a transition from the taxable world (most TIAA accounts, IRAs, 403(b)s retirement assets, etc.) to the tax-free world (Roth IRAs, 529 plans, HSAs, life insurance, your children's Roth IRAs, etc.). To get the best result, it is best to analyze each situation on a case-by-case basis.

In short, the SECURE Act dramatically accelerates the taxes on your retirement plan after your death. For your children, losing the lifetime stretch on an inherited retirement account can carry a huge tax burden. I will cover this idea more in Chapter 12.

One reasonable strategy for some professors with significant IRAs and retirement plans who will not likely spend all their money is to make taxable withdrawals from the retirement plan and/or IRA, pay the tax, and then gift the net proceeds. The gift could be invested in something that grows tax-free like a 529 plan, HSA plan, your children's Roth IRAs, life insurance, etc. That serves the purpose of getting some money out of your estate and allows tax-free growth for your children.

As a result, for many faculty members, an earlier transition from the taxable world to the tax-free world might work better than the standard rule of *"pay taxes later."* We call this strategy transferring assets from the taxable world to the tax-free world. We cover this strategy in greater detail in Chapter 3.

Required Minimum Distributions (RMDs) Explained

You may already know that the SECURE Act raised the age at which you are required to take mandatory distributions from your Traditional retirement accounts to 72 (technically April 1 of the year after you turn age 72)*.

In simple terms, your RMD is the minimum amount you must withdraw from your retirement account each year. That income will be added to your taxable income unless it was contributed on an after-tax basis or if the qualified withdrawals are tax-free, as in the case of the Roth IRA or Roth 403(b). Beginning at age 72, you must withdraw your RMD by December 31 of every year. Roth IRA accounts are excluded from this requirement; they do not require withdrawals until after the death of the Roth IRA owner and his or her spouse.

If you decide to defer your initial RMD to April 1 of the year following the year you reach age 72, you will be required to take two RMDs in that year. For example, if you reach age 72 in November 2023 and decide to take your RMD on March 15, 2024, you will still need to take another RMD before December 31, 2024, to meet your 2024 RMD requirement. This means you will receive two RMDs in the 2024 year.

This is where additional planning can make a big difference in how much tax you will pay. If you are planning on retiring, depending upon the amount of the RMD, you may be better off taking the RMD in the year in which you turn 72, even though you will have taxable wages, instead of taking two RMDs the following year.

Your RMD is calculated by dividing the year-end balance of your IRA or retirement account by a distribution period (or factor) found in *IRS Publication* 590. Table III (also called the Uniform Lifetime Table) applies if you are married and your spouse is NOT more than 10 years younger than you, or if your spouse is not the sole beneficiary of your IRA, or if you are unmarried.

Table I would only be used to calculate your RMDs if you inherited an IRA from someone other than your spouse prior to January 1, 2020. Table I is also

---

* The SECURE Act 2.0 further raised the ages for RMDs. If you were born in 1949 or earlier, RMDs start at age 70 ½ If you were born in 1950, RMDs start at 72. If you were born between 1951 and 1959, RMDs start at 73. If you were born in 1960 or later, RMDs start at 75.

used when a spousal beneficiary elects to defer distributions until the original owner would have turned 72. If you are married and your spouse is more than 10 years younger than you and the sole beneficiary of your IRA, you would use Table II: Joint Life and Last Survivor Expectancy.

You will probably use Table III. Effective 2022, the Table III distribution period (or factor or divisor) for your first RMD at age 72 is 27.4. (That is a change from the old law but isn't part of the SECURE Act). We include it because it is relevant.

It doesn't matter if you're in perfect health and that both of your parents lived to be 100. Table III is based on the government's estimate of the joint life expectancy of the IRA owner, and someone deemed less than 10 years younger than the IRA owner.

The following is an oversimplification and isn't technically accurate, but it is easy to remember. If you're 72, the government assumes under the new life expectancy factors that you will live for roughly 17 more years and then tacks on another 10 years to determine the Lifetime Table life expectancy factor. So, let's look at how your first RMD will be calculated.

Start by looking at how much money you had in your retirement plans as of December 31 of the previous year. To keep the math simple, I'm going to assume that you had exactly $1 million. To calculate your first year's RMD, divide the $1 million by the factor in Table III that matches your age. For this example, I will assume the IRA owner is 72, so the factor is 27.4. Dividing $1 million by 27.4 equals $36,496. That's how much you must withdraw from your IRA and how much additional income will be added to your other existing income.

Here's another way of looking at it. Your first RMD at age 72 will be a little less than 4% because the 27.4 divisor is a little larger than 25. If the factor were 25, it would be 4% exactly. And as you age, the distribution period that you must divide into your IRA balance gets smaller, which means you are required to take out even larger RMDs. If you have $1 million in your IRA at age 90, your divisor is only 12.2, which will cause an RMD of $81,967. Many of our clients have a lot more than a million dollars in their retirement accounts which really equates to massive future taxation.

But that age of 72 for the date when RMDs must begin may not be written in stone. Legislation being considered in Congress as the SECURE Act 2.0 shifts the age for RMDs, depending on the date of birth. For retirement plan owners who turn 72 after 12/31/22 (born between 1951 and 1959), RMDs will begin at age 73. If you turn 74 after 12/31/33 (born in 1960 or later), your RMDs will not start until age 75.

These forced withdrawals cause headaches for many retired professors, not just because they are taxable distributions but because they have an impact on your entire tax return. The distributions can throw you into a higher tax bracket, increase the percentage of taxable Social Security benefits, raise your Medicare B and D premiums, and trigger the Net Investment Income ('NII') tax of 3.8% on investment income. But, notwithstanding the problems you face when you are forced to withdraw money from your retirement plans, the advantages of years of tax deferral usually far outweigh the disadvantages of not saving money in the tax-deferred environment.

Please note that Table II, used if your spouse is more than 10 years younger than you, gives you a much higher divisor resulting in a lower RMD and a lower tax. Additional details about these rules and a description of how your RMD is calculated based on your life expectancy factor can be found in *IRS Publication* 590-B, available online at **https://www.irs.gov/pub/irs-prior/p590b.pdf**.

When mandatory distributions are added to wage income and Social Security benefits, it is not uncommon for us to see the taxable income jump up one full bracket and sometimes two. If you do not need the income to live on, most people are much better off deferring withdrawals from Traditional retirement plans for as long as they can. I'll go into more details about RMDs in Chapter 6.

What if You Work Beyond Age 72

If you are still working full-time at age 72 (and potentially beyond) you will not have to take RMDs from your employer sponsored retirement accounts. Since university professors often continue to work long after their peers in the private sector have retired, they do not have to start their RMDs until they retire. Traditional IRAs do have mandatory RMD requirements at age 72 whether you are working or not, so that may invoke additional planning.

Professors used to be notorious for delaying retirement. I might ask a professor client when he planned to retire. He would say in five years. I meet with the same professor five years later and asked him when he is going to retire? He says in five years. To be fair, I tend to work with the professors who are at the top of their field.

Though this is strictly anecdotal, since Covid and amidst a growing dissatisfaction with some of the changing conditions, I see professors retiring that I would have guessed would have kept working longer. That said, many professors still work beyond age 72. If your university allows it, the IRS allows you to defer RMDs in your 403(b) or 401(k) plan as long as you continue to work. So, if you plan to continue to work beyond age 72, it may make sense to defer distributions from your 403(b) plan until such time that you retire.

What is Retired for the Purpose of Delaying Your RMD?

Over the years, our accounting office has received the question, '*What if I continue to remain an adjunct professor or participate in a phased retirement or even just teach a course after I retire? Can I still defer taking my RMD because technically I'm still working?*'

This is an interesting question and unfortunately sounding like an attorney (again) the answer is it depends. Each institution negotiates its own contract with TIAA or other provider so some universities may have more restrictive rules. You could even have different rules for different contracts with the same university. Professors are unique in that the determination as to what constitutes retirement is how each university defines retirement, and it is up to the university to determine when a professor is deemed retired.

We recommend you contacting the university's HR Department *and* TIAA or the other provider directly about your specific situation as this is a complex area and some of the information is unclear and you may not receive the correct advice.

The IRS does not define how many hours are considered '*still working*' for the RMD exception. As long as your employer considers you as an employee and you are *eligible* to participate in the employer plan and you remain employed after December 31, meaning January 1st, you MAY qualify for the still-working exception.

An important distinction to know—even if you work through the end of the year and retire on December 31, you are required to take your RMD by April 1 of the following year even though you were working through December 31. In addition, you would need to be employed by your current employer into the next year to possibly qualify for this exception (meaning, receive a W-2 the following year *for hours worked* in the following year).

If you defer receiving your accrued sick pay or vacation pay into the following year, this will not qualify *for hours worked*. We are referring to *earned income* that is reported on a W-2 or possibly a 1099 form from the same university you are retiring from.

You can get even more bang for your tax-deferred buck by rolling any IRAs that you may have accumulated over the course of your career into your current work plan assuming your employer permits it.

The rules are designed so you cannot *'retire'* on a certain date, take distributions from your 403(b) plan, and then decide to work as an adjunct professor and say, by the way, I'm working now and am no longer required to take my RMD. There is a lot of complexity in the rules surrounding this exception, so we caution you to plan carefully as there can be some unique tax planning opportunities and blunders if not handled correctly.

You can get even more bang for your tax-deferred buck by rolling any IRAs that you may have accumulated over the course of your career into your current work plan assuming your employer permits it. That way, you can avoid taking RMDs on your old retirement plan or IRA money, too.

Most advisors are anxious to have you roll your retirement plan at work into an IRA but sometimes this actually hurts you because it accelerates income. If you decide to employ this strategy, we strongly recommend a *'trustee-to-trustee'* transfer of the IRA monies into your current work plan since there are limitations on the number of rollover transfers permitted in a given year.

Two quick anecdotes before jumping back into the content. First, I have been working with faculty members for over 35 years, and though I never did a formal study, faculty retirement dates seem to be changing. Earlier in my career, it seemed that many faculty members would just keep working indefinitely.

I always found it interesting that the motivation for working or retiring was usually not financial, but whether they were still productive and still enjoying it. Since so many faculty members that I work with love what they do—and that included my mother—they would often work well past 72.

That trend seems to be diminishing in recent years, with more and more faculty members retiring earlier. I was with a client who I thought was a professor, and I mentioned this phenomenon. I said I had heard that the reason a lot more professors were retiring early was because the administration was getting more and more difficult to work with. The client gave me a stern look and said, *"I am the administration."* Oops.

Also, I fear the consequences of Covid-19 on the entire university environment—remote teaching, faculty cuts, budget cuts, etc., will spur even more *"early"* retirements. Again, anecdotally, I have had a lot more discussions with professors regarding retiring in the short term than I can ever remember for the last 35 years.

Once you do stop working, subject to exception, you should limit your taxable withdrawals to the RMD. The exception is when you are trying to reduce what will become an Inherited IRA because you know that your kids are going to get clobbered with taxes after you die. That is a possibility that we evaluate for all our clients, especially since the SECURE Act eliminated the stretch IRA.

Now that your children are required to distribute their entire Inherited IRA within 10 years of your death, it may make more sense for you to pay tax on the withdrawals. *But paying taxes sooner rather than later is still the exception, not the rule.* An analysis of your future tax bracket (s) and state of residence as well as those of your children also becomes a consideration. I will cover more about evaluating those factors in Chapter 11.

Another exception to the *"pay taxes later"* maxim is that it sometimes makes sense to distribute IRAs before other funds when you can take advantage of an income tax bracket that is temporarily lower than normal. When I run into that situation, I also think about Roth IRA conversions—especially now. The Tax Cut and Jobs Act of 2017 (TCJA) reduced income tax brackets temporarily and that can make Roth IRA conversions much more favorable for more people.

Comparing Current and Future Tax Brackets

In 2017, the 25% income tax bracket topped out at $153,100 for a married couple. In 2023, the 24% tax bracket tops out at $364,200. To oversimplify, income tax rates for most taxpayers were *much* higher in 2017 than they are now, and for a large number of higher-earning families tax rates were much higher in 2017 than they are now.

This means that many individuals who looked into Roth conversions in the past and found that they would not be cost-effective may find that that is no longer true. Because of the *"sunset"* provisions of the 2017 TCJA, these reduced tax rates are scheduled to revert to the higher 2017 rates (plus inflation) starting in 2026. Please see the chart on the next page.

Still, you might be thinking, *"What are you talking about, Jim? My income isn't anywhere near $364,200 now that I am retired."* Maybe so, but if your normal taxable income is $100,000, that means you can now either withdraw more

Comparison of 2017 and 2023 Tax Rates for "Married Filing Jointly"

2017			2023		
$ 0 – 18,650	x	10%	$ 0 – 22,000	x	10%
18,651 – 75,900	x	15%	22,001 – 89,450	x	12%
75,901 – 153,100	x	25%	89,451 – 190,750	x	22%
153,101 – 233,350	x	28%	190,751 – 364,200	x	24%
233,351 – 416,700	x	33%	364,201 – 462,500	x	32%
416,701 – 470,700	x	35%	462,501 – 693,750	x	35%
470,701 *and above*	x	39.6%	693,751 *and above*	x	37%

Notes: Make Roth conversions at 24% now. Otherwise, you might pay 28% or 33% on RMDs later.

from your retirement plans (or better yet, make a Roth IRA conversion of up to $264,200) and still be in the 24% tax bracket assuming you aren't taking additional Medicare premiums and other issues into account. Please see Chapter 16.

In 2017, that same withdrawal would have put you in the 33% bracket. So, before you say that taking more than your RMD from your IRA (or, better yet, making a series of Roth IRA conversions) isn't for you, please be open-minded and examine the data. (In God We Trust, all others bring data.) And if taxes go up in the long run, Roth IRA conversions will be even more profitable for you and your family.

One very valuable service that we provide for our assets-under-management (AUM) clients* is our annual running of the numbers. *"Running the numbers"* is our shorthand affectionate term for preparing a detailed quantitative analysis of a client's finances to optimize financial decisions. We test the tax implications of a variety of different scenarios based on varying assumptions.

----

* Lange Financial Group, LLC is a registered investment advisory firm registered with the Commonwealth of Pennsylvania Department of banking, Harrisburg, Pennsylvania. In addition, the firm is registered as a registered investment advisory firm in the states of Arizona, Florida, New York, Ohio, and Virginia. Lange Financial Group LLC may not provide investment advisory services to any residents of states in which the firm does not maintain an investment advisory registration. This does not in any way imply that we are failing to preserve our rights under the respective states' de minimus rule.

The presence of this book shall not in any direct or indirect fashion, be construed or interpreted to suggest that the firm is offering to sell or soliciting to provide investment advisory services to residents of any state or states in which the firm is not maintaining an investment advisory registration. Again we preserve all rights under each state's de minimus rule, but we wish to emphasize that we are not directly or indirectly soliciting investment advisory clients in states where we have no legal right to do so.

For example, we were relatively sure that the SECURE Act (or something like it) was coming, which would likely include accelerating income taxes on Inherited IRAs, so we included those assumptions in many of the different scenarios in our projections even before the SECURE Act passed. Correctly foreseeing the likely changes in the law led us to make more and bigger Roth IRA conversions which in hindsight worked out extremely well. Then, those numbers become the basis for a Financial Masterplan. Please see the back of the book for more details.

Many financial professionals who neither *"run the numbers"* nor understand critical concepts assume that it does not make sense for retired individuals to make Roth IRA conversions. But after we "ran their numbers," we found ourselves recommending that many 72-year-old+ clients continue executing Roth conversions—even though they were already taking RMDs and receiving Social Security benefits. And if you are not yet retired, many universities now allow you to execute Roth conversions inside your 403(b) plan, assuming the plan document allows in-service conversions.

This is not a *"one-size-fits-all"* proposition, because every taxpayer has unique circumstances. But it is an interesting idea to consider making Roth conversions while you are in the 22% tax bracket that will push you into the 24% bracket if you project that your future RMDs will be taxed at 24% or a higher tax rate.

Three Reasons Your Taxes Will Likely Increase

The recommendations we make to our clients that are based on tax rates increasing are based on three factors we think are likely to occur. First, our current low tax rates are set to expire at the end of 2025, and unless Congress votes to extend them, tax rates will automatically go up. This isn't even to mention the fiscal problems the United States has. The money needed to pay even the interest on our debt must come from somewhere.

Second, we also know that your RMD will increase as you age, which will increase your taxable income, your tax rate, and thus, your taxes.

Finally, for couples currently filing income tax returns using the 'married filing jointly' status, there is an additional future tax increase to take into consideration.

Eventually one of you will die. Excepting the year of death, the surviving spouse, whose taxable income will likely be similar to what it was in the years preceding their husband or wife's death, will have to file their taxes using the 'single' status which subjects them to much higher rates than they had been paying while their spouse was alive. So, for many couples making a series of strategic Roth conversions before these likely tax raises occur could be extremely valuable to your surviving spouse and to your heirs, down the road.

The point is that just because you are taking minimum distributions and Social Security, do not assume you aren't a suitable candidate for Roth IRA conversions.

It should also be noted that due to the overwhelming demand of clients and prospects wanting us to *"run the numbers"* but not engage with our money management services (see the back of the book), we now do a complete Financial Masterplan on a fee-for-service basis, but the fee, subject to exceptions, starts at $12,500. Again, as demand for what we think is a better model for us and the client which is the AUM model that includes our Financial Masterplan, we may stop doing the fee-for-service work.

Important Point About Required Minimum Distributions and Annuities

TIAA investors and faculty members who own annuities inside of their retirement plans (or qualified annuities) need to be aware of one specific feature that can affect your RMD.

Specifically, if you have elected to take a lifetime income from your annuity (also called annuitizing), then the money in that annuity is exempt from the balances you must include when calculating your RMD since you are withdrawing income from your annuity. And if you have a non-qualified annuity (also called a personal or after-tax annuity), you are not required to take a minimum distribution from it at all. But these are just two more reasons why there is no *"one-size-fits-all"* answer when it comes to determining the best spending strategies for profesors and TIAA investors.

As with the old law, you will always be allowed to take out more than the minimum, at least with your CREF, IRA, and other non-TIAA retirement assets. Assets that you have in the TIAA Traditional annuities do have relevant restrictions but are likely good assets to keep. If, however, you can afford to limit your distributions to the minimum, there are significant financial advantages in doing so. Limiting distributions to the minimum defers taxes on the IRA for the longest time available and, subject to exceptions, confers the greatest financial benefits.

The SECURE Act defers the time you are required to take your first minimum distribution until age 72 or later, depending on the year of your birth. For many people, this will allow additional time for your assets to grow tax-deferred and will likely allow an additional two years during which Roth IRA conversions will be beneficial to you and your family.

On the other hand, most professors are far more frugal in their spending than they need to be. I would hate to hear you were reducing your spending because you didn't want to withdraw more than the Required Minimum Distribution even though you could otherwise afford to spend more. Likewise, if the choice is spending more money or making a Roth IRA conversion, most of the time, I will recommend spending more money.

I remember one client saying he had to cut back on his spending and his charitable contributions because he was planning on paying the taxes on a large Roth IRA conversion that year. No. No. No. The point of the Roth conversions is to enhance the quality of your life, not restrict it.

Though I practically begged him not to cut back on his spending, he did indeed cut back on his spending, depriving himself and his family of certain pleasures they could have enjoyed. Then, he died. The difference between what he actually spent and what he could have comfortably spent in the big picture was fairly meaningless. His widow, who was left with way more money than she will ever need, referred to her wealth as *"numbers in a bank."*

So, now that we have an overview of some of the basics of saving and spending retirement assets, let's look at some specific planning issues that university faculty need to consider. Please read on.

KEY IDEAS

- Subject to exception, pay taxes later, except for Roth.

- Take full advantage of employer-provided matches in your retirement plan.

- Use a Health Savings Account if one is available to you.

- Contribute to your Roth 403(b) and Roth IRA while you are working. Also, contribute to your Roth 457(b) plan if you are eligible and can afford it.

KEY IDEAS
(continued)

- Subject to exception, spend your after-tax dollars before your retirement money.

- Most professors should try to limit withdrawals from retirement accounts to the minimum required by law (RMD).

- Spend your Roth accounts last.

2

The Accumulation Years: Fund Retirement Plans to the Maximum

"The most powerful force in the universe is compound interest."
— Albert Einstein

Please note there is some repetition of Chapter 1 in Chapter 2. This chapter provides additional proof for the recommendations made in Chapter 1. In addition, this chapter explores some of the exceptions to our general rule.

We repeat what we said in Chapter 1 in terms of the best order to accumulate money for retirement. Let's assume you have a certain amount of money that you can afford to contribute for your retirement. What is the best order of the different types of retirement plans that you should consider contributing to?

Subject to exception:
1. Take advantage of any employer match.
2. Take advantage of a Health Savings Account (HSAs), if available to you.
3. Contribute to Roth IRAs, subject to exception based on tax brackets.
4. Contribute to Traditional retirement plans or IRAs.
5. Contribute to nondeductible IRAs or nondeductible contributions to a retirement plan.
6. Save money in a plain old after-tax brokerage account.

Why Contributing the Maximum to a Retirement Plan is So Important

A trusted client of mine recently referred to me as her *"guardian angel."* At first, I was totally taken aback—no one had ever called me a guardian angel before. She continued, *"Thirty years ago you advised me to put the maximum into my retirement plan. I didn't know if it was a good idea or not, but I trusted you and did what you recommended. Now I have a million dollars in my retirement plan. What should I do now?"*

Another client recently reminded me of a similar recommendation I made many years ago. He was basically retired but was teaching one course and was paid with a W-2. I recommended that he should maximize his retirement plan contributions even though his net check was close to zero.

These comments compelled me to complete a comprehensive analysis of why it was such good advice to maximize your retirement plan. I wanted to be able to persuasively convince anyone who harbored the least little doubt about the advantages of saving money in a retirement plan over saving money outside of a retirement plan. Also, I didn't think this was a concept I could prove with words. It had to be proven by math and a mini *"running the numbers"* comparison.

I set out to evaluate the outcomes of two different scenarios. For this example, we do not consider the employer match:

1. You earn the money, you pay the tax, you invest the money you earned, and you pay tax on the dividends, interest, and capital gains.

2. You invest money in your retirement plan, and you get a tax deduction. The money grows tax-deferred, and you do not pay taxes on that money until you take it out.

So, which is better: saving inside the retirement plan or outside the retirement plan? *The answer: it is better to save within the retirement plan.* Why? This isn't a touchy-feely issue. It comes down to numbers. Let's take a deeper look into the scenario I briefly presented in Chapter 1.

·············· **MINI CASE STUDY 2.1** ··············
The Clear Advantage of Pre-Tax IRA and Retirement Plan Savings

Professor Pay Taxes Later and Professor Pay Taxes Now are neighbors. From the outside, you wouldn't be able to tell them apart: they own the same type of car; their salaries are the same; and they are in the same tax bracket. Their savings have the same investment rate of return, and they even save the same percentage of their gross wages every year.

They have one big difference. Professor Pay Taxes Later invests as much as he can afford in his tax-deferred retirement plan—his Traditional 403(b)—even though his employer does not match his contributions. Professor Pay Taxes Now feels that putting money in a retirement account makes it *"not really his money"* as he puts it. He doesn't want to have to pay taxes to take out his own money or put up with other restrictions that limit his access to *"his money."* Thus, he contributes nothing to his retirement account at work but invests his savings in an account outside of his retirement plan. Professor Pay Taxes Now invests the old-fashioned way: earn the money, pay the tax, invest the money, and pay the tax on the income that the invested money generates (dividends, capital gains, etc.).

Both men begin investing at age 30.

- In 2022, they start saving $8,000 per year, indexed for inflation.

- Professor Pay Taxes Later has his entire $8,000 withheld from his paycheck and deposited to his tax-deferred 403(b). (The analysis would be conceptually identical if he contributed the money to a Traditional deductible IRA.)

- Professor Pay Taxes Now chooses not to have any retirement funds withheld but rather to be paid in full. He pays income taxes on his full wages—which includes the $8,000 he chose not to contribute to his retirement plan. After the 24% income tax is paid, he has only 76% of the $8,000, or $6,080, left to invest.

Now look at Figure 2.1 *(shown below)*. Professor Pay Taxes Later's investment is represented by the solid line, and Professor Pay Taxes Now's by the dashed line. Look at the dramatic difference in the accumulations over time.

To be fair, Professor Pay Taxes Later will have to pay taxes eventually. When he is retired, for every dollar he wants to withdraw, he must take out $1.32. He pockets the dollar and pays $0.32 in taxes (24% of $1.32). If Professor Pay Taxes Now withdraws a dollar, subject to some capital gains taxes, it's all his, just as he wanted. At age 88, however, Professor Pay Taxes Now has depleted

Figure 2.1

Retirement Assets, IRAs, etc. *vs.* After-Tax Accumulations*

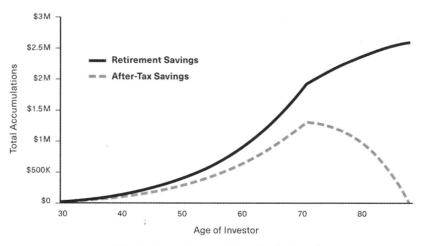

* *Detailed assumptions can be found in the Appendix.*

his funds entirely whereas Professor Pay Taxes Later has $2,606,774 left in his retirement plan.

Given reasonable assumptions and all things being equal, following the adage, *"Don't pay taxes now—pay taxes later"* can be worth over $2 million over your lifetime.

After spending your life working hard, paying the mortgage, paying the bills, raising a family, and paying for braces, putting your kids through college, etc. you may never have expected to have such a substantial IRA or retirement plan and be so well off in retirement. For many of my clients, it seems like a fantasy. But it isn't a fantasy, and you need to think about the best ways to manage that money.

Make Those Nonmatched Contributions to Retirement Plans

What conclusion can we draw from Mini Case Study 2.1? Don't pay taxes now—pay taxes later. Even if your university employer does not offer the additional advantage of matching contributions, you should contribute the maximum to your retirement plan, assuming you can afford it. Money contributed to a retirement plan, whether a 401(k), 403(b), SEP, SIMPLE, 457, deductible IRA, or another type of retirement plan, is a pre-tax investment that grows tax deferred. There are no federal income taxes on the wages contributed.

Some taxpayers view contributions as tax-deductible. Others say those contributions aren't taxable. Whichever way you look at it, you are getting a tax break

**All things being equal, following the adage,
"Don't pay taxes now — pay taxes later" can be worth
over $2 million over your lifetime.**

for the amount of the contribution multiplied by the tax rate for your tax bracket. Furthermore, once the contribution is made, you do not pay income taxes on the interest, dividends, and appreciation *until you take a distribution* (i.e., withdrawal) from the retirement plan. In other words, you pay taxes later.

By not paying taxes up-front on the wages invested in your retirement plan, you reap the harvest of compounding interest, dividends, and capital gains on the money that would have gone to paying taxes, both on the amount contributed, and on the growth, had the money been invested outside of the retirement plan.

In the real world, not only is there a tax advantage to saving in a retirement plan but doing so builds in the discipline of contributing to your retirement plan with every paycheck. The example above assumes that if you are not putting the money in your retirement plan, you are saving and investing an amount equal to what your retirement contribution would have been. But can you trust yourself to be a disciplined saver? Will the temptation to put off saving for retirement until the next paycheck undermine your resolve? Even if you do put it in savings, knowing you have unrestricted access to the money, can you be confident that you would never invade that fund until you retire?

In my practice, the clients who usually have the most money saved at retirement are the ones who religiously contributed to a retirement plan over the course of their long careers.

The idea of paying taxes later and contributing the maximum to your retirement plan(s) is something that I have preached in my practice for over 35 years. Many of my long-standing clients took my advice 20 or 30 years ago, even if they didn't completely understand why, and now they are thanking me.

The Employer Matching Retirement Plan

With all due respect, broadly speaking, you must be pretty *"simple"* (that's a nice word for *"stupid"*) not to take advantage of a retirement plan where the employer makes a matching contribution. As Paul Newman says in the movie, **The Color of Money**: *"Money won is twice as sweet as money earned."*

In my practice, the clients who usually have the most money saved at retirement are the ones who religiously contributed to a retirement plan over the course of their long careers.

The Cardinal Rule of Saving for Retirement

If your employer offers a retirement plan matching contribution, the cardinal rule is: contribute *at least* the amount the employer university is willing to match—even if it is only a percentage of your contribution and not a dollar-for-dollar match. Imagine depositing $1,000 of your money in a bank, but instead of getting a crummy toaster, you receive an extra $1,000 to go along with your deposit. To add to the fun, imagine getting a tax deduction for your deposit and not having to pay taxes on your gift. Furthermore, both your $1,000 and the gift of $1,000 grow (it is to be hoped), and you do not have to pay income tax on the interest, dividends, capital gains, or the appreciation until you withdraw the money.

When you withdraw the money, you will have to pay taxes, but you will have gained interest, dividends, and appreciation in the meantime. That is what employer-matching contributions to retirement plans are all about. If the employer matches the employee contribution on a dollar-for-dollar basis, it is the same as a *100% return on the investment in one day* (assuming no early withdrawal penalties apply, and the matched funds are fully vested).

Over the years, I have heard a lot of excuses for not taking advantage of an employer-matching plan. With few exceptions, all those reasons come down to two words: *ignorance and neglect.* If you didn't know that before, you know it now. If you are not currently taking advantage of your employer-matching plan, run—don't walk—to your plan administrator and begin the paperwork to take advantage of the employer match.

Matching contributions are most commonly found within 401(k), 403(b),

Many eligible 403(b) plan participants also may have access to a 457 plan. You can, in effect, enjoy double the ability to tax-defer earnings through participation in both the 403(b) and 457 plans.

and 457 plans. Many eligible 403(b) plan participants also may have access to a 457 plan. You can, in effect, enjoy double the ability to tax-defer earnings through participation in both the 403(b) and 457 plans. Even if your employer is only willing to make a partial match up to a cap, you should still take advantage of this opportunity. For example, a fairly common retirement plan agreement may provide that the employer contribute 50 cents for every dollar up to the first 6% of salary you contribute. Keep in mind: *This is free money!* Again, this isn't touchy-feely stuff. It is backed by hard numbers.

······························· **MINI CASE STUDY 2.2** ·······························
Running the Numbers for Employer-Matched Retirement Plans

Scenario 1:
- Professor Bill earns $75,000 per year and is subject to a flat 24% federal income tax (for simplicity, I ignore other taxes and assume a flat federal income tax: 24% x $75,000 = $18,000 tax).

- He spends $50,000 per year.

- Because he doesn't use his retirement plan at work, he has $7,000 available to invest: ($75,000 income – [$18,000 tax and $50,000 spending] = $7,000 available cash).

Scenario 2:
Professor Bob also earns $75,000 per year, has the same tax rate, and spends the same amount. But Bob's PhD dissertation advisor was a very wise man— he bought the original *Retire Secure!* After reading the original version of this chapter, he advised all of his doctoral students to be sure to contribute the maximum amounts to their retirement accounts that their future university employers were willing to match because obviously they were all going to continue in academia.

Professor Bob took his advisor's counsel to heart, so he contributes $8,000 to his retirement account and his university matches his contribution 100%. Thus $16,000 goes into his retirement account.

Under current tax laws, Professor Bob will not have to pay federal income tax on his retirement plan contribution or on the amount his university is willing to match, until the money is withdrawn from the plan. By using his employer's university's retirement plan, Professor Bob's picture changes for the better as follows:

- Professor Bob pays tax on only $67,000: $75,000 income – $8,000 *(tax-deferred) = $67,000.* His taxes: 24% x $67,000 = $16,080

- He now has $58,920 *($75,000 income – $16,080 taxes).*

- He makes his plan contribution of $8,000, leaving him with $50,920 outside the plan.
- His employer matches the $8,000 *(also tax-deferred).*
- He now has $16,000 in his retirement plan *(growing tax-deferred).*
- His employer matches the $8,000 *(also tax-deferred).*
- He spends $50,000 per year and is left with $920 in cash.

Which scenario strikes you as more favorable: Scenario 2, with $16,000 in a retirement plan and $920 in cash, or Scenario 1, with no retirement plan and $7,000 in cash? The extreme cynic can figure out situations when a little extra cash and no retirement plan would be preferable, but the rest of us will take advantage of any employer-matching retirement plan.

Please keep in mind that the money in the retirement plan will continue to grow, and you will not have to pay income taxes on the earnings, dividends, interest, or accumulations until you (or your heirs) withdraw the money. But, even without weighing in the advantages of the long-term deferral, at the end of the first year, assuming the employer-matched funds are fully vested, the comparative values of these two scenarios are measured by after-tax purchasing power as follows:

	Scenario 1	*Scenario 2*
After-tax cash available	$ 7,000	$ 920
Retirement plan balance	0	$ 16,000
Tax on retirement plan balance	0	($ 3,840)
Early withdrawal penalty	0	($ 1,600)
Total Purchasing Power	**$ 7,000**	**$ 11,480**

Even if Professor Bob has a financial emergency and must withdraw money from his 403(b) prior to age 59½, resulting in tax and an early withdrawal penalty, and even if he doesn't qualify for any of the exceptions, he still has $4,480 more than Professor Bill, who saved his money in an after-tax account. And if Professor Bob is older than 59½ when he needs to make the withdrawal, the penalty doesn't apply, and the difference is even greater. Obviously, it is better to take advantage of the retirement plan and the employer's matching contributions.

Figure 2.2 *(shown on the next page)* demonstrates that the long-term advantages of the employer match are even more dramatic using the same basic facts and circumstances as in Mini Case Study 2.1 but adding in a 100% employer match of annual contributions. Figure 2.2 compares stubborn Profes-

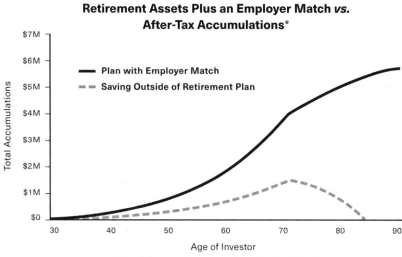

Figure 2.2

Retirement Assets Plus an Employer Match *vs.* After-Tax Accumulations*

* Detailed assumptions can be found in the Appendix.*

sor Bill who refuses to use the retirement plan versus disciplined Professor Bob who contributes to his retirement plan.

Using slightly higher spending assumptions than Mini Case Study 1 to be consistent with taking a RMD *(please see Chapter 3)*, Bill runs out of money at age 84 instead of at age 88 as in Mini Case Study 2.1. However, Bob's matched retirement savings plan has $5,446,284 remaining when he is 84 instead of zero. And despite the large distributions being made after age 84, disciplined Bob's savings are still growing when he reaches 94.

The obvious conclusion again is, if you are not already taking advantage of this, run—don't walk—to your plan administrator and begin the paperwork to take advantage of the employer match.

....

Occasionally, clients moan that they literally cannot afford to make the contribution, even though their employer is willing to match it. I am not sympathetic. I would rather see you borrow the money to make matching contributions. Beg, or borrow to find the money to contribute to an employer-matching plan.

Taking Advantage of the Employer's Match for Your Children Through Gifting

There is an interesting application of this idea if you want to see your child's retirement plan grow, but your child claims he or she isn't making enough to contribute to his or her retirement plan, even though the company offers a matching contribution.

You may want to consider making a gift to your child in the amount that your child would be out-of-pocket, if they contributed an amount that would be matched. Your child can then maintain their spending levels, which are probably way too high by your standards for someone in your child's position. Then, they could use the money you give him to maximize the matching portion of his retirement plan at work.

Let's assume a 100% match of $5,000. Your child puts $5,000 into their Roth 401(k), and the employer matches the $5,000 in the Traditional 401(k). In effect, your $5,000 gift conferred $10,000 of value (and much more if you consider the future tax benefits) for a cost of $5,000.

Alternatively, your child could use the money and put it in a regular pre-tax 401(k), not a Roth 401(k). Here are the numbers for that transaction. Let's say your child's employer matches 100%, up to $5,000, and your child is in the 22% tax bracket. If you make a gift of $3,900 ($5,000 - $1,100 tax), your child should now have enough cash to make a $5,000 retirement plan contribution and would end up with $10,000 in his or her retirement account. That is an example of a leveraged gift. Lots of bang for your gifted buck!

Two Categories of Retirement Plans

Before I get into the details, let me offer a big picture comment. Many people have access to more retirement plans and bigger contributions than they are actually making even though they can afford it. That is still true even if they have read a prior version of this section but for some reasons still didn't take the advice offered here.

Generally, all retirement plans in the workplace fall into two categories: *Defined Contribution Plans* and *Defined Benefit Plans*. Depending on the options available in your state and at your university, you may be able to choose either a Defined Contribution Plan or a Defined Benefit Plan. While many employers offer a Defined Contribution Plan, not all offer a Defined Benefit Plan.

Defined Contribution Plans

Defined contribution plans are relatively easy to understand, and usually offer a wide variety of tax-favored investment options. In a defined contribution plan, each individual employee has an account that can be funded by either the employee or the employer, or both.

Employers frequently tell their employees that their contributions are tax-deductible, which is not technically correct. The employee's taxable income is reduced by the amount that they contribute to the plan, which means that employees who do not have enough deductions to itemize at tax time, will still realize a tax benefit from contributing to the plan. At retirement or termination of employment, subject to a few minor exceptions, the money in a defined contribution plan sponsored by the employer represents the funds available to the employee that can be rolled into his or her own IRA.

If your employer uses TIAA to manage your plan, there are a few additional kinks that I'll discuss in Chapter 8, where I discuss options available for accessing your TIAA and CREF accounts after you retire. In a defined contribution plan, the employee bears the investment risks. In other words, if the market suffers a downturn, so does the value of your investments. Conversely, if the market does well, you are rewarded with a higher balance. The plan illustrated in Figures 1.1 and 1.2 is an example of a defined contribution plan.

Most employers are now offering Roth account options within their defined contribution plans. More information on the advantages of each option is covered in Chapter 4. If offered, the employee can direct all of their contributions to the Roth account or split them between the Roth and Traditional accounts. The Roth accounts are excellent options that provide tax-free growth within defined contribution plans. But unlike employee contributions to Traditional accounts, Roth contributions do not reduce taxable income.

Under the old law, employer matching contributions could not be added to the employee's Roth account; they had to be credited to the Traditional account so that they were taxed when withdrawn. There is, however, recent legislation that allows employers to offer matching Roth contributions. This is a new option and will require that plans be updated to include the Roth choice for matching contributions. Generally, for most employees, we recommend the employer's contribution be funded with Roth dollars. Please see Chapter 3.

Common Defined Contribution Plans

Please note as we go into design for this book, the numbers that follow are accurate. But the proposed regulations would increase these amounts so literally by the time this book goes to press, there could be higher limits. That said, the concepts will not change.

403(b) Plan: If your university offers a defined contribution plan, it will most likely be a 403(b) plan. Most university plans managed by TIAA are 403(b) plans. This plan is similar to a 401(k) plan but is commonly used by certain charitable organizations and public educational institutions, such as universities, colleges, and hospitals. Like a 401(k), the maximum contribution is limited in 2023 to $22,500 for employees under age 50, or $30,000 for those over age 50. 403(b) plans also have a special *"15 years of service"* catch-up provision—so even if you're not age 50 or older, you may be able to contribute more than $22,500 to your plan.

One big difference between a 401(k) plan and a 403(b) plan is that, for non-church employees, 403(b) plans can only invest in annuities and mutual funds. TIAA-CREF is the best known and most common 403(b) provider.

Traditional TIAA plans mitigate the investment risk inherent in defined contribution plans. The overarching goal of TIAA is to provide adequate and secure retirement income for participants. Unlike the mutual funds available as investment choices for most defined contribution plan participants, where account balances may rise and fall with the stock market, contributions are guaranteed a rate of return based on prevailing interest rates at the time of the contribution, generally in the 3% to 3.5% range.

When it's time to retire, TIAA has unique options for accessing your accumulated funds, as we'll cover in detail in Chapter 8. Many of these options are aimed at providing participants with a steady income stream for life, unlike most defined contribution plans, which place the risk of adequate retirement income squarely on the shoulders of plan participants.

457 Plan: After the Economic Growth and Tax Relief Reconciliation Act of 2001 (EGTRRA), 457 plans have become more similar to 401(k) plans. They are commonly used by state and local governmental employers and certain tax-exempt organizations. Typical 457 employees are police officers, firefighters, teachers, and other municipal workers.

An interesting side note is that many eligible 457 plan participant professors do not realize they are eligible to make a 457 plan contribution. They may have a 403(b) plan and do not know they can *"double"* their tax-deferred earnings through participating in both a 403(b) and a 457 plan.

A perfect candidate for using both plans would be a married professor whose spouse has income, and their combined income is more than sufficient for their needs. If they have enough income and if they are age 50 or older in 2023, the professor could contribute a maximum of $22,500 to his or her 403(b), $22,500 to a 457 plan, and make an additional catch-up contribution of $7,500. By doing so, the couple could reduce their taxable income by $52,500. Some 457 plans provide a *"catch-up"* provision for employees who are within three years of normal retirement age, which allows them to contribute even more.

Like other retirement plans, you cannot have a Roth 457 unless the plan allows for Roth contributions. Hopefully, that same plan would allow in-plan rollovers to designated Roth accounts.

A question came up in our accounting office, can a professor contribute to a Roth account within a 457(b) plan? One CPA thought *'no,'* you can only contribute to a pre-tax Traditional account. Another CPA professional said, *'yes'* you can contribute to a Roth. What is the correct answer? Well, despite not being an attorney, after doing the appropriate research, the consensus among the CPAs was *"it depends."*

Governmental 457(b) plans allow employee contributions to a Roth account, provided the plan document permits Roth contributions. The rules do not allow Roth contributions to 457(b) plans sponsored by non-profit organizations. But what if you work for a state university? This is where it gets interesting. Some state universities have adopted the *governmental* 457(b) plan over the *non-profit* 457(b) plan. The professors who work for a state university who have a *governmental* 457(b) plan can contribute to a Roth (for example, University of Michigan, Ohio State University, and University of Pittsburgh).

Bottom line, if you are employed by a state university, you will need to check with your Human Resources Department to see if your employee contributions can go towards a Roth account but more importantly whether your institution allows any 457 contributions.

Note, there is an annual maximum of the amount that can be placed into a defined contribution plan in a given year, which includes the total of your employee elective deferrals to the 403(b) plan and 457(b) plan, and any matching contributions made by the university to your 403(b) plan. The maximum amount for 2023 is $66,000 plus a catch-up contribution of $7,500 if age 50 or older, for a total annual contribution limit of $73,500 or 100% of compensation (whichever is lower). The annual contribution limit usually increases annually.

401(a) Plan: These are also known as money-purchase retirement savings plans and are most commonly offered by government agencies, educational institutions, and not-for-profit organizations. They are highly customizable by the employer, so you may find vastly differing options at different employers, and even different options offered to different subsets of employees. Even professors at the same university are likely to have investments in multiple plans, even all within TIAA-CREF, which is why many of your statements have so many accounts when you think of it as all the same except for the investments themselves.

Many 401(a)s are structured to offer employees an incentive to stay at the organization. They may be funded with dollar, or percentage-based contributions from the employer, the employee, or both.

Employers may match a fixed percentage of employee contributions, or they may make fixed dollar or percentage contributions. Employee participation may be mandatory. The combined limit for employee and employer contributions for 2023 is $66,000, or up the employee's compensation. The contribution limits for 401(a) plans are computed separately from the limits for 457 plans and 403(b) plans, so if you and your employer contribute the maximum, you could theoretically get up to a maximum of $66,000 between all three of these defined contribution plans or $73,500 if over age 50.

401(k) Plan: This plan can accept both employee and employer tax-deferred contributions. The contributions to the plan and the earnings are not federally taxable until they are withdrawn.

Employee contributions to 401(k)s are usually determined as a percentage of salary or wages and are limited to a prescribed amount. In 2023, for taxpayers under age 50, that limit is $22,500. For taxpayers aged 50 and older, the IRS permits additional *"catch-up contributions"* of $7,500 for a total of $30,000. These limits are generally increased for inflation, and as mentioned above, will likely be higher by the time you read this book.

The company—that is, the employer—is responsible for providing the employee with investment choices, typically six to ten choices in either one or two families of mutual funds. Some large employers offering 401(k) plans also allow their employees to purchase individual stock shares in their plans. Fortunately, after the spectacular collapse of Enron, companies are no longer permitted to *require* that their employees own company stock inside their retirement plans.

The employer is also responsible for setting the basic rules of the plan—for example, whether they will offer a matching contribution, or if they will permit loans against the plan. They are also responsible for choosing the investments that are made available to the employee, and for plan administration. The employee is responsible for choosing his or her own investments from the options made available by the employer. 401(k) plans are typically found in for profit entities.

SEP: SEP is an acronym for Simplified Employee Pension. These plans are commonly used by employers with very few employees, and self-employed individuals. Under a SEP, an employer makes contributions to IRAs, which are not taxable for federal income tax purposes, on behalf of employees. Contribution limits are higher with SEPs than with IRAs. Maximum allowable contributions equal 25% of the employee's compensation, up to $66,000 in 2023. If considering a SEP, you must be careful to look at how *compensation* is defined. After you go through the technical hoops, the contribution actually works out to be about 20% of what most self-employed people think is compensation.

SIMPLE: SIMPLE is an acronym for a Savings Incentive Match Plan for Employees. They provide an attractive defined-contribution plan option for small companies that do not sponsor a retirement plan, or self-employed individuals. The maximum allowable contribution ($15,500 in 2023) is lower than that of a SEP, and the employer is required to make either a 2% non-elective contribution for each eligible employee, or a 3% matching contribution for all participating employees. These plans also allow additional *"catch-up"* contributions to be made by employees over age 50 in the amount of $3,500 for 2023.

SEP, SIMPLEs, and One Person 401(k)

Of the three options, we generally prefer a one person 401(k) a.k.a. Solo-K, a.k.a. Super-K.

Solo-K or One-Person 401(k): The Solo-K is commonly used by self-employed individuals (with no employees) who want to contribute the most money possible to their own retirement plan. I recommend these plans for professors who retire from their academic careers, and who have a source of self-employment income such as consulting work. The business owner who has this kind of plan wears two hats—he can contribute to his personal 401(k) as an employee, and then make an additional contribution as the employer. Employee contributions are limited to $22,500 in 2023 ($30,000 if age 50 or over), or up to 100% of compensation if earnings are lower than $22,500. As the employer, the business owner can also make an additional maximum contribution equaling 25% of his or her annual compensation. (As with a SEP plan, be careful to define compensation accurately.) Between his employee and employer contributions, a business owner could contribute $66,000 in 2023 ($73,500 if he is age 50 or older) to his own retirement plan.

For an example of the power of the Solo-K and a calculation, please see Judy's example in Mini Case Study 2.3. These Solo-K plans can also be set up to contain a Roth savings option. This is also the type of plan I usually prefer for the new self-employed retiree that has some type of consulting or other income.

There are also Inherited Roth IRA conversion possibilities with an inherited 401(k), but not with an Inherited IRA. Please see Chapter 11.

Payroll Deduction IRA: This is a relatively newer savings option created in 2013, and it works for businesses of any size. It is probably the simplest and least expensive retirement plan option available to employers, but the contribution limits are low. The employee is responsible for opening an IRA account (either a Traditional or Roth) with any financial institution that offers one. The employer is then responsible for deducting IRA contributions from the employee's pay and depositing the funds into the employee's IRA account. The employer is not permitted to make matching contributions.

The 2023 contribution limit for this type of account is $6,500, with an additional catch-up contribution of $1,000 allowed for employees aged 50 and over. If you think this sounds a lot like a regular IRA, you're right; the major difference is that the payroll deduction by the employer forces the employee to contribute to his or her account.

Deferral Contribution Limits Compared

As a result of a series of tax law changes starting with the Economic Growth and Tax Relief Reconciliation Act of 2001 (EGTRRA), the new deferral contribution limits for employees and owners of many of these individual and defined contribution plans have grown substantially more generous. The government now allows us to put more money in our retirement plans and provides greater tax benefits. I recommend that we take the government up on its offer to fund our own retirement plans to the extent we can afford it.

The maximum deferral contribution limits for 2023 are shown in the chart at the top of the next page. (The maximum contributions for individuals younger than age 50 appear in the first line and the maximum contributions for those age 50 and older are in the second line and in italics). TIAA plans adhere to the contribution limits for 403(b) plans.

Please remember that, with the exception of the Roth accounts discussed more fully in Chapter 3, every one of the retirement plans listed above works basically the same way. Subject to limitations, your taxable income is reduced by the amount you contribute to your plan. Your employer's contribution is not subject to federal income taxes when it is made, nor is your deferral contribution. You pay no federal income tax until you take a withdrawal from the plan,

Maximum Deferral Contribution Limits for 2021-2023

	2021	2022	2023
SIMPLE Plans [a]	$13,500	$14,000	$15,500
50 and older	*$16,500*	*$17,500*	*$19,000*
401(k), 403(b), 457 [b]	$19,500	$20,500	$22,500
50 and older	*$26,000*	*$27,000*	*$30,000*
401(a) [c]	$58,000	$61,000	$66,000
Roth 401(k) + Roth 403(b)	$19,500	$20,500	$22,500
50 and older	*$26,000*	*$27,000*	*$30,000*
SEP [d, e]	$58,000	$61,000	$66,000
50 and older	*$58,000*	*$61,000*	*$66,000*
Solo-K [One-Person 401(k)] [d, e]	$58,000	$61,000	$66,000
50 and older	*$64,500*	*$67,500*	*$73,500*
Traditional and Roth IRA	$ 6,000	$ 6,000	$ 6,500
50 and older	*$ 7,000*	*$ 7,000*	*$ 7,500*
Payroll Deduction IRA	$ 6,000	$ 6,000	$ 6,500
50 and older	*$ 7,000*	*$ 7,000*	*$ 7,500*

[a] SIMPLE plans are for enterprises with 100 or fewer eligible workers.

[b] 403(b) plans are for nonprofits; 457 plans are for governments and nonprofits. In the last three years before retirement, workers in 457 plans can save double the "under age 50" contribution limit.

[c] The limits for 401(a) plan are for combined employer and employee contributions. There are no catch-up contributions for ages 50 and older.

[d] Overall, plan limits for business owners include total of all contributions by the employer (self-owned business), employee (self), and any forfeitures.

[e] Plus amounts for inflation-related adjustments.

and your money can only be withdrawn according to specific rules and regulations. Ultimately, the distributions are taxed at ordinary income tax rates. These plans offer tax-deferred growth because as the assets appreciate, taxes on the dividends, interest, and capital gains are deferred—or delayed—until there is a withdrawal or a distribution.

There are important potential tax considerations depending on which state you live in and which state you retire to, and sometimes you should take appropriate action before you even pack up your belongings and move. For example, one professor client of mine who lived in Washington State was planning to move to California. We made a series of Roth IRA conversions, even higher than we would just for federal purposes. He didn't have to pay Washington tax on the

Roth conversion. After he moved to California he could have tax-free distributions of his Roth IRA not only for federal purposes, but for California purposes also. When he dies and leaves his Roth IRA to his spouse and then their son who lives in CA, neither his wife nor his son will ever have to pay California taxes on the Roth IRA or Inherited Roth IRA.

It is important to know that states tax retirement plans differently. Some states, such as Pennsylvania, do not give employees a tax deduction for their retirement plan contributions but they do not tax retirement plan distributions. So, Pennsylvania becomes a less desirable state to work in, but a more desirable state to retire to.

California, on the other hand, does give employees a tax deduction for their retirement plan contributions, but California taxes IRA and retirement plan distributions, which presumably over time would mean more revenue for the state because the distributions would include appreciation.

A bad scenario for tax purposes would be to live and work in Pennsylvania, not get a tax break for your retirement plan contributions and IRAs, and then retire to California where your IRA and retirement plan distributions would be taxed. A better plan would be to work in California, get the tax break for your retirement plan and IRA contributions, and then retire to Pennsylvania, with no state taxes on retirement plan distributions. You could also retire to a state that doesn't have an income tax, like Texas or Florida. The problem with retiring to Texas isn't Texas taxes. The problem is you have to live in Texas.

Kidding aside, do not let the tail wag the dog. Usually, it is best to live and work where you want and retire to where you want. But sometimes, you can do some tax planning. Sometimes, if it is close, like you spent 175 days in a no or low-tax state, maybe spend an extra week and become a resident of that state. Though time spent is only one test of being a resident. There are other factors to consider when determining residency and we suggest you consult with a tax advisor before making the determination.

Timing and Vesting of Defined Contribution Plans

It is important to understand when employers are required to make their deposits to your retirement plan and when your interest in the plan becomes vested. First, your employer is not allowed to hang on to the money they deduct from your paycheck indefinitely. Department of Labor rules require that your employer deposit your contributions to your retirement plan *as soon as possible, but no later than the 15th business day of the following month.* There are more restrictive rules in place for employers having fewer than 100 plan participants—these employers are required to deposit your contributions within seven business days.

Note, however, that the rules are different for the employer contribution; employers must make their contributions to an employee's retirement plan by the due date of the employer's federal tax return (including extensions). As a result, if your employer is on a calendar year-end, you might not see the matching portion of your 401(k) until well after year-end. Other employers match immediately when a contribution is made.

Also, just because the money is credited to your account doesn't necessarily mean it is all yours immediately. The portion you contribute will always be yours, and if you quit tomorrow, your contribution remains your money. The employer's contribution might only become available to you after working a certain number of years—once you have put in your time. Your employer may refer to this as being *"vested"* in the plan. A common vesting schedule is 20% per year that an employee remains with the company until five years have passed. At that point, the employee is 100% vested. This is called graded vesting. Other plans allow no vesting until the employee has worked for a certain number of years. Then, when he or she reaches that threshold, there is a 100% vesting in the employer's contributions. This is called *cliff vesting*.

A Quick Note about Retirement Plan Loans

Loans against IRAs and IRA-based plans (SEPs and SIMPLEs) are prohibited by law, but loans are permitted against 401(k), 403(b), 457(b), profit sharing and money purchase plans. Some employers offering these types of defined contribution plans allow their employees to take loans against their retirement accounts. Federal tax laws specify that, if loans are permitted, the amount cannot be more than 50% of the participant's vested account balance, up to a maximum of $50,000. Federal laws also specify that the loan must be repaid within five years unless the proceeds were used to buy your primary residence.

Remember, the employer is responsible for setting the rules of their own plan, so some employers might only permit loans in the event of financial hardship, and some might not permit them at all. If loans are permitted, the employee must sign a written loan agreement that specifies the repayment schedule. Most employers require that the loan be repaid through payroll deductions.

If someone needs a loan, many people prefer to take one against their retirement plan because the interest rates are generally lower than what they can get from a bank, and they pay that interest back to themselves. There are some negatives with this strategy that you need to be aware of though. The money taken out of the plan is no longer earning an investment rate of return and, even if the loan is repaid with interest, the interest rate will likely not be as high as the investment rate of return that would have been earned if the money had remained in the account.

Because most employers require repayment via payroll deduction, many employees cannot afford to continue their 401(k) contributions while they are repaying their loan—which affects their ability to reach their long-term retirement goals. And if your employer offers a matching contribution, you lose their matching contribution (which I call free money) during the time you are not contributing to the plan. In some plans, when you take out a loan, you are prohibited from making employee contributions to the plan for one year. This rule is specific to the employer's plan document and not an IRS rule.

While these might seem like relatively minor points, I think you will really regret taking a loan from your retirement plan if you are separated from service before it is repaid. If you lose your job for any reason, you are generally obligated to repay the full balance remaining on the loan, within 60 days.

What do you think the chances are of a bank giving you another loan to repay your retirement plan loan, when you are unemployed? If you are unable to repay it, then your employer is required to treat the loan as a distribution, and you will receive a 1099-R that you will have to include on your tax return the following year. In addition to having to pay taxes on the unpaid balance of the loan, you may also owe a 10% penalty if you are under the age of 59½.

And while you might not plan on leaving your job, that decision could be made for you by a change in university priorities. Then, you are left with a tax problem that you didn't see coming when you were filling out your paperwork for your loan.

We have seen people that had to file for bankruptcy because they could not pay the massive taxes on the distributions from their IRA or retirement plan. To add to their misery, their IRA or retirement plan which is now reduced was one of the assets that would have been protected from creditors in a bankruptcy.

Defined Benefit Plans

With a defined benefit plan, the employer contributes money according to a formula described in the company plan to provide a promised monthly benefit to the employee at retirement. Many people refer to these types of plans as *"my pension."* While most commonly offered by federal, state, and local govern ments, there are a few private employers who still offer them. Many state school universities offer defined benefit pension plans which are sometimes an option among several types of plans. These tend to be public universities, and have widely varying benefit amounts, participation rules, and vesting schedules. The amount of the benefit is determined based on a formula that considers the number of years of service, salary (perhaps an average of the highest three years), and age.

In the private sector, defined benefit plans usually do not allow the employee to contribute his or her own funds into the plan, and the employer bears all of the investment risk. Universities frequently require employees to contribute funds, which will be matched by the employer at some ratio.

For example, schools in the University of California system, such as UC Berkeley, offer a plan where employees contribute 7% of annual pay and the University of California contributes 8% of annual pay. When it is time for the employee to collect his monthly benefit, the employer is responsible for paying the benefit—regardless of how the investments have done from the time of the employer's contribution to the time of the employee's distribution.

If your university offers a choice between a defined benefit and a defined contribution plan, think carefully before making your choice. This is a situa- tion where *"running the numbers"* can help you see the financial implications of your decision.

Defined benefit plans were far more common 30 years ago than they are today. For people with defined benefit plans, there are few opportunities to make strategic decisions during the working years to increase retirement ben- efits. It might be possible to increase the retirement benefit by deferring salary or bonuses into the final years or working overtime to increase the calculation wage base. These opportunities, however, depend on the plan's formula, and they are often inflexible and insignificant.

At retirement, the employee is often given a wide range of choices of how to collect his or her pension. Distribution options generally involve receiving a certain amount of money every month for the rest of one's life.

Receiving regular payments for a specified period, usually a lifetime, is called an annuity. (Please do not confuse this type of annuity with a tax-deferred an- nuity or a 403(b) plan, which is also often called an annuity.) The annuity period often runs for your lifetime and that of your spouse. Or it might be defined with a guaranteed period for successor beneficiaries; maybe it is guaranteed for the life of the longest living spouse, or perhaps for a 10-year term regardless of when you die, or your spouse dies.

Guaranteeing Income for Life

Employees who have defined benefit plans have some very important options to consider at the time of retirement. For example, let's assume that you are in good health and want the highest monthly income for the rest of your life. That often seems like the best option. However, choosing this option means that, if you die first, your surviving spouse is out of luck because your monthly pension payments stop at your death. More times than not, if we need to protect the income for both spouses' lives, I will recommend a reduced pension but with a 100% guarantee for the surviving spouse.

Sometimes pension plan owners take my usual advice and choose a lower monthly payment because it will last through their life and their spouse's life. Sometimes the owner will take a large annual payment and his or her surviving spouse will receive a fraction, perhaps half or two-thirds throughout his or her life. But there is another option to consider.

One of the options frequently pushed by insurance agents is to buy a one-life (not two-life) annuity and use some of the extra income to purchase life insurance on the owner's life. Should the owner die, the life insurance death benefit can go toward the surviving spouse's support. When you look at the numbers, as we have, this usually isn't the best strategy if you still have the option to choose a pension benefit that protects your spouse after your death.

You can see that there are many important decisions to be made at your retirement. In these situations, *"running the numbers,"* that is, comparing different potential scenarios, can provide guidance towards making a decision that is right for your family. And if you have already retired and made an irrevocable choice, it might not be too late to improve your situation. For example, if you already decided to take the highest pension without a survivorship feature, it might not be too late to get insurance, if you are still insurable. In other words, if you are retired and, after reading this book, are now concerned that by taking a one-life annuity with the highest monthly payment you did not sufficiently provide for your surviving spouse, you might want to consider purchasing life insurance*.

---

* Life insurance can be offered by a CPA through Lange Life Care for those interested. It would be offered in their role as a CPA and not as an attorney. There would be no attorney-client relationship. There is no solicitation being made for legal services by the author nor by Lange Legal Services, LLC.

In many, if not most situations, it is often simplest and best to choose a two-life option ensuring full income to you and your spouse. But these questions are so complex that I strongly encourage you to consult with a retirement planning specialist, and who can objectively *"run the numbers."* That way, you can make a decision with full knowledge and understanding of the alternatives available for your family.

Risk of Default

One other issue to consider—although hard to quantify and anticipate—is state retirement systems failing to make their promised payments. The number of announcements about reduced payments and no payments has reached crisis proportions and is getting worse. Retirees in many states and industries have suffered serious reductions in their pension income, and many people who are not yet retired have been notified that their plans have been frozen, meaning that they will get the benefit accrued up to the frozen date, but no additional credit for more years of service or increases in pay.

The Pension Benefit Guaranty Corporation is a federal agency that administers the pensions of companies that cannot meet their obligations to their employees, but even they are stretched to the limit because of the sheer number of pension plans that are inadequately funded. If you are a participant in such a plan, you might want to consider establishing a defined-contribution account in addition to this plan, to supplement your retirement income.

Failing pension plans may soon be the cause of another financial crisis in this country. As if the inadequate funding (formally known as the stated deficit) isn't enough to scare the daylights out of many pension plan participants, what about the understated liability? Many defined benefit plans use interest rate assumptions of 7% or higher, which is not realistic. If a plan is currently paying out to pensioners, as most are, it is extremely imprudent for the plan assets to be invested aggressively.

A safer strategy would be to invest the plan assets in a mix of stocks and bonds. So, let's assume that the plan has 50% of its assets in stocks, and 50% in bonds. If stocks pay 7% over the long term and bonds pay 2% over the long term, the plan as a whole will not earn a 7% rate of return. It will earn an average rate of return of 4.5%. There are also costs associated with pension plan administration—maybe 0.5% to 1%—that have to be considered as well.

The solution, unfortunately, is not to try and earn a higher rate of return by investing all of the plan assets in stocks.

Pension plan owners, especially government agencies, must bite the bullet and contribute more to the pension plan. And when they do not have the money in their budget to do so, they make the plan deficit disappear (on paper, anyway) by increasing the assumed rate of return.

I really feel the problem of underfunded pension plans is going to blow up on us and, to a large extent, it already has. As part of the American Rescue Plan Act of 2021, the Pension Benefit Guaranty Corporation ("PBGC") created a Special Financial Assistance ("SFA") Program to address the immediate financial crisis of underfunded pension plans. The program will provide an estimated $94 billion in assistance to more than 200 eligible plans that are severely underfunded. For example, according to Joel Anderson in an article published by **gobankingrates.com** dated May 10, 2022, New Jersey has $254.4 billion in unfunded pensions. That is up 29% since 2019 despite a good market at that time.

My brother, like thousands of others who worked for a university or entity in Oregon that had a state pension plan had his payment reduced significantly and he didn't get a lot of notice. Perhaps this will put you on notice and you might want to access the viability of the pension plan in your state or company before relying on a 100% payment.

Cash Balance Plan

A relatively new and unique version of a defined-benefit plan is known as a *cash balance plan*. Technically, this is a defined-benefit plan, but it has features similar to a defined-contribution plan. Though on the rise, this type of plan is not common. Each employee is given an account to which the employer provides contributions or pay credits, which may be a percentage of pay and an interest credit on the balance in the account. The account's investment earnings to be credited are usually defined by the plan, and the employer bears all downside risk for actual investment earnings shortfalls. The increase in popularity of cash balance plans has been spurred by the increased number of small business owners who are getting closer to retirement age.

Most cash balance plans are established for the primary benefit of the owner(s) of the company, so contributions from the company for the owners are usually very large with a smaller contribution provided to employees. In our accounting practice, we see Cash Balance plans for physician or dental practices where the owner professional is looking to retire in a few years and wants to significantly increase their retirement plan balances and receive a corresponding tax deduction not only for the contributions to the employee accounts but also to the owner's account.

There is a good possibility that you have the opportunity to invest more money in your retirement plan or plans than you realize. If you have access to more than one retirement plan, Mini Case Study 2.3 might be one of the most important sections of the book.

How Many Plans Are Available to You?

There is a good possibility that you have the opportunity to invest more money in your retirement plan or plans than you realize. For many readers who are still working, applying the lessons of this Mini Case Study could save you thousands of dollars a year. If you have access to more than one retirement plan, the following study might be one of the most important sections of the book.

···   **MINI CASE STUDY 2.3**   ···
Contributing the Maximum to Multiple Retirement Plans*

Tom and his wife, Judy, both 55, want to make the maximum retirement plan contributions allowable. Tom earns $51,000 per year as a professor at a university that has both a 403(b) plan and a Section 457 plan. Judy is self-employed, has no employees, and shows a profit after expenses on her Schedule C, Form U.S. 1040, of $80,000 per year.

Tom and Judy have a 16-year-old computer-whiz child, Bill, who works weekends and summers doing computer programming for Judy's company. Bill is a legitimate subcontractor, not an employee of Judy's company. Judy pays Bill $40,000 per year. What is the maximum that Tom and Judy and Bill can contribute to their retirement plans for calendar year 2022?

Tom: *Calculating Maximum Contributions to Multiple Plans*

Under the 2001 EGTRRA, Tom could contribute $27,000 to his 403(b) plan in 2022 ($20,500 normal limit plus another $6,500 because he is over 50). Under a special rule specifically relating to 457 plans, he could also contribute another $20,500 to his 457 plan in 2022. He is also eligible to contribute

---

* We have used 2022 amounts for this example. The retirement plan contribution limits for future years are likely to be even higher. The current year contribution limits are available on our website at **https://PayTaxesLater.com**. You can also receive these updates as soon as they happen, by signing up for our free e-mail newsletter.

$7,000 to a Roth IRA ($6,000 per year limit plus $1,000 because he is over age 50). (Roth IRAs are discussed in more detail in Chapter 3). Please note the new law allows contributions to all three plans—something not previously permitted. Ultimately, Tom was able to contribute more than his entire income to retirement plans. Now, for most people, this isn't realistic, but here, we're just looking at the maximum that this family *could* contribute, disregarding any other financial needs.

Judy: *Calculating Maximum Contribution to a Solo-K*

The following example is a little complicated but offers many readers with self-employment income an opportunity to contribute more money in their retirement plan than they are contributing right now.

After rejecting a more complicated and more expensive defined benefit plan, Judy chooses the one-person 401(k) plan, or the Solo-K plan. Judy could contribute as much as $41,870 into her personal 401(k) plan. This plan for self-employed taxpayers has the equivalent of an employee and employer share.

The first component is the 401(k) elective employee deferral amount that is limited to $27,000 in 2022 (the same limits as Tom's 403(b) plan). Most Solo-Ks are set up so that you can deduct this portion on your tax return and have it taxed like a regular 401(k). If you want this portion to enjoy the tax-free benefits of a Roth IRA, which we generally recommend, you can set up a Roth Solo-K, and elect to put this $27,000 into the Roth Solo-K. So, she has options—Traditional Solo-K or Roth Solo-K. Please see Chapter 4 for a detailed comparison of a Roth 401(k) *vs.* a Traditional 401(k).

The second component is a $14,870 discretionary profit-sharing, or employer's contribution. Please note that, as with a Traditional 401(k) plan, the employer contribution cannot be made to the Roth account. To arrive at the $14,870, Judy's net self-employed income of $80,000 must be reduced by half of her computed self-employment tax, which is $80,000 x 92.35% x 15.3% = $11,304 x 50%, or $5,652. Then that amount is subtracted from her net income, $80,000 ($80,000 – $5,652 = $74,348). The $74,348 is multiplied by the 20% contribution rate limit (for self-employed individuals, and equal to 25% of earnings net of the contribution itself) to yield the maximum profit-sharing contribution amount of $14,870. (If Judy's income had been higher, the total of both the employer and employee contributions to her Solo-K could be as high as $67,500 in 2022.

The maximum contribution allowed to the plan is $61,000 in 2022 and she can also make a $6,500 catch-up contribution). Judy also can make an additional $7,000 contribution to her Roth IRA including the catch-up contribution since she is over age 50. *Note: if Judy's self-employment income is from an eligible small business, the qualified business income deduction ("QBID") would need to be subtracted from the Solo-K employer contribution computation. Since this calculation is beyond the scope of this chapter, we have not included the QBID deduction in the calculation.*

Bill: *For Parents Who Are Considering Funding Retirement Plans for Their Children*

Although Bill is young, if he can afford it, he should use his $40,000 income to begin making contributions to his retirement plan. Bill will owe $6,120 of self-employment tax, half of which is deductible, so his net earned income for the purposes of retirement plan contributions is $36,940.

Bill could open a SIMPLE plan and contribute $14,000 in 2022, plus a 3% SIMPLE matching contribution, which would be $1,108 (3% of $40,000 x .9235). The net earned income less these amounts is $18,772 which is enough to fully fund his Roth IRA with $6,000. If he already spent some of his income, his parents could make him a gift of the money.

The tax-free benefit of the Roth IRA and the tax-deferred benefit of the SIMPLE plan are so important to a child during his or her lifetime that some parents who have sufficient money are willing to fund their child's retirement plan. This is a wonderful idea. However, in order to contribute to a retirement plan or IRA, the child must have earned income. Some parents will be tempted to create a sham business for their child or even put their child on the payroll as a sham transaction. I do not recommend this approach. I advocate that the child does legitimate work, complying with all child labor laws. All retirement plan contributions should stem from legitimate work or businesses, and if based on self-employed earnings, be a real business. (I had to say that in case the IRS reads this. In all seriousness, however, there are also nonfinancial benefits in having a child do legitimate work to receive money.).

I have seen parents paying infants to model, characterizing the payment to the infant as self-employment income and making a retirement plan contribution for the infant. I think that goes too far. Any situation where a child younger than 11 years old receives employment compensation is highly suspect. Even at age 11, legitimate compensation should not be too high.

Let's assume that Tom, Judy, and Bill max out their retirement plan contributions. Even though Tom and Judy earned only $131,000 and Bill earned only $40,000, the family could contribute nearly $124,478 into their retirement plans and Roth IRAs for 2022. For subsequent years, or maybe even this year, the contribution limits are likely to be even more generous. I am assuming, of course, the family could afford these contributions. Even if they cannot and have substantial after-tax funds held in a brokerage account, they should still consider these high retirement plan contributions and get their money to live from their brokerage account. Is this a great country or what?

This example intentionally exaggerates the family's likely contributions. The point is to show the maximum contribution limits and the variety of plan options available. In this particular case, Tom and Judy and Bill may choose not to maximize their contributions because they may not receive any income tax benefits beyond a certain level of contribution. It is worthwhile, however, to review this case study to help with choosing and implementing a new plan.

....

Minimize Your Life Insurance Costs to Maximize Your Retirement Contributions: The Ladder Approach

Many old classic whole life insurance agents are going to hate me (many already do) for writing this section of this chapter. Many of our younger faculty clients complain that they face a choice between fully funding their retirement plan contributions or paying for enough life insurance to adequately protect their families (among other competing costs). Even though some universities are more generous in the amount of life insurance they provide to faculty members, and even though professors can often purchase additional optional coverage at a discount, which may not be enough to fully protect their family.

I am extremely leery of whole life, especially for young faculty members. Term insurance is almost always a better solution for individuals who want to make sure of a guaranteed and needed sufficient death benefit at a relatively low cost.

The objective of term life insurance is to protect a family from the financial devastation that can ensue from the untimely death of a primary bread winner(s). It is also important to insure the value of the services of a stay-at-home parent. It is critically important insurance, but it is also to your advantage to try to get the appropriate level of coverage for the most reasonable price.

The following section, though by no means complete, presents my favorite idea for many young families to protect themselves in the event of an early, unexpected death, but to do so relatively cheaply. I am working from the premise that I do not like to see people underinsured, but I also want everyone to be thinking ahead to retirement.

One of the most common mistakes my younger clients make is not having sufficient term insurance. Most healthy young people survive until retirement age and paying for term insurance is not something anyone really wants to do.

In my or for that matter virtually any large estate planning practice, we see young healthy people who died much too early. In my experience, it is rarely the result of a catastrophic car or plane accident, but more frequently because of the sudden onset of cancer or some other fatal disease.

Most people, however, also have this vague sense that the responsible thing to do is to purchase insurance to protect their families. Some people seek out an insurance provider and initiate a policy; others do something when a life insurance professional approaches them. In either case they usually end up with some kind of policy. The key is to find a policy that balances adequate insurance and minimum premiums. I do not like to see people, especially younger people who are working on a limited budget, pay high life insurance premiums.

The best way to start thinking about how much life insurance you need is to consider *"How much income will your survivors require to live comfortably?"* Let's say that after some analysis, you decide that an appropriate income is $60,000 per year in today's dollars. Please note I did not derive this number as a multiple of current salary; it is based purely on projected need.

I am not going to delve into the intricacies of calculating a safe withdrawal rate—that is to say, how much as a percentage of principal you can withdraw and have the money last for a lifetime—but I would say for young people with a long-life expectancy, 4% would probably be on the high side for a safe withdrawal rate. This means if there is no other source of income, an individual will need at least $1,500,000 of life insurance ($60,000/4% = $1,500,000).

First, I hope I didn't just bum you out and make you realize you are vastly underinsured because $60,000 of income doesn't sound that high, and you do not have anywhere near $1,500,000 of insurance. Admittedly, whatever resources you have can be used to reduce the need for life insurance. If both spouses work, the income of the survivor can certainly be factored in. If you have significant investments or savings, they can also be used to reduce the need for insurance.

Many insurance professionals make a convincing case for permanent insurance, which is a type of policy that ultimately has cash value. There is a payout when you die, or sometimes upon reaching a certain age. Term insurance, on the other hand, at least the way I use it, will likely not pay out if you survive to a normal life expectancy. It is designed to protect your heirs if you do not survive to a normal life expectancy.

Permanent insurance is expensive, so many families who like the idea that there will always be a payout in the future go ahead and buy permanent insurance. They are usually woefully unprotected at the insurance premium levels they can afford. Term insurance is less expensive, so when cost is an issue, which it nearly always is for younger families, I recommend considering laddered term insurance to help keep premiums more affordable but to also provide you with sufficient protection. Even though you give up a permanent benefit, I would rather see the money going toward sufficient term insurance, so the surviving spouse and other family members are protected rather than having a permanent policy but with an insufficient amount of coverage.

What is the *"Ladder Approach?"* Let's assume that you do projections and determine that you will have sufficient money to retire at age 60 (assuming you are age 30 now). You might logically think—as premiums are guaranteed never to go up—*"Okay, I need a 30-year level term policy for $1,500,000."*

If you work and save for ten years, you may only need $1,000,000 at that point in time. Perhaps in the ten years beyond that, your need may drop to $500,000. I am trying to keep it simple to make a point. The point is as you age, your insurance needs will change, usually getting smaller, and thinking within this more flexible framework offers some new options.

Since I am being frugal with your insurance budget, consider the following set of policies, assuming the above situation.

- Get a 30-year term policy for $500,000 coverage
- Get a 20-year term policy for $500,000 coverage
- Get a 10-year term policy for $500,000 coverage

If you die between the date the policy is issued and year ten, your heirs get $1,500,000, which is what we determined was the needed amount. At the end of ten years, the first policy ends, and you will only have $1,000,000 of coverage. That is okay. By this point you should have $500,000 in retirement plans and savings. In addition, the need for insurance will be down a little bit because your heirs will have a shorter life expectancy.

After 20 years, the second policy ends, and you will only have $500,000 of coverage remaining. That is okay because by this time you should have $1,000,000 of retirement and savings, and your need will only be $500,000. At the end of 30 years, you will have no coverage, but again, that is okay because hopefully by then you will have accrued sufficient resources for your surviving spouse.

Of course, in the above example, I have kept things really simple. I have not included relevant factors like inflation, children's true needs, timing of education needs, the ability of the surviving spouse to work, and so forth.

But you get the idea. We have helped a number of our clients reach their goal of adequate coverage through this laddered system. Frequently, a 30-year level term policy costs more than individuals might want to pay or can afford, so they compromise by not getting the insurance coverage they really need. I would prefer to see you get the coverage you need by using some variation of the laddered approach that I have suggested. Remember, the goal is sufficient coverage for a reasonable cost. That said, my recommendation for many younger clients is to have most of your coverage through term insurance, but also consider adding a small permanent policy to the mix.

In all fairness, I didn't invent this layered approach. I learned it from Tom Hall, an excellent broker I work with in Pittsburgh. This brings up another point. After you decide to get the insurance you need, I recommend purchasing your insurance through an ethical insurance broker (someone who can purchase insurance from many different companies). In our experience, working with a broker is the way to get the best policies at the best rates.

Consider Conversion Options Before You Buy Term Life Insurance

Also, when considering term insurance, a key consideration should be the policy's conversion features. Conversion features provide additional flexibility in case your insurance needs change in the future. Suppose you become uninsurable due to health issues, or you decide you need coverage for a longer period. Without conversion options, you might have to buy a new policy with a higher premium because you're older and likely have medical issues or—worst case scenario—those options may be unavailable.

Conversion options allow you to convert to an insurance company's 'permanent' product without medical underwriting at the same rate class as you were originally approved. Most insurance companies have an expensive conversion feature, but some insurance companies offer conversions to any product available in their portfolio at the time of conversion. Having the option to convert to the lowest cost product available can be a game changer as we get older and medical issues begin to arise. Also, if you should become uninsurable and you have a good conversion option, you may have the ability to sell your policy. Please refer to Chapter 26 where we include Exit Strategies for your life insurance policy in the event you do not want to pay the premiums anymore.

Let's look at an example. One of our clients had a ten-year term policy that was expiring when he was age 64. He was originally approved at the best rate class (preferred plus) and became uninsurable. He had a valuable conversion option that allowed him to convert to the lowest cost permanent product in the insurance company's portfolio. He decided to convert his original $1 million term policy to a $1 million permanent policy without any medical underwriting. Not only did he have a greatly reduced life expectancy, he was able to obtain a valuable asset at a reduced rate to protect his family which also included a chronic care provision which he did not previously have with his term policy. It was a wonderful investment and offered additional protection for the future needs of his spouse and family.

For more information on how to get the best deal on life insurance, and how to use life insurance as a tool to protect your family after you die, be sure to read Chapter 26, *Life Insurance As An Estate Planning Tool*.

What If You Think You Cannot Afford to Make the Maximum Contributions?

What if you think you cannot save more than the minimum amount to get your employer match? The truth is you may very well be able to afford to save, but you do not realize it. That's right. I am going to present a rationale to persuade you to contribute more than you think you can afford.

Let's assume you have been limiting your own contributions to the amount that your employer is willing to match and yet you barely have enough money to get by week to week. Does it still make sense to make nonmatched contributions assuming you do not want to reduce your spending? Maybe.

If you have substantial savings and maximizing your retirement plan contributions causes your net payroll check to be insufficient to meet your expenses, I still recommend maximizing retirement plan contributions. The shortfall for your living expenses from making increased pre-tax retirement plan contributions should be withdrawn from your savings (money that has already been taxed). Over time this process, that is, saving the most in a retirement plan and funding the shortfall by making after-tax withdrawals from the after-tax account, transfers money from the after-tax environment to the pre-tax environment. Ultimately, it results in more money for you and your heirs.

A final point worth mentioning is that you should consider your personal tax bracket when making contributions to your retirement plan. Your tax bracket will likely change over the course of your lifetime because of your marital status, and changes in your income and likely changes in the tax law. While I still want you to contribute the maximum you possibly can to your retirement plan, in some instances it may make more sense to contribute to the Traditional account rather than the Roth account, and vice versa. These strategies are covered in detail in Chapter 4.

Pending Changes

As we go to press, SECURE 2.0 became law. The contribution amount to retirement plans will increase with inflation. However, the concepts and the advice will be the same, which will usually be to max out your Roth first and Traditional for the rest.

KEY IDEAS

- You should contribute the maximum you can afford to all the retirement plans to which you have access in the order recommended in this chapter.

- Most professors have the ability to contribute more money to a retirement plan than they thought.

- Do not neglect life insurance during your accumulation years. Using a laddered approach can be an affordable way to protect your family as your retirement savings accumulate.

- Conversion privileges may be a future game changer when securing term life insurance. The lowest price is not the sole consideration when purchasing term life insurance products.

3

Traditional IRAs *vs.* Roth IRAs

"Saving is a very fine thing. Especially when your parents have done it for you."
— Winston Churchill

For the majority of people, the primary vehicle for retirement savings will be in an employee-sponsored retirement plan such as a 403(b) plan, and I'll discuss those plans at length in the next chapter. But some of you may have spouses or partners whose only option for accumulating retirement assets is with an IRA. Or you may have IRA accounts funded by rollovers from retirement plans from other institutions. Or perhaps you've contributed enough to your employer's retirement plan and HSA to get the full employer match, and you want to explore IRA options. Or you've retired or even if you are still working but have a side business as a self-employed speaker/writer/consultant and you want options for continuing to accumulate your savings.

What is the Difference Between an IRA and a Roth IRA?

Prior to the SECURE Act, individuals could not contribute to Individual Retirement Accounts (IRAs) past age 70½. After passing the SECURE Act, effective in year 2020, individuals at any age can contribute to an IRA. The only requirement is the contribution cannot exceed the smaller of earned income or the IRA contribution limit.

There are two major types of IRAs, the Traditional and the Roth. Traditional IRAs were created in 1974 as an incentive for taxpayers to begin saving for their retirements. Owners of Traditional IRAs enjoy tax-deferred growth on their investment, but the contributions and earnings are taxed at the federal level when a qualified withdrawal is made. IRA owners can also take a tax deduction for their contributions if they meet either of these two requirements:

- They (and their spouse, if married) do not have a retirement plan at work.

- They earn less income than the Adjusted Gross Income (AGI) limit for deducting IRA contributions. (Please see the following discussion regarding Traditional IRA eligibility rules.)

If IRA owners have income above the limit for which they are permitted to deduct the contribution, they may still contribute to an IRA, but without the benefit of a tax deduction. These are commonly referred to as *nondeductible IRA contributions.*

With the exception of the Roth IRA (discussed below) and the Defined Benefit Plan, all the other retirement plans mentioned in Chapter 2 can usually be rolled into an IRA, income tax-free, at retirement or service termination.

Roth IRAs were first established by the Taxpayer Relief Act of 1997. The main characteristic of the Roth IRA is that the investment grows tax-free and is not taxed when qualified withdrawals are made. However, unlike the Traditional IRA, there is no income tax deduction up front. The Roth IRA income limit on contributions is much higher than the Traditional deductible IRA income limit on contributions. This allows many higher income earners who are not eligible for a deductible IRA to participate in a Roth IRA.

I was a big fan of Roth IRAs even before they became law. I wrote the first peer-reviewed article on Roth IRAs and Roth IRA conversions that was published in *The Tax Adviser* in 1998. At the time, few understood how fabulous the Roth plans could be. I am still advocating IRA owners strongly consider Roth IRAs and Roth IRAs conversions in many situations.

Here is a comparison of the differences between Roth and Traditional IRAs: The essence of a Roth IRAs (in contrast to a Traditional IRA) is that you pay tax on the seed (i.e., the contribution, because you don't not get a tax deduction), but you can reap the harvest tax-free (i.e., the distribution). With a Traditional IRA, you deduct the seed, but pay tax on the harvest.

Contribution Limits for Both Roth and Traditional IRAs

The permitted contribution amounts are the same for both Roth IRAs and Traditional IRAs. Note that the *total* permitted contribution amount applies both to IRAs and Roth IRAs, which means that for 2023, you can only contribute a total of $6,500 ($7,500 if you are 50 or older) to IRAs and Roth IRAs.

> The essence of a Roth IRA is that you pay tax on the seed *(the contribution)*, but you can reap the harvest tax-free *(the distribution)*. With a Traditional IRA, you deduct the seed, but pay tax on the harvest.

Unlike the contribution limits for most employer-sponsored qualified retirement plans, the maximum contribution limits for Traditional and Roth IRAs have not changed since 2019. The total IRA and/or Roth IRA contributions cannot exceed your *earned* income, and, as with Traditional IRAs, a married individual filing a joint return may make a Roth IRA contribution for the nonworking spouse by treating his or her compensation as his or her spouse's. The contribution limits for 2019 through 2023 are shown in Figure 3.1 below.

Figure 3.1
IRA Contribution Limits for 2019 through 2023

	Roth IRA	Traditional IRA
Investment	Grows tax-free	Grows tax-deferred
Withdrawals *(qualified)*	Tax-free	Taxed as ordinary income
Contributions	Income level	Income level
Income Limits	Affects ability to contribute	Affects deductibility of contribution
Contribution Limits	Same as IRA	Same as Roth IRA
Required Distributions	Not if you are the original owner	Yes

Contribution Limits for Individuals 50 and Older

Year	Annual IRA *and* Roth IRA	Catch-Up Contribution Limits
2019	$6,000	$1,000
2020	$6,000	$1,000
2021	$6,000	$1,000
2022	$6,000	$1,000
2023	$6,500	$1,000

Sharp-eyed readers may notice that, while the IRS found it necessary to adjust the maximum contribution limits for most employer-sponsored qualified retirement plans for inflation in 2023 and three years prior, they only recently changed the contribution limits for Traditional and Roth IRAs in 2023 as part of the SECURE Act 2.0.

Traditional IRA Eligibility Rules

1. All taxpayers who have earned income are allowed to contribute to a Traditional IRA without regard to income level.

2. If neither you nor your spouse participates in an employee-sponsored retirement plan, you both can deduct the full amount of your Traditional IRA contributions.

3. If you are covered by a retirement plan at work, there are AGI limits for allowing full deductions, partial deductions, and limits above which no deductions are permitted. They are shown in Figure 3.2 on the next page.

A spousal contribution can be made for a nonworking spouse if the other spouse has earned income, and a joint tax return is filed. A spousal IRA has been around for decades, but as of 2013, it has a new name: the Kay Bailey Hutchison Spousal IRA.

And while the dollar amounts for contributions were increased for inflation, the basic rules for spousal IRAs are still the same. IRA contributions for both spouses are still limited by the amount of income earned by the working spouse.

If the working spouse earns $8,000, then the maximum that can be contributed to both IRAs combined, is $8,000. Please note *"contribution amounts"* and *"deduction amounts"* are two different things. If the working spouse is not covered under a retirement plan at work, the non-working spouse's IRA contribution (a maximum of $6,500 - $7,500 if over age 50 in 2023) is fully deductible. If the working spouse is covered under a retirement plan at work, the nonworking spouse can still contribute the same amount, but the tax deduction may be limited, as shown in Figure 3.3, also on page 59.

4. If you have too much income to deduct your Traditional IRA contribution, you can still make a nondeductible IRA contribution if you are eligible. You will not get the income tax deduction up front, but you will still gain the advantage of the tax-deferred growth in the account.

Roth IRA Eligibility Rules

1. As with a Traditional IRA, an individual can contribute to a Roth IRA after reaching age 70½ as long as he or she has earned income. Earned income includes wages, commissions, self-employment income, and other amounts received for personal services, as well as long-term disability benefits received prior to normal retirement age, taxable alimony, and sepa-

Figure 3.2

**2022 and 2023 AGI Limitations for Deducting a Traditional IRA
if You are Covered by a Retirement Plan at Work**

Year	Fully Deductible	Partially Deductible	Not Deductible
Single & Head of Household			
2022	$ 68,000 *or less*	$ 68,001 - $ 77,999	$ 78,000+
2023	$ 73,000 *or less*	$ 73,001 - $ 82,999	$ 83,000+
Married Filing Jointly			
2022	$109,000 *or less*	$109,001 - $128,999	$129,000+
2023	$116,000 *or less*	$116,001 - $135,999	$136,000+
Married Filing Separately			
2022	N/A	*Less than* $10,000	$ 10,000+
2023	N/A	*Less than* $10,000	$ 10,000+

Figure 3.3

**2022 and 2023 AGI Limitations for Deducting a Traditional IRA
if You are NOT Covered by a Retirement Plan at Work**

Year	Fully Deductible	Partially Deductible	Not Deductible
Single & Head of Household			
2022	No Income Limit	–	–
2023	No Income Limit	–	–
Married Filing Jointly or Separately *(Spouse Does Not Have a Plan at Work)*			
2022	No Income Limit	–	–
2023	No Income Limit	–	–
Married Filing Jointly or Separately *(Spouse Does Have a Plan at Work)*			
2022	$204,000 *or less*	$204,001 - $213,999	$214,000+
2023	$218,000 *or less*	$ 218,001 - $227,999	$228,000+
Married Filing Separately *(Spouse Does Have a Plan at Work)*			
2022	–	*Less than* $10,000	–
2023	–	*Less than* $10,000	–

rate maintenance payments received under a decree of divorce or separate maintenance.

2. Individuals must meet the income tests, which exclude higher income tax-payers from contributing to Roth IRAs. (See Figure 3.4 below.)

3. A married individual filing a joint return may make a Roth IRA contribution for the nonworking spouse by treating his or her compensation as his or her spouse's but must exclude any of his or her own IRA contributions from the income treated as his or her spouse's. (For example, in 2023, if you are not yet age 50 and make $8,000, you can contribute $6,500 to your Roth, but only $2,000 to your spouse's Roth.) Total contributions cannot exceed your income.

Figure 3.4

2022 and 2023 Income Eligibility Rules for Roth IRAs

Year	Full Contribution	Reduced Contribution	No Contribution
Single & Head of Household			
2022	*Up to* $129,000	$129,001 - $143,999	$144,000+
2023	*Up to* $138,000	$138,001 - $152,999	$153,000+
Married Filing Jointly			
2022	*Up to* $204,000	$204,001 - $213,999	$214,000+
2023	*Up to* $218,000	$218,001 - $227,999	$228,000+

Advanced Distribution Rules for Traditional IRAs

1. Traditional IRA withdrawals are generally taxable at the federal level, but not necessarily at the state level. If you make nondeductible contributions to your IRA, you will have *basis* (in other words, money that you put into the account, that you already paid tax on, and on which the IRS cannot tax you again). If all of your IRA contributions were tax deductible, you have no basis in the account. It is important to know if you have basis in your nondeductible IRA, because you do not want to pay more taxes on your IRA withdrawal than are required.

The burden of proving that a portion of the withdrawal is not taxable falls on you, so I hope you filed a Form 8606 to keep track of the basis in your IRA. This form should be filed every year as an attachment to your tax return once you have any basis in your IRA. When a withdrawal is made from an IRA with basis, a calculation is made to determine what percentage of the money in the account is your contribution, and what percentage reflects earnings on your contributions.

Let's say your non-deductible contributions were $20,000 and the value of your IRA at year-end after taking a $10,000 withdrawal is $90,000. In this case, 20% of the withdrawal is considered a return of your own money and is not taxable. The remaining $8,000 is taxable. (My book, *The Roth Revolution*, covers in detail a great technique for converting after-tax or nondeductible IRAs or after-tax dollars inside a Traditional 401(k) to Roth IRAs without paying any tax. Please visit **https://PayTaxesLater.com**, for more information about that book.) An example of this strategy is also presented in Chapter 7.

2. All Traditional IRA withdrawals prior to age 59½ are subject to an additional 10% penalty (for amounts exceeding basis) unless the withdrawal falls under one of the following exemptions:

- They are made to a beneficiary (or the individual's estate) on or after the individual's death.

- They are attributable to the individual with a total or permanent disability.

- They were used for qualified first-time home purchase expenses.

- The distributions are not more than your qualified higher education expenses.

- They were used for qualified medical expenses exceeding 7.5% of AGI.

- The distributions are not more than the cost of your medical insurance due to a period of unemployment.

- They are part of substantially equal periodic payments over the life of the participant—that is, distributions qualifying under Section 72(t) (which we do not cover in this book) for exemption from the premature distribution penalty.

- They are due to an IRS levy on the account.

- The distribution is a qualified reservist distribution.

- The distribution is a coronavirus-related distribution from January 1, 2020 to December 30, 2020, up to an aggregate limit of $100,000. The

CARES Act allows you to spread out your taxes for the withdrawal over three years (2020-2022). If you repay some or all of the distribution back into your IRA, the IRS considers that amount a 'rollover' and not subject to income tax

3. All Traditional IRAs are subject to RMDs after age 72, subject to changes in SECURE Act 2.0.

Distribution Rules for Roth IRAs

1. In order to take completely tax-free (or qualified) withdrawals from a Roth IRA that has grown in value, five years must have elapsed since opening the account. There is a separate five-year holding period for each Roth IRA conversion as well (conversions are discussed in more detail in Chapter 15). Do you want the practical wisdom regarding the 5-year rule? In the vast majority of cases, it isn't relevant. Roth IRAs and Roth IRA conversions are long-term strategies, and it almost always makes the most sense to keep them for longer than five years. That said, I get asked about the 5-year rule a lot.

Distributions must be made on or after age 59½, unless one of the following special circumstances applies:

- A distribution is made to your beneficiary (or your estate) on or after your death.

- A distribution is attributable to your disability.

- A distribution is made for a qualified first-time home purchase expense up to $10,000 (lifetime maximum).

2. This restriction also applies to the beneficiary of a Roth IRA whose owner dies before the five-year period has ended. The beneficiary may withdraw funds tax-free as long as they do not exceed the contribution amount, but he or she must wait until the five-year period has passed before being able to enjoy tax-free withdrawal of the Roth IRAs earnings.

3. Withdrawals prior to age 59½ may be taken without tax or penalties to the extent of previous annual contributions.

4. Withdrawals in excess of previous contributions made before the five-year holding period is met are taxable, but penalty-free under the following circumstances:

- For qualified college expenses.

- For qualified unreimbursed medical expenses that exceed 7.5% of AGI.

- For health insurance premiums paid for certain unemployed individuals.

- If withdrawals are part of substantially equal periodic payments over the life of the participant.

- If the distribution is part of an IRS levy.

- You are the beneficiary of a deceased IRA owner.

- If you are withdrawing up to $5,000 in the year after the birth or adoption of your child.

- The withdrawal was made when you were a reservist.

All other withdrawals prior to age 59½ that are in excess of previous contributions are taxable and subject to a 10% penalty.

5. Roth IRA amounts are not subject to RMDs during the original owner's lifetime.

Furthermore, a Roth IRA owner can designate his or her spouse as the beneficiary who, upon the Roth IRA owner's death, would have the option of postponing RMDs until the second death. After the surviving spouse's death, the subsequent beneficiary (usually a child) would be required to take nontaxable minimum distributions of the Inherited Roth IRA over 10-years in accordance with the new rules in the SECURE Act.

A distribution does not necessarily have to be taken every year, but all of the Roth IRA money must be distributed by year 10. (Please see Chapter 11 for distribution rules for Inherited IRAs and Inherited Roth IRAs.)

The five-year holding requirement for Roth IRAs is intended to promote long-term savings. The five-year clock starts ticking on January 1 of the tax year associated with the first contribution or conversion, which actually results in making the five-year waiting period less than five years. The period begins on the first day of the tax year for which a contribution is made.

If you open a Roth IRA account for the 2023 tax year by making a contribution on April 15, 2024 (the last day you can make your Roth IRA contributions for 2023), the five-year period is from January 1, 2023, to December 31, 2027. To achieve the same five-year period, start date when opening a Roth IRA account using a Roth IRA conversion, you must make the conversion by December 31, 2023 (the last day you can make your Roth IRA conversions for 2023). Pursuant to these Roth IRA rules, if you suddenly need the money the day after or at any time after you make the contribution, you can take out the amount you contributed, free of tax. Any interest or gains, however, have to remain in the account for five years, in order to become tax free. Note, however, that the IRS has a process called *"ordering rules"* that determine if there is tax due on your distribution. Distributions are ordered as follows:

- your contributions,
- conversion and rollover contributions, on a first-in, first out basis (generally, taken from the earliest year first), and
- earnings on contributions.

Assume you converted $80,000 from a Traditional IRA to a Roth IRA in 2018, and that $20,000 of that amount was your basis. At the time of the conversion, you would have included $60,000 in your taxable income. In 2019, you made a $7,000 contribution to the Roth IRA. In 2022, at age 60, you take a $9,000 distribution from the Roth IRA. How much of your distribution is taxable? Well, our accounting office can always figure it out for you, but if you'd rather do it yourself, use the above rules.

The money you contributed is considered first. You contributed $7,000, so $7,000 of the $9,000 is not taxable. The next $2,000 isn't taxable either, because that was part of your conversion, and it was taxed in 2018. There is no early withdrawal penalty because you are over 59½. But suppose that your Roth IRA has grown to $150,000 and you want to withdraw everything so that you can buy a second home.

Following the same rules, the $7,000 you contributed is not taxable, and the $80,000 conversion amount is not taxable. The gain of $63,000 is taxable because a second home is not a qualified exception to the five-year holding period rule. You should wait until 2023 to withdraw the final $63,000 because it will not be taxable then.

Advantages and Disadvantages of Roth IRAs

The Principal Advantages:

- With limited exceptions, they grow income-tax free.
- More liberal contribution rules are in place. Taxpayers may also elect to convert all or part of their Traditional IRAs to Roth accounts, by paying the taxes at the time of the conversion. The future growth on the converted amount is tax-free.
- They are not subject to the RMD rules mandating withdrawals beginning

at age 72. As of this writing, you are not required to take distributions during your lifetime. (You may *choose* to, but you do not *have* to). If you die and leave your Roth IRA to your spouse, your spouse will not have to take RMDs either.

- If needed, all of your after-tax annual contributions are always eligible for withdrawal at any time without tax consequences.

- If you have earned income after age 72, you can keep contributing money to your Roth IRA (and so can your spouse, based on your income).

- In cases where maximum retirement contributions are made and there are also after-tax savings, forgoing a tax deduction helps to lower the amount of after-tax savings while putting more value in the tax-free environment. Keep in mind that after-tax savings have inefficient tax consequences on their investment returns.

The long-term advantage of the Roth IRA is that, in many cases, your heirs receive a 10-year stretch on the income earned on the Roth IRA. The 10-year limit does not apply to spouses or other eligible designated beneficiaries.

The Principal Disadvantages:

- You do not receive a tax deduction when you make a contribution. You will then have less money to invest in after-tax funds or to spend. But remember, after-tax funds are not tax efficient due to income taxes. And if you simply spend the tax savings, the Roth alternative will look even better because it forces you to save and build a more valuable IRA.

- If you drop into a lower tax bracket once you begin taking your IRA distributions, you may sometimes do better with a Traditional IRA. In this case, the tax savings from the deductible contribution would exceed the taxes paid upon withdrawal. This disadvantage can often be offset by a longer period of tax-free growth.

- The Roth IRA account may go down in value. In that case, if the decline becomes large enough, you would have been better off with a deductible IRA because at least you would have received a tax deduction on your contributions. As always, I recommend that you use prudent investment strategies so that the possibility of losses in your Roth account are minimized.

- If Congress ever eliminates the income tax in favor of a sales tax or value-added tax, you will have given up your tax deduction on the Traditional IRA. And since the distribution will be tax-free anyway, in retrospect, the choice of a Roth IRA would have been a mistake. This situation is similar to the extreme example of having lower tax brackets in retirement.

People who have earned income, and who are ineligible to make Traditional deductible IRA contributions because their income is above the limits, can still make contributions to an IRA, but *without* the tax deduction. These nondeductible IRAs are also available for people who are above the income limits to make Roth IRA contributions.

Nondeductible IRAs

If your income is below the threshold and you are eligible to make Roth IRA contributions, it is important to understand that the Roth is always a much better choice than the *nondeductible* IRA. Remember, you do not get a tax deduction for either, but all the money in the Roth IRA will be tax-free when the money is withdrawn, but the growth in the nondeductible IRA will be taxable. Roth IRAs can provide a much better result over the long term. Many people make the mistake of contributing to a nondeductible IRA instead of a Roth IRA when they have a choice. Although the mistake can be mitigated if caught in time, this mistake results in future taxes that could have been avoided.

Nondeductible IRA contributions that provide tax-deferred growth, however, are still of great benefit for many high-income people who do not qualify for Roth IRA and deductible IRA contributions. Better yet, as of this writing, high income individuals are still eligible to convert their nondeductible IRA accounts into Roth IRAs with little or no tax cost.

A recent IRS ruling also permits individuals who have both deductible and non-deductible contributions in their retirement plans, to split the plan assets. This means that the pre-tax portion of the plan can now be rolled into a Traditional IRA, and the after-tax portion can be rolled into a Roth IRA—effectively allowing a tax-free Roth IRA conversion. (See Chapter 7 for more information on Roth IRA conversions.) This is opportunity knocking, given a little forethought.

What Makes a Roth IRA So Great When Compared with a Traditional IRA?

The advantages of compounding interest on both tax-deferred investments and on tax-free investments far outweigh paying yearly taxes on the capital gains, dividends, and interest of after-tax investments. As you saw in Chapter 2, you are generally better off putting more money in tax-deferred and tax-free

The Roth is always a much better choice than the nondeductible IRA. You do not get a tax deduction for either, but all the money in the Roth IRA will be tax-free when it is withdrawn. The growth in the nondeductible IRA will be taxable.

accounts than in less efficient after-tax investments. Remember that with regular after-tax investments, you must pay income taxes on annual dividends, interest, and, if you make a sale, on capital gains.

The advantage the Roth IRA holds over a Traditional IRA builds significantly over time because of the increase in the purchasing power of the account. Let's assume you make a $6,000 Roth IRA contribution (not including the $1,000 catch-up contribution if over age 50). The purchasing power of your Roth IRA will increase by $6,000, and that money will grow income tax-free.

On the other hand, let's assume you contribute $6,000 to a deductible Traditional IRA and you are in the 24% tax bracket. In that case, you will receive a tax deduction of $6,000 and get a $1,440 tax break (24% x $6,000). This $1,440 in tax savings is not in a tax-free or tax-deferred investment. Even if you resist the temptation to spend your tax savings on a nice vacation and put the money into an investment account instead, you will be taxed each year on realized interest, dividends, and capital gains. *This is inefficient investment growth.*

The $6,000 of total dollars added to the Traditional IRA offers only $4,560 of purchasing power ($6,000 total dollars less $1,440 that represents your tax savings). The $1,440 of tax savings equates to $1,440 of purchasing power, so the purchasing power for both the Roth IRA and the Traditional IRA are identical in the beginning. However, in future years, the growth on the $6,000 of purchasing power in the Roth IRA is completely tax free. The growth in the Traditional IRA is only tax-deferred, and the $1,440 you invested from your tax savings, is taxable every year.

One of the few things in life better than tax-deferred compounding is tax-free compounding. If your income is not over the limit and you can afford to do so after making your employer-matched contribution and the appropriate non-matched contributions to your retirement plan, I generally recommend making additional annual contributions to a Roth IRA. Although you do not get an income tax deduction for your contribution to a Roth IRA, as you might with a

> One of the few things in life better than tax-deferred
> compounding is tax-free compounding.

Traditional IRA, the tax savings you realize from a Traditional IRA contribution are neither tax-free nor tax deferred. When you make a withdrawal from your Traditional IRA, the distribution is taxable. But when you (or your heirs) make a qualified withdrawal from a Roth IRA, the distribution is income-tax free.

Should I Contribute to a Traditional Deductible IRA or a Roth IRA?

As stated earlier, a Roth versus a nondeductible IRA is a no-brainer: if given the choice, always go for the Roth. But for those individuals with a choice between a Roth IRA (or work retirement plan) and a fully deductible IRA (or work retirement plan), how should you save? The conclusion is, in *most* cases, the Roth IRA is superior to the deductible IRA (and nonmatched retirement plan contributions like 401(k)s).

To determine whether a Roth IRA would be better than a Traditional IRA, you must take into account:

- The value of the tax-free growth of the Roth versus the tax-deferred growth of the Traditional IRA including the future tax effects of withdrawals.

- The tax deduction you lost by contributing to a Roth IRA rather than to a fully deductible IRA.

- The growth, net of taxes, on savings from the tax deduction from choosing a deductible Traditional IRA.

In most circumstances, the Roth IRA is significantly more favorable than a Traditional IRA. (A number of years ago, I published an article in *The Tax Adviser*, a publication of the American Institute of Certified Public Accountants, which offered the mathematical proof that the Roth IRA was often a more favorable investment than a Traditional IRA.) The Jobs and Growth Tax Relief

> The conclusion is, in most cases, the Roth IRA is superior
> to the deductible IRA and nonmatched retirement plan
> contributions like 403(b)s.

Reconciliation Act of 2003 (JGTRRA) and subsequent tax legislation changed tax rates for all brackets and reduced tax rates for dividends and capital gains.

After these tax laws changed, I incorporated the changes into the analysis of the Roth versus the Traditional IRA. The Roth was still preferable in most situations, although the advantage of the Roth was not quite as great as before JGTRRA. However, our country is currently facing unprecedented financial challenges, and I would be surprised to hear that our government intends to reduce our tax rates any time soon. And, if the tax rates on dividends and capital gains, or even the ordinary tax rates increase, the Roth's advantage will be even greater.

Figure 3.5

Roth IRA Savings *vs.* Traditional IRA Savings*

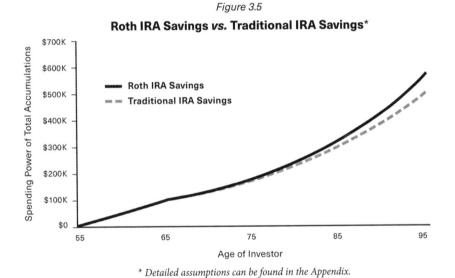

* Detailed assumptions can be found in the Appendix.

Figure 3.5 shows the value to the owner of contributing to a Roth IRA versus a regular deductible IRA measured in purchasing power.

The amounts reflected in the figure show that saving in the Roth IRA is always more favorable than saving in the Traditional IRA, even if the contributions are made for a relatively small number of years. If tax rates become higher in the future, or if a higher rate of return is achieved, the overall Roth IRA advantage will be larger. Given a long-time horizon (such as when monies are passed to succeeding generations), the Roth IRA advantage becomes even bigger. The spending power of these methods at selected times is shown in Figure 3.6 on page 70.

Figure 3.6 may seem to show that there is not a significant difference between the two, but keep in mind that this illustration was purposely created using a

Figure 3.6
Total Spending Power of Traditional *vs.* Roth IRA

End of Year Age	Traditional IRA	Roth IRA
55	$ 7,207	$ 7,210
65	$ 118,688	$ 119,948
75	$ 208,237	$ 214,809
85	$ 359,336	$ 384,694
95	$ 607,278	$ 688,931

very limited (11-year) contribution period and very conservative (6%) rate of return. In short, it demonstrates that, even with minimal contributions, shorter time frames and very conservative rates of return, the Roth IRA will still provide more purchasing power than a Traditional IRA.

The Effect of Lower Tax Brackets in Retirement

I will usually recommend the Traditional IRA over a Roth IRA if you drop to a lower tax bracket after retiring and have a relatively short investment time horizon. Under those circumstances, the value of a Traditional deductible IRA could exceed the benefits of the Roth IRA. It will be to your advantage to take the high tax deduction for your contribution and then, upon retirement, withdraw that money at the lower tax rate.

For example, if you are in the 24% tax bracket when you are working, and you make a $6,000 tax-deductible IRA contribution, you save $1,440 in federal income taxes. Then, when you retire, your tax bracket drops to 12%. Let's assume that the Traditional IRA had no investment growth—not an unrealistic assumption for a taxpayer who chooses to invest his IRA in a certificate of deposit which, at the time of writing, paid historically low interest rates. If he makes a withdrawal of $6,000 from the Traditional IRA, he will pay only $720 in tax—for a savings of $720.

$ 1,440   Initial Tax Savings from IRA Contribution
− 720   *Tax Due on IRA Withdrawal*

$ 720   **Final Tax Savings**

With that caveat, however, my analysis shows that the Roth can become more favorable when a longer investment period is considered. The tax-bracket ad-

If you drop to a lower tax bracket after retiring and have a short investment time horizon, I usually recommend the Traditional IRA or 403(b) over a Roth IRA or Roth 403(b).

vantage diminishes over time. So I ran the analysis again, starting with the same assumptions as in the previous example, except that, beginning at age 66, the ordinary income tax bracket is reduced from 24 to 12%.

The spending power of these methods at selected times is shown in Figure 3.7 on the next page. You can see that, under this particular set of circumstances, the Traditional IRA would be more beneficial to you during your lifetime. Note, however, that the Roth offers more spending power from age 100 on. Of course, most people will not survive until 100, but we show the analysis to point out that even facing a reduced tax bracket, the Roth IRA will become more valuable with time—an advantage for your heirs.

Figure 3.7
Total Spending Power of Reduced Tax Bracket in Retirement

End of Year Age	Traditional IRA	Roth IRA
55	$ 6,692	$ 6,695
65	$ 99,438	$ 100,235
	(Lower Tax Bracket)	
75	$ 193,216	$ 179,506
85	$ 336,783	$ 321,468
95	$ 577,168	$ 575,700
100	$ 751,200	$ 770,416
105	$ 974,773	$1,030,990

If you anticipate that your retirement tax bracket will always remain lower than your current tax rate and that your IRA will be depleted during your lifetime, I will usually recommend that you use a Traditional deductible IRA over the Roth IRA.

Unfortunately, once the RMD rules take effect at age 72 for tax-deferred IRAs and retirement plans, many individuals find that they are required to withdraw so much money from their IRAs, that their tax rate is just as high their pre-retirement tax rate. And, when their RMDs are added to their Social Security income, some taxpayers find themselves in a higher tax bracket than when they were working. For these people, a Roth IRA contribution is usually preferable to a Traditional IRA.

These numbers demonstrate that even with a significant tax-bracket disadvantage, the Roth IRA can become preferable with a long enough time horizon. Furthermore, when you consider the additional estate planning advantages, the relative worth of the Roth IRA becomes more significant. (Please see Chapter 15 for a more detailed discussion of making a Roth conversion in a higher tax bracket when you will likely be in a lower tax bracket after retirement.)

Comments on Your Actual Tax Brackets: A Subtle Point for the Advanced Reader

The previous analyses reflect simple assumptions of 24% income tax savings on your deductible IRA or retirement plan contributions. This is in essence the cost of the Roth IRA or Roth 401(k)/Roth 403(b) in the comparisons we have shown. However, the U.S. tax code has several complications that create actual incremental tax brackets that are much higher than the tax brackets listed on the federal tax tables based on your taxable income. These items must be considered in the context of measuring the advantages of Roth IRAs to deductible IRA contributions.

These tax code complications can have extreme effects on the actual tax bracket for some people, most notably retirees with Social Security income, significant capital gain income, and less frequently with the increase in the standard deduction included in the Tax Cut and Jobs Act, and itemized deductions that involve medical expenses.

For example, consider Fred Jones, a single 65-year-old retiree who has pension income of $36,000, Social Security income of $25,000, and part-time wage income of $5,000. He also has itemized deductions of $30,000, including $10,000 of medical expenses which, because he is 65, are partially deductible this year to the extent that they exceed 7.5% of his AGI.

After looking at Figure 3.5, Fred is considering the potential advantages of using his wage income to make a $5,000 Roth IRA contribution, rather than a $5,000 deductible IRA contribution. If he makes the Traditional deductible IRA contribution, he pays $5,063 in federal income tax. If he chooses the Roth IRA, his tax is $7,538 or $2,475 more. This is nearly 50% of the IRA contribution amount. This means his actual tax bracket is almost 50% even though the IRS tables indicate he is in the 25% tax bracket! The main reason that this happened is because the additional income from losing the IRA deduction caused much more of his Social Security income to be taxable. He also lost some of the medical expense deduction, due to its 7.5% of AGI limitation. Thus, Fred felt the cost of choosing the Roth IRA was too high that year and wisely chose the deductible IRA.

Although Fred's future situation may not always be so extreme, his numbers did not appear to be that unusual. Fred's example illustrates why careful tax planning is so important. There are many things in the tax code that result in a different actual tax bracket than the IRS tables would indicate. Before finalizing Roth contribution or conversion decisions, it is best to *"run the numbers"* or see a competent tax advisor to determine the actual effects.

When we analyze Roth IRA advantages and disadvantages for our clients (when compared to deductible contributions), we keep referring to the marginal tax rates to help us decide if the conversion makes sense in the long term. For most people, the current actual marginal tax rate is not hard to determine and is similar to what the IRS tables would indicate. Therefore, we will continue to use simply calculated tax bracket rates in our analyses of Roth accounts. But please keep in mind that it is prudent to calculate the actual current year tax cost of the Roth.

Wealthy clients and readers raise a lot of questions about the five-year holding period. As stated earlier, what I really want to do when I hear that question is yell, *"Why do you care?"* It is extremely unlikely that anyone would need to spend all of their money at one time. Let's face it—if you did, you'd be broke, and the five-year holding period on the Roth account would be the least of your worries.

Realistically, most people will spend their retirement savings over a period of many years. And the people who have a Roth IRA as part of their retirement accumulations generally have some after-tax money and some Traditional IRA or retirement plan funds—at least, this would be my advice.

But because the Roth IRA is the last money I want people to spend, it should not matter that there is a five-year waiting period to achieve tax-free growth. The Roth's advantages almost always more than make up for any lack of liquidity resulting from the five-year rule. In most cases it is best to not even consider the five-year rule because the investment period of a Roth IRA is likely not only greater than 5 years—it's your entire life.

> **Wealthy clients and readers raise a lot of questions about the five-year holding period. In most cases it is best not to even consider the five-year rule because the investment period of a Roth IRA is likely not only greater than 5 years— it's your entire life.**

The fact that individuals can continue to contribute to a Roth IRA if they continue to work past age 72 is a great opportunity to continue saving, especially since more and more people earn income well after the Traditional age of retirement. The no-RMDs rule gives rise to significant estate planning opportunities to stretch savings for those willing to leave the money in the tax-free account for a long time. Depending on the lifespan of the beneficiary, the funds can grow tax-free to their great advantage.

KEY IDEAS

- The Roth IRA is always preferable to a nondeductible Traditional IRA and is usually better than a deductible Traditional IRA contribution.

- For Roth IRAs, no taxes are due upon the eventual distribution.

- No distributions from Roth IRAs are required during the owner's or the owner's spouse's lifetime.

- Withdrawals from Roth IRAs prior to age 59½ are free from tax and penalties to the extent of previous contributions.

4

Traditional 403(b)s *vs.* Roth 403(b)s

"The question isn't at what age I want to retire, it's at what income."
— George Foreman

The ideas in this chapter comparing Traditional 403(b)s with Roth 403(b)s are pretty much equally applicable to comparing Traditional 401(k)s to Roth 401(k)s. Conceptually, they are similar to comparing Traditional IRAs to Roth IRAs.

What Are Roth 403(b)s?

Many—but not all—employers offer a Roth option inside their retirement plans. If this option is available to you, subject to exception, I highly recommend you take advantage of it. In Chapter 4, we touched on some of the basic differences between Traditional and Roth 403(b)s.

The Roth 403(b) combines the features of a Traditional 403(b) with a Roth IRA. Employees are permitted to deposit part or all of their own contribution, which is the amount deducted from their paychecks, as a contribution to a Roth account, meaning it will receive tax treatment similar to a Roth IRA. The laws governing retirement plan contributions, however, require that the employee always has the option to defer money into the Traditional deductible account when the Roth account is offered as an option. No one is forced to use the Roth account if they prefer to take the tax deduction.

Unlike Traditional contributions to a 403(b) plan, employee contributions to a Roth 403(b) account do not receive a federal tax deduction. But the growth on these contributions will not be subject to taxes when money is withdrawn, because the Roth account grows tax-free.

In short, if you have two options for your retirement plan, one a Traditional account and the other a Roth account, with the same amount of money in each, the Roth account, over time, will be of greater value since the income taxes imposed on withdrawals from the Traditional 403(b) greatly reduce its overall value. By this, I do not mean to imply that the Roth retirement plans are better than the Traditional plans for everyone, but they are for many. The choice is similar

> **Unlike Traditional contributions to a 403(b) plan, employee contributions to a Roth 403(b) account do not receive a federal tax deduction. But the growth on these contributions will not be subject to taxes when money is withdrawn, because the Roth account grows tax-free.**

to deciding whether to make a Roth IRA contribution or a *deductible* contribution to a Traditional IRA as discussed in Chapter 3.

Roth retirement plans were first offered in 2006, but under temporary rules. Many employers did not add the Roth feature to their existing plans because of the additional paperwork, plan amendments, reporting, and recordkeeping involved. Since then, the law has become permanent, and more and probably most universities are now offering Roth 403(b) features. These significant additions to the retirement planning landscape offer many more investors an extraordinary opportunity to expand, and, in many cases, to begin saving for retirement in the Roth environment where their investment grows *tax-free*. Coupled with the increased contribution limits for the Traditional 403(b) plans, employees and even self-employed individuals will be able to establish and grow their tax-free retirement savings at a rate greater than ever before.

How Do Roth 403(b) Accounts Differ from a Roth IRA?

One of the most significant advantages of the Roth 403(b), and the one that distinguishes it from a Roth IRA, is that Roth 403(b) plans are now available to a much larger group of people. Roth IRA contributions are only available to taxpayers who fall within certain Modified Adjusted Gross Income (MAGI) ranges. The 2023 income limit for Roth IRA contributions for married couples filing jointly is $228,000 and for single individuals and heads of household, less than $153,000. If your income exceeds these limits, you are not permitted to contribute to a Roth IRA.

High income earners might get around that limitation through a backdoor Roth IRA. But even then, we are talking about a contribution of $7,500 per year in a Roth IRA for a taxpayer aged 50 or over versus $30,000 for a Roth 403(b). The restrictive MAGI limitations do not apply to Roth 403(b) plans, providing higher income individuals and couples easy access into the tax-free Roth environment.

This increased accessibility is really important. Roth IRAs have always appeared to be ideal savings vehicles for wealthier individuals, but up until January 1, 2006, or more recently if their employers just began offering the 403(b) option, wealthier individuals had been precluded from establishing Roth accounts due to the income limits.

In Chapter 3 we demonstrated the Roth IRAs great advantages as part of a long-term retirement and estate plan. And wealthier individuals can generally afford to let money sit in a Roth account and gather tax-free growth. The longer the funds are kept in the tax-free Roth environment, the greater the advantage to both the Roth IRA owner and his or her heirs.

Advantages and Disadvantages of Roth 403(b) Contributions

The Roth 403(b) plan option offers advantages and disadvantages similar to those of Roth IRAs discussed in Chapter 3, but they are worth repeating and expanding upon here.

Advantages of the Roth Plans:

1. By choosing the Roth, you pay the taxes up front on your contributions. (Can we say this often enough?) While you might have taken the tax savings from your Traditional plan contribution and invested the money in after-tax investments, over time, you will receive greater value from the tax-free growth.

2. If your tax bracket in retirement stays the same as it was when you contributed to the plan, you will be better off (assuming the Roth account grows, and possibly even if it goes down in value somewhat).

3. If your tax bracket in retirement is higher than when you contributed to the plan, you will be much better off. (Please note that we will look more closely at the effect of higher and lower tax brackets in retirement later.) There are many reasons why you could move into a higher tax bracket after you retire. Here are a few examples:

a. The federal government will decide to raise tax rates (highly likely).

The longer the funds are kept in the tax-free Roth environment, the greater the advantage to both the Roth IRA owner and his or her heirs.

b. You need to increase your income with taxable withdrawals from your Traditional IRA plan, perhaps because you have medical expenses that were not covered by insurance.

c. You own or inherit income-producing property or investments that begin to give you taxable income.

d. You own annuities or have other lucrative university or state pension plans that begin paying you income because of Required Minimum Distributions (RMDs).

e. The combination of your pension, Social Security, and RMDs are higher than your former taxable income from wages.

4. While you are alive, there are no RMDs from the Roth IRA accounts. Roth 403(b)s are subject to RMDs, but, as of this writing, these plans can easily be rolled into a Roth IRA upon your retirement. Traditional plans have RMDs beginning at age 72 for retirees. The Roth IRA provides a much better long-term, tax-advantaged savings horizon, as shown in Chapter 3.

5. Your heirs will benefit from ten years of tax-free growth if the Roth is left in your estate. Whatever advantage you achieved with the Roth can be magnified by your heirs over their lifetimes. If they qualify for one of the exceptions, tax-free growth will to some extent continue for the rest of their lives.

6. The Roth provides greater value for the same number of dollars in retirement savings. This may lower federal estate and state inheritance taxes in an estate with the same after-tax spending power.

7. If you are in a low tax bracket now, or even if you have no taxable income (possibly because of credits and deductions), contributing to the Roth plan instead of the Traditional plan will not cost you a significant amount now, but it will have enormous benefits later.

8. If you were previously unable to consider Roth IRAs because your income exceeded the income caps, contingent on your university's retirement plan options, you may now be eligible to consider Roth accounts.

9. If you need to spend a large amount of your retirement savings all at once, withdrawals from a Traditional plan would increase your marginal income tax rate. The Roth has a significant advantage in these high spending situations. Because Roth withdrawals are tax-free, they do not affect your marginal tax rate.

10. Having a pool of both Traditional plan money (funded by the employer contributions and taxable upon withdrawal) and Roth plan money (funded by the employee and tax-free to withdraw) to choose from, can provide you an opportunity for effective tax planning in retirement. With both types of plans, the Roth portion can be used in high income years and the Traditional plan can be used in lower income years when you are in a reduced tax bracket. These low tax brackets may occur during years after retirement, but before the RMDs from the plan holding the employer's contributions begin.

11. Simply put, however, the tax-free growth in the Roth will give both you and your heirs purchasing power.

Disadvantages of the Roth Plans:

1. You are close to retiring and your income will be lower after you retire than while you are working. That is the most likely exception where you would be better off contributing to a Traditional plan rather than to a Roth plan.

2. Your paycheck contributions into the Roth 403(b) are not tax deductible, as is a Traditional 403(b) contribution. You will get smaller net paychecks if you contribute the same amount to a Roth account, rather than a Traditional account, because of increased federal income tax withholding.

   Losing the tax-deferred status means that by the time you file your tax return, you will have less cash in the bank, that is, in your after-tax investments. (Keep in mind, however, when compared to tax-deferred or tax-free retirement savings accounts, after-tax investments are the least efficient savings tool.)

3. The retirement investments may go down in value. Retirement assets held in CREF accounts, unlike TIAA accounts, are subject to market fluctuations. If the decline becomes large enough, it is possible that you would have been better off in a Traditional tax-deferred plan, because, at the very least, you would have received a tax deduction on your contributions.

4. If Congress ever eliminates the income tax in favor of a sales tax or value-added tax, you will have already paid your income taxes. However, it seems unlikely that such a system would be adopted without grandfathering the rules for plans in place to prevent such inequities.

5. If your tax bracket in retirement drops, and you withdraw funds from your retirement assets before sufficient tax-free growth, the taxes you save on

your Roth 403(b) plan withdrawals are less than the taxes you would have saved using a Traditional plan. This can be the case if you earn an unusually high amount of money in one year, maybe from speaking fees or writing a textbook that puts you in a very high tax bracket, but ultimately you do not end up with such high income after retirement.

If that were the case, a better approach might be to use the Traditional account for deferrals in that year or other years where your income is unusually large. (Please note that later we will look more closely at the effect of lower tax brackets in retirement.)

6. This is a hard one to quantify, but many retirement plan owners, including my wife and I, are extremely reluctant to spend our Roth. Even though we have a seven-figure Roth, psychologically we are treating it as sacred and consider it part of our daughter's inheritance. We have gone through spending contortions, even borrowing money, so we do not touch that Roth. This is not unusual. If instead of making Roth conversions we had Traditional IRAs, we likely would have spent the after-tax dollars that we used to convert to the Roth IRAs to pay certain expenses. My wife has a large Roth, but it doesn't feel liquid.

I have many clients who could afford to spend a lot more money than they do and having large Roth accounts that they are reluctant to spend compounds the problem.

Availability of the Roth 403(b)

Employers that now offer a 403(b) plan may choose to expand their retirement plan options to include the Roth 403(b) but they are not required to do so. Some institutions were early adopters; others may take more time to incorporate the new plans into their offerings; still others may never offer them. SECURE Act 2.0 now allows employers to offer Roths for employer contribution.

Contribution Limits for Roth and Traditional 403(b)s

For 2023, the Traditional and Roth 403(b) employee contribution limits are $22,500 per year, or $30,000 if you are age 50 or older). Employer matching contributions do not affect this limit. If you participate in both a 401(k) plan and a 403(b) plan, this limit applies to all your contributions to both plans.

In 2023, a 50-year-old employee cannot make a $30,000 contribution to a Traditional 401(k) account and a $30,000 contribution to a Roth 401(k) account; the contributions to both accounts combined cannot exceed $30,000. The Roth

Employers who now offer a 403(b) plan may choose to expand their retirement plan options to include the Roth 403(b), but they are not required to do so.

401(k)/403(b) contributions will be treated like a Roth IRA for tax purposes.

Some universities also offer a 15-year catch-up option. If you have 15 or more years of service, you may be allowed to contribute an additional $3,000 per year, above the annual limits. This option has two important limitations. First, this is only available if you have contributed on average less than $5,000 per year to your 403(b) plan. Second, there is a lifetime limit of $15,000 for catch-up contributions. If you contribute $3,000 each year for five years, you will use up the lifetime limit.

Perhaps an example of a Traditional *vs.* Roth contribution would help.

·· **MINI CASE STUDY 4.1** ··

Contributing to a Traditional 403(b) *vs.* a Roth 403(b) – Lower Income Tax Bracket

Joe, a prudent 55-year-old history professor, participates in his university's 403(b) plan. He has dutifully contributed the maximum allowable contribution to his 403(b) plan since he started working. This means he is also taking full advantage of the employer match, which at his university is a generous 12% of his salary. Until his employer adopted the new Roth 403(b) option, his expectation was to continue contributing the maximum into his Traditional 403(b) for 2023 and beyond.

Now Joe has a choice. In 2023, he can either continue making his regular deductible 403(b) contribution ($30,000); he could elect to make a $30,000 contribution to the new Roth 403(b); or he could split his $30,000 contribution between the regular 403(b) portion and the Roth 403(b) portion of the plan. His decision will not have an impact on his employer's contribution—the employer's matching contribution remains unchanged and goes into a Traditional tax-deferred account.

With Joe's $30,000 contribution, however, there is a fundamental difference in the way his Traditional 403(b) is taxed and the way his new Roth 403(b) is taxed. With the Traditional 403(b), Joe gets an income tax deduction for his contribution to the 403(b). After Joe retires, however, and takes a distribution from his Traditional retirement plan, he will have to pay income taxes on that distribution. If Joe contributes to the Roth 403(b), he will not get a tax deduction for making the contribution, but the money will grow income-tax free.

When Joe takes a distribution from his Roth retirement account, he will not have to pay income taxes, provided other technical requirements are met. These other requirements are usually easy to meet and include such things as waiting until age 59½ before making retirement account withdrawals and waiting at least five years from the time the account is opened before the first withdrawal.

Because Joe has some after-tax savings already and does not really need more income tax deductions, he is advised to contribute to the Roth 403(b). Assuming Joe takes my advice and switches his annual contributions to the Roth 403(b), he will have three components to his university retirement plan. He will have the employer's matching contributions in his Traditional account, plus the interest, dividends, and appreciation on those contributions, to the extent that he is vested in the plan. He will have his own (the employee's) Traditional portion of the plan, which consists of all of his contributions to date plus the interest, dividends, and appreciation on those contributions. Then, starting in 2023, he will have a Roth portion for his Roth contributions.

If Joe is married and filing a joint tax return and his 2023 adjusted gross income is less than $218,000, he may have already been making contributions to a Roth IRA outside of his employer's retirement plan. In 2023, he would have been able to make the maximum Roth IRA contribution of $7,500 ($6,500 for people under age 50) to the plan.

Remember Joe can contribute the maximum ($30,000) to his Roth 403(b), plus the maximum ($7,500) to his Roth IRA, assuming that his income is below the exclusion limits. As long as Joe is working, the Roth 403(b) through his university will remain separate from any Roth IRA he may have outside of his employer's plan.

If his 2023 adjusted gross income was more than $218,000, he would not have been allowed to contribute to a Roth IRA (the income phase-out range is between $218,000 and $228,000). What is much different for Joe is that the amount of money he will be allowed to contribute into the income tax-free world of the Roth will see a dramatic increase, because there is no income limit for employees who want to contribute to a Roth 403(b) plan at work.

....

Choosing Between the Roth and Traditional 403(b)

The following analysis is equally important for individuals considering a Roth IRA conversion. I do not repeat this analysis in Chapter 15, but people who are con-

sidering a Roth IRA conversion, or interested in learning more about them, should read this material with the Roth conversion in mind.

Many clients come to us wondering whether they would be better off making contributions to a Roth account or to a Traditional retirement account. If the choice is between using a Roth IRA versus a nondeductible Traditional IRA, it is pretty easy to make the case for the Roth. However, because of the nature of the Roth's advantages and disadvantages, which are contingent on your current and future income tax brackets, there is no one size fits all answer if the choice is between a Traditional deductible IRA and a Roth. So, I have formulated some different scenarios showing how the Roth accounts become advantageous for some people and a bad idea for others.

Setting the Stage

Assume that we have a professor named Gary who is 55 years old, and who is able to contribute $27,000 to his 403(b) plan for eleven years, until he retires at age 66. His employer offers a Roth account in their 403(b), and Gary wants to know if he should direct his contributions to the Roth or the Traditional side of the plan. We ran the numbers using the following assumptions:

1. Gary earns a conservative rate of return of 6% annually on all of his accounts.

2. At age 72, Gary rolls the Roth 403(b) part of his CREF over to a Roth IRA to avoid RMDs. (This is a very important step; we'll cover more about it later).

3. Gary knows that he will save a significant amount in taxes if his contributions are made to the tax-deductible Traditional account. Gary is more disciplined than most savers, because he is willing to take all of the money that he saved on taxes and contribute it to an after-tax brokerage account environment.

4. In this scenario, Gary's income tax rates are as follows:

    a. 24% ordinary incremental tax rate during his working years.

    b. 24% ordinary incremental tax rate during his retirement years.

    c. Capital gains tax rates are 15%.

5. Gary is taking the Minimum Distribution Option (MDO) from his TIAA account to satisfy his RMDs beginning at age 72. (We'll look at the other distribution options that you may have available to you at your university in Chapter 8.) He pays ordinary income taxes on the distributions and uses the rest of the money to pay his living expenses. The Roth account has tax-

free spending withdrawals taken in the same amount.

6. The calculated income tax rate on all growth of the after-tax account averages 18%. (24% is the marginal tax rate, not the actual tax rate.)

7. At the end of each year, we measure the spending power for each scenario. To measure the spending power of pre-tax Traditional 401(k) plan balances, an allowance is made for income taxes. The tax rate of this allowance or liquidation rate is, initially, 24%, comparable to the ordinary tax rate.

Now we are able to "*run the numbers*" and see the resulting spending power of the remaining assets as shown in Figure 4.1 on page 85.

Calculating the Results

Figure 4.1 shows that there is an increasing advantage from investing in the Roth 403(b) instead of the Traditional 403(b) plan. Although it's difficult to see, the advantage begins in the first year. At Gary's retirement age of 66, the advantage has grown to $6,652, or 1.58%.

By age 75, after RMDs have begun, the advantage is 4.10%; by age 85, it is 9.45%; and by age 95, it is a 21.71% advantage resulting in an additional $169,962 for the Roth owner.

For an individual whose circumstances match the assumptions of Figure 4.1, the cumulative advantage over the 40-year projection period should provide the incentive to use the Roth rather than the Traditional 403(b). And if a rate of return greater than 6% is assumed, the advantage to the Roth owner increases significantly. In addition, if there is a tax increase, the Roth would be of even greater advantage.

Under current rules, if Gary should pass away and leave his Roth account to his surviving spouse, she will not have to take RMDs from the account over her lifetime. If he leaves the Roth account to someone other than his spouse, perhaps a child, the SECURE Act requires that the entire account balance be distributed within 10 years. The rules regarding RMDs are discussed in detail in Chapter 6, but for now it's important to know that RMDs force money out of a tax-deferred or tax-free environment, into a taxable environment. And remember Professor Pay Taxes Now and Professor Pay Taxes Later from Chapter 2? Professor Pay Taxes Later was the clear winner.

If you're trying to figure out the most opportune strategies for naming beneficiaries of your IRAs, you should refer to Chapter 11 for an in-depth discus-

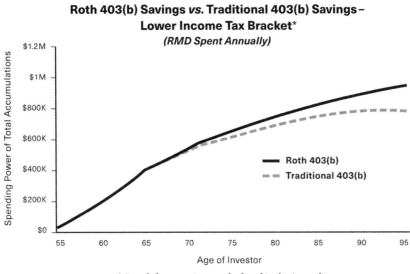

Figure 4.1

**Roth 403(b) Savings *vs.* Traditional 403(b) Savings –
Lower Income Tax Bracket***
(RMD Spent Annually)

* *Detailed assumptions can be found in the Appendix.*

sion on the subject, but here is a simplified explanation of the inheritance rules for a spouse:

- If you leave behind a Traditional IRA, your spouse can treat the IRA as his or her own and ultimately take RMDs based on his or her own life expectancy (technically the life expectancy of her and someone deemed ten years younger than her.)

- If you leave behind a Roth, your spouse is never required to take RMDs.

With the confiscatory SECURE Act, the rules have changed drastically—and not for the better—if your beneficiary is not your spouse or does not qualify for an exception. We'll cover those changes in Chapter 12. In fact, the new rules for Inherited IRAs under the SECURE Act could provide an additional incentive for committed couples who have not legally married, to do so. We'll take a deeper look at financial reasons that committed couples might want to marry for the money in Chapter 25.

Even though we are not talking about Roth IRA conversions at this point in the book, the reasoning that goes into deciding to put money in a Roth 403(b) versus a Traditional 403(b) is conceptually similar to the reasoning that goes into deciding to make a Roth IRA conversion. So, although you may be retired, the following analysis is relevant for retirees thinking about a Roth IRA conversion.

Additional Advantages for Higher Income Taxpayers

One great feature of the new Roth options for 403(b) plans is that it allows higher income taxpayers to save money in the Roth environment. How does the advantage change in their situation? Figure 4.2 (above) uses the same assumptions as Figure 4.1; except that Gary's ordinary income tax rate has been in-

Figure 4.2

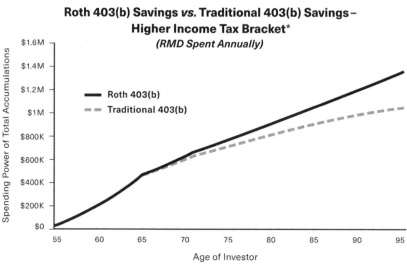

* Detailed assumptions can be found in the Appendix.

creased to the current maximum of 37%, including the liquidation tax rate used for measurement.

In Figure 4.2, we discover that the Roth 403(b) advantage for a higher income taxpayer is greater than for the lower income taxpayer in the 24% tax bracket (Figure 4.2). The advantage has now become a higher 29.41%, or $308,766, after 40 years.

Why such a large difference? There are several reasons why this happened, and they relate to the ever-changing tax laws. First, the maximum federal income tax rate was increased from 35% to 37%. Second, there were several new taxes imposed on high income taxpayers. Higher earners (in 2022, single individuals whose adjusted gross income exceeds $200,000 or married taxpayers filing jointly whose income exceeds $250,000) are now subject to the Net Investment Income Tax, which adds on an additional 3.8% tax to certain investment income earned outside of the Roth account. Higher income earners are also subject to an additional 0.9% Medicare tax on all wages in excess of $200,000 for individual taxpayers and $250,000 for married taxpayers. These and other factors all combine to make the Roth an even more attractive option for higher income taxpayers than in prior years.

And guess what? The higher income taxpayer is less likely to spend the Roth investments, thus making the long-term benefits more achievable. The bottom line is that the Roth 403(b) is dollar for dollar more valuable for the higher income retirement plan owner than a middle-income retirement plan owner. The counter argument is that the amount of savings to middle income taxpayers, though smaller, is more meaningful in terms of the impact on their lives.

The Roth savings options can change people's lives for the better. Subject to a few exceptions discussed above, if you have access to a Roth option in your university's retirement plan, I highly recommend that you take advantage of it, and if you can afford it, contribute the maximum allowed. Also, please keep in mind that this analysis is also quite valuable for someone interested in Roth IRA conversions because there are a lot of similarities in the calculations and the sensitivity of tax brackets.

Making It Happen

Notice, however, there is a caveat. I said, *"If you have access."* Though Congress has made Roth 401(k)s and Roth 403(b)s available for employers to use, that doesn't mean your employer has adopted these features or has made plans to do so. University retirement options vary greatly between states, between institutions within a state, and even between TIAA contracts at a particular institution. Some options are set by state law, while others are determined at the university level.

If your university does not provide options for a Roth 403(b) and you like to waste time attempting to argue with your human resources department who is responsible for those decisions, you can gently (or not so gently depending on

> **The Roth savings options can change people's lives for the better. Subject to the exceptions discussed in this chapter and in other parts of the book, if you have access to a Roth option in your retirement plan at work, I highly recommend you take advantage of it, and if you can afford it, contribute the maximum allowed.**

your personality and faculty politics) suggest that your university include a Roth 403(b) option in its retirement plans and allow you to participate.

KEY IDEAS

- Roth 403(b) plan options offer professors a powerful entrée into the world of tax-free wealth accumulation.

- Roth 403(b) plans are most valuable over the long term for high income participants.

- Saving at least a part of your retirement funds in a Roth account can be one of the best things you can do for yourself and your family.

5

Optimal Spending Strategies for Retirees

"I am having an out-of-money experience."

— Author Unknown

First, subject to exceptions, the following is the best order to spend your money after you retire:

1. Spend your existing income first, which includes things like any pension, interest, dividends, Social Security, and any self-employment income because you have to pay tax on that money anyway.

2. Spend after-tax dollars that are not in an IRA or a Roth IRA, and that do not have any or much appreciation.

3. Spend highly appreciated after-tax dollars that do incur a capital gain.

4. Spend your Traditional retirement assets like IRAs and 403(b)s.

5. Spend your Roth IRA dollars last.

Of course, there will be exceptions based on individual tax brackets, and on individual and family situations, and one big exception that is covered in Chapter 15, transferring your money from taxable to tax-free, but that is primarily for higher net worth professors. But, subject to those exceptions, this is generally the best order for spending to minimize taxes.

This and the following chapters have a nitty gritty analysis of how we reached the above conclusion to determine the optimal spending order when you need to take money from your portfolio to meet your living expenses. We also examine the exceptions which are important, particularly for high income and high net worth professors.

Which Assets Should I Spend First?

Recent changes in tax laws that affect capital gains and tax brackets, and new taxes aimed specifically at high income individuals have made it increasingly difficult to simplify spending strategies for retirees. Under the old laws, it was much easier and generally more accurate to recommend spending after-tax dollars first, then IRA dollars, and Roth dollars last. Even under the old laws, that was not always accurate for everyone, but this simplistic advice is no longer accurate for an ever-growing number of taxpayers.

Sometimes it is the best course of action, but sometimes it now makes sense to spend Roth IRA dollars before Traditional IRA dollars in order to stay in a lower tax bracket. In addition, the Tax Cuts and Jobs Act (TCJA) of 2017 added the extra wrinkle of temporary tax rate cuts which will expire in 2026 unless they are extended, so your long-term strategy could incorporate an eventual tax hike from today's relatively low rates. Plus, as I'll discuss in greater detail in Chapter 12, the SECURE Act drastically accelerates taxes on Inherited IRAs and retirement plans, which may change the kinds of assets you are planning to leave to your children and grandchildren. In addition, we now must consider SECURE Act 2.0 which at press time was recently passed as law.

In order to get the best answer for your specific situation, you could have a qualified advisor or CPA *"run the numbers"* for you. Or you might prefer to do the calculations yourself if you like to pack your own parachute.

That wasn't fair. Certain things, like drafting wills and trusts you should almost always have a competent expert do. Other things, like working out the best spending order for retirement assets, while tricky, may not be out of reach for quantitative individuals who have a lot of time and like the challenge of figuring this stuff out.

However, it would not be helpful for me to tell you that it is best to *"run the numbers,"* and not give you general guidelines which illustrate the points I'm talking about. Therefore, please understand that the information presented in this chapter is just that—general guidelines—that may not produce the optimal result for your own situation.

Finally, perhaps the most important exception to our recommended spending order involves shifting taxable assets to tax-free assets. Please see Chapter 15, *Roth IRA Conversions Before and After the SECURE Act.*

At retirement an individual moves into distribution mode—that is to say, he begins to spend retirement savings. This is *not* to say that accumulation stops. Income and appreciation on the investments, Social Security funds, and any pension plan proceeds might still be exceeding your expenses. In fact, most of my retired clients have more money now than they did when they retired.

You may be fortunate enough to find that your Social Security, pension, Required Minimum Distributions (RMD) from your IRA (if any) and from your TIAA accounts, and dividends and interest on your after-tax investments pro-

In general, it is preferable to spend principal from your after-tax investments rather than taking taxable distributions from your IRA and/or retirement plan.

vide enough funds for your living expenses. Let's assume, however, that is not the case, and you need to either tap into your after-tax funds (you might think of that as your *"nest egg"*) or make additional taxable withdrawals from your IRA or retirement account to make ends meet. In general, it is preferable to spend principal from your after-tax investments rather than taking taxable distributions from your IRA and/or retirement plan.

I've been in the accounting, legal and tax minimization business for over thirty years. Most of my clients actually listen to me, but I always have a few who do not. Instead of following my recommendations, they choose to spend their IRAs first. It drives me crazy. When I used to prepare taxes, when the exception applied even less frequently, I used to see clients spending the wrong money first.

With this one particular client, every year, when I delivered his tax return, while I was still preparing tax returns, I would include a personal note saying, *"I really hate to see you pay income taxes on this."* I would also call him. He said his stockbroker wanted to maintain a balance between his IRA and after-tax dollars. Now, I'm all for an appropriate and well-balanced portfolio. I agree that you do not want to have all your eggs in one basket. But I am not into this allocation between IRA and non-IRA dollars at the expense of considerable extra taxes right now. If you are older than 59½, you do not have to worry about maintaining the liquidity of your after-tax dollars because you can take money out of an IRA whenever you want without a penalty. I would much rather that, subject to some exceptions. Most taxpayers follow my *"pay taxes later"* rule.

Mini Case Study 5.1 and Figure 5.1 (on page 92) provide a comparison of the benefits of spending after-tax savings before pre-tax accumulations.

·· **MINI CASE STUDY 5.1** ··
Spend Your After-Tax Money First

Both Professor Pay Taxes Now and Professor Pay Taxes Later start from an identical position in 2022. They are both 65 years old and both have $300,000 in after-tax funds and $1,100,000 in retirement funds. They both receive

$25,000 per year in Social Security income. They want to spend $86,000 per year, after paying income taxes.

Their investment return is 6.5% and the rate of inflation on expenses is 3.5%. Income tax assumptions include ordinary income and capital gains tax rates established by the Tax Cuts and Jobs Act of 2017 and subsequent tax laws. State income taxes are ignored.

Professor Pay Taxes Now does not spend any of his after-tax funds until all the retirement funds are depleted. By spending his retirement funds first, he triggers income taxes on the withdrawals, reducing the tax-deferral period, and his balance goes down. He also subjects a larger share of his after-tax funds to income taxes on the dividends, interest, and potential capital gains.

All income taxes due on the retirement funds and the after-tax funds cause a greater amount to be withdrawn from his retirement account. In 25 years, by paying taxes prematurely, he has sacrificed a fortune in tax-deferred growth. Shortly after his 89th birthday, Professor Pay Taxes Now is out of money.

Professor Pay Taxes Later first uses his after-tax funds to meet expenses. Only when the after-tax funds are depleted are withdrawals made from the retirement accounts. He fully uses the tax-deferred features of the IRA. Professor Pay Taxes Later has over $350,000 on his 89th birthday. Both he and Professor Pay Taxes Now enjoyed an identical lifestyle, investments, and so forth, but there is a significant difference in the amount each has remaining at their age 89.

Figure 5.1

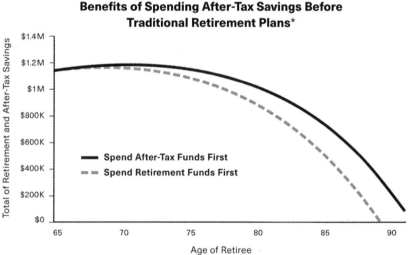

Benefits of Spending After-Tax Savings Before Traditional Retirement Plans*

* Detailed assumptions can be found in the Appendix.

Professor Pay Taxes Now is broke, and Professor Pay Taxes later has enough funds to support himself for an additional 3 years. In states such as Pennsylvania that do not tax retirement income but do tax after-tax investment income, the benefits of spending the after-tax money first is even greater.

The conclusion would most likely be the same for any reasonable set of assumptions in terms of how much money each individual has, and what rate of return you want to assume. The principle stands: don't pay taxes now—pay taxes later even after you retire.

The Big Picture

Once the after-tax money is spent, there is no longer a one size fits all answer as to whether it is more advantageous to spend Traditional IRA or Roth IRA money. In late stages of spending and under certain other circumstances, it does not hold true that no Roth dollars should be spent while Traditional IRA dollars remain.

If you live long enough to fully deplete your Traditional IRAs and are left with only Roth dollars and little taxable income other than Social Security, you will likely be in the 0% tax bracket. From that point on, you will be missing out on what could have been tax-free Traditional IRA withdrawals. Before the Traditional IRA is all gone, it makes sense to spend a combination of Traditional and Roth IRA dollars so that 0% tax brackets never get wasted.

In 2023, a married couple filing a 2023 tax return jointly could withdraw up to $27,700 from their Traditional IRA and, if they have no other taxable income, would pay zero tax on the withdrawal! Also, there are strategic times when spending Roth dollars can save more in taxes than the 12% tax bracket you expect to be in.

Your actual taxes on incremental additional IRA withdrawals may be 27% or more because of the phase-in rules on the taxability of Social Security and the addition of the new Net Investment Tax. There may be other situations where spending some Roth dollars before Traditional IRA dollars could benefit you in retirement.

Keep in mind also that the current low rates are scheduled to go up in 2026, due to the sunset provisions of the 2017 Tax Cut and Jobs Act at which point we will go back to the 2017 rates (plus inflation). So, it may be wise to spend more Traditional IRA and TIAA dollars now, and more Roth dollars later if and when the rates go up. As I said, it is more difficult now to make blanket recommendations for spending order. A case-by-case analysis is needed.

··· **MINI CASE STUDY 5.2** ···
Capital Gains May Affect Spending Order

What follows is a detailed mathematical analysis regarding whether it is a good idea to spend highly appreciated dollars that will incur a capital gain or spend IRA dollars. We try to be even handed and use a *"running the numbers approach"* to produce recommendations. The problem in real life, however, is that the highly appreciated assets often comprise a large percentage of the portfolio. Furthermore, frequently those assets have been good performers in the past and clients often have strong emotional ties to the stock, especially if it is the stock of their former employer. Though hard to quantify, there is significant value that might even exceed any tax disadvantage in reducing your exposure to any concentrated positions in stocks or funds, even if you have to incur a capital gain.

One of the primary reasons people think it may be better not to spend the after-tax money first is because of capital gains. Changes to the capital gains tax rules in 2012 make this an issue for far fewer people than in the past. Capital-gains tax rates now vary depending on whether the gains are short-term or long-term, and they no longer apply *at all* to taxpayers whose taxable income falls in the 10% or 12% marginal tax bracket. Yes, you read that right. If you are in the 10% or 12% tax bracket, your capital gain is not subject to federal tax unless your capital gain pushes you above the 12% bracket.

In this case study, we are using the tax brackets and rates in effect for 2022. While the exact numbers will be different for subsequent years, conclusions remain the same.

Example:

You are married and your joint taxable income before any capital gains is $60,000 which places you in the 12% marginal bracket. (For 2022 the MFJ top ordinary income level at 12% is $83,550.) You incur a $23,550 long-term capital gain. There is not any capital gains tax on that realized capital gain.

High income taxpayers who fall into the 35% tax bracket are subject to a 20% capital gains tax plus the 3.8% Net Investment Tax for a total of 23.8% tax. Taxpayers whose income falls into a bracket higher than 12% but less than 35% are subject to a 15% capital gains rate and possibly the 3.8% net investment income tax. Let's assume that the after-tax assets in the previous example have a zero-cost basis, and that the entire $300,000 will now be taxed as capital gains. Is that a problem? The answer is, not necessarily.

Professor Pay Taxes Later is a single man in Figure 5.1, so let's assume he's single here too. If he liquidated 100% of his after-tax stock account all at once, he would have a $300,000 capital gain. That's nowhere near enough to put him into the highest income and capital gains tax brackets, but 85% of his Social Security is now taxed. The tax he owes on just his Social Security and the capital gain is $40,824. It doesn't stop there, though. He also has to pay Net Investment Tax of $4,608. Since he has such a high income this year, Professor Pay Taxes Later is going to have to pay the IRS $45,432 on April 15th.

If Professor Pay Taxes Later had talked to us or another firm that actually does advance planning to help clients reduce their tax bill before liquidating all of his stock, we would have told him that he could save a lot of money in taxes by liquidating only as much as he needs to meet his expenses each year. Let's assume that Professor Pay Taxes Later cashed in only $69,000 of his stock each year. This is approximately the amount he has to withdraw if he needs $86,000 to live on after he pays his taxes. 85% of his Social Security will still be taxed, but he's in a lower tax bracket because his total income is significantly lower. His income is so much lower, in fact, that he does not have to pay the additional Net Investment Tax at all.

This year, he will owe the IRS only $6,174. If he liquidates the $300,000 stock account at an equal rate over four years ($75,000 each year), the tax savings compared to liquidating it all at once are significant ($17,136 in savings)!

The really surprising news, though, comes if we make Professor Pay Taxes Later a married man. We're going to assume that he has a wife who is his age, and that she collects the same amount of Social Security that he does. In this scenario, they will have more to spend ($90,000) by liquidating less (only $40,000) of the after-tax stock account each year. When he was a single man, he had to liquidate $69,000 each year in order to be able to spend $86,000. How on earth is that possible?

One obvious reason is that his wife is receiving her own Social Security benefits (I used $25,000 for purposes of this illustration), and they can use that money toward their spending needs. The not so-obvious reason lies in their tax return. Their standard deduction is double that of a single person, which reduces their taxable income.

Because their taxable income is lower, only 48% (as compared to 85%) of their Social Security benefits are taxed. Their taxable income for the year is only $37,950 (as compared to $77,300 when he was single), and because of the favorable capital gains rates, they pay nothing—yes, zero—in federal income tax.

In this scenario, Professor Pay Taxes Later liquidated $40,000 of after-tax stock with a zero-cost basis, paid almost nothing in tax, and still has more spending money than he needs! They have $50,000 in Social Security benefits and $40,000 in proceeds from the sale of the stock, which leaves them with $90,000 and nothing owed to the IRS!

Let's even go so far as to consider what happens if the married Professor Pay Taxes Later decides to listen to his buddy, Professor Pay Taxes Now, instead of me. Accordingly, he withdraws the additional money he needs from his retirement plan instead of his after-tax account. He didn't know that the money he takes from his retirement plan is subject to ordinary income tax rates. If he withdraws just enough to meet his living expenses, $36,000, from his retirement plan instead of his after-tax account, he will owe the IRS $3,255 on April 15. If he had cashed in his after-tax stock that had a cost basis of zero and the income was from a $36,000 capital gain, he would have owed the IRS nothing. Zero. Nada.

Unfortunately, Professor Pay Taxes Later doesn't have enough money to pay the tax bill, because his Social Security and the $36,000 retirement plan withdrawal were just enough to cover his normal monthly expenses. That means that he must withdraw even more from his retirement plan to pay the tax, which is going to increase his tax bill next year. The amount he needs to withdraw to cover his spending needs in addition to the tax due on his retirement plan distribution is $40,000, which increases the tax amount due to $4,143. And as you can imagine, paying all of these unnecessary taxes will cause him to burn through his retirement plan very quickly.

For higher income taxpayers, the outlook for very high taxes is even gloomier, because they are in higher income tax brackets and are potentially subject to the additional Net Investment Income Taxes as well.

When considering spending in retirement, there are many factors that need to be taken into consideration in order to make sure that there are no unpleasant surprises by the time April 15th rolls around. This is one area where it is well worth your time and money to consult with an accountant who is highly skilled in tax planning. It is a specialty in my asset-under-management practice, and it allows us to make recommendations concerning Roth IRA conversions to our clients with confidence. But above all, I hope I have made it very clear that the old assumption that you can never cash in highly appreciated investments without getting hit with a huge tax bill is simply not true.

....

There is one point to consider, though, which may be of interest to readers who have more than enough income from other sources, and who expect to have money in their estates to leave to their children.

The 'step-up in basis rule' states that, if property is inherited, it assumes a basis equivalent to its fair market value at the date of the decedent's death. It is referred to as a 'step-up' because frequently the fair market value of the property at the date of death is much greater than the decedent's basis—which was the cost when it was first acquired.

If you have $100,000 of Google stock for which you paid $10,000, your basis is $10,000. If you sold the stock, you would have to report a $90,000 capital gain. If instead of selling it before you die, you die owning the stock and leave the stock to a child, though, his basis in the stock would be $100,000 because that was the value at the time of your death.

So, if you are preparing an estate plan assuming that your life expectancy is short, it may be advantageous for you to not spend highly appreciated after-tax investments before your retirement funds. If you anticipate being in a situation like this, either on your own or with a qualified advisor, run some numbers. Most of the numbers we have run indicate that unless you are going to die in a few years, you are usually better off spending your after-tax dollars first, even if you will incur capital gains tax and give up your step-up in basis.

On the other hand, it is possible, even likely, the step up in basis rules will be repealed in the near future.

Another factor to consider when deciding which assets to leave to your children and grandchildren is the impact of the SECURE Act on Inherited IRAs and retirement accounts. As I will cover in more detail in later chapters, the SECURE Act will cause a massive income tax acceleration for beneficiaries of retirement accounts.

Under the old law, beneficiaries could stretch distributions of retirement account assets over their lifetimes, which allowed those assets to continue to appreciate, and to spread the tax bite over years. But now, beneficiaries have no choice but to take full distribution of those accounts within ten years, unless they qualify for an exception.

This change may make it even more beneficial to spend your retirement accounts and to leave your highly appreciated after-tax investments to your children. Your children will be able to take advantage of the step-up in basis and will have money that they can access according to their timetables.

You can potentially spare them the pain of the huge tax bills they would incur if their inheritance had fewer high-dollar TIAA, IRA, and other retirement accounts, which would have to be distributed—and taxed—in ten years. Later in this book, I cover strategies to minimize the tax bite. As with all my recommendations, you have to *"run the numbers"* to see what the best spending strategy is for your unique situation.

·· **MINI CASE STUDY 5.3** ··

Which Accounts Should I Save for My Children?

Phyllis Planner is 65 years old and widowed (though the conclusion would be basically the same for a married taxpayer). She is thinking ahead. She wants her money to provide her with a comfortable standard of living, and also wants to leave some money to her three children. How should Phyllis evaluate which pool of money to spend first and which to save for as long as possible? There are four general categories of money to support her retirement. They are ranked in order of how I recommend Phyllis spend her money, exhausting each asset category before breaking into the next asset category.

1. After-Tax Assets Generated by Income Sources:
    • Pension distributions
    • Dividends, interest, and capital gains
    • Social Security

Of course, when Phyllis is 72, under the current rules, she will be required to take minimum distributions from her IRA. Since she will have to pay income taxes on the distributions, the proceeds that remain after she pays taxes on the IRA distributions could also be spent before any of the following assets or sources of income.

2. After-Tax Assets (investments that are not part of a qualified pre-tax retirement plan that would generate income subject to taxes annually):

   • Investments that will either sell at a loss or break even
   • Then, more highly appreciated investments

3. IRA and Retirement Plan Assets (assets subject to ordinary income tax):

   • IRA, 403(b), 401(k), and so forth, dollars over and above Required Minimum Distributions

4. Roth IRA:

   • Roth IRA dollars

The assets in the income category should be spent first since she has to pay tax on that money anyway. But let's assume that Phyllis' Social Security, and the pension, dividends, and interest are not sufficient to meet her spending needs. Then the question becomes, *"Which pool of money should be spent next?"* If we keep in mind the premise of *"don't pay taxes now—pay taxes later,"* the answer is obvious: the after-tax dollars.

If we spend our after-tax dollars, except to the extent that a capital gain is triggered on a sale, those dollars will not be subject to income taxes and the money in the IRA can keep growing tax deferred. Then, when Phyllis has exhausted her after-tax funds, she can delve into her IRA or pre-tax funds.

Whenever you make a withdrawal from an IRA or from your TIAA accumulations, you are going to have to pay income taxes. To get an equivalent amount of spending money from the IRA assets and the after-tax assets, you have to take the taxes into consideration.

Assuming that you are in a 24% tax bracket, you need $1.32 from the IRA assets to get $1.00 of spending money ($1.00 cash + $0.32 to pay the taxes). We get $0.32 cents because $1.32 x 24% = 0.32.

On the other hand, the after-tax money is withdrawn tax-free, so to get $1.00, you withdraw $1.00 unless capital gains tax applies. Even if you are subject to capital gains tax, the rate is 15% for taxpayers who are in the 24% tax bracket. You are still ahead by 17 cents for every dollar you withdraw.

Finally, when Phyllis exhausts her IRA and pre-tax funds, she spends her Roth IRA. Why should she spend her Traditional IRA before her Roth IRA? If tax-deferred growth is a good thing, then tax-free growth is even better. By spending taxable IRA money before Roth IRA money, she increases the time that the Roth IRA will provide income tax-free growth.

If your plan is to leave money to your heirs, their tax situations should be considered as well. If you have heirs who have tax deferral/avoidance as a goal and their tax bracket is the same as yours or higher, then the Roth assets are the best assets for them to inherit. The opposite conclusion may be reached if you have other heirs who plan on spending the money soon after they inherit it and are in a lower tax bracket. If that is the case, you could be better off spending the Roth IRA yourself. The facts of each case should be considered. Please see the discussion of *"Who Gets What?"* in Chapter 19.

···   **MINI CASE STUDY 5.4**   ···
Using Tax Planning to Determine the
Best Spending Order

One possible exception to spending after-tax dollars first is to make small IRA withdrawals, or small Roth IRA conversions if your current tax bracket is lower than your future tax bracket once you retire. This strategy saves some taxes since you are getting some money out of your IRA before you must take Required Minimum Distributions (RMD), which will be taxed at your higher post retirement rate. If you withdraw just enough to take you to the top of your current (low) tax bracket, then you get that money out at a lower tax rate without pushing yourself into a higher tax bracket. But first, let me clarify a common misunderstanding about taxes and tax brackets.

What many people do not understand is that tax brackets are tiered. A married couple who is filing their joint tax return in 2024 (for their 2023 taxes), and who has taxable income up to $22,000 is taxed at 10%. If they earn more than that, then the next tier of their income is taxed at the next bracket (income from $22,000 to $89,450 is taxed at 12% for married filing jointly), and so on.

Some people are deathly afraid of getting one more dollar. They think, *"Oh no! If I get one more dollar, I'm going to be thrown into the 24% tax bracket, and my taxes are going to explode."* But that's not right.

What happens is that *the one additional dollar* will be in the 24% bracket. This is illustrated in Figure 5.2 which shows the tax brackets for returns filed for the tax year 2023. You can see that a taxpayer, who falls into the maximum tax bracket of 37%, does not actually lose 37% of his income to taxes.

Determining a strategy for the distribution years is where the rubber meets the road. I've had clients who, after meeting with me or reading my materials realize they made costly mistakes along the way. That's water under the bridge. If that's you, that's par for the course. Just do the best you can with your starting point now. Most of us are in *"clean up mode"* meaning mistakes were made in the past and we are planning to do the best we can with whatever we have now, no matter how we got to where we are now.

In this case study, we are using the tax brackets and rates in effect for 2022. While the exact numbers will be different for subsequent years, conclusions remain the same.

Let's look at a hypothetical example. Though Joe and Sally Retiree, aged 65, have an estate of $1.5 million, their taxable income is only $30,000. (Taxable income is arrived at after subtracting itemized or the standard deduction.) Right now, they are in the 12% tax bracket, but when Joe reaches age 72, his minimum distribution will push his income well into the 22% tax bracket. Joe decides to make voluntary withdrawals from his IRA every year until he reaches his RMD date as follows. Please note that depending on your year of birth, under SECURE Act 2.0 your RMD date could be later than age 72. Please see Chapter 6, *Required Minimum Distribution Rules*.

Figure 5.2

Tax Brackets for Use in Filing 2023 Returns in 2024

Married Filing Jointly and Surviving Spouses

Taxable Income:	Tax:		
$ 0 – 22,000	10% of taxable income		
$ 22,001 – 89,450	$ 440 +	*12% of the excess over*	*$ 22,000*
$ 89,451 – 190,750	$ 9,385 +	*22% of the excess over*	*$ 89,450*
$ 190,751 – 364,200	$ 13,200 +	*24% of the excess over*	*$190,750*
$ 364,201 – 462,500	$ 42,336 +	*32% of the excess over*	*$364,200*
$ 462,501 – 693,750	$ 56,211 +	*35% of the excess over*	*$462,500*
$ 693,751 *and above*	$ 70,086 +	*37% of the excess over*	*$693,750*

Single

Taxable Income:	Tax:		
$ 0 – 11,000	10% of taxable income		
$ 11,001 – 44,725	$ 220 +	*12% of the excess over*	*$ 11,000*
$ 44,726 – 95,375	$ 4,693 +	*22% of the excess over*	*$ 44,725*
$ 95,376 – 182,100	$ 6,600 +	*24% of the excess over*	*$ 95,375*
$ 182,101 – 231,250	$ 21,168 +	*32% of the excess over*	*$182,100*
$ 231,251 – 578,125	$ 28,106 +	*35% of the excess over*	*$231,250*
$ 578,126 *and above*	$ 39,668 +	*37% of the excess over*	*$578,125*

> Determining a strategy for the distribution years is where the rubber meets the road. I've had clients who, after meeting with me or reading my materials, realize they made costly mistakes along the way. That's water under the bridge. Most of us have made mistakes in the past. Do the best you can with whatever you currently have, no matter how you got to where you are now.

The top income limit of the 12% bracket for married filing jointly (using 2023 tables) is $89,450. Joe and Sally already have $30,000 in taxable income before any IRA withdrawal. If Joe makes a voluntary $59,450 IRA withdrawal now, assuming no additional tax on Social Security, Medicare Part B, etc. he still pays tax on the withdrawal at the same 12% rate as the rest of his income. If he waits until age 72, when he is required to make a withdrawal, much of the later distributions will be taxed at 22%.

Depending on the circumstances, it might be a reasonable strategy for him to begin distributions before he turns age 72. Calculations reveal that the higher distribution yields a slight long-term advantage, although not as much as you might think because of the simultaneous loss of some tax deferral.

For many clients, particularly frugal clients, I would prefer a variation of this strategy that provides better long-term benefits. Instead of making an IRA withdrawal of $59,450, paying tax on the funds, and then being left with after-tax dollars that will generate taxable income, I would recommend Joe make a $59,450 Roth IRA conversion.

Many clients will resist this advice, but I urge you to at least consider it. My wife and I have made Roth IRA conversions well into the six figures of our own money, paid an enormous tax bill, and I still recommend that clients take advantage of the lower tax bracket this way. This advice is perfectly consistent with Jonathan Clements' article in *The Wall Street Journal*, in which Jonathan quoted me giving this identical analysis. We will cover the reasons to consider Roth IRA conversions in more detail in Chapter 7. For now, suffice it to say that I am a big fan of Roth IRA conversions.

If Joe does not want to make a Roth IRA conversion, he should at least consider taking IRA distributions even before he is required to, based on his tax bracket. Please note that adding income in the form of extra IRA distributions and/or Roth IRA conversions may have an impact on the taxability of Social Security benefits and other items (refer back to *"Comments on Your Actual Tax Brackets"* in Chapter 3), which should be worked into the numbers for the amount to withdraw or convert.

KEY IDEAS

- Subject to exception, spend after-tax dollars before IRA or Roth dollars.

- Leave money in tax deferred and tax-free environments as long as possible.

- Determining the best spending strategy depends on your individual situation.

- Sometimes the strategy of shifting from the taxable environment to the tax-free environment will change the optimal spending order.

- Future changes in tax rates may make it more beneficial to spend funds from Traditional IRA and TIAA accounts now while tax rates are low.

- The SECURE Act will have a big impact on how Inherited IRA and retirement plan assets are taxed.

- Determining which assets to leave to your children requires consideration of their financial situations and their income levels, which will determine the magnitude of any tax burden they face from inherited assets.

6

Required Minimum Distribution Rules

"There was a time when a fool and his money were soon parted, but now it happens to everybody."

— Adlai Stevenson

Eventually Everyone Must Draw from Retirement Savings

Even if you stick to the game plan to spend your income and after-tax dollars first, eventually, by law, you will have to withdraw funds from your Traditional IRA or qualified retirement plan by taking Required Minimum Distributions (RMDs). Roth IRAs are currently exempt from this requirement, though Democratic tax proposals in recent years have included provisions to change this—most recently for *"mega-Roth IRAs"* over $10 million. For now, though, I will limit the discussion to the rules governing Traditional retirement plans.

If your 70th birthday is July 1, 2019, or later, you must take your first RMD by April 1 of the year after you reach age 72. The key word here is minimum. Keeping in mind the *"Don't pay taxes now—pay taxes later"* rule of thumb, I want you to continue to maintain the highest balance in your IRA. If you take a RMD the year you turn 72 and a distribution the following year, you may remain in a lower tax bracket which would be advantageous. You can always take out more if you need it.

As I mentioned in Chapter 1, depending on your age, you may be taking your RMDs at a different age than 72. As a result of SECURE Act 2.0, other changes are increases to the ages for RMDs, depending on the year of birth.

- If you turn 73 after 12/31/22 *(born in 1951 to 1959)*, your RMDs begin at age 73.

- If you turn 74 after 12/31/33 *(born in 1960 or later)*, your RMDs begin at age 75.

Since these changes passed after the book went to press, if you fall into any of these age groups as you read the rest of this chapter, keep these adjusted ages for starting RMDs in mind.

> **Eventually, by law, you will have to withdraw funds from your Traditional IRA or qualified retirement plan.**

During the financial crisis of 2009 and in response to the Covid-19 pandemic during 2020, the federal government temporarily suspended the RMD rules. The reasoning was that older retirees should not be forced to sell their investments when the value of the investments is low.

That reasoning didn't make sense to me because investors have always been allowed to take their RMD in stock instead of cash, if they prefer—it's called an in-kind distribution. So, if the investments in your IRA have decreased in value, you can have the investment shares transferred directly to a non-IRA account and leave them alone until they increase in value again. You still have to pay tax on the amount of the transfer, but the only reason you would be forced to sell when the value is low would be if you did not have a lot of cash on hand and you needed to sell some of the securities to pay the tax on the RMD or to meet living expenses.

Another point to consider is that, while the IRS requires that you calculate the RMD for every IRA account that you own, you are not required to withdraw a minimum distribution amount from every IRA you own. You can add up all of your RMDs and take the total amount from one account, preferably from one that has not gone down in value. Hopefully, being aware of these little-known rules will help you avoid having to take a loss on your investments if you need to take a RMD when the markets are down.

On the other hand, taking smaller distributions from one IRA and larger ones from a different IRA could lead to attention by either the organization investing the money or the IRS. Personally, I would rather not deal with a pain in the butt problem than save a few dollars, but potentially you could save more than a few dollars and maybe you do not mind dealing with notices and issues because you love getting the last drop out of the tax code.

Calculating Your RMD After Age 72

Currently, RMDs are calculated by taking your projected distribution period, based on your age and the age of a beneficiary deemed to be 10 years younger than you, and dividing that factor into the balance of your IRA or qualified plan as of December 31st of the prior year. Bear in mind that your projected life expectancy factor or the projected distribution period is not based on your personal eating and exercise habits or even your genetic history! It is an actuarial calculation from the IRS determined solely by age.

Many large financial institutions offer tools on their websites that automatically calculate RMDs. If you would like to do the math yourself, the IRS's Supplement to the *Publication 590* contains worksheets that you can use to work through the calculation, as well as the tables that you will need to use to find your RMD factor. For those who would just like a quick glance, the tables are published in the Appendix at the end of this book.

The IRS provides three life expectancy tables in *IRS Publication 590-B*. After more than 20 years, these tables were updated in February 2022, to a new version to be used for distributions made in calendar year 2022 and beyond. The most frequently used table is Table III, not Table I. I present them here in the reverse order.

1. **Table III: Uniform Lifetime Table** (for use by unmarried IRA owners and married owners whose spouses are not more than 10 years younger). This table is available in the Appendix of this book.

2. **Table II: Joint Life and Last Survivor Expectancy Table** (for IRA owners with spouses 10 or more years younger). This is not covered in the Appendix of this book because it is too long. See *IRS Publication 590*.

3. **Table I: Single Life Expectancy Table** (for IRA beneficiaries). This table is available in the Appendix of this book.

Table III: Uniform Lifetime Table for IRA Owners

Generally speaking, most IRA owners will use Table III. In effect, the age-dependent projected distribution periods in Table III are based on the joint life expectancy projections of an IRA owner and a hypothetical beneficiary not more than 10 years younger.

Using a joint life expectancy is advantageous because the longer joint-life expectancy factor reduces the annual RMD. But rather than using the actual life expectancy of the beneficiary for the calculations, the IRS simplifies the terms. Table III deems all beneficiaries—from children to grandmothers—to have a life expectancy 10 years longer than that of the owner.

At age 73, the projected distribution period is 26.5 years (roughly the single life expectancy from Table I plus 10 years, although you must refer to the tables for the precise factor).

If you are already receiving RMDs (born before July 1, 1949), your distribution that is required to be paid by December 31, 2022, will be based on the new factors effective January 1, 2022.

·· **MINI CASE STUDY 6.1** ··
RMD Calculation for IRA Owners

Bob turns 77 in 2022. As of December 31, 2021, he has two IRAs that are each worth $500,000. He names his son, Phillip, as the beneficiary for one IRA and his 74-year-old wife, Mary, for the other. To calculate his 2022 RMD for the IRA with his wife as beneficiary, he takes the life expectancy at his age 77 from Table III, 22.9, and divides that into his balance, $500,000, to arrive at $21,834. He uses the same table and the same factor to arrive at the same RMD from the IRA that has his son as the beneficiary. When Bob dies, the amounts that his wife and son will be required to take from the IRAs they inherited from him will be different. I'll go into more detail about that later in this chapter.

·· **MINI CASE STUDY 6.2** ··
RMD Calculation with IRA Owner and Spouse
More Than Ten Years Younger

Bob will have to use a different calculation for the RMD for the IRA with his wife as the beneficiary if Mary is only 65 years old. According to Table II, Bob's and Mary's joint life expectancy factor based on the ages they will be on their birthdays in 2022 is 24.3. Bob calculates his RMD by dividing 24.3 into his balance of $500,000 to arrive at $20,576. Bob's RMD for the account with his wife as the beneficiary is lower than for the account with his son as the beneficiary because Bob and his wife were permitted to use their actual *joint* life expectancy factor for his calculation.

We will cover more about IRA beneficiaries in Chapter 11. For now, please look at the Figure 6.1 on the preceding page to see how the age of his spouse affects Bob's RMD.

···

Table II: Joint Life and Last Survivor Expectancy Table for IRA Owners with Spouses Ten or More Years Younger

Because nothing that the government does is ever without complications, there is an exception for married individuals when the IRA owner is 10 or more years older than his or her spouse. Those individuals are permitted to use their actual joint life expectancy factor, which will result in smaller RMDs.

Figure 6.1

IRS Table III Spouse Who is *Not* 10 Years Younger (or Child) as Beneficiary				IRS Table II Spouse Who is 10 Years Younger as Beneficiary			
Bob's Age	IRA Balance ($)	Factor	RMD	Bob's Age	IRA Balance ($)	Factor	RMD
77	500,000	22.9	21,834	77	500,000	24.3	20,576
78	478,166	22.0	21,735	78	479,424	23.4	20,488
79	456,431	21.1	21,632	79	458,936	22.5	20,397
80	434,799	20.2	21,525	80	438,539	21.6	20,303
81	413,275	19.4	21,303	81	418,236	20.7	21,303
82	391,972	18.5	21,188	82	398,031	19.9	20,205
83	370,784	17.7	20,948	83	378,030	19.0	20,002
84	349,836	16.8	20,824	84	358,133	18.2	19,896
85	329,012	16.0	20,563	85	338,456	17.4	19,678
86	308,449	15.2	20,293	86	319,004	16.5	19,451
87	288,156	14.4	20,011	87	299,671	15.7	19,334
88	268,145	13.7	19,573	88	280,583	14.9	18,831
89	248,573	12.9	19,269	89	261,752	14.2	18,433
90	229,304	12.2	18,795	90	243,319	13.4	18,158

Table I: Single Life Expectancy Table for IRA Beneficiaries

When a spouse dies before age 72, the younger spousal beneficiary of the IRA has two options. He or she can roll the Inherited IRA into his or her own IRA and begin RMDs when he or she reaches age 72. Or he or she can decline to treat the IRA as his or her own and simply defer distributions until the year that the original IRA owner would have attained age 72. At that point, he or she would begin distributions based on his or her Table I life expectancy factor. This is an extremely important decision that you will have to make if your spouse predeceases you, and the advantages and disadvantages of each option are covered in detail in Chapter 14.

Non-spouse beneficiaries (there are some exceptions) of Inherited IRAs have no options. And, under the SECURE Act, effective January 1, 2020, a radically different law governs Inherited IRAs and retirement plans from what we had in the past. Now, subject to exceptions, the beneficiary of a Traditional Inherited

IRA must withdraw and pay taxes on that Inherited IRA within 10 years of the IRA owner's death. The IRS issued Proposed Regulations on February 24, 2022, that are not law as we go to press but are likely to become law to clarify the SECURE Act and they included the requirement that most beneficiaries will also have Required Minimum Distributions until the Inherited IRA is fully distributed (required by the end of year 10).

The exceptions, in addition to your spouse mentioned earlier, include beneficiaries with disabilities or chronic illnesses, the IRA owner's children younger than age 21 (clarified under the Proposed Regulations), and beneficiaries who are not more than 10 years younger than the IRA owner.

These non-spouse exceptions (or beneficiaries inheriting prior to 2020) are not subject to the 10-year rule and must begin to take distributions based on their own life expectancy (as projected in Table I) as of the year following the year of the IRA owner's death. For each subsequent year, the non-spouse beneficiary subtracts one (1) from his original factor, because his life expectancy is diminished by one year for every year he survives. This is frequently referred to as the *"minus one method."*

Calculating Your Life Expectancy after the Initial Year

It is interesting to note that Table I life expectancies are reduced by one full year as each year passes. Tables II and III, however, reduce the life expectancy of the IRA owner by less than one year. This is analogous to the old double recalculation method. (Readers who remember those rules get bonus points.) The idea is that as we age, our life expectancy declines, but it does not decline by an entire year.

So, if you are a surviving spouse who inherits an IRA, but you do not treat the Inherited IRA as your own IRA, your life expectancy is recalculated each year based on the life expectancies shown in Table I (the full year decline).

When you die, your non-spouse heirs must use your life expectancy at the time of your death, reduced by one for each subsequent year, for their RMD calculation. For a discussion on whether a spouse should treat an IRA as his or her own IRA, refer to Chapter 12.

With the new Single Life Tables taking effect as of January 1, 2022, there is a transition rule for Inherited IRA beneficiaries to reset the life expectancy calculation in line with the new tables. This redetermination requires the beneficiary to go back to the year after the year of the IRA owner's death and find the beneficiary's single life expectancy factor as of his/her age in that year under the new tables. Subsequently, one year will be deducted from the new life expectancy for each year since the first distribution year to arrive at the new factor for the relevant post-2021 year.

Here's an example of how that works. In 2019, Gina inherited an IRA from her father when she was 33. From the old Single Life Table, her life expectancy was 50.4. She used that as a denominator to calculate her RMD for 2020. For 2021, using the *"minus one method,"* she used 49.4 (50.4–1). With the new Single Life Table, her life expectancy at age 33—her age when she inherited the IRA—has increased to 52.5. To calculate her RMD for 2022, she takes her new initial factor of 52.5 and reduces it by the two calendar years since 2020 (2020 and 2021) to get a new factor of 50.5.

Timing Your First Required Distribution

If you were born after June 30, 1949, then your first distribution will be required in the year that you turn age 72, though you have the option to take it as late as April 1 of the following year. For example, retirement plan owners born in 1950, will have to take one distribution in 2022 and one in 2023, or two distributions in 2023 if they do not take a distribution in 2022.

If you do not take a distribution in 2022, the first distribution in 2023 will have to be taken prior to April 1, 2023 (in effect, for what should have been taken in 2022), and the second distribution will have to be taken by December 31, 2023. Annual minimum distributions would continue for the rest of the participant's life.

So, if you have a choice regarding when and how to take your first distributions, should you take one distribution per year or should you wait and take two the following year? That decision might rest on the implications for your tax bracket. If you take a minimum distribution the year that you turn age 72 and one distribution the following year, you may remain in a lower tax bracket, which would be advantageous. Taking two distributions in one year, though, could push you into a higher tax bracket and possibly accelerate the phase-out of certain tax credits or deductions. If that is the case, you will likely be better off violating our *"Pay Taxes Later"* rule by taking one distribution and paying some tax before you have to. On the other hand, if you will remain in the same tax bracket even with two distributions, then it makes no difference if you wait until you are required to begin distributions. This allows you to take advantage of the additional period of tax-deferred growth.

In the previous example, for participants born after 1950, there is no RMD for 2022. Unless the participant needs the money or is pursuing the early distribution of an IRA because of a lower income tax bracket or estate plan strategy, he or she is better off leaving the money in the IRA and taking the first RMD in 2023 or later.

There can be a significant planning opportunity when deciding the year to take your initial RMD, especially if you have taxable wages from your current employer to consider. Our advice is to either actually make the calculations yourself or consult with the appropriate financial professional, even your tax preparer before making the decision as to which year to take your initial RMD in order to *'smooth out'* the taxable income and *'manage'* the tax brackets when possible.

Failing to take a minimum distribution when required, however, or not taking a large enough minimum distribution has very expensive consequences. As of this writing, the IRS charges a 50% excise tax on the amount that was not distributed as required. So, if you were required to take a $10,000 minimum distribution and didn't do so, you will owe $5,000 in excise tax. And that's in addition to the normal income tax you will owe on the distribution, as well as general penalties for underpayment of tax.

Special Rule for Qualified Plan Owners Who Are Still Working Past Age 72

RMD rules apply to Traditional IRAs (not Roth IRAs) and qualified plans [401(k)s, 403(b)s, Roth 401(k)s, and Roth 403(b)s, etc.]. However, the rules governing 401(k)s and 403(b)s are slightly different than for IRAs.

- If you are still working after age 72, the IRS does not require you to take a distribution from the retirement plan connected to your current job as long as you do not own more than 5% of the company. Remember, though, that your employer is responsible for setting the rules for your plan. Even though the IRS doesn't require you to take a distribution, your employer might.

- If you have a plan such as a 401(k) associated with a job from which you have retired, the IRS says you will have to take your initial RMD by April 1st of the year following the year in which you reach age 72. Some employers allow you to keep your retirement plan with them when you start to take withdrawals, and some employers require that you roll the account into an IRA before you start to take withdrawals.

- If you have two or more retirement plans associated with jobs from which you have retired, the IRS requires that each plan calculate a minimum distribution for you when you reach age 72. This is different from their rules for calculating RMDs on IRAs, which allow you to add up the values of all of your IRAs, calculate the RMD, and then take the full distribution from one account.

  This can be a very important consideration for people whose old plans happen to include stock in the company they worked for, because the RMD requirement might cause you to have to sell stock when the value is low. As long as you have enough other assets to pay the tax on the RMD, though, you can take your company stock as an *"in-kind"* distribution and keep it in a brokerage account until the time that it increases in value again.

  The one exception to this rule is for 403(b) plan owners. The IRS allows participants in 403(b) plans to add up the values of all their accounts, calculate the RMD, and then take the full distribution from one account. For individuals such as retired university professors who have multiple 403(b) plans, this makes the paperwork much simpler to deal with at year end.

- If you had a 401(k) plan from a former job and rolled that 401(k) plan into a plan associated with the job at which you are still working, then you will have to check with the plan administrator of your current plan to see whether you will be forced to take RMDs upon attaining age 72 from the portion of that 401(k) plan that is attributable to your former employment.

  Private Letter Ruling (PRL) 200453015, published in January 2005, states that the IRS permits deferral of the RMDs on all of the funds in the new employer's account *including the rollover contributions* from the former employer until April 1st of the year after the employee retires from the new employer. You must, however, make sure that your employer's plan will allow you to do what the IRS will allow you to do.

I have a client who became really excited about the prospect of avoiding his minimum distribution. He wanted to start his own retirement plan (actually a one-person 401(k)] based on his small self-employment income). Then he wanted to roll his IRA into a one-person 401(k) and suspend his RMDs on his IRA. It was a good thought, but with a fatal flaw. He is more than a 5% owner of his consulting business, and the rule about deferring the RMD after age 72 if you are still working does not apply to individuals with a 5% or greater ownership in the company.

················· **MINI CASE STUDY 6.3** ·················
RMD If Still Working Past Age 72

Joan continues to work even though she is older than 72. She has a total of $1 million in her 401(k) plans: $500,000 associated with her current job and $500,000 from a former job. She has never consolidated the two plans. Her new plan includes both her and her employer's most recent contributions.

By April 1st of the year after she turns age 72, she will be required to take minimum distributions from the $500,000 associated with the job she left, but not from the account that is still active due to her employment. Whether she could take the money from the 401(k) from the job she retired from, roll it into her current plan (by trustee-to-trustee transfer), and avoid an RMD is not clear. The IRS will allow it, but her current employer may not.

If your employer does permit it, this may be an incentive for someone still working after age 72 to consider rolling money out of their IRA and into a retirement plan at work. Usually, I prefer money going the other way, which is from 401(k) to IRA, or my current preferred strategy, from a work 401(k) or IRA to a one-person 401(k) plan that you control.

Special Rules for 403(b) Participants for Pre-1987 Retirement Plan Funds

Participants in 403(b) plans are subject to some special rules that do not apply to participants in other types of plans. Both employee and employer contributions to a 403(b) plan made before January 1, 1987, are not subject to RMDs until age 75. As a result, the balance that was in your 403(b) as of December 31, 1986, is not subject to RMDs until you reach age 75, not age 70½ or 72, even if you have retired.

If you fall into this special category of 403(b) account holders, you should consult with your organization's benefits office to determine the balance in the account as of December 31, 1986.

Surprisingly, many institutions, including TIAA, do a good job of tracking that balance. If your 403(b) plan included pre-1987 contributions and you roll it into an IRA, the *"grandfathered"* status of those contributions is lost, and you will be required to take minimum distributions on them at age 72. Contributions made on January 1, 1987, and later are subject to RMDs at age 72. Note, however, that the growth and appreciation on pre-1987 dollars is not grandfathered and is treated like a regular 403(b).

On the other hand, when you actually calculate the tax advantage of keeping the funds in the 403(b) to defer a portion of the minimum distribution, it is relatively small. If you think you could get even a slight investment advantage by doing a trustee-to-trustee transfer from your 403(b) to an IRA to gain additional investment options, it would still be worthwhile.

Retired public safety officers, including law enforcement and firefighters, have a special exception to the distribution rules. They can receive a distribution of up to $3,000 completely tax-free from their 403(b), as long as the proceeds are used to directly pay for accident, health or long-term care insurance.

A Possible Compromise for Those Who Do Not Need Income and Are Charitably Inclined—Use QCDs

Although there is no way to avoid taking RMDs from Traditional (not Roth) IRAs, there is an option available to those individuals who do not need that income for living expenses, and who are inclined to donate to charity. The Pension Protection Act of 2006 created something called a Qualified Charitable Distribution, which allows IRA owners to specify that a payment of up to $100,000 from their RMDs be sent directly to a **qualified** charity upon reaching age 70½.

Here is how it works. IRA owners electing this option are still required to take their RMD, but the amount of the distribution is sent directly to the **qualified** charity and can be excluded from their gross income. For individuals who are charitably inclined, this can make a lot more sense than having the RMD sent to them, and then issuing a separate check to the charity, particularly if the taxpayer doesn't itemize deductions. (The Tax Cuts and Jobs Act of 2017 made it more difficult for many Americans to itemize their charitable contributions.)

So, if you do not itemize, the charitable contribution isn't tax deductible, and the IRA distribution is taxable. With a Qualified Charitable Distribution (QCD), you still cannot deduct the charitable donation, but at least you're not taxed on the IRA distribution. In essence, you are making charitable contributions on a *"pre-tax"* basis versus an *"after-tax"* basis. In addition, there are many potential tax benefits from reducing your adjusted gross income using a QCD:

- Less of your Social Security income may become taxable.
- The phase-out of medical expenses you claim as itemized deductions is reduced.
- The phase-out of total itemized deductions is reduced.
- The Net Investment Income tax surcharges can be reduced.

- You may avoid future increases in your Medicare premiums.
- Your Alternative Minimum Tax may be reduced.

QCDs were originally supposed to be effective only in 2006 and 2007, but over the years Congress extended them on a temporary basis and finally made them permanent as part of the Consolidated Appropriations Act of 2016. It is worth pointing out that the while the SECURE Act increased the RMD age to 72, the qualifying age for a QCD remains at age 70½. However, there is one major drawback that all of your post-70½ deductible IRA contributions must be tracked against your QCDs and your otherwise tax-free QCD will be reduced by your contribution amount.

Qualified Charitable Distributions have three criteria you must be aware of:

1. You have to make sure that the charitable organization is a *qualified* charity. A qualified charity is one that has a valid tax-exempt status, according to the U.S. Treasury. There are some very good causes that I personally donate to, but they do not meet the definition of a qualified charity. As such, I cannot deduct those contributions, nor could I send them a QCD. The organization will be able to tell you if they're tax-exempt or not, or, if you want to be 100% sure, you can search on the IRS.gov website.

2. You have to be at least age 70½ to make a QCD.

3. QCDs are only available for IRAs, or inactive SEPs and SIMPLE plans. QCDs from an employer-sponsored retirement plan are currently not permitted.

Please see Chapter 20 for a dedicated chapter on Qualified Charitable Distributions written by Steve Kohman, CPA.

When Should You Schedule Taking Your RMD?

Theoretically, you should take your RMD on December 31st to delay as long as possible withdrawing money from the tax-favored environment. In the real world, however, it is difficult to get any work done with financial firms in December and trying to comply with a deadline between Christmas and the last day of the year is a total nightmare. Remember, if you miss taking a withdrawal

If you do not need the cash, I recommend scheduling your distribution for Thanksgiving or early December.

by year-end, you face the 50% penalty under the current law for failing to take your RMD—an expensive penalty. If you do not need the cash, I recommend scheduling your distribution for Thanksgiving or early December. If you need the RMD for your spending needs, it may be best to schedule 12 equal monthly distributions throughout the year.

How to Get Your Interest-Free Loan from the IRS

I do not understand why anyone would have extra tax taken out of their paycheck to ensure that they get a big refund. Why on earth would you give the IRS an interest-free loan? It should be the other way around! Would you like to get an interest-free loan from the IRS?

One way to do so is to take your RMD in December and have federal income tax withheld from it, rather than paying quarterly estimated taxes on your retirement income throughout the year. From the IRS's perspective, tax that is withheld is treated as if it has been withheld at an even rate throughout the year as opposed to being treated like a single estimated tax payment you made late in the year—so you will not get penalized for paying all of the tax due in December.

How to Avoid Paying Tax Estimates and Float the IRS at the Same Time

Here's an even better idea for those of you who hate paying estimated taxes and who love getting an interest free loan from the IRS. If you are currently paying quarterly estimated taxes on your non-IRA income, you can forgo your estimates completely and instead ask your IRA custodian to do up to a 100% tax withholding on the RMD you take at the end of the year.

Let's say that you have been paying estimates of $1,500 each quarter, and you have been told that you will have to take a RMD of $6,000 this year. In December, you can instruct your IRA custodian to withhold federal income tax from your RMD at a rate of 100% and have them send the entire $6,000 directly to the IRS. This strategy allows you to earn interest on the money you are required to take from your IRA for as long as possible, and also allows you to earn the interest on the estimated tax payments that you were going to send to the IRS.

The best part is that, under current rules, as long as the amount of taxes withheld from your RMD is sufficient to cover the amount of tax you owe for the entire year, there is no penalty for paying 100% of your tax liability in December! I cannot understand why so few people use this strategy.

KEY IDEAS

- Subject to the transferring from the taxable environment to the tax-free environment and other exceptions, keep your RMD to the required minimum. Do not take out more money than you need so that you keep the balance in your tax-deferred accounts as large as possible.

- If you turn 70 after July 1, 2019, you do not need to start taking your RMD until you turn 72.

- If you do not need the cash, make a habit of taking your RMD at Thanksgiving or in early December.

- If you are paying quarterly estimated taxes, consider having your IRA custodian withhold the full amount of your annual estimates from your RMD. This is not only an interest-free loan from the IRS and avoids late payment penalties, but it is easier than sending in estimated taxes.

7

Should You Transfer Your 403(b) to an IRA at Retirement?

(Rollovers vs. Trustee-to-Trustee Transfers and Other Strategies)

"They say it is better to be poor and happy than rich and miserable, but how about a compromise like moderately rich and just moody?"

— Diana, Princess of Wales

When someone retires or is *"service terminated,"* the big question is: *"What should I do now?"*

Without getting into specific investment ideas, let's consider whether it makes sense for you to keep your money in your existing retirement plan, transfer it to an IRA, take a lump-sum distribution or make a trustee-to-trustee transfer into your new one-person 401(k) plan. We'll be discussing some of the TIAA-specific complexities in Chapters 8 and 9, but in this chapter, we'll be looking in detail at moving your retirement asset distribution options but not your TIAA. Contingent on the specifics of any given retirement plan, the basic options are as follows:

1. Transfer the money into a separate IRA.
2. Leave the money in your current plan.
3. Annuitize the balance *(for more information on annuitizing, see Chapter 9)*.
4. Use some combination of options 1, 2, and 3 *(often my favorite choice)*.
5. Take a lump-sum distribution.
6. Transfer money to a one-person 401(k) plan.

An Important Consideration Before You Do Anything

The first question that you should be asking yourself before making any transfers is whether you have any after-tax dollars in your retirement plan. These dollars would likely be the result of contributing more than you were allowed to deduct in your retirement plan, but you did it anyway in order to get deferred earnings.

If you have after-tax dollars in your retirement plan, and do not think carefully, you could end up transferring them to an IRA or doing something else. You already paid tax on these dollars, but that fact could easily get lost if you move them with the rest of your pre-tax dollars to an IRA. The result is overpaying on taxes when you start taking distributions from your IRA. You may potentially be missing a big opportunity to do a tax-free Roth conversion. Please see Chapters 15 and 16, where I talk about Roth conversions after the SECURE Act without having to pay any taxes if you have after-tax dollars in your IRA or retirement plan and about the possible impacts that Roth conversions can have on Medicare premiums.

Rolling Over to an IRA

Retirees often talk about rolling over to an IRA or rolling money out of a retirement plan and into an IRA. Technically we should use the term *transfer*, simply because the IRS makes a significant distinction between the mechanics and regulations of a rollover versus a trustee-to-trustee transfer.

The trustee-to-trustee transfer is simpler, and what I usually recommend. I'll explain the distinctions between rollovers and transfers later in this chapter. (In keeping with common usage, when referring to a transfer I will use the terms *rollover* and *transfer* interchangeably throughout this book, but please understand that what I am referring to is following the technical procedures of a trustee-to-trustee transfer.) (See the section in this chapter called *The Mechanics of IRA Rollovers and Trustee-to-Trustee Transfers.*)

> **Retirees often talk about rolling over to an IRA or rolling money out of a retirement plan and into an IRA. Technically we should use the term *transfer*, simply because the IRS makes a significant distinction between the mechanics and regulations of a rollover *vs.* a trustee-to-trustee transfer. In addition to using the term *transfer*, we should actually employ the mechanics of a trustee-to-trustee transfer as opposed to an IRA rollover.**

Though there are a few downsides, transferring retirement plan accumulations into an IRA or into your own one-person 401(k) via a trustee-to-trustee transfer is usually the best option. The most likely exception where that doesn't apply is if your retirement plan accumulations are in Traditional TIAA. Please see Chapters 8 and 9, where I discuss options for TIAA accumulations. As with most decisions, there are advantages and disadvantages.

Tax Advantages of Transferring a University 403(b) or Company 401(k) into an IRA

Proper planning requires taking the appropriate steps while you are alive and having in place the appropriate procedures after you and your spouse have died. Prior to the SECURE Act, with a bit of planning, your heirs could stretch taxable distributions from an Inherited IRA and certain retirement plans for decades. But, as we'll describe fully in Chapter 14, unless the beneficiary of your IRA is your spouse or qualifies for an exception, the SECURE Act will force your heir to completely drain that account within 10 years of your and your spouse's death, drastically accelerating the income taxes due on those funds.

On top of that, if your employer's retirement plan document stipulates the wrong provisions, even the measly 10-year stretch may be replaced by a screaming income tax disaster. Your heirs could be in for a tax nightmare if you never transferred your 403(b) to a 401(k) retirement plan or an IRA. Different rules apply if a spouse inherits a 403(b) or 401(k) versus someone other than your spouse—say a child—so it is important to understand how your decisions can affect the outcome.

The old Westinghouse 401(k) plan in Pittsburgh forced non-spousal beneficiaries to withdraw their inherited 401(k) and pay taxes on the withdrawal much faster than the IRS would have required if the retirement plan owner had done a trustee-to-trustee transfer to an IRA and the beneficiary could have *"stretched"* the Inherited IRA.

The old engineers did not like transferring out of their plan because it had a high guaranteed income investment similar in concept to your Traditional TIAA. Their compromise position was since the income acceleration provision did not apply to the surviving spouse, they left the money in the plan at work until the first spouse died. Then, they made the trustee-to-trustee transfer to an IRA.

That might be a reasonable compromise if you want to keep some of your TIAA where it is, and your university does accelerate distributions on non-spousal beneficiaries at death. On the other hand, few universities have that provision.

Some employees prefer to keep their retirement plan balance where it is rather than transferring it to an IRA, especially if TIAA manages that plan, simply because TIAA plans offer favorable fixed-income investments. Unfortunately, many employees fail to realize that the specific plan rules that govern their individual 403(b) or other retirement plan take precedence over the IRS distribution rules for Inherited IRAs or retirement plans.

The distribution rules that come into play when a retirement plan participant dies are found in a plan document created by the employer that few employees or advisors ever bother to read. You would like to think that, since employers participate in the plans they offer to their employees, they would design the rules of the plan to be as beneficial as possible. Unfortunately, that is not necessarily the case. Most people would not even think that the rules that their employers set could affect their estate distribution after their death, but, since the plan rules always take precedence over the IRS rules, it is possible that your employer's decisions could haunt your beneficiaries long after your death. Here is how it works.

IRS Options for a Spouse Inheriting a 403(b) or Other Retirement Plan

You have three IRS options if you inherit your spouse's 403(b) or retirement plan:

1. The first option is to leave the money in the plan. You have to change the name on the account, but sometimes there are advantages to keeping it where it is. For instance, even if you are not yet age 59½, you can take withdrawals and not have to pay the 10% penalty. You might also like the investment choices that the plan has.

   If you elect this option, though, you cannot change the beneficiary designations that were chosen by your spouse. They would continue to apply after your death. If your spouse was already taking Required Minimum Distributions (RMDs), you will have to continue taking distributions. If your spouse had not started taking distributions, you will have to start taking distributions in the year that the original account owner would have been required to start taking their RMDs.

   In either case, you can calculate the distributions based on your own life expectancy. For TIAA accounts, if you leave the money in the plan, you will still earn interest with the same investment choices that the original owner had.

2. The second option is to roll the money over into an Inherited IRA. You would be required to take (at least) the Required Minimum Distributions (RMD) based on your own life expectancy. Withdrawals would not be subject to the 10% penalty even if you are not yet age 59½, and you can name your own beneficiaries. I have never recommended this option in practice but include it because there may be situations when it makes sense, but only if the surviving spouse is younger than 59½.

3. The third option is to roll the 403(b) into your own IRA. This is the best option if you do not need the income, because you will not be required to take distributions until you reach age 72. You can also name your own beneficiaries with this option.

As I have touched on previously, and as I will explain in further detail in Chapter 14, the SECURE Act radically changed the rules for non-spouse beneficiaries.

The SECURE Act eliminated the options for most non-spouse beneficiaries to stretch RMDs over their lifetimes. Unless the beneficiary qualifies under one of the limited exceptions, all money must be withdrawn from the plan within ten years, a drastic acceleration of income and taxes. Technically, it must be withdrawn in the year of the tenth anniversary of death, but for simplicity, I will just refer to this date as ten years after the death of the IRA or TIAA owner. Retirement plan sponsors can also add their own requirements, which may require plan assets to be fully withdrawn shortly after the death of the original owner. Most plans managed by TIAA allow beneficiaries to keep their inherited accounts with TIAA so they can take advantage of the more favorable TIAA rates for payouts.

But at the very least, non-spouse beneficiaries of any retirement plan, whether it is an IRA, a 401(k), or a 403(b), will have to withdraw the entire balance within ten years, if not sooner. Let us assume you inherit a $1 million 403(b), and the plan requires that you withdraw all of the money within 10 years.

Many 401(k)s and 403(b)s used to require non-spouse beneficiaries to remove 100% of the proceeds of the plan within one year after the death of the owner, which meant that the beneficiaries had to pay tax on the entire plan balance. In prior years, those kinds of rules provided an enormous incentive to roll the money into an IRA rather than keeping it in a 401(k) or 403(b). Employers are no longer permitted to require that beneficiaries withdraw the money from the plan within one year. Even though the SECURE Act drastically limits the ability of non-spouse beneficiaries to defer distributions—and thus taxes—over their lifetimes, at least the limited 10-year rule allows impacted beneficiaries some ability to defer taxes. I'll discuss the implications of the SECURE Act on your family and your estate planning in detail in Chapter 12.

·· **MINI CASE STUDY 7.1** ··
True Story of the Disastrous Consequences of
Not Making a 401(k) Rollover to an IRA*

Even before the divorce papers were final, the mother of a young son had her divorce attorney draft a new will and retirement plan beneficiary designation. In her will and in her retirement plan, she cut out her ex-husband and left everything to her son via a trust that provided for his education, among other things. Making provisions for her son was particularly important because she was in poor health and was no longer able to work.

She saw a financial planner about the possibility of rolling her retirement plan into an IRA. She hated to pay fees and found the idea of moving the account particularly distasteful because she liked the fixed-income account of her former employer's 401(k) plan which was similar to the guaranteed TIAA account.

She was not aware that the rules of her retirement plan, as stated in the plan document, stipulated that the entire plan balance must be withdrawn within a year of her death. Her retirement plan would not permit her son to use his own life expectancy or even the ten-year deferral for RMD purposes.

The financial planner used only investment-related reasons to try to convince her to roll over her 401(k) into an IRA and was not successful. The attorney who prepared the will and the beneficiary designation of the 401(k) never recommended an IRA rollover at all.

The mother died with over $250,000 in her former employer's retirement plan. Because the plan rules said that the money had to be taken out by the last day of the year after her death, the trust she established for her son had to pay massive income taxes on the entire balance of the retirement plan. Even worse, the trust for her son had a much higher income tax rate than he would have had individually, which meant the retirement monies were taxed at the highest rate—which at the time was 35%.

Had the mother taken her retirement plan and rolled it into an IRA the day before she died, and if she had used the appropriate beneficiary designation, the money would have remained in a tax-deferred environment as an

---

* The details have been changed to meet confidentiality requirements.

Inherited IRA. Distributions and thus taxation could have been spread over ten years. Since this happened before the SECURE Act, it could have been stretched over the child's life.

If the client, the attorney, or the financial advisor had read and internalized **Retire Secure!**, they would have seen the potential for the problem of accelerated income taxes lurking in the rules of the employer's plan. The advisor could have pointed to compelling reasons to transfer the money into an IRA that went beyond investment issues. They might have considered rolling everything but the fixed-income fund into an IRA, but they didn't. The result of the lack of planning and the lack of a knowledgeable advisor left the son financially handicapped, in addition to suffering the loss of his mother.

Rolling the 401(k) into an IRA

Retirees who still have their money in a retirement plan that does not even allow the remaining 10-year stretch should strongly consider rolling their retirement plan, or at least a major part of it, into an IRA.

To be fair, today there would not be massive income tax acceleration in one year (no plans are like that anymore). Mistitling the beneficiary form would also only lead to a five-year payout in a worse-case scenario. Also, the deferral period even if done right today, would be ten years, not the life of the beneficiary.

The moral of the story: If you are unaware of your plan's death distribution rules, please inquire about them right away. It could save your family a bundle in the long run.

> Retirees who still have their money in a retirement plan
> that does not even allow the remaining 10-year stretch
> should strongly consider rolling their plan, or at least a
> major part of it, into an IRA.

Reasons to Transfer an Old 401(k) or 403(b) to an IRA or to a One-Person 401(k)

One of the most compelling reasons to transfer money out of a 401(k) or 403(b) retirement plan and into an IRA is the opportunity to take advantage of the universe of investment choices offered by IRAs.

The challenge facing most IRA owners is choosing among the thousands of available investments such as index funds, mutual funds, stocks, bonds, etc. Leaving the money in the company plan will often limit your options to those your employer makes available to you. The argument for greater investment choices becomes even more critical if your plan does not offer good investment choices.

A second reason to consider moving an old 401(k) or 403(b) is that, nowadays, most people do not stay employed with one company for their entire career. Most people have several—even many—employers over the course of their careers. This might lead to the existence of several 403(b) or 401(k) plans, all of which are likely to have different rules. It is possible to put different beneficiaries on different accounts that could lead to unintended and/or unfair allocations at death.

If you have a good plan where you work, you can ask your plan administrator if the plan accepts rollover contributions. If so, you can transfer your old 401(k) into your current 401(k) or 403(b). If not, you can roll your old 401(k) into an IRA.

Some financial writers, like Jonathan Clements of *The Wall Street Journal*, feel that naive retirement plan owners are likely to be the victims of unscrupulous financial advisors. The argument goes that if you stay in your 403(b) or 401(k) plan, you will avoid some of these unscrupulous advisors. I hate it when I see an *"advisor"* who has convinced their client to transfer their 403(b) or 401(k) to an IRA, and then has that money invested in products that pay them a high commission and/or charging high fees to the client.

Advantages of Retaining a 401(k) or 403(b) Rather than Rolling It into an IRA

1. *Deferred Required Minimum Distributions:* Special rules allow employees of universities to defer taking their RMDs until they retire, even after they turn age 72. For example, let us assume you are such an employee, aged 72, and still working. Half of your retirement assets are in a 403(b) at the university where you currently work. The other half is in an IRA, which came from a rollover from a previous employer. There is no RMD requirement from your current employer's plan, as long as you continue to work there. You must take your annual RMD from your Traditional IRA, even though you are still working.

   If your university allows you to transfer your IRA into your 403(b), then you do not have to take a RMD on your money in the 403(b) including the money you just rolled into the 403(b). If you just left your money in an IRA, you would have had to take RMDs on the IRA.

2. *Superior Credit Protection:* Many ERISA (Employee Retirement Income Security Act of 1974) type plans enjoy federal protection against creditors and bankruptcy that IRAs do not enjoy. This means that if you file for bankruptcy or if you owe money to creditors, no one can touch the funds in an employer-sponsored retirement plan such as a 403(b) or 401(k). IRAs have some state and federal protection from creditors, but not as strong protection as ERISA plans.

   The Bankruptcy Abuse Prevention Act of 2005, signed in April 2005 by President Bush includes an exemption for contributory IRAs and Roth IRAs. At the time we went to press, the exemption is $1,512,350. Fortunately, any rollovers from employer-sponsored retirement plans to IRAs as well as SEP or SIMPLE IRAs are fully protected from bankruptcy, regardless of the account's value. The balances in these accounts do not count towards the $1,512,350 limit that protects contributory and Roth IRAs from bankruptcy.

   Outside of bankruptcy, Traditional contributory IRAs and Roth IRAs only have creditor protection under state law. Rollover IRAs from ERISA plans also lose their federal creditor protection outside of bankruptcy and are only protected to the extent that state law allows.

   There is one exception to the rule that protects contributory and Roth IRAs from bankruptcy. In 2014, the U.S. Supreme Court determined that

Inherited IRAs and retirement plans are not subject to this exemption, and therefore are not protected from creditor claims in bankruptcy cases. Because there are two different types of creditor protection (federal and state), I usually advise owners of large IRAs to keep their rollover IRA in a separate account from their contributory IRA. IRAs usually have state law protections, but over time, even these state law protections have diminished.

For the vast majority of participants, a good umbrella insurance policy providing coverage of at least $1 million or possibly $2 million or more (to protect against unexpected liabilities) is the cheaper and easier solution than keeping funds in a 403(b) and which might have better creditor protection.

For those who may have personal liability issues, such as emergency room doctors or surgeons, the superior credit protection may be more important than the investment and estate planning advantages of the IRA.

For example, I recently worked with a physician who decided to keep his money in his existing 403(b) plan when it would have given him more investment options to roll the plan balance into an IRA. For the physician, the additional protection of keeping his money in his 403(b) plan from work intact was more important than the investment flexibility of an IRA.

Recent case law has held that one-person 401(k) plans are not ERISA plans, so they are not federally protected against bankruptcy claims better than an IRA. Depending on the state you live in, though, your state laws may provide creditor protection to your personal 401(k) that is somewhat superior to that of an IRA.

3. *Borrowing Privileges:* The 403(b) plan may have provisions that allow you to borrow against the plan. I talked about the dangers of 401(k) and 403(b) loans in Chapter 2, but there can be situations when it may be handy to borrow money from a 403(b) plan. Borrowing from an IRA is not permit-

> **For the vast majority of participants, a good umbrella insurance policy providing coverage of at least $1 million or possibly $2 million or more (to protect against unexpected liabilities) is the cheaper and easier solution than keeping funds in a 403(b) and which might have better creditor protection.**

ted, with one caveat. The IRS does permit you to withdraw funds from an IRA and, as long as the funds are re-deposited within 60 days, there is no tax consequence. This is not a loan. If you do not redeposit the funds within 60 days, the distribution is fully taxable, and penalties apply if you are under age 59½.

4. *Roth IRA Conversion Possibility for Non-Spouse Beneficiary:* This is a sleeper advantage of keeping money in a 403(b) or 401(k) or opening your own 401(k) that I have never seen anyone execute in practice, with the exception of clients in our firm. Notice 2008–30 from the IRS provides a unique opportunity for a non-spouse beneficiary to do a Roth IRA conversion of an Inherited 401(k) or 403(b) plan. Non-spouse beneficiaries of Inherited IRAs are not allowed to do an Inherited Roth IRA conversion of an Inherited IRA. This ability for non-spouse beneficiaries of qualified plans to convert is an additional reason to retain assets in a qualified plan.

This could be a huge opportunity if you are in a higher income tax bracket than your beneficiaries. That is, die with your 403(b) and have one or more of your beneficiaries make a conversion from an Inherited 403(b) to an Inherited Roth 403(b).

Please note the plan document, which describes the rules of the plan, must allow this Inherited 403(b) to Inherited Roth IRA transfer. Many, if not most, plan documents do not allow conversion of the Inherited 401(k) or 403(b). Beware that if you roll an IRA into a one-person 401(k), the IRS will most likely disallow a non-spouse beneficiary from converting that Inherited 401(k) to a Roth IRA. The step doctrine says you can't do in two steps what's not allowed in one step.

Further discussion on this strategic concept is discussed later in Chapter 13 when the beneficiary is a disabled or chronically ill beneficiary when this strategy can be enormously favorable, even sometimes measuring in additional tax savings of tens, sometimes hundreds of thousands of dollars.

> **Notice 2008–30 from the IRS provides a unique opportunity for a non-spouse beneficiary to do a Roth IRA conversion of an Inherited 401(k) or 403(b) plan. Non-spouse beneficiaries of Inherited IRAs are not allowed to do an Inherited Roth IRA conversion of an inherited IRA.**

5. *Direct Roth IRA Conversion from 401(k) and 403(b) Plans:* It used to be that you had to transfer your 401(k) balance into a Traditional IRA before you could convert that Traditional IRA to a Roth IRA. Under current laws, it is possible to transfer your 403(b) account directly to a Roth IRA, eliminating the need for the extra step. But the good news doesn't stop there.

For years, taxpayers who had after-tax contributions in their 401(k) or 403(b) accounts tried to roll those directly into their Roth IRA too. The IRS rules weren't clear, and the process was complicated. Many 401(k) plan sponsors simply issued one check for the amount in the Traditional account, and another check for the amount in the after-tax account and passed the responsibility for the legality of the rollover on to the new custodian. Some taxpayers were audited because of the transaction, and some were not.

In September of 2014, the IRS issued Notice 2014-54 that formally permits what taxpayers have been trying to do all along. If you have after-tax contributions in your 401(k) or 403(b), you can now directly roll those contributions in to a Roth IRA, tax-free. Please do not miss this opportunity if this applies to you!

Music to the Ears of a CD Investor

I bet all you CD investors are tired of hearing everyone talk about the benefits of a well-balanced portfolio, are you not? You do not want to hear that inflation will eat at the purchasing power of your CD investments. You just want some good advice on how to manage your CDs. Okay. Fair enough. This is for you.

Maybe you just do not want to be in the market no matter what all the financial advisors say. Many people feel this way in light of the recent market volatility. If you feel this way, you will be happy to know that the FDIC insurance for CDs has been increased from $100,000 per person to $250,000 per person. Those seeking additional security can add a transfer on death designation to the CDs adding $250,000 of FDIC insurance protection per beneficiary named on the transfer on death designation.

Conservative retirees are also attracted by the offers made by some banks to allow seniors to upgrade their CDs annually to a higher interest rate and for a longer term. When the maximum term, typically 10 years, is reached, the annual upgrade in rates is still permissible, but you have to ask for it. Conservative investors should also be aware of the one-year rule, which restricts IRA owners from transferring their IRAs from one bank to another, to take advantage of higher CD rates. This type of transfer is only permitted once per year. Choosing CDs with a term of 5 to 10 years should alleviate some of the worry about market ups and downs but is certainly not advisable when interest rates are as low as they are when we went to press.

Also, many retirees are unaware that most banks permit annual RMDs to be taken from CDs without breaking the CD or incurring any penalty or loss of earnings. But do not just arbitrarily roll over a sizeable portion of your 401(k) into CDs that you buy from your current bank. It would be better to get quotes from at least three or four banks. Share the quotes with the bank manager you really want to do business with and ask him/her for their best and final rates.

My Somewhat Unique Recommendation: The One-Person 401(k) Plan

Throughout this chapter and in other parts of this book, I have mentioned the possibility of creating a one-person 401(k) plan and using that as your primary retirement plan vehicle in the same way that many people now use IRAs. The difficult part to using this strategy is that you need self-employment income to open your own one-person 401(k) plan. Many retirees, by definition, do not have self-employment income. If that is your case, the best solution might be to roll the money into an IRA or if your retirement funds are in an IRA now, to leave them there.

If possible, it would be better if you could get some self-employment income. Do some consulting, work on a project, do something where you earn some income and based on that self-employment income, set up a one-person 401(k) plan. You will have control of the plan, and you can do a trustee-to-trustee transfer of all your retirement plans to this one-person 401(k) plan.

If you are retired and still have money in your former employer's 403(b) plan, subject to exceptions mentioned in this chapter, I would consider rolling at least a portion, if not all, of your existing 403(b) plan from your former job into your new one-person 401(k) plan.

This offers the following benefits:

- Extremely flexible investment choices.
- Your beneficiaries would still be able to make a Roth IRA conversion of the Inherited 401(k). (See Chapter 12.)
- Expanded Roth IRA conversion possibilities (new).
- Depending on the state you live in, you may have better protection from creditors than with a Traditional IRA.

> **Many retirees are unaware that most banks permit annual RMDs to be taken from CDs without breaking the CD or incurring any penalty or loss of earnings.**

Having a lot of money in a university 403(b) or even a Traditional IRA is not bad, but, having it in a one-person 401(k) plan that is completely under your control is, for many retirees, a better strategy. If you do not have any self-employment income and have no realistic way of getting self-employment income, the classic trustee-to-trustee transfer to an IRA will usually be best with at least the majority of your retirement assets.

However, to be fair (as mentioned above), there are some advantages to leaving your university 403(b) plan where it is and not rolling the money into an IRA or one-person 401(k).

A Quick Note About the Aggregation Rules

Under the old Section 408(d)(2) IRA aggregation rules (also called the pro-rata rule), a retirement plan participant who wanted to transfer the balance of his plan, including the basis from after-tax contributions, to a Traditional IRA was not permitted to isolate the after-tax contributions and convert that money to a Roth IRA, and then transfer the balance of the account to a self-employed retirement plan or a qualified retirement plan with another employer without first considering the balances of his other existing IRAs.

It was unbelievably complicated, so I want to give you some historical perspective. Think of all of your retirement assets as being different pots of money. In the past, you would have needed to first determine the value of all of your after-tax contributions to your IRA and retirement plan. Second, you would have needed to add up the value of all of your Traditional IRA accounts—Roth IRAs are not included. Finally, you needed to figure out the ratio of the after-tax contributions to the Traditional IRA accounts. That ratio was the percentage of your Roth IRA conversion that was not taxed. Let's look at an example.

Assume you had a $1,000,000 IRA with no basis and had an old $300,000 403(b) with basis of $50,000 from your after-tax contributions. You wanted to convert the $50,000 to a Roth IRA. Under the IRA aggregation rules, if you wanted to convert the $50,000 of after-tax contributions in your 403(b) to a Roth IRA, you would have had to previously convert the entire balance of the other Traditional IRAs as well as the $300,000 403(b). This would have caused a whopping income tax bill in the neighborhood of $437,500 ($1,250,000 total taxable conversion amount with taxes at 35%) to get the $50,000 of after-tax contributions into a Roth IRA. That would likely be a far too high Roth conversion than is appropriate.

Many retirees tried to circumvent the aggregation rules by taking advantage of a special rule that allowed them to roll the pre-tax contributions in their 403(b) directly to an IRA and take the after-tax contributions back. The plan administrator would issue two checks for the distributions, and the idea was that the pre-tax contributions would be rolled into an IRA, and the after-tax contributions would be deposited into a brokerage account where they would presumably earn taxable interest and dividends.

What actually happened was that retirees would roll the pre-tax contributions directly to an IRA, and then try to roll the after-tax contributions directly to a Roth IRA—in effect, giving themselves a tax-free Roth IRA conversion.

How to Successfully Convert your Non-deductible IRAs and After-Tax Dollars in Retirement Plans Without Having to Pay Any Taxes (Sometimes)

Of course, the IRS fought this strategy for years and said that the pro-rata rule which they considered the standard rule should still apply to those transfers. In October of 2014, though, the IRS finally gave up and issued a clarification stating that the after-tax amounts can, assuming certain requirements are met, be rolled directly into a Roth IRA *(IRS Notice 2014-54)*.

The next couple of paragraphs are tough to understand, but there may be an opportunity here. This ruling gives high-income taxpayers an unprecedented opportunity to save money which ultimately can end up in a Roth environment. In the past, there was a smaller incentive for them to contribute to the after-tax account in their 401(k)s or 403(b)s, and their contributions to the pre-tax accounts were limited ($22,000 in 2023, or $30,000 if they were age 50 or older.) Assuming that their plans allow it, they can now contribute the maximum to

> **In October of 2014, the IRS finally issued a clarification stating that the after-tax amounts can, assuming certain requirements are met, be rolled directly into a Roth IRA.**

their pre-tax account and the maximum to their after-tax account inside the retirement plan (in 2023, the total contribution limit is $66,000 or 100% of compensation below $66,000 or $73,500 if age 50 or older).

Thanks to this new ruling, they now can roll the after-tax contributions into a Roth IRA at retirement. The following is an example with numbers to show how this works.

The Mega-Back Door Roth

Professor Anna earns $100,000 from her university. In 2023, she contributes the maximum $22,500 to her 403(b) plan, and her employer matches that, up to 6% of her salary, and adds $6,000 to her 403(b) account. Like all employer matches, the employer match is always added to Anna's pre-tax contributions. Anna now has $28,500 in her 403(b) account. If her retirement plan permits, she could contribute an additional $37,500 to her after-tax account to get to the maximum of $66,000.

If Professor Anna's 403(b) plan allows her to make in-service withdrawals from her account while she's still employed as well as allowing after-tax contributions, she can then immediately convert her $37,500 of after tax-funds from her 403(b) and roll them into a Roth IRA before the after-tax contributions generate returns that would be taxable during a rollover. This is what's known as a mega-backdoor Roth, a fantastic method of quickly building up a large Roth IRA balance.

If your plan does not permit in-service withdrawals or additional contributions to the after-tax contribution inside the retirement plan, you can still do a mega-backdoor Roth after you leave your current employer, but you will most likely owe taxes on any investment earnings during the rollover. Remember, you cannot make the after-tax contributions required for a mega backdoor Roth until you've reached your 403(b) employee contribution limit of $22,500 in 2023 if under age 50 or $30,000 if over age 50.

This means, the maximum amount of after-tax dollars that can be converted through the mega back-door Roth conversion is $43,500 in 2023 if age 50 or older since you must contribute the maximum employee contribution limit of $30,000 first.

It is important to know the pro-rata rules still apply to partial withdrawals. Let's say that you have a $1,000,000 403(b) that is still with your former employer and $200,000 of that is your after-tax contributions. You are reading this section and you want to convert the $200,000 to a Roth IRA. If you request a distribution of only $200,000, then $160,000 will be considered pre-tax contributions and $40,000 will be considered after-tax contributions, because the pro-rata rules apply. If you want to move the entire $200,000 to a Roth IRA, then you have to take the entire $1,000,000 out of the plan. If you transfer $800,000 to a Traditional IRA and $200,000 to a Roth IRA, the transfer to the Roth IRA will be tax-free.

Roth Conversions Without Taxes

It is possible under certain conditions to make a Roth IRA conversion without having to pay any taxes. You can do this if you meet certain requirements and have after-tax dollars inside your retirement plan. In practice, taking an asset that is growing tax-deferred and turning it into an asset that is growing tax-free—without paying any tax on the transaction—almost seems too good to be true. But, given the right conditions, you can do it.

Let's assume you have some after-tax IRA money and pre-tax money in your IRA. First, let's start with what you are not allowed to do that I bet you want to do. Let's assume you have some after-tax IRA money that you could convert to a Roth IRA for free—but you also have some pre-tax IRA money that you would have to pay tax on if you converted that money. I bet what you would like to do is to convert only the after-tax portion of your IRA to a Roth IRA, not paying the tax; and then be left with a Roth IRA and a Traditional IRA and go your merry way.

The problem is that you are not allowed to do that. You must combine all your IRAs (including SEP and SIMPLE IRAs) and take them all into account when making a Roth IRA conversion because you are subject to the proration rules as outlined above.

No matter how many IRA accounts you may have, the Tax Code considers all your IRA money to be in 'one pot.' Any already taxed money in the IRA environment is your basis, regardless of which specific IRA account contains the after-tax money. For every dollar removed from the IRA environment, the ratio of your total after-tax IRA basis to your total tax-deferred IRAs (year-end values plus the conversion amounts) determines the proportion of the distribution that is taxed.

So, can we get around the aggregation rules? Fortunately, there is a way as of this writing. There is legislation proposed in the Build Back Better Act to eliminate conversions of retirement accounts with 'basis' in them. While we are expecting future conversions of 'basis' in retirement accounts to be minimized for certain high-income levels and/or eliminated, we wanted to include this important content in the event it is still available to you when you are reading this book.

I've written and hosted many webinars regarding this unintended loophole for many years. And now, the IRS has caught on, and there is pending legislation to disallow tax-free conversions of basis in IRAs. But, as of the writing of this book, you are still permitted to make Roth conversions of your after-tax basis if done properly. Let's hope you are able to take advantage of the loophole and if they close it later on, you will be *'grandfathered'* because you took advantage of it while it was still allowed.

I will be referencing a 403(b) plan, but the same concept works for 401(k) plans. The assumptions are you are still working and participate in an employer 403(b) plan and your 403(b) plan accepts IRA rollovers (that is to say, you can roll your IRAs into your 403(b)), and your 403(b) plan states that it will ***not*** accept after tax-dollars in your IRA for the rollover, as it will only accept the Traditional or pre-tax dollars in your IRA.

You can also do this plan after you *"retire"* from your regular job if you have consulting income, as the consulting income will then give you the capability of setting up your own one person 401(k) discussed above and below.

You then initiate a *'trustee-to-trustee'* transfer of ***only*** the pre-tax dollars in your IRA to your 403(b) or one person 401(k) plan. The most crucial part of this transaction is that you do a *'trustee-to-trustee'* transfer and not a direct rollover, as you are only permitted one direct rollover every 365 days. If you have multiple IRAs with pre-tax dollars and after-tax dollars and you do a direct rollover *vs.* a trustee-to-trustee transfer, you will blow the tax-free Roth conversion.

An Example of a Tax-Free Roth Conversion

Let's look at a client example of a tax-free Roth conversion that was completed by one of our clients based upon our recommendation. Our client who was age 50 had a total of seven IRAs including SEP, SIMPLE and regular IRAs, including both after-tax and pre-tax monies for a total combined IRA balance of $1.7 million. Of the $1.7 million, there was $150,000 in after-tax contributions.

Since he was still working and had a 401(k) plan that accepted IRA rollovers of pre-tax contributions only, he requested *'trustee-to-trustee'* transfers of the pre-tax dollars only from all of the IRA accounts into his employer's 401(k) plan. By doing so, this left only the after-tax monies in his IRAs, and he was able to do a tax-free Roth conversion of $150,000. The increase in the overall net asset values at age 100, using a 6.5% rate of return was $364,600, with his Roth IRA accounts increasing by approximately $819,000! Is this a great country or what?

Figure 7.1, below, is based on a PowerPoint slide that I have been presenting for 20 years or more to demonstrate this strategy. The employer qualified plan also includes a one person 401(k) where you are the employer! The Traditional IRA money goes into the one person 401(k) and the after-tax dollars inside the IRA become a Roth IRA. All without having to pay Uncle Sam a nickel.

Figure 7.1

Slick Idea to Bypass the Allocation of Basis on IRA to Roth Conversions

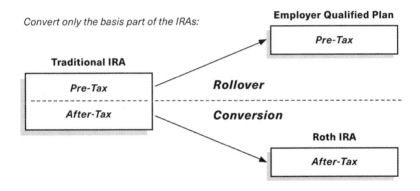

To be fair, I have to mention the potential disadvantage of this plan. If you prefer to make your own investments, or you have a money manager who you think can outperform the 403(b), you are giving up control. After the transaction, that $1,550,000 will be held in your 403(b) plan at work. Presumably, your 403(b) will offer you a number of options but you will not have the entire universe of possibilities that you would if the money were in an IRA. At some point after the conversion, however, you could consider rolling money from your 403(b) back into an IRA.

What if you are retired? Is there a loophole for you? Maybe. What you would need to do is to establish your own solo 401(k) plan. The biggest problem you are likely to face in setting up your own solo 401(k) plan is that you need to have earned income. If you are completely retired and will never have earned income again, this entire plan will not work. But if you are doing some consulting work for your former university on a contract basis or you can develop any earned income, you can establish your own Solo 401(k) plan.

It is important that you are paid as an independent contractor and not a W-2 employee, most likely filing a Schedule C with your Form 1040. If you had your own Solo 401(k) plan, then you could execute the same strategy as shown in the previous section. Our client was able to roll the pre-tax dollars into his 401(k) plan at work and isolate the after-tax dollars in his IRA, avoid the proration and aggregation rules and make the Roth IRA conversion for free.

Actually, a slew of Westinghouse retirees utilized this strategy. I give a talk every year to this group and after a few did it, some clients and frankly some non-clients did it and many followed. There are few things in life a Westinghouse retiree likes better than making a Roth IRA conversion without paying the taxes. They also like to talk about it. It's like finding a great bargain or better yet something you really want, and you find out you can get it for free.

Fair warning: The rules on this topic are very complicated. If you have any basis from after-tax contributions in your qualified plan account, you should consult with a qualified advisor who can review your situation prior to completing a rollover to an IRA.

Alternately, you could study the rules in depth, make certain there are no mechanical screw-ups and try doing it on your own. Some of the Westinghouse retirees did do it on their own. But then again, many of them would rather have a root canal than pay an advisor. I do not hear about the ones that tried it and screwed it up. They do not talk about it when they screw it up.

Combining Distribution Options

Frequently, sometimes due to my advice, my clients who have been associated with TIAA-CREF decide to leave the fixed-income component of their retirement plan (their Traditional TIAA) in their 403(b) plans because of the favorable rate of return. Incidentally, I agree with that reasoning.

Some of them will choose to transfer their CREF balances to an IRA because of the diversity of investment options. Finally, some participants will annuitize part of their TIAA-CREF balance to guarantee a set amount of income regardless of how long they live. I'll go into more detail about options for TIAA-CREF funds in Chapter 8 and will cover annuitizing in Chapter 9.

Although not all plans offer an option to annuitize, it is still beneficial for retirees to consider splitting their retirement accumulations between their 401(k) plans or 403(b) plans, and their IRAs in situations where there are investment and/or tax reasons to maintain a separate IRA and 401(k) or 403(b) plan account.

Lump-Sum Distribution

First, let's get the terminology straight. When I refer to the *lump-sum distribution*, I am referring to the special tax treatment afforded retirees when they withdraw their entire account and pay income tax on the entire amount. Ouch!

Many retirees say they *"took the lump sum,"* but what they really mean is that they chose not to annuitize their retirement plan accumulations—that is, not to accept regular monthly payments for the rest of their lives. (For more information on annuitizing, see Chapter 9.) What actually happened was that they rolled or transferred the money into an IRA or left the money in the existing retirement plan. Few retirees actually elect the special tax treatment per Internal Revenue Code (IRC) Section 402(d), which is the proper meaning of *taking a lump-sum distribution*.

So why is a lump-sum distribution significant? The advantage of a lump-sum distribution is that it qualifies for a special tax calculation. The tax calculation is called 10-year averaging, and it is available only to individuals born before 1936. The essence of the 10-year averaging calculation is that you may withdraw your entire retirement plan balance and pay income taxes on it immediately, but at a reduced income tax rate. In addition, a capital gains tax rate is applied to the amount attributable to pre-1974 contributions to the plan. This amount will often be less than the ordinary income tax that would otherwise be due.

A lump-sum distribution is only permitted when the employee reaches age 59½, or is separated from service, or dies. If the owner is self-employed and becomes totally or permanently disabled, they may take a lump-sum distribution as well. Lump-sum distributions must be made within a 12-month period from the triggering event for the distribution (i.e., death, attainment of age 59½, separation from service), subject to certain exceptions, to qualify as a lump-sum distribution.

Ten-Year Averaging is a Hellish Calculation

Do you qualify? Should you do it? The answer in both cases is usually no. I will spare you the details. Even assuming you are willing to jump through enough hoops to qualify, for most employees, it will result in a needless acceleration of income taxes, though admittedly at a lower-than-normal rate.

In practice, I have never recommended a 10-year averaging plan but have preferred to take advantage of the net unrealized appreciation (NUA) provisions when available and roll the rest into an IRA. The NUA provisions apply to retirement plans that include appreciated employer securities, which is not something that most university faculty have. But if this does apply to you, see Chapter 9 in the third edition of the original *Retire Secure!* which can be accessed at **https://PayTaxesLater.com/Books/**

My reason for not getting too excited about the 10-year averaging is not the restrictions, but the fact that you must come up with money to pay the taxes now. Remember the bedrock principle: *Pay Taxes Later—Except for Roths*. Nonetheless, asking your financial professional to *"run the numbers"* for you is a prudent approach.

The general idea behind the lump-sum distribution is that if you successfully jump through a series of hoops, the IRS will discount your taxes. That said, even at a reduced tax rate, it would require some very compelling arguments backed by serious number crunching to persuade me that accelerating taxes is a good idea—especially if large sums of money are involved, which is often the case.

In theory, I can picture the lump-sum distribution (LSD) being useful in three situations.

1. You have a phenomenal use for the money. Some professors, who have pensions in addition to a 403(b), have taken an LSD and used the money to speculate in real estate. They paid the reduced tax on the LSD and used the remaining proceeds as a down payment on commercial real estate. If the rent covered the mortgage, the idea was that the building appreciation would be on the entire purchase price of the real estate and not the amount invested (the down payment). During the boom real estate markets of past years, that strategy actually worked for a number of taxpayers. Unfortu-

nately, it also leads to unrealistic expectations for the next generation of would-be landlords. During the best of times, that strategy was too aggressive for me, and in today's environment, I would not even think about it.

2. I could picture considering the LSD if the retirement plan owner was rich and either terminally ill or extremely old and if the value of the total estate was worth well more than the estate tax exemption equivalent amount ($12.92 million in 2023). In that case, he might want to consider the LSD to avoid the combined income and estate taxes on the IRA after death.

3. It might be a way of getting the money out at a cheaper tax rate than dying with the retirement plan and have the distributions be subject to the SECURE Act.

Other professionals certainly disagree with me. My natural bias is toward keeping retirement assets in IRAs or retirement plans rather than withdrawing the money and paying the tax earlier than necessary, except if you are making a Roth conversion or paying the taxes and gifting the net proceeds to be invested tax-free by your heirs. If there were a good reason to make early IRA or retirement plan withdrawals, then the LSD becomes attractive. I just hate paying taxes up-front.

There could be times when the LSD may be a good choice, but I suggest that you approach it with a predisposition against the LSD and make a qualified financial professional prove to you with hard numbers that it would be a good thing to do in your specific situation. If you take that approach, you will likely be safe from making a bad decision.

Deciding on a good strategy for handling your retirement assets is an area where a good financial advisor can provide enormous value, particularly if he is a number runner. Getting good advice at this point can have a significant impact on your future.

The Mechanics of IRA Rollovers and Trustee-to-Trustee Transfers

Let's assume the goal is to move your retirement plan funds from one retirement plan to either another retirement plan or an IRA or your new one-person 401(k) plan (what I generally recommend). Most people call this kind of transfer a rollover. But if you are a do-it-yourselfer you need to be aware that according to the proper terminology, there are, in fact, rollovers and trustee-to-trustee transfers.

Individuals planning to move money from a 403(b) retirement plan (or similar plan) to an IRA generally will want to conduct a trustee-to-trustee transfer.

A rollover from a 403(b) or other type of qualified retirement plan into an IRA is tax-free, provided you comply with the rules. IRC Section 402 states that retirement plan distributions are not taxed if rolled over to a retirement plan or an IRA. Technically, a rollover is a distribution from one retirement plan or an IRA to the owner and then taken by the owner to the new retirement plan. If you affect a transfer of funds through a rollover, you have to worry about the following rules:

- The 60-day rule
- The 20% withholding-tax rule
- The one-rollover-every-12-months rule

The best way to avoid the problems of the 60-day rule, the 20% withholding-tax rule, and the one-rollover-per-12-months rule is to complete a trustee-to-trustee transfer of a retirement plan to an IRA. In a trustee-to-trustee transfer, you never touch the actual money. It is an electronic blip; a few pieces of paper (not green) and/or some digital data pass from one financial institution to another. Some institutions make the check payable to the new trustee but send it to the participant who is then responsible for forwarding the check to the new trustee. Although this is a permissible method of completing a trustee-to-trustee transfer, please speak to a qualified advisor and the plan administrator before completing a trustee-to-trustee transfer under these circumstances.

The following three sections provide a short description of the problems you may encounter if you do not do a trustee-to-trustee transfer. If the merit of doing the trustee-to-trustee transfer rather than a rollover is established in your mind, you may safely skip the next three sections and jump to What You May Roll Over and What You May Not.

Avoiding the 20% Withholding-Tax Rule

When someone elects to roll over a 401(k) or 403(b) or other retirement plan to an IRA without using a trustee-to-trustee transfer, the transferring company must withhold 20% of the amount rolled over and send it to the federal government as an estimate of what you will owe on April 15th. (If you live in a state that taxes retirement income, they might be required to withhold state income tax as well.) This can be a nightmare if your intent was to roll over the entire amount.

By not doing a trustee-to-trustee transfer, you create an unnecessary 20% withholding of income taxes. This withholding trap has caught many unwary 401(k) owners off guard. Since your former employer is required to withhold

20%, the only way you will not have to pay any income taxes on the rollover is for you to come up with the 20% amount yourself, from other sources. If you do not have the 20% amount to restore to your retirement plan, you'll have even more headaches because you will have to pay income taxes on the rollover to the extent that the 20% withholding is insufficient to cover the tax that you owe based on your final situation at year end.

The best way to avoid the 20% withholding-tax rule is by simply doing a trustee-to-trustee transfer.

Note: the 20% withholding-tax rule does not apply when transferring one IRA to another.

The 60-Day Rule

Let's assume you can get around the 20% withholding problem. Another problem remains. You must comply with the 60-day rule. You must restore the funds to another retirement plan or an IRA within 60 days of receiving the distribution. Otherwise, income taxes must be paid on the entire amount; furthermore, if you are age 59½ or younger, you have the added 10% premature distribution penalty—a nightmare.

Are there exceptions? A few—but basically, you do not want to go there. If you are planning to do a rollover as opposed to a trustee-to-trustee transfer, you must get the money back in a retirement plan or IRA within 60 days.

Most of the reasons the IRS will accept as excuses for not doing so are so terrible that you would never want to plan for any of them to happen. If you do miss the 60-day rule accidentally, then you can start looking at the reasons the IRS will waive the rule, but do not expect to obtain relief.

In practice, people who want to do a rollover versus a trustee-to-trustee transfer may be looking for a short-term loan, and the only source of money is the IRA or a qualified plan. Loans are not permitted against IRAs, and the amount of the loan that was allowed by their qualified plan might not be enough, and some people who think they are clever might choose to withdraw their IRA or retirement plan and attempt to repay the money within the 60 days. That might work, but it is risky at best.

The classic reason for trying to finesse the system is to use the money for some type of real estate transaction. However, that is what bridge loans at the bank are for. If avoiding those fees is so critical, and you are certain that there will be no hang-ups with either the sale or purchase of whatever the money is needed for, good luck. But if the deal goes sour because of some unforeseeable event, do not expect the IRS to have any sympathy.

Perhaps the Horse's Ass Award goes to the guy who wants to take advantage of some type of financial tip on an investment that isn't listed on one of the popular exchanges. He is told he can double his money in a month. The Horse's Ass has no other funds to invest except his IRA or retirement plan. He goes to his retirement plan, withdraws funds as a loan, invests in his sure winner, and plans to restore the retirement plan before 60 days pass. The sure winner implodes, and the Horse's Ass has not only lost money on his investment, but he will have to pay income taxes on money he doesn't have anymore. The $3,000-per-year loss limitation on deducting the capital loss will virtually make the tax benefits of the loss meaningless, and the income tax he must pay on the retirement plan withdrawal will be draconian.

If the hot tip were a stock or mutual fund that is traded over any of the recognized stock exchanges, he would have been better off rolling the money into an IRA and purchasing the security in his IRA account. That way, when the account gets clobbered, at least he will not face the tax liability in addition to the loss.

The One-Rollover-Per-12-Months Rule

An individual is allowed only one rollover per any 12-month period, but the number of trustee-to-trustee transfers anyone can make is unlimited. If you have different IRAs or different retirement plans, you may have one rollover per separate IRA or separate retirement plan.

Also, the one-rollover-every-12-months rule applies only to IRAs. For example, a reader who initiates a direct rollover from a 401(k) to an IRA on January 3, 2023, can roll over to another IRA on January 17, 2023, if he or she so desires. This move is permissible because the first distribution was not from an IRA.

Again, life is complicated enough. Do a trustee-to-trustee transfer, and do not worry about this rule, the 60-day rule, or the 20% withholding-tax rule.

What You May Roll Over and What You May Not

My general rule of thumb under the new expanded portability rules is that an individual can roll anything into anything. Of course, that is a slight exaggeration, but the general idea now is that, if the paperwork is done correctly, pre-tax funds can go from one qualified plan to another without taxation, though some restrictions may apply.

The general idea now is that, if the paperwork is done correctly, pre-tax funds can go from one qualified plan to another without taxation, though some restrictions may apply.

Most of the recommended rollovers—or to be more technically correct, trustee-to-trustee transfers—will be from taxable retirement plans to IRAs. For example, a retired or service terminated employee owning a fully taxable account, such as a 401(k), a 403(b), a 457 plan, a SEP, a Keogh, and so on, will usually be well served to institute a trustee-to-trustee transfer to an IRA.

The employee is allowed to transfer from account to account if he or she likes. However, if you leave your university job and go into the private sector, you might think it's a good idea to consolidate your old 403(b) with your new company's 401(k). You can, but it may not be in your best interests.

I generally prefer that you transfer the old 403(b) into a separate IRA or your own one-person 401(k) and then start new contributions in the 401(k), which will eventually leave you with balances in an IRA, or your own 401(k) and a 401(k) from work. As I cover more fully in Chapters 8 and 9, keeping your TIAA account intact may allow you to take advantage of higher-than-average fixed income rates, so there may be reasons to leave your 403(b) plan assets where they are.

There will be times when it might be advisable to go backwards. For instance, if a working or self-employed IRA owner wanted to use retirement funds to purchase life insurance, he or she might take his or her IRA (through which he or she is not allowed to purchase life insurance), transfer it into a different qualified plan, and then purchase his or her insurance inside the qualified plan. Caution is advised, however, for retirement plan owners who want to purchase life insurance inside a retirement plan. We do not cover that interesting but risky strategy in this book.

In summary, you cannot do the following:

- Transfer or roll over the Required Minimum Distributions (RMD) from a retirement plan or an IRA into another retirement plan. You must pay tax on that money. (But I liked that you may have at least at one time thought you had a great idea.)
- Make a Roth IRA conversion from your RMD.
- Open a Roth IRA with your RMD.

- Transfer or roll over Inherited IRA distributions.
- Transfer or roll over Section 72(t) payments (a series of substantially equal payments distributed from a qualified plan for the life of the employee or the joint lives of the employee and his designated beneficiary that qualifies for an exception from the 10% penalty otherwise imposed on 72(t) payments).

Special Exception for 403(b) Owners with Pre-1987 Balances

Even if retired, a 403(b) owner's pre-1987 balance is not subject to RMDs until he or she is age 75, not age 72. To qualify for this exception, the plan sponsor has to have separately accounted for and kept records for the pre-1987 contributions. If records were not kept for the pre-1987 contributions, then the entire plan balance is subject to the age 72 RMD rules.

If there are pre-1987 contributions, retirees might want to keep their 403(b) plans with their previous employer because the RMDs at age 72 would be less. If the 403(b) is rolled into an IRA, you will be required to take the RMD at age 72 on the entire balance in the account (including the pre-1987 dollars).

If the terms of the 403(b) retirement plan allow the non-spouse beneficiary to keep the assets in the plan for five years, then there is no tax incentive to do the rollover (assuming the retiree is happy with the investment accounts offered). In fact, there is a tax disincentive because of the acceleration of the RMD.

The tax disincentive ends up being so minor, however, that if you think you can do even a tiny bit better by investing outside of the 403(b) with an IRA, then do not worry about the minor acceleration of income you will make by losing the option to defer the pre-1987 RMD until you would have reached age 75.

Inexact Language on a Beneficiary Form Can Spell Disaster

If you do decide to roll your 401(k) into an IRA, or transfer your IRA to a new custodian, you will have to fill out new beneficiary forms. Most people take this step for granted, but I have to caution you about it because sloppy titling

> **Sloppy titling could accelerate the taxes on the Inherited IRA even faster than the dreaded SECURE Act for non-spouse beneficiaries of an IRA. It is imperative that the deceased IRA owner's name remain on the account.**

could ruin the 10-year stretch IRA concept for your non-spouse beneficiaries. I discuss this in detail in Chapter 11, but for now it is important to know that the deceased IRA owner's name must remain on the account.

·· **MINI CASE STUDY 7.2** ··

The Difference Between Proper and Sloppy Language
on a Beneficiary Form

Grandpa and Grandma both name a well-drafted trust for their grandchild, Junior, in the beneficiary designations of their respective IRAs. They both die during the same year. Due to a quirk in estate administration, Detailed Danny becomes the administrator for Grandpa's IRA, and Sloppy Susan becomes the administrator for Grandma's IRA.

Detailed Danny, when transferring the Inherited IRA to the trust for Junior, follows the advice of Grandpa's financial planner and titles the account *"Grandpa's IRA (deceased, December 2022) Trust for Benefit of Junior."* Junior, being only 21-years old at Grandpa's death, is able to stretch payments from Grandpa's IRA for 10 years. Even when Junior is 31 years-old and he takes his final distribution, the account continues to have Grandpa's name. Because the Inherited IRA makes a tremendous difference in Junior's life and since his financial security as a young adult is assured, he often thinks of Grandpa's thoughtfulness and also appreciates Detailed Danny's care in handling the Inherited IRA.

Sloppy Susan, when doing similar work for Grandma's IRA, titles the account *"Trust for Junior."* The trust is audited, and the IRS requires the trust to pay income tax on the entire balance which could lead to a five-year income tax acceleration instead of a ten-year acceleration. If the beneficiary meets one of the exceptions to the ten-year acceleration, then the mistake could amount to a million dollars or more.

···

Make sure that your executor or administrator knows how to title the Inherited IRA correctly. If you are a financial planner, I hope I have made a compelling case for the correct titling of an Inherited IRA. If you are in charge of internal office procedures at a financial institution, create a policy that ensures that all Inherited IRAs retain the name of the deceased IRA owner; you will avoid costly mistakes for a lot of beneficiaries.

Also, please do not assume that your financial professional, whether a CPA, financial planner, or (with all due respect) an attorney, will know about proper titling and act accordingly.

Sloppy titling could accelerate the taxes on the inherited IRA even faster than the dreaded SECURE Act for non-spouse beneficiaries of an IRA. It is imperative that the deceased IRA owner's name remain on the account.

Other Titling Notes

If there are multiple beneficiaries (as is typical with accounts left to *"children equally"*), the accounts should be split after death and the Inherited IRAs should then be kept separate. Please note that under the new rules, each minor child will be forced to take RMDs from the Inherited IRA until age 18, and then drain the balance within ten years. But, if one of the beneficiaries qualifies for one of the exceptions, that money could be taxed over his or her life expectancy. In addition, although the deceased IRA owner's name will remain on the account, the Social Security number of the beneficiary should be used.

KEY IDEAS

- Before you transfer any retirement plan assets to an IRA, check to see if there are any after-tax dollars or net unrealized appreciation for money in your plan. Converting those after-tax dollars to a Roth IRA will prevent you from paying taxes on the same dollars twice. Be aware of any pro-rata limitations when making Roth IRA conversions with after-tax dollars.

- Look into the ability to make a mega back-door Roth conversion if your institution allows you to make after-tax contributions to your retirement plan and immediate in-service distributions.

- For many individuals approaching retirement, initiating a trustee-to-trustee transfer of a qualified retirement plan to an IRA or a one-person 401(k) is a good decision.

- There are circumstances where a retiree will be well-served by retaining at least a portion of his or her retirement plan in the original university 403(b).

KEY IDEAS
(continued)

- Professors who continue to work after age 72 **may** be able to defer their RMDs until they actually retire. Check with your plan documents to see if this is permitted.

- If you have self-employment income, moving your retirement plan assets into a solo 401(k) plan can provide many advantages, including flexible investment options, options for Roth conversions, and, depending on state law, you may have additional creditor protection.

- Professors and TIAA investors who have pre-1987 balances in their 403(b) plans do not need to take RMDs of their pre-1987 balances until age 75.

- Weigh your decision carefully and look at all circumstances of your situation, including your estate plans.

- If you decide to move your 403(b) assets to an IRA or to a solo 401(k) plan, the easies—and less prone to error—method is to conduct a trustee-to-trustee transfer. With a trustee-to-trustee transfer, you avoid the 60-day rule, the 20% withholding rule, and the one-rollover per year rule.

- Deciding how to manage your retirement assets at the time you retire is important and deserves your full attention.

- Inherited retirement plan assets must be clearly titled with the original owner's name, the word "inherited," and the beneficiary's name. Failing to do so may result in accelerated distribution—and taxation—of the entire balance within 5 years of death instead of ten or if the beneficiary qualifies for one of the exceptions, over the life of the beneficiary.

8

One of the Great Mysteries of Life:
How Should Professors and TIAA Investors Access their TIAA and CREF Accounts after Retirement?

"The only mystery in life is why kamikaze pilots wore helmets."
— Al McQuire, Marquette Basketball Head Coach
(1964-1977)

Before we start looking at the trees, let's look at the forest. Many, if not most professors, TIAA investors and even advisors do not appropriately apply the lessons of the next two chapters. It is well worth your time to read and internalize this information.

There are important restrictions on the liquidity of many Traditional TIAA annuities. When I refer to liquidity here, I mean the ability to withdraw funds from the particular account and do whatever you want with the money. While liquidity is usually preferable, there are reasons you might be willing to own assets with restrictions on your liquidity that offer other advantages. For example, if you are a TIAA participant, you likely own *"vintage TIAA"* that has liquidity restrictions but pays a better than average fixed income rate of return. So, our general approach is to learn about your restrictions and your options and only then decide what is the best course of action.

You likely remember when your retirement plan used to be known as TIAA-CREF. TIAA-CREF underwent a significant overhaul in 2016. Now it is simply known as TIAA. Over the years, they instituted many changes, and we attempt to cover both the classic information as well as incorporating the more recent changes.

The great mystery of how professors should access their TIAA and CREF accounts at retirement is complicated. You want to optimize your strategy, which usually involves minimizing taxes for both you and your heirs. To complicate life even further, different TIAA contracts have different distribution rules that vary not only among universities, but even different contracts with the same

153

university. These TIAA distribution rules must be considered to devise the best plan for retiring or retired professors and other TIAA investors.

If you've had a long career, you likely have multiple contracts, even if you've been with the same employer the entire time. That is why your retirement account statements have different line items for what seem to be the same investments. Each contract could have its own set of distribution rules and restrictions. If you've been with multiple employers, that complicates things even further.

It's essential to get the basics down and know your options before making critical decisions that will affect both you and your family. Let's start with summarizing the available options for accounts not subject to some of restrictions common to contracts that include the TIAA Traditional Annuity.

Let's assume for the moment you have tax-deferred funds in a Traditional retirement account (where all your contributions and your employer contributions were on a pre-tax basis). This tax status is consistent with many types of retirement plans, including IRAs, TIAA and CREF accounts, a 403(b) plan, and retirement plans in the private sector like 401(k)s. It is also consistent with a 457(a) plan that is often available to professors.

Unlike with Roth accounts, income taxes will eventually need to be paid on withdrawals. Let's also assume that you are deemed retired or service-terminated from the organization that was the source of your TIAA or CREF account, or other retirement plans generally offered through their 403(b) or 401(a) plans.

Most of the 632 university faculty clients I work with have far more money in their retirement plans than outside their retirement plans. If you are in the same boat, unless you plan to leave all this money to charity, someone, either you or your heirs, will eventually have to pay income taxes on the portion not being left to charity. The SECURE Act exacerbates the tax consequences.

Figuring out the best strategies for mitigating taxes has always been a nightmare for professors with large retirement accounts. That nightmare became much worse when the SECURE Act passed. And with the likelihood of higher tax rates for both you and your heirs down the road, planning to constrain a potentially enormous income-tax punch to your retirement plan becomes critical.

Distribution Options for IRAs, CREF, and Other Retirement Plans

Let's start by looking at the retirement distribution options for everything other than your TIAA Traditional accounts. This includes your IRAs, CREF, Vanguard, Fidelity, and other pre-tax accounts. Depending on the type of investments you have and your age, you may have full or partial liquidity of some of your retirement funds even if you are still working. Your IRAs are liquid whether you are working or not. But the crux of this chapter assumes that with regard to the contracts or accounts in question, that you are retired, or service terminated. So, what are your options?

Withdraw Everything

You could withdraw all your accumulations. Doing so would be just about the stupidest thing you could do because you would incur massive immediate income taxation. Money withdrawn from a Traditional account would be subject to income tax, and you would lose future tax deferrals. Money withdrawn from a Roth account generally would not be taxable, but you would lose the tax shelter on future earnings.

Tax-Free Rollover (Trustee-to-Trustee Transfer)

You could execute a tax-free rollover from your Traditional tax qualified CREF (or Vanguard or Fidelity or other retirement account) to a Traditional IRA. This would preserve the income tax shelter on these funds. There are many reasons you might want to make this rollover; for now, the simplest reason might be that you would like more investment options.

Convert to a Roth

You may be able to convert your Traditional (pre-tax) CREF or a portion of your account to a Roth CREF account. If your employer allows it, you may even be able to do that conversion directly in your plan. If not, you can transfer your pre-tax CREF holdings to an IRA and then convert that IRA (or a portion of that IRA) to a Roth IRA.

If you have a choice between converting a Traditional IRA account to a Roth or converting your CREF into a Roth, I'd prefer you convert the IRA. Converting the IRA allows better paperwork control and reduces the chances of problems that might stem from making a Roth conversion inside any account that isn't an IRA. It also stops your minimum required distribution which is better than converting it to a Roth 403(b) that will have a RMD after age 72, 73, or 75.

The tax consequences of converting all your Traditional accounts would probably be horrendous, but a partial IRA to Roth, or even a Traditional 403(b) to a Roth 403(b), conversion at some point during your retirement will likely be a good strategy depending on your circumstances. While this Roth conversion would trigger income tax on the money converted, future earnings on that money can be completely tax-free. Pay taxes once and never again (that is the subtitle of my Roth IRA conversion book).

Withdrawals

Depending on the contract you own, you could withdraw a lump sum amount or have a specific amount systematically withdrawn from your CREF (or Vanguard, or Fidelity, etc.) account on a monthly, quarterly, semi-annual, or annual basis. The amount of your withdrawal can be changed at any time, and there is no limit on the number of withdrawals. Again, these withdrawals will be subject to income tax unless coming from a Roth account.

Interest Payment Retirement Option

Another possibility is the Interest Payment Retirement Option (IPRO). With an IPRO, you withdraw only the interest earned from when you retire to the time you reach age 72 or the age when Required Minimum Distributions start.

Annuitize

Yet another option is to annuitize your CREF (or Vanguard or Fidelity, etc.) holdings. Annuitizing means surrendering all or a portion of your accumulated annuity in exchange for receiving regular payments for a period of years or, more likely, the rest of your life. In the old days, like when my mother retired, she didn't have all the other options. She had no choice but to annuitize her TIAA and CREF accounts. The most significant advantage of annuitizing is that you, or, if you are married and choose a two-life annuity, you and your spouse will have a monthly income stream guaranteed for life. Married participants who annuitize often choose to receive payments that last for the remainder of their own and their spouse's lives.

One idea is to annuitize enough money that your monthly annuity payment plus your Social Security will cover *"the basics."* That way, you would have a guaranteed income for life, and you will know that—no matter what happens to the market—you will always have food on the table, a roof over your head and a little money for Saturday night.

On the other hand, while the security of guaranteed income may sound appealing, there are significant cons to annuitization, including a loss of financial flexibility. Once the annuity is set up, it cannot be changed to reflect changing life situations or financial needs. Another negative aspect of annuities is that they are not generally an effective means of providing for your heirs. If you

> **One idea is to annuitize enough money so that your monthly annuity payment plus your Social Security will cover *"the basics."***

choose to annuitize, any funds remaining in your retirement plan at the time of your death will vanish unless you have selected the surviving spouse or guaranteed period option. Choosing either a two-life annuity or even a guaranteed number of years annuity, however, will reduce the total amount of your monthly annuity payments.

Another problem with annuitization, at least right now, is the amount the insurance company will pay you on a monthly basis doesn't seem overly attractive when I have examined these options in recent years. This was partly the result of a sustained period of low interest so getting a higher annuity payment will likely become a reality as interest rates climb. Even if annuitization of at least a portion of your retirement assets is a good idea, as we go to press, and I suspect for a while after that, it will be a lousy time to annuitize because the interest rate factors are so low.

Presumably when interest rates on fixed income starts going up higher, the amount TIAA and/or other insurance companies will pay you will also go up. In addition, the longer you wait, the bigger your payment. Please see Chapter 9 for more details on annuitizing.

Minimum Distribution Option for CREF

If you have other sources of income or money to support yourself, you could just let your IRAs, CREF and other retirement plan assets continue to grow undisturbed until necessary. For non-Roth accounts, if you are age 72 or older and retired, you will be required to take out the Required Minimum Distributions (RMDs) according to IRS regulations.

Subject to restrictions in your institution's contract with TIAA, you retain the right to make additional withdrawals above the RMD from your CREF investments at any time and for any amount. The ability to take more than the minimum is critical and often not available with some TIAA Traditional holdings. This will also give you liquidity. If you have not depleted your CREF by the time of your death, the remainder will go to your named beneficiaries. This same minimum distribution strategy is an option for IRAs as well.

Your Most Likely Best Bet: Some Combination of the Above

Combining several of the above options is most likely your best bet. For example, if you have a million dollars in TIAA and CREF, you could consider annuitizing enough TIAA money that, when added to your Social Security, it gives you a basic income for the rest of your and your spouse's life. You could also consider a Roth conversion for a portion of the funds. If you have been feeling pent up because of Covid and you are bursting to take a vacation and think it is now safe (or at least safer), you can just take a taxable withdrawal. If you need additional income on a regular basis, you could take it monthly just by making withdrawals. Other combinations should also be considered depending on your circumstances.

But, what if, in addition to having CREF, you have TIAA Traditional? This is where things get complicated.

Distribution Options for TIAA Traditional Accounts

Only some of the options described above for CREF accounts are also available to TIAA participants. The distribution options for TIAA Traditional accounts will depend on which contract(s) you own, as well as rules put in place by the IRS and the contract or contracts your employer signed with TIAA. I cannot guarantee that the rules I will go through are the rules of your organization's specific contract with TIAA. Also, you are likely to have multiple contracts, even with the same employer, and each contract might have its own set of distribution rules.

According to TIAA, the TIAA Traditional annuity is designed to meet long-term retirement income needs. It is not meant to be a liquid asset. TIAA Traditional annuities, especially *"vintage TIAA"* typically pay a higher rate of return than other fixed income assets. Accordingly, there are often quite a few restrictions on how you can access it.

Retirement Annuity and Group Retirement Annuity

Let's focus on the two most common TIAA Traditional contracts: the RA (Retirement Annuity) and the GRA (Group Retirement Annuity). These contracts have much in common, with a few differences. Some of these differences will be discussed next.

TIAA Traditional RAs do have important restrictions in terms of withdrawals. For certain TIAA Traditional RA contracts, you are not able to withdraw all of your accumulations as a lump sum, make a tax-free rollover to an IRA, or take systematic withdrawals unless you elect the Transfer Payout Annuity (discussed later).

If you own the Group Retirement Annuity (GRA) or the Retirement Choice Annuity (RC), you can take lump-sum withdrawals from the TIAA Traditional account if your employer's plan allows it. The catch is that you must make the withdrawal within 120 days after the termination of your employment. Even then, the amount that you withdraw will be subject to a 2.5% surrender charge, so I do not recommend doing this unless you have no other option.

What if you do not make that 120-day deadline? The only option you have to quickly withdraw your money is to use the Transfer Payout Annuity (TPA), discussed below, which again we do not like because you are giving up an investment that may pay a better rate of return than other fixed income investments. *So, how can you access your TIAA RA or GRA accounts?*

You Can Die (Harsh, but True)

Your heirs will not be constrained by the limitations noted above if you have not yet annuitized your contracts.

Transfer Payout Annuity

You can transfer the balance of your RA or GRA into another investment (either within or outside of TIAA) over a defined period. This is called a Transfer Payout Annuity (TPA). These transfers take a significant amount of time to complete, being paid out in 10 annual installments. For an RC account, the transfer is paid out in 84 monthly installments. If the installments are not rolled over to an IRA or another tax-deferred account, TPA payments will be included in your taxable income.

You can start this process while you are still working. It has the great advantage of making you more liquid. It is also, as we will see, like throwing the baby

Our general approach for many clients is to get your liquidity from funds outside of the Traditional TIAA annuities while still enjoying the higher rates of return you may be receiving from your TIAA contracts.

out with the bathwater. Please read below why I do not like the TPA for most investors. Please note that my dislike of the TPA is the minority opinion for financial advisors.

Minimum Distribution Option

You can take the MDO option (age 72 or older). To over-simplify, at age 72 your distributions will be a little less than 4% of your balance and the percentage increases every year after that. But, subject to potential restrictions in your institution's contract with TIAA, you do not retain the right to exceed the Required Minimum Distribution, or to make additional withdrawals whenever and for whatever amounts you desire. This contrasts with the MDO option for most CREF or other retirement plan contracts.

Annuitize

While annuitizing is currently out of fashion, and currently not paying a high rate for non-vintage TIAA, it could be a good choice for at least a portion of the retirement accumulation for many professors. As I mentioned previously, when my mother retired, she didn't have all these choices. She had to annuitize, which means she had to forego the entire balance in her retirement plan in exchange for a regular income that would last the rest of her life.

TIAA calculated the income they would pay her based on a number of factors like the current interest rate when she retired and how long someone her age and sex would live (an actuarial calculation, not a guess based on her health)! She annuitized at age 70. Though I will never be certain, my guess is TIAA figured she would live to about age 85. She survived until 95. That means that in addition to what would have been a regular income with a reasonable fixed income return from age 70 to age 85, she got an extra ten years of payments. On the other hand, if she had died at 75, she and our family would have missed ten years of payments. Though she never had a lot of money, she never worried about money after retirement and always had a good income.

Annuitizing, subject to exception, is generally irrevocable, so it is important that you understand the consequences as it applies to not only you, but also your heirs. Because annuitizing is such an important yet overlooked strategy, we've devoted the entire next chapter to the topic.

Interest Payment Retirement Option (IPRO) Annuity

You can take the IPRO and receive only the interest from when you retire until you reach the age when your Retired Minimum Distributions must start.

What Are Your Options if You Are Not Satisfied with the Choices You Made—IPRO or MDO?

Suppose more than 120 days have elapsed since you terminated your employment, and you aren't happy with the IPRO or MDO options mentioned earlier, most likely because you want more money from your TIAA contracts. In that case, your only option is to transfer or withdraw your money using a Transfer Payout Annuity (unless you agree to annuitize). Under the current rules, RAs and GRAs are paid out in ten annual installments, and Retirement Choice (RC) annuities are paid over seven years, with 84 monthly installments.

Choosing between annuitization and systematic withdrawals can be difficult, especially since annuitizations are permanent; once you annuitize, there's no going back. TIAA has recently introduced an option for some CREF variable annuities that allow you to see if annuitization makes sense for you without making a permanent commitment. The program, called Income Test Drive, provides you with a monthly income equivalent to what your annuity payment would be.

Your *"test drive"* can last up to two years, and you can cancel at any time. At the conclusion of the two-year trial period, if you do not cancel your test drive, your accounts are converted to actual annuities with all the pros and cons discussed earlier. If you do cancel, the amount you have received is treated as a withdrawal. Note, the Income Test Drive is currently not available for the TIAA Traditional Annuity. For more details on the kinds of changes you are allowed to make with your TIAA annuities, please see **https://www.tiaa.org/public/pdf/ How-to-make-changes-to-annuity-income.pdf**

The Little-Known Downside of the Transfer Payout Annuity

One common mistake I have seen many professors make is to start the Transfer Payout Annuity based on only a partial understanding of their options. They do this because they are afraid of losing liquidity.

Yes, the TPA will provide you additional liquidity, but often at a steep cost. Sometimes the TPA can result in unnecessary income-tax acceleration especially if the transfer is made from a TIAA Traditional Annuity in a tax-qualified 403(b) and the proceeds are directed to a non-IRA account. Other times, it forces distributions from a higher-than-average fixed income guaranteed investment (your Traditional TIAA), only to be transferred to an investment that pays a lower return or subjects you to additional market risks.

It's essential to have a thorough understanding of all your options before initiating a TPA because once you begin, other than the exception I just mentioned, you cannot change your mind and cancel. While it is possible to redirect the TPA installments into other IRAs, annuities, etc., the installments will still be paid on the original schedule of ten annual payments, severely limiting your options.

TIAA Vintages

TIAA accounts are like wine in that they come in vintages. Today, interest rates are extremely low (though probably rising). Years ago, when many of you were making contributions to your TIAA accounts, the interest rates on TIAA investments were higher. At this point, you likely still have some of those vintage TIAA years.

TPA payments are withdrawn pro-rata across all vintages, taking away your ability to hold on to your higher-interest vintages while withdrawing from those that have a lower rate. With the TPA, you are potentially sacrificing the better-than-average fixed-income instruments for a less advantageous position.

KEY IDEAS

- A well-thought-out financial plan should have a combination of a well-diversified portfolio and appropriate liquidity while providing sufficient cash flow. Because of the liquidity restrictions and other reasons, it can make sense to annuitize a portion of your TIAA Traditional Annuity holdings.

- It is possible for most university faculty members to put together a retirement plan that will provide the necessary cash flow to ensure they and their spouses can live well for the rest of their lives, minimize their tax liability, and allow them to pass along an inheritance to their beneficiaries.

  Given the importance and the complexity of making such a plan, college professors should get the best information to make these critical decisions and/or get help from an expert, preferably one with proven expertise in minimizing taxes, investing, and understanding of the options professors have at retirement, an understanding of the unique investment and distribution limitations with TIAA, and beyond.

9

Does Annuitizing Your TIAA or CREF Retirement Accumulations Make Sense for You?

"I advise you to go on living solely to enrage those who are paying your annuities."

— Voltaire

Before I get into the meat of the chapter, I must get some definitions and terminology out of the way. We do include a glossary of terms in the book, but many readers probably skipped over it and in this chapter, it is particularly important for the reader to understand the terminology. If you currently have holdings in TIAA and/or CREF, you likely think of them as investments. But TIAA calls them an annuity. And technically, they are an annuity.

Please note we are not talking about investments that are called variable annuities, fixed index annuities, equity index annuities or commercial annuities. If someone is trying to sell you one of these annuities, hang on to your wallet. Though I am sure there are a lot of annuity salespeople that would disagree with me, I think of these types of annuities as having high costs and not a great investment for most retirees. For me to sell or recommend one of these types of commercial annuities to anyone, I would have to move to the dark side. To be fair, however, these types of commercial annuities are not in my world, and they might be better than I think for some investors.

But that doesn't mean that if you already bought one you should dump it. Many times, the products have a high fee but offer downside protection. The costs are front loaded and my advice to people that have them is usually to hold on to them until at least they are past the penalty period for early distributions. And, as I discuss in Chapter 10, if you find yourself with an annuity that's not suited for you, you may be able to exchange that annuity or life insurance for a more suitable annuity. The section on *Purchasing Deferred Annuities with Existing Annuities and Life Insurance* explains how to do that. If you have one of these types of annuities, please read that section. But I digress…

> **For me to sell or recommend one of these types of commercial annuities to anyone, I would have to move to the dark side.**

What is an Annuity?

An annuity is an investment vehicle (financial product) offered by a life insurance company. Annuitizing your annuity investment means that you exchange your lump-sum savings for a stream of income that lasts for a specified period of years or the remainder of your life or your and your spouse's life. Annuities can be fixed (meaning that they pay a set interest rate and are guaranteed to never go down in value) or variable (meaning they will fluctuate in value depending on the chosen investments). Both fixed and variable annuities can be annuitized.

In simple terms, if you annuitize your TIAA and/or CREF or other annuity contracts for that matter, you convert your investments into an income stream. You surrender all or a portion of your money (typically in your TIAA or CREF account) to purchase regular, recurring payments for a defined period. The most common period to receive these recurring payments is the rest of your life or, if you are married, the rest of your and your spouse's lives.

Annuitizing your TIAA and/or CREF has a bad reputation these days. The argument is that if you and/or your spouse die young, you will have disinherited your children. That can be true, but that isn't the only important consideration to take into account.

Let's start with professors and other investors who contributed to 403(b) or 401(a) plans established by their employer. Many organizations used a firm formerly known as TIAA-CREF (now it's simply called TIAA) to manage those plans. In the past, your accumulation options with TIAA-CREF were more limited than they are today. You could contribute to either the TIAA Traditional Annuity and earn a fixed rate of interest or to the CREF side and earn potentially higher returns by investing in the stock market. Over time, more options were introduced and today you likely have many options.

Under the old rules, when you retired, you could turn your savings into an income stream that was guaranteed for life. But if you wanted to take a big chunk of money out of your account, you could have been in for a rude awakening. Withdrawal options on some products were very limited, and many professors found they did not have the liquidity they thought they would have. Please see Chapter 8 which outlines the historic and current choices for distribution options from your TIAA and CREF accounts at retirement.

Readers who cannot stand the roller coaster ride of the stock market may derive some comfort from annuitizing a portion of their retirement savings, which will provide a monthly income (guaranteed if they annuitize some of their TIAA savings) to last their entire lifetime. But that sense of security can also impose limitations on access to your money. Finding the appropriate balance and the factors you should consider in your situation is what this chapter explores.

The Big Changes to TIAA and CREF

If you choose to annuitize (except for the Income Test Drive), you cannot undo that choice, so it must be thoroughly thought out before making that commitment.

A Brief Anecdote

Please allow me to interject a quick story about using the word *"annuitizing."* My mom was a journalism professor. She was old-school. Strunk and White's classic text, *The Elements of Style*, was her Bible for the English language. Accordingly, she hated when a noun or adjective was turned into a verb by adding *"-ize"* or, even worse, *"-izing."*

Before she died, she graciously agreed to help with the editing of the original version of *Retire Secure!* Oh my, it was a struggle to get her to accept the word *"annuitizing."* But, for the life of me, I could not think of a better or more concise term to describe the process. Also, I like to be consistent with the language TIAA uses. Fortunately, we had an excellent relationship, and it never came to blows. Eventually, she grudgingly agreed to turn a blind eye to my lazy gram-

Choosing to annuitize your retirement plan is essentially the same as what an educator covered under many State Employees Retirement System (SERS) is forced to do in their defined-benefit plan. That is, you get regular guaranteed payments, usually for your life and/or the life of your spouse as opposed to having access to a large chunk of money .

mar, and we continued to happily enjoy attending concerts at the Pittsburgh Symphony Orchestra together for many years until she passed.

Annuity Basics

Though we include a glossary, the word annuity in this context invites confusion. The normal meaning of the word *"annuity"* is a stream of income or an asset that will be converted into a stream of income at some time. But, in this context, particularly with TIAA, you will see the word annuity even though you will never be required to turn that annuity into an income stream. So, when you get your statement from TIAA, and you see the word annuity, whether the investment is in TIAA or CREF, you will never be required to annuitize.

If you own a Traditional (meaning pre-tax) annuity in your retirement plan, which you most likely have, you will pay tax on the entire withdrawal unless you have basis in that annuity. (Basis represents the after-tax balance in your account. If you made non-deductible contributions to your IRA or retirement plan, the amount of your contributions equals your basis, and this money is not subject to tax upon distribution.)

If you never spend the money and pass it on to your heirs, they will have to pay taxes on their Inherited TIAA funds. That is similar to the treatment of an IRA or a 401(k), which are common in the private sector. If you leave your *"annuity"* or IRA or 401(k), etc. to a registered charity, it will pass tax-free because charities are tax-exempt.

If you own a Roth annuity in your retirement plan, you will generally pay no tax on your withdrawals, nor will your heirs. Donating a Roth annuity to charity is almost always a bad idea unless you are leaving everything to charity. Whether it is a Roth or a Traditional (pre-tax) annuity makes no difference to them—taxes are a non-issue. It makes a big difference to your heirs. I'll be covering more about which type of account is best to leave to a charity in Chapters 19 and 20.

You may also have contributed to annuities outside of your retirement plan. If you did so with TIAA, TIAA calls these *"personal annuities,"* but the IRS refers to them as non-qualified annuities. If you annuitize a non-qualified annuity, it is only partially taxable because some of it is considered a return of your own money, money you already paid taxes on.

If you are interested in the safety of a deferred income stream that starts at a future date, and readers with long life expectancies might be good candidates, please see Chapter 10 on longevity annuities and qualified longevity annuity contracts (QLACs).

The TIAA Traditional Annuity

The TIAA Traditional Annuity is a fixed annuity, meaning that it is guaranteed to never go down in value. You can contribute to a fixed annuity on a regular basis by contributing through your employer's retirement plan, or you can purchase a fixed annuity with a lump-sum contribution.

Two things set the TIAA Traditional Annuity apart from fixed annuities offered by other insurance companies. First, they pay different interest rates depending on when your contributions were made. These are known as *vintages*. Second, other insurance companies generally invest the money you contribute to their fixed annuity contracts into government and high-quality corporate bonds.

TIAA seeks to earn a higher rate of return on their Traditional annuity than commercially available annuities by investing a portion of their assets into real estate and other assets. Since real estate assets and some other assets are less liquid and less predictable than bonds, the Traditional annuity managers must protect their investments by limiting your ability to take withdrawals whenever you feel like it. For this reason, if you want to maintain at least a portion of your TIAA Traditional Annuity, and in many cases you probably should, you should understand the restrictions on liquidity. Again, our general approach, subject to exception, is get your liquidity from other sources but not liquidate your vintage Traditional TIAA.

Assuming your employer offers more than one option, you might be allowed to purchase a Retirement Annuity (RA) or the Group Retirement Annuity (GRA), or even a Retirement Choice (RC) contract. And you may have the ability to direct your contributions to Traditional (pre-tax) or Roth (tax-free) accounts.

If you own your TIAA Traditional in a Supplemental Retirement Annuity (SRA) or Group Supplemental Retirement Annuity (GSRA), you can generally access the money that you have invested in it without restrictions or surrender charges.

If you own your TIAA Traditional within an older contract such as an RA, you usually cannot take a lump-sum withdrawal, even after retirement. The RC allows a lump-sum withdrawal on a very limited basis—it must be done within

120 days of retirement, but again, there is a penalty for that withdrawal that I do not like to pay. Then, there is the Transfer Payout Annuity (TPA)—*see below.*

To withdraw money from one of those contracts that restricts your liquidity, unless you are interested in the minimum distribution option or annuitizing that is discussed in Chapter 8, you must initiate a series of transfers that TIAA calls a Transfer Payout Annuity (TPA).

If you own the RA and choose the TPA you will receive your money in 10 annual installments. If you own the RC, you will receive your money in 84 monthly installments.

In general, I like Traditional TIAA as a fixed income guaranteed investment. I generally do not like the TPA as the TPA forces the liquidation of the better-than-average fixed-income investment. As a result, I look for alternatives to the TPA for liquidity purposes. That said, if you have a large amount of retirement savings in the RA or the RC, it may make sense to start the TPA with just a portion of your TIAA Traditional while you are still working. That way, you can move some of your assets to an IRA, which will have more flexible withdrawal options. But that is the exception. Usually, we can find sufficient liquidity from other sources.

Initiating the TPA can, in some cases, be an irrevocable decision. Please see Chapter 8 for details on why such an important decision should not be taken lightly.

The CREF Variable Annuity

The CREF Variable Annuity is different than the TIAA Traditional Annuity in that your principal is not guaranteed. In general, the Traditional stock market or one measure of a limited segment of the stock market such as the S&P 500 has over a long period of time outperformed fixed income investments. Most of the stock-based options in CREF accordingly, have also outperformed the guaranteed TIAA fixed income accounts. There are many CREF options, called subaccounts, ranging from stocks and bonds to real estate and foreign investments. Your contributions can be made on a pre-tax (Traditional) or after-tax (Roth) basis. You are responsible for choosing the subaccounts for your retirement contributions. Depending on your choices and market performance, your CREF accounts can fluctuate significantly in value.

Like the TIAA Traditional Annuity, you can buy the CREF Variable Annuity in more than one type of contract. Each of those contracts has different rules, and one of their most popular contracts is the Intelligent Variable Annuity.

I generally do not like the TPA as the TPA forces the liquidation of the better-than-average fixed-income investment. As a result, I look for alternatives to the TPA for liquidity purposes.

Unlike the TIAA Traditional Annuity, the CREF Intelligent Variable Annuity has no restrictions on withdrawals for retirees. However, just because you can access your money immediately doesn't mean that you *should*. If your CREF assets are in a Traditional (meaning pre-tax) annuity, the withdrawal will be taxable. Also, money invested in CREF accounts are equity assets that can fluctuate in value, and you do not want to be forced to liquidate them when the market is down.

Another option for your CREF assets would be to make a tax-free rollover (technically, a trustee-to-trustee transfer) to a Traditional IRA. This might provide you with more investment options while preserving the income tax shelter on the money.

You might also be able to convert all, or a portion, of those Traditional CREF assets to Roth assets. Some employers allow you to do a conversion directly within your plan. If your employer plan does not and you are retired, you can transfer your pre-tax CREF assets to an IRA and make a Roth IRA conversion. While a Roth conversion triggers income tax on the money converted, future earnings on that money are completely tax-free.

Depending on the contract you own, you may be able to make a one-time withdrawal or have a specific amount systematically withdrawn on a monthly, quarterly, semi-annual, or annual basis. Other possibilities include the Interest Payment Retirement Option (IPRO) or the Minimum Distribution Option (MDO) (covered in Chapter 8).

Immediate Annuities

While TIAA and CREF annuities are most commonly associated with retirement, it is also possible to purchase an immediate annuity that is not part of a retirement plan. For example, if you receive an inheritance, purchasing an immediate annuity with money that has already been taxed would allow you to receive a steady income stream for the rest of your life.

I am going to focus on retirement annuities, specifically annuities purchased inside a qualified retirement plan. But much of this discussion will also apply to non-qualified immediate annuities. The primary difference is the income tax treatment of the annuity payments from Traditional pre-tax retirement plan annuities are fully taxable, while those from after-tax or non-qualified purchased with after-tax dollars are only partially taxable because the money used to buy the annuity has already been taxed, and each payment represents a return of capital (nontaxable) and interest (taxable).

Payment Schedules for Annuitization

The terms and the duration of the annuity payments depend on what your annuity company, including TIAA, offers and the choices you make. Possible options include receiving payments for:

- the remainder of your life.
- the remainder of your and your spouse's life.
- a fixed number of years.
- one of the plans above with an additional provision to extend benefits to your heirs.

There are many variations in payment schedules, including various guarantee periods. For example, one option offers payments for life with 10 years of payments guaranteed. In that case, if you die within 10 years of annuitizing, the remaining payments within the 10-year period are paid to your heirs. Sometimes you can choose a higher payment while both you and your spouse are alive and a lower payment after your death, such as a 100% benefit initially and a 50% or 60% benefit for the surviving spouse. Since I like to provide for both spouses, I usually prefer a 100% benefit for the surviving spouse even though it means a lower payment for both spouses.

Remember, unless you pick a payment option that includes a survivorship or guarantee option, there will be no money left to pass on to your heirs. On the other hand, if you live a long time, you will get a guaranteed income for as long as you live. So, if you live longer than projected (an actuarial calculation, not a guess based on your health), you are the big winner.

Once you annuitize your contract, there's no going back. It's therefore critical that you understand all of your options as well as the consequences of your decision before you sign on the dotted line.

What is the Best Deal?

Which is the better deal? It depends. An ideal candidate for annuitization is a healthy, single person with a long-life expectancy who doesn't care about leaving any money behind. If you are married without heirs, a joint life annuity that will last throughout your and your spouse's lifetimes is often the best choice of at least a portion, if not a major portion of your retirement assets.

Those are both more clear-cut situations. Even forgetting the *"break-even analysis"* that I will present later, most of the recommendations I have made for married professors who choose to annuitize at least a portion of their retirement assets is to take a 100% joint annuity that guarantees an income stream as long as one person in the couple survives. This is also consistent with what most clients want.

I cannot tell you how many times I've had married clients say this—or something similar—to me: *"Our first goal is to make sure we are financially comfortable for both of our lives and for the survivor of the two of us to remain comfortable for the rest of their life."* A 100% joint life annuity goes a long way toward meeting that goal. Along with receiving their Social Security checks, the annuity enables them to count on a guaranteed amount of income every month.

If circumstances indicate a reduced life expectancy for one partner, a single-life annuity option might make sense. Even then, I would only recommend this if there were sufficient funds to provide for a survivor, on the chance that the healthier spouse dies prematurely.

One way to protect a survivor if you take a single-life annuity is to purchase a separate life insurance policy—an approach advocated by many insurance salespeople. Most of the numbers we run, however, have shown that a two-life annuity often gives a better result than a single-life annuity with additional life insurance—assuming that both spouses have a reasonable life expectancy.

While guaranteeing a *"base"* income seems desirable, few investors want to (or should) annuitize 100% of their TIAA Traditional or CREF accumulations. Striving for a balance is important. Annuitizing a portion of a retirement plan ensures that a portion of your money will last at least as long as you do. Annuitizing too much of your retirement money could lead to a lack of flexibility and liquidity that you might later regret.

Most insurance companies, including TIAA, will calculate your annuity payment according to a life expectancy table based on your age and sex, their experience with participants that have annuitized, and expected future interest rates. Please note that if you had reason to believe you would not live to your actuarial life expectancy determined by a measurement of the general population that chooses to annuitize, you should not likely annuitize. On the other hand, if you were in excellent health and had significant longevity in your family, you would be more likely to annuitize. In general, your actual physical condition does not generally enter the insurance company's calculation of your payment. Sometimes, if you prove to the insurance company you have a short life expectancy, they may increase the annuity payment.

This contrasts with the process of buying life insurance. When you buy life insurance, you want the life insurance company to recognize how healthy you are so that they give you the best possible rate for the coverage. With an immediate annuity, you want the life insurance company to project that you have a much-reduced life expectancy. If they do not expect you to live long, the amount you receive in each payment will be higher. It's a question of odds, and you want them in your favor! If you live a long life after annuitizing, preferably well past your actuarial life expectancy, the better it will work out for you and your family—however, they, too, are aware of those parameters.

I do not recommend annuitizing if you have a reduced life expectancy. Usually, the annuity company or retirement plan does not give sufficient weight to the applicant's health for me to recommend an annuity for someone with a dramatically reduced life expectancy. An insurance company may consider these factors, but not to the extent that they give you what I would consider a reasonable increase in payments. If I had a significantly reduced life expectancy and needed funds, I would likely look at viatical settlement, but that is something we briefly touch upon in Chapter 26 regarding life insurance.

TIAA Traditional Retirement Accounts: Vintages, Returns, and Payout Rates

The interest rate you are paid on your TIAA Traditional Annuity assets varies, depending on your contract. You are paid the highest interest rates in the contracts that allow the least flexibility for withdrawal such as the Retirement Annuity (RA). For purposes of this example, I am going to focus on the Retirement Annuity (RA) since that is typically the TIAA account with the highest balance.

When the accumulations in your TIAA Traditional Retirement Annuity (RA) are annuitized (converted into an annuity upon your retirement), your annual income payout is calculated based on a guaranteed lifetime income for you, or you and your spouse, or whether you want a guaranteed payout period (for example, 10 years) *vs.* a lifetime income. Another variable affecting the income payout is the vintage of the accumulations, i.e., when the funds were deposited (referred to earlier).

The vintage determines your annual return on your investment in the TIAA Traditional Annuity during the accumulation stage. For example, as of this writing (July 31, 2022), money deposited in a Retirement Annuity (RA) contract between July 1, 2022, and July 31, 2022, will earn an annual interest rate of 5.25%.

These rates of return have fluctuated with changing market conditions, hitting a low in 2020-2021, and now are at an all-time high. Each March 1, the rates for all vintages are reviewed for a possible reset, so the rates for particular vintages shown below may be different in the future.

Please see this website for the current rates: **https://www.tiaa.org/public/pdf/ Yale_TIAATraditionalCreditingRatesFlyer.pdf**

Vintage *(Date Deposited)*	Current Rate of Return
7/1/22 – 7/31/22	5.25%
6/1/22 – 6/30/22	5.00%
5/1/22 – 5/31/22	4.75%
3/1/22 – 4/30/22	4.25%
1/1/22 – 2/28/22	4.00%
2020 – 2021	3.70%
2012 – 2019	4.10%
2006 – 2011	4.35%
Prior to 2006	4.65%

When you retire and annuitize your TIAA Traditional RA accumulations, a payout rate is determined based on the vintages of the accumulation and the specific guarantees you elect. This chart shows the current payout rates (as of January 2022) for two common annuitization choices, *single lifetime*, and *joint lifetime*, calculated for a professor who is retiring at age 67.

Vintage	Single Life	Joint Life
2022	6.0%	5.10%
2021	6.1%	5.20%
2016-2020	6.2%	5.30%
2012-2015	6.3%	5.40%
2002-2011	6.8%	5.90%
Pre-2002	8.4%	7.50%

An illustration may help understand how the annual payout of a TIAA Traditional RA would be determined, using the current rates above. Imagine a professor who has a total TIAA RA accumulation of $1,000,000, divided between vintages like this:

Vintage	Accumulation
2022	$ 5,000
2021	$ 20,000
2016-2020	$ 75,000
2012-2015	$ 100,000
2002-2011	$ 300,000
Pre-2002	$ 500,000

The table below calculates the annual payout for these accumulations for a single lifetime (the professor only) if the professor retired at age 67.

Amount	Vintage	Payout Rate	Annual Payout
$ 5,000	2022	6.0%	$ 300
$ 20,000	2021	6.1%	$ 1,220
$ 75,000	2016-2020	6.2%	$ 4,650
$ 100,000	2012-2015	6.3%	$ 6,300
$ 300,000	2002-2011	6.8%	$ 20,400
$ 300,000	Pre-2002	8.4%	$ 42,000

Total Annual Payout: $74,870 ($6,239/month)

This annuitization would pay out $74,870 annually, or $6,239 per month. If the professor only lived long enough to receive 10 years of annuity payments, the total paid out would be $748,700, which is less than the initial investment of $1,000,000. However, if the professor lived for 20 years after retirement, they would receive $1,497,000 from their $1,000,000 investment.

But remember about all these rates. TIAA stops paying at the professor's and/ or the spouse's death. Each payment you receive, typically monthly because you are using this for cash-flow, is a little bit of interest (about 1%) and mostly return of capital. You get more interest on the vintage pre-2002 years. If you live a long time, you will get way more than your capital, and some interest. It could go the other way too.

I think the psychological reassurance that you will never run out of an income is a good thing, even if you do not like the idea that you could have premature deaths and money is lost. Get over it. It is cheap insurance. Do not think like an actuary. Think like an economist.

If you annuitize, the majority of the time with two healthy spouses with long life expectancies I often recommend a two-life annuity, so TIAA has to pay not only you, but the survivor for life.

Sometimes, if one spouse has a significantly longer life expectancy than the other, I might recommend a single life annuity, even for a married couple. Then, if you want to protect the partner with the shorter life expectancy, get life insurance on the one likely to live longer which could also in effect be tax-free.

The illustrations above are rough estimates; they do not take into account potential increases to TIAA's payout rates, which could result in higher annual and total payouts. These estimates are meant to provide a ballpark idea of an individual TIAA Traditional RA annuitization.

Standard or Graded Option to Protect from Inflation

Electing a standard or graded payout is another possibility to consider when annuitizing a TIAA Traditional RA. A standard payout would remain the same throughout the life of the annuity (with possible small increases over time). A graded payout would initially be lower and gradually increase over time. For an accurate calculation of a graded payout from a TIAA Traditional RA, contact TIAA directly. However, as of November 15, 2022, the graded payment method is no longer an option for new annuity elections.

Ultimately, you are making a hedge on inflation. Please note, even with the graded option there is no guarantee that the amount will truly keep up with inflation. It probably will not. That said, one simple way to look at it is if you want a certain amount of money per month, you are likely thinking in today's dollars. So, without even analyzing the math, the graded payout seems to be simpler.

Again, going back to the theory of annuitizing enough so that when added to Social Security, it provides basic shelter, food, and necessities. Let's say in today's dollars that is $80,000 per year. Let's say you and your spouse get $40,000 and $20,000 respectively on your Social Security.

Count $40,000 guaranteed from Social Security (because one will eventually die, and the survivor gets the higher of the two Social Security benefit amounts.)

You need another $40,000, so you would annuitize enough that you get the $40,000. But, if this is a long-term plan, then electing the graded option makes sense so you do not have to think about inflation, or at least not much. The payments in the early years will be lower, but assuming that both spouses are alive, both of you will be receiving Social Security benefits, so you may not need as much cash in the early years. The amount you would have to annuitize for two 70-year-olds is roughly $600,000.

Now, you have in effect income insurance for life for you and your spouse without the gargantuan expenses of the *"commercial annuities"* which are appropriately looked down on by sophisticated investors. With the graded option, your payments increase and hopefully that increase keeps up with inflation, and hopefully, at least one of you lives long enough to at least break even on where you would have been in cumulative payments with the standard option.

However, Larry Kotlikoff says that's the wrong way to think about it. You're essentially buying *"longevity insurance,"* which Larry says is the best way to avoid running out of money. Larry says, *"Do not think like an actuary on this issue. Think like an economist."* If you're more worried about not living long enough to break even, that's *"thinking like an actuary."* But by including longevity insurance in your long-term planning, you're thinking like an economist.

If you die early and do not break even, it will not make any difference to you because you will be dead. Dead people do not have financial problems.

Notwithstanding my logic, most people get the standard and I think the people at TIAA typically recommend standard. People who chose standard before likely did very well up until recently (2022) so far because we have been in a period of low inflation. And for some people, choosing the standard with larger payments upfront, may be preferable to the uncertainty of how much and when the payments under the graded option will increase. As the saying goes, *"A bird in the hand is worth two in the bush."*

CREF Annuities (Variable)

A CREF immediate annuity is a variable annuity. But CREF doesn't offer the high fee types of annuities that I mentioned at the beginning of this chapter. The other difference is what most people call a variable annuity is not an immediate annuity. With the CREF annuity, assuming you decide to annuitize part or all of it, the annuity payment starts the following month of annuitizing. The payment amount will go up or down depending on the fund's financial performance.

Over time, CREF funds tend to have a higher rate of return than TIAA, but in the short-term can sometimes pay out less. They ultimately reflect the market. You would expect a market-based investment to do substantially better over time than a guaranteed investment.

Some retirees would rather have the stable guarantee of TIAA's fixed annuity, rather than worrying about the market's ups and downs and its effect on their CREF annuity. I tend to like to annuitize TIAA and use CREF or other market-based investments for actual investment.

TIAA Annuities (Fixed)

TIAA annuities, on the other hand, are fixed annuities; that is, they have a defined, guaranteed benefit.

One thing I like to do in practice is to compare the interest rate you would receive with a TIAA annuity versus just going to the private market and purchasing a qualified annuity. In virtually every case I have examined, a TIAA annuity that included older vintages paid a higher rate than a fixed annuity purchased on the open market. Your vintage TIAA (pre-2002) is a fixed income Ferrari.

Annuitizing: A Conservative Strategy?

One view holds that annuitizing over a lifetime or joint lifetimes is a practical, conservative strategy because it ensures that you will not outlive your money. Although you lose access to the lump sum of money immediately after you annuitize, and the lifetime-based payments stop after your death unless you choose a survivorship option or a guaranteed number of years options. But, in either case, the payments will not run out in your lifetime, no matter how long you live.

Annuitizing a large amount of money is sometimes an emotionally hard choice to make. It feels like you are giving it all away even though you are actually ensuring a secure income source. One solution to the fear of annuitizing is to annuitize only a portion of your available funds. Annuitizing a portion of your assets is probably sound for many situations. Jonathan Clements, a great financial writer and defender of the consumer, wrote the following in one of his columns for *The Wall Street Journal* where he quoted me.

> *"I often suggest that income-hungry retirees take maybe a quarter of their nest egg and use it to purchase an immediate fixed annuity, thus buying a lifetime stream of income. But if you really want to generate a lot of income and you think you will live to a ripe old age, here is an even better strategy. Buy that immediate annuity—but wait until age 75, so you get a generous income stream based on your shorter life expectancy."*

Some people do not like the idea of annuitizing because they are afraid that, if they die early, the money they paid into the account will be lost—it wouldn't

> **If you die early and do not break even, it will not make any difference to you because you will be dead. Dead people do not have financial problems.**

matter to them, but it would be bad for any heirs. TIAA Traditional GRAs allow you to choose a payout method that guarantees that your heirs will receive some of the capital you invested if you die early.

For example, one option would be to choose payments for life with a guaranteed 10-year payout to your heirs if you die prematurely. Sometimes, the annuity contract will specify that a large portion of the original cost will be returned to the family if the owner dies early. Asking for these types of guarantees is common, but they come at a cost—the amount you receive monthly will be reduced. Alternatively, you might want to consider forgoing the extra expense of an annuity guarantee feature in exchange for a higher monthly income. My personal preference is to keep it simple: when you annuitize your TIAA accumulations, make it for your life or the lives of both you and your spouse.

The common advice among financial planners and attorneys is, *"Do not sell a client an immediate annuity without a guaranteed feature because if the client dies early, the heirs might sue you or at least give you plenty of grief."* From a financial planner or insurance agent's viewpoint, that is probably good advice. For the client, however, it may not be the best advice.

One idea that I have expressed before is to annuitize enough so that, in combination with Social Security, your *"base expenses"* like shelter, food and transportation are covered no matter what the market does.

·· **MINI CASE STUDY 9.1** ··
When Annuitizing a Portion of Your Assets is a Good Choice

Jim and Mary Davies are both age 67, have both had successful careers at State University, where Jim is a history professor and Mary is an economics professor. They had planned to keep working until their 70s, but the stress of remote teaching during the Covid-19 pandemic took its toll on them, so they are considering retiring this year. Between them, they have $1,000,000 in TIAA Traditional RAs. If they claim their Social Security benefits this year, their combined annual benefits from Social Security will be $64,000. They are in excellent health and look forward to a pleasant retirement of leisure and traveling the world. They have no children. For simplicity's sake, we will assume that they must begin taking their RMDs at age 72.

Their basic expenses are $85,000 per year. Mary, being an economist, wants to "run the numbers" and see if annuitizing part of their TIAA accounts would make financial sense. They would like to annuitize enough of their TIAA accumulations to generate $21,000 with the standard method to protect against inflation and to cover the shortfall so that they have no worries about keeping a roof over their head, food on the table, and all their bills paid. Any extra income from their TIAA accumulations will be earmarked for travel or will be saved for future needs.

One option, among many they are considering, is to each annuitize $200,000 of their balances, beginning at age 67, and with full benefits paid to the survivor upon the death of the first spouse. The example below shows what would happen if they both invested $200,000 in a fixed annuity:

	Monthly Payment	Paid Annually
Fixed Payments for Jim	$ 893	$ 10,716*
Fixed Payments for Mary	$ 893	$ 10,716*
Combined Payments	**$ 1,786**	**$ 21,432**

*Calculated with the TIAA Retirement Calculator

Because they are considering retiring before age 72, when they must start taking Required Minimum Distributions from their retirement assets, they will take the IPRO (Interest Payment Retirement Option) to withdraw the interest earned until they need to start taking their RMDs.

Based on the vintages of their TIAA assets, their IPRO payments will be an average 3.4% of their current balance of $600,000 in TIAA accumulations. Then, at age 72, they will switch to MDO (Minimum Distribution Option) payments to satisfy their RMD.

The table, on page 178, shows that by annuitizing $400,000 of their TIAA accumulations, Jim and Mary will have adequate funds for the rest of their lives. The first column shows the income generated by the remaining $600,000 in their TIAA accounts. The first few years through age 71 are interest-only payments based on 3.4% of their $600,000 balance. Starting at age 72, their MDO payments, begin at roughly 4% of the balance of their TIAA assets. This percentage comes from IRS life expectancy tables and increases each year, gradually depleting their TIAA account balances. If they both live to age 95, their RMD will be $35,196. If we assume that the Social Security benefits will include an estimated annual cost-of-living-adjustment of 2.5%, and that annual expenses will increase by 3% with inflation, even at age 90, the Davies' income will still exceed their expenses.

Age	TIAA IPRO/MDO	TIAA Annuity	SSA Income	Total Income	Expenses	Savings	Total Annuity Paid
67	$20,400	$21,432	$64,000	$105,832	$(85,000)	$20,832	$21,432
68	$20,400	$21,432	$65,600	$107,432	$(87,550)	$40,714	$42,864
69	$20,400	$21,432	$67,240	$109,072	$(90,177)	$59,610	$64,296
70	$20,400	$21,432	$68,921	$110,753	$(92,882)	$77,481	$85,728
71	$20,400	$21,432	$70,644	$112,476	$(95,668)	$94,288	$107,160
72	$21,898	$21,432	$72,410	$115,740	$(98,538)	$111,490	$128,592
80	$27,943	$21,432	$88,225	$137,600	$(124,825)	$230,644	$300,048
85	$31,851	$21,432	$99,818	$153,101	$(144,707)	$281,898	$407,208
90	$34,835	$21,432	$112,935	$169,202	$(167,755)	$304,423	$514,368
95	$35,196	$21,432	$127,776	$184,404	$(194,474)	$279,773	$621,528

The column labeled Savings shows the cumulative excess that the Davies will have. This shows they will have a nice cushion that can be used to fund travel, entertainment, and to spend on the causes they care most about. The final column shows the cumulative annuity payments they receive. By age 85, they will break even on the amount they annuitized and will have received back their initial annuity investment in benefits. Because they both chose full survivor benefits, this income stream will continue as long as at least one of them is still alive. If at least one of them lives to age 95, the Davies will receive a 155% return on their investment of $400,000 in their annuities.

So, how do they lose with this strategy? They both die young. But, again to quote Larry Kotlikoff, dead people do not have financial problems. Think like an economist, not like an actuary.

Now to be fair, I picked the facts and made close to the ideal couple to annuitize. The big thing with the Davies is they do not have any children and it isn't important to leave any money for their heirs. I also said they were in excellent health which would favor longer life expectancies. In the real world, there will likely be one or more heirs, competing demands, the income from annuitizing might come too soon, or a myriad of other problems. But it makes sense for more professors to consider utilizing annuities as an income strategy than currently do so.

If this type of thinking is appealing to you, you should also read about long term deferred annuities and qualified longevity annuity contracts (QLACs) in Chapter 10.

Based on this very simple projection, the Davies are reassured that it appears they will not outlive their assets, and that they will have an ample excess of funds that they can use for travel and to live perhaps a bit better than they do now. This example, of course, is a simplification, and ignores their other financial assets—which, with an economist in the family—they certainly have in abundance. Including all their other assets would make this too complicated. The point of this projection was to see if annuitizing a portion of their TIAA accumulation combined with Social Security would generate enough income for them to live on, without dipping into their other investments.

It also ignores the impact of income taxes, but as a first estimate of their finances, this scenario puts their minds at ease that they will not have to endure another challenging year of teaching in an uncertain, pandemic-influenced environment.

....

Annuitizing Retirement Accumulations

Retired professors are faced with taking RMDs from their retirement plans once they reach age 72, the required beginning age under current law before SECURE Act 2.0 passed. Instead of taking these payments based on the annual value and life expectancy factors, they can choose to annuitize the balance. This way, they no longer must worry about managing the money and what happens if the balance dwindles or becomes depleted. The risk and responsibility are transferred to TIAA.

In many situations, annuitizing at least a portion of the retirement assets is a good choice. In the late 1990s, and even more lately when the market was up and you could smell confidence in the air, annuitizing was frowned upon.

If you are reading this book, you have likely lived through some turbulent financial times. There is a lot to be afraid of these days: Heightened fears of global warming, economic disruption, economic downturns, the recent Russian assault on Ukraine, the enormous problems in the U.S. political system, the failure of major financial institutions, terrorism, federal deficits, stock market downturns, inflation and world pandemics have increased the attractiveness of a steady guaranteed income. Many professors want to ensure they have financial security for themselves and their spouse for the rest of their lives, no matter what happens to the market or the economy.

In many real-life situations, annuitizing a portion of your retirement holdings is consistent with a desire for security. It provides a stable income that, combined with Social Security, will provide a minimum base of income and a sense of financial security not available with other strategies.

Timing of Annuitizing

The income you receive from annuitizing a certain amount of money will be mainly determined by two factors: your age (or the age of you and your spouse, assuming you pick a two-life annuity) and the current interest rate.

The higher the interest rate and the older you are, the higher the annuity payment will be. Through the tone of this chapter, you can see that for many retired professors, I do like annuitizing a portion of your retirement accumulations, but for most professors, not now.

Before we went to press, interest rates were low, but starting to creep up. This means that if you annuitized now, the locked-in amount you would receive would be less than if interest rates were higher.

Interest rates have been low for many years, and I am not a market timer. That said, they are still low historically and likely to go up. Remember when you could earn 18% interest on a CD? I do not know if those days are coming back, but even if the CD rate went up to 3%, the payout on annuitizing would go way up.

If the CD rate went up to 5%, there would be an enormous difference in your expected payment from annuitizing.

Also, I do not like the idea of annuitizing early in your retirement because, frankly, it is much harder to predict your needs and expenses. Going in, you might think you want to spend conservatively for the rest of your life and live where you are now. Maybe later, your daughter has a child and moves to Texas or somewhere you never even considered purchasing a second home. Your idea of conservative spending is out the window as you find yourself supporting two houses and helping your children with their expenses or the expenses of your grandchildren.

In many real-life situations, annuitizing a portion of your retirement holdings is consistent with a desire for security. It can provide a stable income that, combined with Social Security, will provide a minimum base of income and a sense of financial security not available with other strategies.

I have one client who has two children, both of whom had children. One child moved to a warm sunny Southern state and the other to a colder state in the North. Though my clients were native Pittsburghers and thought they would spend the rest of their lives in their Pittsburgh house, they now support two houses, and neither of the houses is in Pittsburgh. They bought houses in the same cities as both of their children and are enjoying the snowbird life. They spend roughly 6 months with each child and their families and then return to where the other daughter lives. This lifestyle also allows an *"endless summer."*

Please note that even though I continue to work full time, I spend about half my time in Tucson and the other half in Pittsburgh. So, we are supporting two households, three if you include my daughter, and frankly having financial flexibility is important.

The point is if it is early in your retirement, you might end up in a situation that you could never have expected. Since annuitizing cannot be undone after you make that election, I would prefer you have a better handle on what your retirement years will look like before making an irrevocable decision.

Annuitizing Worked Out Well for Many Older Investors

Annuitizing worked out well for many of my older clients, many of whom have since passed, who retired in the 1980s or before and were forced to annuitize most of their TIAA and CREF holdings. (They may also have been able to take some taxable withdrawals.) Those retirees enjoyed both a fixed payment stream from their TIAA annuities and a variable payment stream from their CREF annuities.

In addition to whatever they saved, they could count on a monthly income from their TIAA and CREF annuities and Social Security. They may not have been rich, but they were usually comfortable. There was no need for trusts, no money management, and no messing around. When the market was up, they

> I am particularly familiar with professors who had
> to annuitize because one of them was my mom.

got larger distributions from CREF but still enjoyed a steady income from the TIAA fixed annuity that outperformed the guarantee.

Although the CREF annuities experienced periods of declines over the years, the payment amounts received from CREF annuities greatly exceeded the TIAA annuity payments over the last 20 years. Over the long term, the CREF annuities have provided income, albeit a variable income, that surpasses that provided by the TIAA annuities.

The previous example was not limited to TIAA and CREF participants. It applied to many taxpayers who either had to or chose to receive a regular payment for life in the form of a pension or to take a lump sum.

I am particularly familiar with professors who had to annuitize because one of them was my mom. When she retired from her job as a professor of journalism (back then in her department, retirement was mandatory at age 70), she had to annuitize her retirement plan accumulations. My dad predeceased her, so I recommended taking out a one-life annuity without a guaranteed number of years. Since I preferred she get more income, I told her to forget the survivorship feature and just get the most possible for herself. Against my advice, she chose an annuity with a survivorship feature.

If she died within 10 years of her retirement, my brothers and I would have received some income until she would have turned 80. But she died at age 95. The reduced payment she received on the survivorship guarantee for her children was wasted, but she took great delight in knowing that the insurance company still lost a bundle of money on her. I do not know the formula that TIAA uses to calculate the amount they will pay for the monthly benefit of annuitizing. But they certainly didn't assume she would live till age 95.

Whatever it was, they had to pay her for many more years than they likely expected. Between her Social Security, her annuity payment, and the payment that I made to her for the purchase of the family home where I live now, she had a great income for her retirement years though she never had a lot of money.

In case you are wondering, I bought *"the family homestead,"* where I was born and grew up when my wife and I were looking for our first house. It is a big old house in Squirrel Hill, a neighborhood within walking distance of Carnegie Mellon University (CMU) and the University of Pittsburgh (Pitt). Many professors live in Squirrel Hill and enjoy a walking or bicycle commute to CMU or Pitt. I could walk or bike to work also, but since I usually run late and tend to work well into the night—like I am as I write this book—I drive anyway.

Annuitizing: A Risky Strategy?

Another view of annuitizing is that it is not a conservative strategy but rather a gamble. Since most annuities are based on actuarial life expectancy, you are gambling that you will outlive your actuarial life expectancy, and TIAA is gambling that you will not. (To quickly calculate your actuarial life expectancy, visit: **https://www.ssa.gov/OACT/population/longevity.html.**)

But the tables do not take into account information you know about your own health and the longevity in your family. TIAA also doesn't take those factors into account—but you should.

- If you have reason to believe that you will not survive your actuarial life expectancy, then annuitizing is probably a mistake.

- If you think, however, that you and your spouse are going to substantially outlive your actuarial life expectancy and the life expectancy of people that have chosen to annuitize, then annuitizing on a two-life basis, that is the payment will continue for your and your spouse's life, which is longer, will provide both of you an assured income stream for a long life.

- If you have a terminal illness and your spouse has a long-life expectancy, consider having your spouse purchase an immediate annuity on his or her life only. If you do that, please make sure the spouse with the reduced life expectancy will still be okay financially if you die. If not, consider term life insurance for the healthier spouse.

Although annuitizing will provide fixed monthly amounts for a lifetime, there are other risks involved that make even this conservative strategy a gamble. One risk is that the issuing insurance company will go bankrupt and will be unable to meet its obligations to pay the annuity. State governments provide state guarantee funds to protect consumers against insurer insolvency, but some of those plans are stretched to the maximum.

You can minimize your risk by choosing insurance and annuity companies with Standard & Poor's quality ratings of at least AA or preferably AAA, even if it means that the interest rate offered to you is not as high as through a lesser-rated insurance company. TIAA is currently rated AA+/Stable by Standard & Poor's. That is a pretty good rating. As I mentioned earlier, when we compare rates to other insurance companies, TIAA participants with vintage TIAA will usually do better getting a TIAA annuity than from other insurance companies.

Another risk involves the effect of inflation on fixed annuity payments. If the payout is the same amount every month, the long-term effects of inflation can lead to the annuity income becoming inadequate to meet growing expenses in later years. Inflation may be higher in the future, so it may be wise to seek out an inflation-protected annuity.

Unfortunately, effective November 15, 2022, TIAA's graded payment method, which offered lower payments to start and increase each year, is no longer an option for new annuity elections. For more information on distribution options for a TIAA Traditional annuity, please visit **https:// www.tiaa.org/public/pdf/ TT_FAQ_.pdf**

CREF annuities may help to protect your annuity payment stream from inflation by providing a payment that changes based on market investment returns. This can be both good and bad. If the stock market (or another investment index) does well, then you will be better off, but if the market returns are negative, you face the risk of the payments decreasing. Either can happen in times of high inflation. Pick your poison—do you risk the effects of inflation or a market decline?

My personal preference for most clients is not to annuitize their CREF holdings. If annuitizing is appropriate, then annuitize a portion or all of your TIAA. That way, the amount you receive on a guaranteed basis when combined with Social Security can be counted on as a base income.

If you do not need the money, annuitizing retirement plan assets needlessly accelerates income taxes on your retirement accumulations. In theory, at least in the early years, the annuity payment will be somewhat higher than RMDs since it reflects a return of principal.

Also, if you incur unexpected expenses and need more than your monthly annuity payment amount but have no other savings, you are just plain out of luck unless you can borrow from a bank or other lending institution. If you are taking RMDs from a retirement plan, you can always eat into the principal for a larger distribution if you need it. This is, of course, the fundamental risk of annuities.

Finally, let me end this chapter with some excellent advice from Larry Kotlikoff, a professor of economics at Boston University. He is also the author of a wonderful book regarding Social Security called **Get What's Yours**. Of course, I still like my book on Social Security where I also cover the synergy between delaying your Social Security and making Roth IRA conversions. Please go to **https://PayTaxesLater.com/Books/** for your free digital copy of *The $214,000 Mistake: How to Maximize Your Social Security & IRAs*. That said, Larry is a well-regarded economics professor who provides sage advice.

Larry gave me this life advice regarding when to take Social Security, but it also applies to annuitizing: *"If you die young, you are dead and dead people do not have financial problems. The legitimate financial fear is not dying young but outliving your money."* Annuitizing addresses this legitimate fear.

For most retirees, Larry is a fan of annuitizing at least some of your accumulations, as are Jane Bryant Quinn, a popular financial writer, now retired, known as a champion for consumers, and Jonathan Clements, former personal finance writer for *The Wall Street Journal.*

I have worked with a number of professors who had already made all of the critical decisions regarding annuitizing their retirement assets prior to becoming clients or who, despite already being clients, made those decisions without seeking input and recommendations from our accounting firm. For some of those clients their decisions regarding whether to annuitize, how much to annuitize and which options they ultimately selected worked out well for them.

However, I have also seen my fair share of financially disadvantageous consequences befall professors who made bad decisions about the timing, amount, or retirement plan options.

I have seen professors where their bad choices weren't disastrous, but they gave up a great opportunity that they could not undo. And I have seen professors in situations similar to the Davies who decided not to annuitize *any* portion of their retirement assets, which unnecessarily restricted their disposable income during retirement.

Obviously, consulting our team of experts doesn't guarantee perfect results. But when consulted, we do use our experience, subject-matter expertise, and nuanced understanding of the complexities of each client's financial situation and goals to ensure that our clients are aware of all the options available to them and what the potential long-term financial pros and cons of each option are. To learn more about what we do for our clients and how to take the first step towards working with us, read the section at the back of this book titled *How Professors Can Put Financial Success on Autopilot.*

KEY IDEAS

- Annuitizing a portion of your TIAA accumulations, using the graded method if you want to protect against inflation, is often a good strategy to ensure that you never run out of money.

- Take time to understand *all* of your options *before* you commit to something you cannot undo.

- TIAA vintage investments pay a higher amount when annuitized than most other insurance companies would likely pay.

10

A Variation on the Annuity Theme:
The Longevity Annuity and the Qualified Longevity Annuity Contract (QLAC)

"Money often costs too much."

— Ralph Waldo Emerson

The longevity annuity is something that I and many financial experts that I respect including Jane Bryant Quinn, Jonathan Clements, and Larry Kotlikoff believe is a great solution for a limited number of individuals. That said, to the best of my knowledge, no client of mine has bought one. For that matter, I do not know anyone that ever bought one.

When I write books or deliver webinars, there is always the tension between presenting what you know people want to read or consume and what I think readers should consider for their planning.

This section is what I think some people should be thinking about, even though I know most people do not like the idea. And, to bolster my argument, since the last edition of *Retire Secure!* when I wrote about longevity annuities, the IRS has approved a variation called a Qualified Longevity Annuity Contract (QLAC) that I like much better for most retirement plan heavy college professors or TIAA investors.*

Eliminate the Fear of Running out of Money Before You Die

If your most consuming, most sleep-depriving worry is running out of money before you die—despite all your best planning, perhaps a longevity annuity is something you should consider. In effect, a *longevity annuity* is a type of annuity that requires immediate payment for a deferred benefit. It is a longevity insurance contract.

---

* QLAC annuities and life insurance can be offered by a CPA through Lange Life Care for those interested. It would be offered in their role as a CPA and not as an attorney. There would be no attorney-client relationship. There is no solicitation being made for legal services by the author nor by Lange Legal Services, LLC.

You buy the annuity now, but you receive nothing immediately other than the guarantee that, in a number of years from your purchase date, if you are still alive, you will begin receiving annual or monthly benefits. The longevity annuity can take the place of a *'pension'* in your later years, especially for someone who does not have a pension—someone whose only guaranteed monthly income source is their Social Security check. An example might be helpful.

Assume you are age 65, healthy, and think you have a long-life expectancy. You do not need any additional income now and you think you have more than enough money to last you for the next 20 years. Your fear is that you might very well live beyond those secure 20 years and then you would outlive your money. You do not want to buy an immediate annuity because you really do not need the income now. So, you purchase a longevity annuity that will provide you with an income 20 years from now.

If you're like most people, it's not the first 20 years of retirement that scares you, it's the years beyond those years that keeps you restless at night. In its purest form, if you die before 20 years, too bad, you get nothing, your heirs get nothing from the insurance company, and having bought the annuity would have been a mistake, unless you purchased a guaranteed income protection rider. Of course, when you add riders to your annuity contract, the cost of your annuity increases and/or the benefit decreases.

If, however, you live until age 95, the decision to buy this type of annuity will have proven to be of tremendous benefit. Obviously, if you live longer, the annuity would be even more valuable. It is like many forms of insurance. If you need it, you will be very glad that you have it. Not needing it is the risk that you take. But being the number runners that we are, let's look at specific examples to help quantify the benefits and drawbacks. As you would expect, you can purchase longevity annuities, also known as deferred income annuities (DIAs), with various survivorship features.

·············· **MINI CASE STUDY 10.1** ··············
Buying a Longevity Annuity

Phil is age 65, and he is confident that he will have sufficient income for the next 20 years to maintain his standard of living. He also has $100,000 of discretionary after-tax dollars to immediately fund a longevity annuity. He is single and has a son to whom he would like to leave something. Phil is intrigued by the idea of the deferred income annuity, for which he would pay $100,000 now and receive no benefit from now until he turned 85. He wants to look at the cost and benefits of the deferred income annuity and also compare and contrast the numbers for purchasing the longevity annuity on a life-only basis versus an installment refund basis. If he opts for the life-only option, and then dies before turning 85, without any income protection riders, there would be no benefit paid to his son, and the insurance company gets to keep all the money Phil paid for the annuity. If he opts for the installment refund option, though, and then dies before turning 85, his son or other heirs will be guaranteed the monthly income for 15 months—guaranteeing some return of his original investment.

Once Phil reaches age 85, the longevity annuity with the life-only option will provide him with a fixed lifetime monthly income of $4,356.21 ($52,274.52 per year). If he chooses to go with the installment refund option, his monthly income will be $2,854.30 ($34,251.60 per year). The interest rates used in these calculations were from 2022 and were relatively low at the time. If rates are higher when you're reading this, then the income will be greater.

If we assume an inflation rate of 2.5% per year, these amounts provide an annual income in today's dollars of about $31,902 for the life-only option or $20,903 for the installment refund option at age 85. Each year thereafter, the real income in today's dollars drops due to the continued effects of inflation.

These two amounts mean that, if we do not take into account interest or the time value of money, or if Phil lived 12 or 15 months beyond his 85th birthday, this would be a winner. However, that isn't a fair analysis. A fair analysis must take into account the time value of money and taxes on the annuity income. If we make certain assumptions and *"run the numbers,"* we have a much less favorable break-even point.

Let us *"run the numbers"* assuming investment income on an alternative investment generating rates of return of four, six, or eight percent. The annuity income received at age 85 is taxable to the extent that the income exceeds the $100,000 investment. For example, let us also assume that the annuity company has determined that the income at age 85 is considered 28% withdrawal of cost basis and the rest is ordinary income (and therefore taxable) until the total cost of $100,000 is returned. Also assume an average tax rate of 24% for both scenarios. Figure 10.1, shown on the following page, illustrates the various break-even points.

Figure 10.1 shows that, if Philip dies before age 85, purchasing the annuity would have been a bad decision. But if Philip lives to age 90, he'll receive more money through the annuity than his after-tax investments paying 4% and 6%. If he lives beyond 95, the annuity beats his 8% investment as well.

The figure also assumes that Phil does not spend any of his after-tax money. This may prove difficult in real life, especially if his assets needed to pay for long-term care in a nursing home. Philip also has the option to elect the return-of-premium guarantee option. This would reduce the amount he receives monthly, but also guarantees that his heirs will receive some money from the account.

Now that Phil has the numbers, his options are much better defined, but he still must decide if his fear of running out of money outweighs the risk of not realizing a return on the investment.

Figure 10.1

Longevity Annuity Illustration*

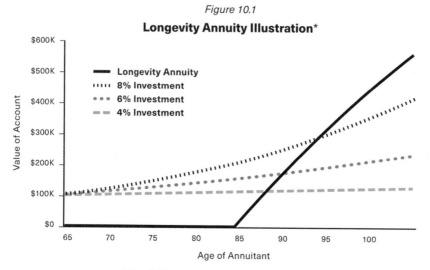

* *Detailed assumptions can be found in the Appendix.*

How Much is Peace of Mind Worth to You?

That is a dilemma that people must assess for themselves. But I offer this observation from Larry J. Kotlikoff, a Boston University economics professor and developer of important software that does a dynamic analysis of multiple variables affecting retirement spending. His model is superior to other models that use constant and static spending targets. Larry says if the whole point is to never run out of money, we should be willing to pay a premium over the actuarial break-even number—in effect, for peace of mind. The reason it has so much appeal to me and other advisors is that it helps alleviate the #1 fear facing most retirees—outliving their money.

An important consideration is that if you are married what I have described does not protect both spouses, just one individual. I would not recommend it in its simplest form if you are married. In that case, unless there are extenuating circumstances (such as one of you has life insurance or a pension or other resources), you should purchase the deferred income annuity for both lives so that your surviving spouse does not lose the income at your death. The above example does not analyze these numbers. For now, suffice it to say that the annuity payment would be reduced because the insurance company must continue paying until both the husband and wife die.

As always, for professors with most of their retirement holdings in TIAA accounts, the specific options available for a QLAC depend on the plan or plans offered by your university. While TIAA does offer QLACs, you will have to check with your university to see if your plan offers QLACs, and if so, whether single life, joint life, or a plan that will pay a refund upon your death is available. Both you and your spouse can purchase a QLAC up to the limit allowed by the IRS which is currently currently $200,000 of your qualified retirement assets and you each can choose separately a single life, joint life, or a refund death benefit. Of course, if you choose a refund death benefit or joint life QLAC, the annual payments you receive from the QLAC will be less.

Some other advantages to the deferred income annuity include knowing exactly how much income you will be receiving in the future. There is not any stock market or interest rate risk, as the future income amount is guaranteed. You are protecting your savings from market downturns. The longevity annuity relieves you of the responsibility of managing your monthly income so you can let go of that responsibility without having to worry about running out of money.

What Are the Disadvantages of a Longevity Annuity?

What are the biggest arguments against it? Well, right off the bat, you are writing a check for $100,000 (actually, it could be for any amount), and you are not getting any immediate benefit. You could die before 85 or whatever age you are expected to receive payments, and your decision would not have worked out well for your family. Longevity annuities do not have any real liquidity, as you no longer have access to that money. For many people with heirs to consider, that will be the end of the discussion. For you hearty souls who are worried about running out of money and are willing to take some extra risks to address your fear, please read on.

The insurance company that issued your annuity could fail, and you end up with nothing. However, almost every state has a guaranty fund, much like FDIC, that pays claims if your insurer becomes insolvent. During the bailout of

AIG and other financial companies, stockholders suffered, but owners of their annuities and beneficiaries of life insurance policies were completely protected. Of course, I cannot deny there is some amount of risk, even with highly rated companies.

Another reason not to buy it now is that today, interest rates are relatively low, though at press time they are rising, and as a result, the future annuity payments will be less than they would be if interest rates were higher. In addition, we could face hyperinflation and even if you survive, you will get paid in devalued currency.

On the other hand, if you recognize the downsides of this investment and you want a guarantee of not running out of money, and you can live with the downsides that I pointed out, this is a great idea. In the end, perhaps the best use for a longevity annuity comes not from purchasing one outright, but rather from trading up.

Purchasing Deferred Annuities with Existing Annuities and Life Insurance

I often rely on Tom Hall, an insurance broker with Pittsburgh Brokerage Services, LLC, to find my clients the best deals on life insurance. Tom often has astute recommendations. This *"aha"* moment came from Tom.

Before introducing Tom's idea, I have to give you some background information on one problem I often encounter as an estate planner. Many of my clients, at some point in their lives, have purchased a commercial, high commission annuity. A discussion of that type of annuity is beyond the scope of this chapter. In any event, sometimes they work out well, but sometimes retirees who have purchased a tax-deferred annuity do not have a good plan for their eventual disposition.

Tom Hall says, *"That's fine. Do a tax-free exchange of your tax-deferred annuity for this longevity annuity."* What a great idea! The reason this is such a good idea is a taxpayer can do a tax-free exchange disposing of an asset he or she did not want to keep in exchange for guaranteed payments in the future as long as

With a longevity annuity, even if you survive, if we experience hyperinflation, you will get paid in devalued currency.

the client lives long enough. This could be a much better choice than electing the annuitizing option that is usually part of a tax-deferred annuity contract.

The reason is, if you annuitize a tax-deferred annuity contract now, the payments will be much lower than if you elect to defer payments for a number of years in the future. Furthermore, the regular annuity usually isn't a great asset to leave behind because all the growth on the annuity will usually be subject to ordinary income to your heirs.

If you are doing long-range planning, and there is an issue with potential income shortfalls in later years, you could also do a tax-free exchange of the cash value in a life insurance policy you no longer need into a longevity annuity. You would only consider this option if you no longer need the life insurance death benefit or the potential riders, such as chronic care.

The positive is you do not have to furnish out-of-pocket dollars to pay for the annuity. Instead, you are using the cash surrender value to purchase the longevity annuity. This strategy can *'true up'* the long-term plan and remedy any income shortfalls if you have a life insurance policy that you no longer need or want, and it has cash value in it.

Qualified Longevity Annuity Contract (QLAC)

For most professors, a QLAC is better than a Traditional deferred long-term annuity.

In 2014, the IRS decided to allow longevity annuities to be purchased within qualified retirement accounts, including 401(k)s, 403(b)s, 457(b)s, and IRAs, and they are called *'Qualified'* Longevity Annuity Contracts (QLACs). Until 2014, employees in the private sector could not purchase longevity annuities within their qualified plans—and this was largely because of the RMD rules. The reason the IRS issued rules to permit owners of 403(b)s, IRAs, etc. to purchase QLACs within their plans was to allow people to save a portion of their retirement accounts for the later years of their retirement.

For most professors, I prefer a QLAC to a Traditional after-tax long-term annuity. The obvious reason is most professors have a lot of retirement plan assets and less after-tax assets.

Another big benefit to QLACs purchased within retirement plans is they are exempt from RMD rules as long as the plan participant does not use more than $200,000 lifetime maximum to buy the annuity. This means a husband and wife could potentially allocate a total of $400,000 to QLACs, assuming both had suf-

> **Another big benefit to QLACs purchased within retirement plans is that they are exempt from RMD rules as long as the plan participant does not use more than $200,000 lifetime maximum to buy the annuity.**

ficient retirement accounts to justify this retirement strategy. The benefit to the RMD exemption is to allow the retiree to keep more in savings for longer periods of time. The distributions must start by age 85.

Remember, it is up to your employer to decide what options are available to you within your qualified plan, so you may have to suggest that they add a new option for longevity annuities. Even if they do not, you can transfer money to an IRA to purchase one on your own. If you are thinking about rolling your 403(b) plan into an IRA to fund your QLAC, you will not be able to fund your QLAC until the year following your rollover. The reason is the amount you add to a QLAC is based upon your IRA balance on December 31 of the prior year.

Note: Inherited IRAs do not qualify for QLAC treatment. Being able to avoid $200,000 of retirement income is an immediate tax savings and the guaranteed income can provide you with a lifetime of financial security.

A QLAC can be a wise addition to your retirement strategy if you are concerned about outliving your savings. Essentially, a QLAC provides an RMD tax break between the ages of 72 and up to age 85. The lower RMDs can save you more than just the income tax on the lower RMD. By keeping your AGI lower, you will reduce your income taxes, possibly avoid the 3.8% Net Investment Income Tax, minimize any Medicare Part B premium surcharges, and possibly reduce taxes on your Social Security benefits.

An annuity must be designed and labeled as a QLAC to qualify; buying a longevity annuity is not sufficient to qualify for the RMD relief rules.

What are the Disadvantages of the QLAC?

The obvious disadvantage is that you buy one and then die before the scheduled payouts. In addition, while you are deferring your RMDs and the taxes on the RMDs, you are not reducing taxes forever.

For example, if you are age 72 and buy a QLAC that doesn't pay until age 85, you are deferring minimum required distributions for 13 years that could by itself save many thousands of dollars in taxes. But you are not permanently avoiding income taxes unless you die before the payoff period begins.

Keeping money invested inside your retirement account could help it earn more income than the payments from the QLAC. Annuities are insurance products, not investments. As we mentioned above, if you die sooner than you expected, you may not collect more than you paid in.

To protect against this disadvantage, there are QLACs that provide a return of premium option that will pay out to your beneficiaries, but if you opt for it your monthly income while you are alive will be lower. If your goal is to reduce your RMDs and manage taxes in retirement, making Roth Conversions or Qualified Charitable Distributions (QCDs) discussed in Chapters 6 and 20 should be considered first. But, if your health and genetic history indicates you will likely live to a ripe old age and you fear running out of money when you are quite old, I still like QLACs.

Also, as with the disadvantage of the deferred annuity, the QLAC is not excellent protection against high inflation.

It should also be noted as of this writing, the SECURE 2.0 Act has passed. This legislation removed just the 25% cap on QLACs and increased the overall maximum amount allowed in a QLAC from $145,000 to $200,000. As a practical matter, $145,000 premium is probably more than most professors want to pay anyway.

KEY IDEAS

- The longevity annuity is purchased now for income later and is a useful hedge against running out of money before you die.

- The longevity annuity provides a fixed level of income that's not subject to market fluctuations.

- Since 2014, the IRS has allowed for the purchase of Qualified Longevity Annuity Contracts (QLACs) within qualified retirement plans, making those funds exempt from the RMD rules. This is likely a better option than Traditional longevity annuities for most professors.

Key Ideas continue on the following page.

KEY IDEAS
(continued)

- QLACs can be used to defer RMDs and income tax due on those RMDs.

- The chief disadvantages of either a longevity annuity or a QLAC are:

  1. If you die young, you lose your money.

  2. The loss of liquidity and earning power from those funds used to pay the premium.

  3. They are not great solutions to protect you from inflation.

11

What Happens to Your IRA When You Die?
Contrasting the Old Regulations and the New Rules within the SECURE Act

"Certain things they should stay the way they are.
You ought to be able to stick them in one of those big glass
cases and just leave them alone."

— J.D. Salinger
(The Catcher in the Rye)

The following information is critical for university faculty members and TIAA investors and all retirement plan owners. Put simply, if you do not make proactive plans for your IRA and retirement plans, your estate will take a huge unnecessary tax hit. This is especially true if your retirement plans are the largest asset in your estate, which is true of many older investors. Not understanding how the change in the law will affect your beneficiaries and not taking proactive measures to protect yourself and your family could make a difference of hundreds of thousands of dollars.

What Hasn't Changed: The Basic Transfer of Retirement Accounts After the Death of the First Spouse

Let's start with a simple case. You are married, and if your IRA and/or retirement beneficiary form is completed correctly (it usually isn't) and there is appropriate estate administration after your death (there often isn't), your IRA or TIAA accumulations will likely pass to your spouse as the primary beneficiary.

Your surviving spouse can transfer your retirement account assets into their own IRA using a technique called a spousal rollover, but we would prefer that they make the transfer using a similar, but safer, process called a trustee-to-trustee transfer.

The trustee-to-trustee transfer electronically moves the funds from your IRA or retirement account directly to your surviving spouse's IRA, avoiding the potential mix-up and withholding tax problems caused by cutting a check. This trustee-to-trustee transfer, assuming it is done correctly, eliminates the possibil-

> Your surviving spouse can transfer your retirement account assets into their own IRA using a technique called a spousal rollover, but we prefer they make the transfer using a similar, but safer, process called a trustee-to-trustee transfer.

ity of horrendous tax consequences caused by human error. This was true before the SECURE Act, and it is still true.

If you were taking Required Minimum Distributions (RMDs) from your IRA or TIAA account before your death and your spouse is your beneficiary and roughly your age, he/she must continue to take RMDs from the IRA (which is now his/hers after the trustee-to-trustee transfer). His/her RMDs will be similar to those you received because they will also be based on a joint life expectancy. This time, though, it's the joint life expectancy of your spouse and the life expectancy of someone deemed ten years younger that determines his/her RMD. There are also special rules that apply to spouses who are more than ten years younger than their spouse. Please see Chapter 6 for more information on RMDs while you are still alive.

Required Minimum Distribution of the Inherited IRA Under the Old Law

We include this section in case your beneficiary qualifies for a critical exception so we can show you how much tax savings can result from savvy planning.

Under the old law (which continues to set the rules for deaths prior to 2020) and depending on your situation, it was probably to your spouse's and your family's advantage to continue to defer the taxes and take only the RMDs from the IRA for as long as possible. Pay taxes later. The benefits of doing so are illustrated in Chapter 1, where we show the advantage of keeping the money in the IRA while spending after-tax money first.

But what happens after both spouses are gone, or you leave at least a portion of your IRA to a non-spouse beneficiary, most likely your child or children? Or, what happens if one spouse *"disclaims"* to the children and/or the children disclaim to the grandchildren? (We will explore disclaimers more in Chapter 14.) This is where the intense pain of the SECURE Act should strike terror in the hearts of university faculty and every TIAA investor and IRA owner.

Under the old law, if your beneficiary were a child or grandchild, or anyone other than your spouse, they had the option to *"stretch"* distributions from the

Inherited IRA over their lifetimes. (An IRA that is inherited by a non-spouse beneficiary becomes a special asset called an Inherited IRA.) The RMD for the Inherited IRA was calculated by dividing the balance in the Inherited IRA as of December 31st of the previous year by the beneficiary's life expectancy found in *IRS Publication 590B*.

Even though they were required to begin taking taxable distributions from the Inherited Traditional IRA the year after their parents or grandparents died (the beneficiary of an Inherited IRA was not permitted to defer distributions until age 70½ as the original owner was), the RMDs of the Inherited IRA were much smaller than the RMD of the original IRA owner because of the child's/ grandchild's much longer life expectancy. These rules allowed your Inherited Traditional IRA to continue to grow tax-deferred *for a very long time*.

Don't pay taxes now. Pay taxes later. And even after you're dead, we still want your beneficiaries to pay taxes later too.

Required Minimum Distribution of the Inherited IRA Under the SECURE Act

Inherited Traditional IRA (Non-Spouse Beneficiary)

Under the SECURE Act, an Inherited Traditional IRA, subject to exceptions, must be fully distributed and taxed by December 31st of the year that includes the tenth anniversary of the IRA owner's date of death. For shorthand, we will typically refer to this date as ten years after the IRA owner's death. This causes a massive income tax acceleration and many lost years of income-tax-deferred growth compared to the pre-SECURE Act law.

According to Proposed Regulations released by the IRS in February 2022, beneficiaries who do not qualify for one of the exceptions to the 10-year rule are split into two groups, depending on whether the original account owner was already taking distributions or not. If the account owner was 72 or older at the time of their death and had begun taking distributions, beneficiaries must take annual distributions for nine years in addition to completely emptying the account within ten years after the death of the IRA owner. Those annual distributions need to be made *"at least as rapidly"* as the account owner was taking them before he died.

What does *"at least as rapidly"* mean? This means that distributions for the first nine years will be made as if the original account owner were still receiving them. For example, suppose the decedent died at age 75 and had been using the IRS Table III for calculating distributions. That means that the next year, when the beneficiary needs to take the first distribution, he would divide the account balance by 23.7, which would be the factor for a 76-year-old account owner, to get the minimum amount of the first distribution. The beneficiary could also take a larger distribution, maybe one-tenth of the balance, but he would need to take a distribution of at least 1/23.7 of the account balance.

The good news about the Proposed Regulations is that they won't take effect until 2023, according to Notice 2022-53, released by the IRS in October 2022. For deaths in 2020 and 2021, if the decedent was old enough to be taking distributions, the beneficiary will not need to start taking annual distributions until 2023. If the retirement account owner dies before he starts taking distributions, the beneficiary does not need to take annual distributions, but must empty the account completely by the end of the tenth year.

Granted, there are some additional tax-planning opportunities for the beneficiary of the Inherited IRA, especially if the beneficiary is only subject to the 10-year rule and does not need to take annual distributions. For example, if the beneficiary of the Inherited IRA is in a low tax bracket but is expected to be in a much higher tax bracket soon, it would likely make sense to make some taxable distributions of the Inherited IRA while the beneficiary is in a low tax bracket even before he is required to do so.

Depending on circumstances and tax bracket, the beneficiary of the IRA owner dying before age 72 may choose to take distributions roughly equally over the ten-year period in order to smooth out the income taxes paid on the distributions.

For beneficiaries who are subject to the annual distribution requirement and the 10-year rule, those annual distributions can serve as a floor for planning the most tax-efficient method for emptying the account within ten years. As stated earlier, it may make sense to make larger distributions in years when the beneficiary is in a lower tax bracket, and smaller ones when the beneficiary's tax bracket increases. Or it may make sense for the beneficiary to take roughly equal distributions over ten years, provided those annual distributions are greater than his RMDs.

Inherited Roth IRA (Non-Spouse Beneficiary)

In the case of an Inherited Roth IRA, the distributions to the beneficiary are not taxable because the original Roth IRA owner paid the taxes. Inherited Roth IRAs continue to grow income-tax-free. Under the old law, the Roth IRA beneficiary could *"stretch"* the tax-free distributions over his or her life expectancy, similar to an Inherited Traditional IRA.

Under the SECURE Act, an Inherited Roth IRA, subject to exceptions, must be fully distributed within ten years of the original owner's death. This doesn't cause a massive income tax acceleration, but it does mean the beneficiary is losing many years of income-tax-free growth that were available to him under the old law. This also means ten years after the death of the Roth IRA owner, future dividends, interest, or realized capital gains are subject to income tax, just like a regular taxable investment.

And while you might not think that the old mechanism for stretching an IRA was all that important, those rules allowed owners of IRAs and other retirement plans to create tax-deferred and tax-free dynasties that ultimately provided lifetime incomes in the millions of dollars to their children and grandchildren.

Even with more modest inherited IRAs and Roth IRAs, it allowed children of IRA owners to have a lifetime of income that was a valuable supplement to their own income. Now it will be much harder to leave that kind of legacy to your heirs through your retirement accounts.

In 2019, time took its toll and, sadly, a number of our clients died. Some of the deceased IRA owners had more than $2,000,000 in IRAs, and some had substantial Roth IRAs. Children of clients who died in 2019 with IRAs had enormous opportunities for income tax deferral. Children of clients who died in 2019 with Roth IRAs had enormous opportunities for tax-free distribution deferral.

We had a death in the last few days of 2019 of a tax-savvy client who we all liked and, while we were genuinely sad, we both had the same thought—much better that the client died before year-end than after. Because he died before the effective date of the SECURE Act (January 1, 2020), his children were ultimately left in a much better position because they could *"stretch"* both the Inherited IRA and Roth IRA over their lifetime instead of being forced to withdraw the entire balance within ten years of his death. Going forward, children will have fewer opportunities to maximize the Inherited IRA and Inherited Roth IRA you leave them.

One lesson you should take from reading these rules is the status quo is likely to cause massive income tax acceleration of the Inherited IRAs and to consider methods to reduce the amount of money you leave to your non-spousal heirs through IRAs.

Figure 11.1

Old Law for IRA Distributions

Old Law – Inherited IRA Distributed Over Lifetime

YEAR	AGE	INHERITED IRA BALANCE	ANNUAL DISTRIBUTIONS	TOTAL DISTRIBUTED
2020	*80*	*$ 1,000,000*		
2021	46	$ 1,063,566	$ 26,132	$ 26,132
2022	47	$ 1,074,284	$ 27,060	$ 53,192
2023	48	$ 1,084,468	$ 28,022	$ 81,214
2024	49	$ 1,094,066	$ 29,020	$ 110,234
2025	50	$ 1,103,025	$ 30,055	$ 140,289
2026	51	$ 1,111,287	$ 31,128	$ 171,417
2027	52	$ 1,118,791	$ 32,242	$ 203,659
2057	82	$ 471,136	$ 100,242	$ 1,994,933
2058	83	$ 390,216	$ 105,464	$ 2,100,397
2059	84	$ 301,514	$ 111,672	$ 2,212,069
2060	85	$ 203,815	$ 119,891	$ 2,331,960
2061	86	$ 94,870	$ 101,511	$ 2,433,471
2062	87	—	—	**$ 2,433,471**

* Detailed assumptions can be found in the Appendix.

Demonstration of RMDs With Old Law

Figure 11.1, on previous page, demonstrates the advantage of inheriting an IRA under the old law. It assumes the beneficiary elects only to take RMDs from the Inherited IRA. As shown in the chart below, the first year is the RMD of the IRA owner who died at age 80. His 45-year-old beneficiary must begin taking an RMD from the Inherited IRA the year after the owner's death when he is age 46. We skipped some middle years and picked up towards the end of the beneficiary's life to save space. Look at the bottom line...

Under the old law, the total distributions to the beneficiary of this $1M Inherited IRA could have been $2,433,471.

What Happens to Your IRA When You Die Now Under the SECURE Act?

With the new 10-year rule for distributing an Inherited IRA, one class of beneficiaries (e.g., beneficiaries of the original owner who had not started taking distributions) could take zero distributions for the first nine years after the death of the parent or grandparent, but then, they would have to take out the entire

Figure 11.2

IRA Distributed Under the SECURE Act

SECURE Act – Inherited IRA Distributed Over 10 Years

YEAR	AGE	INHERITED IRA BALANCE	ANNUAL DISTRIBUTIONS	TOTAL DISTRIBUTED
2020	80	$ 1,000,000		
2021	46	$ 927,500	$ 142,500	$ 142,500
2022	47	$ 849,925	$ 142,500	$ 285,000
2023	48	$ 766,920	$ 142,500	$ 427,500
2024	49	$ 678,104	$ 142,500	$ 570,000
2025	50	$ 583,071	$ 142,500	$ 712,500
2026	51	$ 481,386	$ 142,500	$ 855,000
2027	52	$ 372,583	$ 142,500	$ 997,500
2028	53	$ 256,164	$ 142,500	$ 1,140,000
2029	54	$ 131,595	$ 131,595	$ 1,271,595
2030	55	—	—	$ 1,271,595

* Detailed assumptions can be found in the Appendix.

amount in the tenth year. Depending on the amount of the Inherited IRA, that would likely push the beneficiary to a high-income tax bracket. Or, if the IRA owner was already taking distributions before they died, the beneficiary will be required to take annual distributions *"at least as rapidly"* as the account owner was receiving distributions. To make things simple for this example, I treated the distributions to come out more evenly. Look at the bottom line.

Though it isn't exactly an apple-to-apple comparison because I am not properly accounting for the time value of money, please note that in the example above, the beneficiary inheriting under the old law received $1,161,876 more from distributions from a million-dollar inherited IRA than the beneficiary under the new law.

Please note that in Figure 11.2 on page 203, I have assumed the beneficiary chose to take the distributions evenly over ten years. In reality, the best time to take a taxable withdrawal from a Traditional Inherited IRA would be when your beneficiary is in their lowest tax bracket, as long as it is within ten years of the death of the IRA owner.

Planning for the Inherited Roth IRA

A beneficiary of an Inherited Roth IRA should have a completely different distribution strategy than the beneficiary of an Inherited Traditional IRA. Unless they meet one of the exceptions to the ten-year rule (which I discuss in Chapter 12), the entire balance of an Inherited Roth IRA will also need to be withdrawn within ten years of the original owner's death. If the beneficiary of a Roth IRA doesn't need the money currently, he should just let the Inherited Roth IRA grow income-tax-free for ten years after the death of the original Roth IRA owner. At the ten-year mark, the entire Roth IRA would be withdrawn.

To oversimplify, if the beneficiary inherited $1,000,000 in a Roth IRA and the money was invested at 7%, he would have a $2,000,000 account after ten years. Again, the distributions from that account are not taxable, as well as dividends, interest, and realized capital gains during the 10-year period. At that point, the money in the Inherited Roth IRA becomes a plain after-tax brokerage account.

The new law governing post-death RMDs for most non-spouse beneficiaries is not at all advantageous—in fact, it is the opposite.

Unless you take pro-active measures, a massive income tax acceleration—one I have spent much of my career trying to help people avoid—is exactly what this law accomplishes. If you have a substantial IRA or TIAA accumulations, as

The beneficiary inheriting under the old law received $1,161,876 more from distributions from a million-dollar inherited IRA than the beneficiary under the new law.

most older professors and TIAA investors have, the effect on your heirs will be devastating *unless* you make significant changes to your retirement and estate plan. Roth IRA conversions are one important defense against the SECURE Act.

Planning for the Small Stretch that Survived is Still Critical

At this point, let me also add this cautionary note. Even with its diminished value, *taking full advantage of the 10-year limited stretch is still important.* Unfortunately, the *"stretch IRA"* is more often botched than done correctly. If the beneficiary meets one of the exceptions to the SECURE Act, taking advantage of the stretch IRA is even more critical.

Someone, whether it is the attorney, advisor, CPA, or client, usually makes a mistake that destroys the stretch IRA, causing a major tax acceleration for the beneficiary. For example, if Dad dies leaving his IRA to Junior and the advisor unwittingly titles Junior's Inherited IRA as *"Junior, IRA,"* the ability to stretch the Inherited IRA would likely be reduced from a ten year-stretch to a five-year stretch. Consequently, Junior suffers a major tax acceleration. The correct name for the account should be something like *"Inherited IRA of Dad for the Benefit of Junior."* If you do not have the magic language in the new account title or don't do exactly as you should in many other ways, your heirs will be taxed—literally and figuratively.

To realize the *"stretch IRA,"* however limited, you need appropriate estate planning and administration after the IRA owner's death. This was true under the old law and remains true with the new.

Please note there are special *"stretch"* opportunities for minors, and beneficiaries with disabilities or chronic illnesses, and beneficiaries who are ten or fewer years younger than the owner, which I will cover in Chapter 12.

What if the Beneficiary of the IRA or Roth IRA is a Trust?

If the end beneficiary is a trust, it must meet certain technical requirements to be deemed a designated beneficiary and receive *"stretch IRA"* status. Please see pages 307–8 in **Retire Secure!**, 3rd edition for details. (Call us to send you a copy, order it from Amazon or download a copy from **https://PayTaxesLater.com/ Books/** for a list of conditions that the trust must meet.) Otherwise, the trust will suffer enormous income-tax acceleration. In the case of an inherited Roth IRA, it could cause a needless acceleration of tax-free distributions.

Please note that many attorneys, banks, and even CPAs are touting the benefits of "IRA Trusts." They typically name the bank or financial institution as the trustee. I generally prefer to name a family member as trustee; that way, you can achieve the same tax result but still have the advantage of a family member as trustee. The advantages of having a family member as a trustee or even executor is keeping control in the family and usually lower fees. On the other hand, sometimes there are no good choices for the trustee in the family or acquaintances and you must look to some type of corporate trustee.

Remember that there are critical exceptions to the 10-year rule for beneficiaries with chronic illnesses or disabilities. For more information about those exceptions, please see Chapters 12 and 13. A special needs trust is often the best way to leave money to a beneficiary with a disability or chronic illness. An important goal of a special needs trust is to provide money to the beneficiary in a way that does not interfere with any type of government benefit the beneficiary might be receiving or may receive in the future.

Drafting a special needs trust that is named the beneficiary of your IRA requires special language to protect the beneficiary's government benefit and minimize income-tax implications. When drafting a trust for a beneficiary with a disability or chronic illness, it is critical that your attorney understands the consequential language that allows beneficiaries to (1) continue to qualify for government benefits and (2) to qualify as a designated beneficiary to the pre-2020 lifetime stretch for the trust. Please see Chapter 13 if you have a beneficiary with a disability or chronic illness.

Our accounting firm can help you with developing a Financial Masterplan. We can provide assistance to your local attorney in getting your estate plan on the right track. In conjunction with our money management partners, Lange Financial Group can offer investment management services. As I'll discuss further below, we find major errors in more than 50% of the more current trusts and 90% or more of the older trusts we have seen when the underlying asset is an IRA or retirement plan.*

---

* Please see restrictions and disclaimers at the end of the book in the section titled *"Save More, Have More, Leave More! The Lange Edge! A Truly Integrated Long Term Financial Masterplan".*

Another common situation is naming minor children as beneficiaries of a trust. As I'll discuss in more detail in the next chapter under *Exceptions to the SECURE Act*, minor children of a deceased IRA owner are only *partially* exempt from the income tax acceleration rules.

Under current law, a minor child (or a trust for a minor child) may defer distributions of the Inherited IRA or Roth IRA until they reach the age of majority at age 21. At that point, the 10-year clock starts ticking. Therefore, if a 10-year-old inherits an IRA from a deceased parent, they could have 21 years of income-tax deferral. So, it is crucial that the trust be drafted appropriately.

Accumulation Trusts *vs.* Conduit Trusts and the Potential Need to Redraft Your Trusts

Accumulation trusts are typically permitted to accumulate income. This might be appropriate if the income from the trust exceeds the needs of the beneficiary, and the trustee doesn't want to give the beneficiary more money than he or she currently needs (or the owner of the IRA wanted to keep total control over the money from the grave)! So, while the trust does not have to pay out all the RMDs to the beneficiaries, the minimum distribution amounts that were not distributed to the beneficiary will be taxed within the trust at trust tax rates that are generally significantly higher than individual tax rates.

An accumulation trust still falls within the 10-year income-tax acceleration requirement of the SECURE Act. The advantage of an accumulation trust after the SECURE Act is that the trustee will have more discretion over when and how the income and principal are distributed during the 10-year term following the IRA owner's death and after. For instance, if a beneficiary is in college and has little or no income, the trustee may want to distribute income before the beneficiary graduates from school and gets a job that will put them in a higher tax bracket.

In contrast, a conduit trust requires the trustee to distribute all income from the trust. In the example of the college student who might do better to receive money before graduation, the trustee of a conduit trust has less control over the timing of the payout.

If a conduit trust is named a beneficiary of the IRA, all the RMDs from the Inherited IRA must be paid to the trust and then to the beneficiaries who pay tax at their income tax rate (avoiding the high taxes on undistributed RMDs). Many conduit trusts with an IRA as the underlying asset were drafted to avoid the high income-tax rates if the income and distributions were just left in the trust.

Now, however, after the SECURE Act, with the loss of the lifetime stretch, beneficiary designations of IRAs and retirement plans that have conduit trusts as the beneficiary must be re-examined and probably transitioned (while the IRA owner is still alive) to accumulation trusts. Even though they avoid high trust tax rates, any control the IRA owner was trying to exert will be moot both during and after the ten years in which the balance must be distributed.

The trustee may want to keep money in the trust for the same reasons that the trust was set up in the first place. That might include protecting the money from a spendthrift beneficiary, creditor protection, preserving a government benefit, protecting a beneficiary from a no-good spouse, or, for that matter and more commonly, a future ex-spouse. By that I mean your current son or daughter-in-law that will become an ex-son- or daughter-in-law in the future.

In such cases, a trustee might not want to distribute the remaining balance of the trust within ten years of the IRA owner's death. If you want to give the trustee options for more control, and if your current beneficiary is a conduit type trust, that alone might be a good reason to review your wills and trusts and beneficiary designations of your IRAs and retirement plans and possibly add a codicil or redo at least a portion of your estate plan.

The recommended change would often be to change the conduit trust to an accumulation trust. If you do not even have a conduit trust now, you can go straight to the best choice and skip your intermediate estate plan and set of wills and trusts. That is like going from a young baseball player skipping the minor leagues and going straight to the major league. That might be true of many readers in many areas of their retirement and estate plan.

This conduit vs accumulation trust was not as big a problem before the SECURE Act because the taxable distributions could have been extended over the life of the beneficiary. So, a conduit trust would be fine. Now that the inherited IRA cannot be stretched more than 10 years, it is a big problem.

On the other hand, by the time you finish reading more of this book you will likely want to completely redo your entire retirement and estate plan, so do not do anything until you have read the book or at least Chapter 14, *Lange's Cascading Beneficiary Plan*. Though it sounds self-serving, for a lot of professors and TIAA investors, it would be advantageous to have our accounting firm get involved in both reviewing your current estate plan* and making sure your local estate planning attorney is getting things right, which again 50% or more of the more current plans and 90% or more of the older plans have not, at least in our experience.

Examples of Estate Plans That May or May Not Need Attention

Here is an example of an estate plan that includes a trust that urgently needs attention. Assume a spendthrift trust is the primary beneficiary of a multi-million-dollar IRA. Please also assume that if the money were left outright to the beneficiary, the beneficiary of that trust would buy a new guitar and spend money on drugs and alcohol before paying rent. Then assume that the spendthrift trust is a conduit trust, and the IRA owner is old and sick. That is an urgent situation that needs immediate attention. The terms of the trust should be changed from a conduit trust to an accumulation trust.

On the other hand, a conduit trust that is for the benefit of young grandchildren who are the second contingent beneficiaries after the spouse and the children would not be as pressing. If there is not much money in the IRA and both the spouse and the children have significant needs, perhaps that estate plan doesn't merit spending any time and money to amend. Of course, these two situations represent the extremes; most of our readers and clients are somewhere in between.

The point, however, is if you have a conduit trust as the beneficiary, or even the contingent beneficiary, of your IRA or retirement plan, you may need to update your wills, trusts, and beneficiary designations of your IRAs and retirement plans.

If you are getting the idea that the rules around trusts are complicated and that any estate plans that include trusts need special expertise, you are right. That is especially true when the underlying asset is an IRA. The unfortunate news is that most attorneys botch the basic rules for drafting trusts to qualify as a designated beneficiary of an IRA. We find errors in approximately 50% of the estate plans that we have seen and as high as 90% or more of the older estate plans where a trust is the beneficiary or contingent beneficiary of an IRA or retirement plan. This is particularly surprising because many of these trusts

---

* Lange Accounting Group offers guidance on retirement plan distribution strategies, tax reduction, Roth IRA conversions, saving and spending strategies, optimized Social Security strategies and gifting plans. Although we bring our knowledge and expertise in estate planning, it will be conducted in our capacity as a number crunching CPA. However, we will likely make recommendations that clients could have a licensed estate attorney implement. Life insurance can be offered by a CPA through Lange Life Care for those interested. It would be offered in their role as a CPA and not as an attorney.

Asset location, asset allocation and low-cost enhanced index funds are provided by the investment firms with whom Lange Financial Group is affiliated. This would be offered in our role as an investment advisor representative. Please see the front of the book for disclaimers related to these services.

In our role for each of these instances, we will not be acting as the clients' attorney and there will not be an attorney/client relationship. There is no solicitation being made for legal services by the author nor by Lange Legal Services, LLC.

are drafted by attorneys that often have good reputations and work for large, expensive law firms.

The Consequences of Getting It Wrong Can Be Dire for the Beneficiaries

We rarely give our seal of approval when we review *"estate plans"* prepared by other attorneys. Part of it is we are particular and want the strategy optimized. It is the beneficiary designations of TIAA, IRAs and other retirement accounts that usually need the most attention. Many clients assume that the problem with their estate plan where a trust is the beneficiary is that they are out of date. We find more often than not they were terribly flawed the day they were prepared.

The rest of this chapter describes how our accounting firm handles these problems in practice. I am not sure how to do a great job for a client if you do not take these steps. If you have no interest in how we do it, then please skip to the *Key Ideas* section.

When we develop a Financial Masterplan for a client, we conduct a review of their existing estate plan. And, during our review of estate plans we rarely see a new client's existing plan that could not be significantly improved by redrafting or updating based on our recommendations. Many of our recommendations are life changing for the beneficiaries.*

As mentioned earlier, in the majority of cases, even if expensive downtown firms prepared the estate plan, there are usually huge gaps. One of the biggest issues is not having the proper language to help the beneficiaries get the most of their inherited TIAA, IRAs, and retirement plans.

A common mistake that just might be a consequence of the SECURE Act is whether or not trusts designated as beneficiaries of IRAs that qualified as conduit trusts also contain the proper language to qualify as accumulation trusts since there are now many occasions where conduit trusts designated as beneficiaries of IRAs give beneficiaries too much money too quickly.

---

* Lange Accounting Group offers guidance on retirement plan distribution strategies, tax reduction, Roth IRA conversions, saving and spending strategies, optimized Social Security strategies and gifting plans. Although we bring our knowledge and expertise in estate planning to this review, it will be conducted in our capacity as a number crunching CPA.

However, we will likely make recommendations that clients could have a licensed estate attorney implement. In this capacity, we will not be acting as the clients' attorney and there will not be an attorney/client relationship. There is no solicitation being made for legal services by the author nor by Lange Legal Services, LLC.

Many clients assume that the problem with their wills and trusts, and retirement plans and IRA beneficiary designations where a trust is the beneficiary is that they are out of date. We find more often than not they were terribly flawed the day they were prepared.

We can and do consult with and provide guidance to your local estate attorney who drafts, redrafts, or updates your estate plan. We have even identified excellent estate attorneys in a number of states across the country to whom we refer our out-of-state clients who need to establish or amend their estate plans.

Please note that reviewing existing estate plans and making recommendations is a service that we do for our assets-under-management clients and for clients who engage our firm to develop a Financial Masterplan for them on a fee-for-service basis.

KEY IDEAS

- If the largest asset in your estate is your IRA or retirement plan, the beneficiary designations of your IRAs and retirement plans are the most important estate documents you have. Please be sure the beneficiary designations on all your retirement accounts are filled out appropriately.

- The SECURE ACT does not change the surviving spouse's ability to roll over or make a trustee-to-trustee transfer of an IRA inherited from a spouse.

- Subject to exception, the surviving spouse should continue to limit withdrawals to the RMDs for as long as possible.

- Taking advantage of the 10-year limited stretch is still critically important

Key Ideas continue on the following page.

KEY IDEAS
(continued)

- If your IRA or retirement plan is the underlying asset for a trust, you should think about reviewing the trust with an estate attorney who understands the concepts and the appropriate language when drafting trusts when the underlying asset is an IRA or retirement plan.

- Conduit trusts that were a reasonable choice in the past should probably be redrafted to protect the beneficiary and made into accumulation trusts.

12

The Impact of the SECURE Act on Your Family—Followed by a Special Section on the Proposed Regulations

"The more hidden the venom, the more dangerous it is."

— Margaret of Valois

Effective January 1, 2020, the SECURE Act accelerates taxes on Inherited IRAs and retirement plans and is Trump's and Congress' devastating penalty on hard-working families.

A Special Asset—The Inherited IRA or Inherited Retirement Plan

If you die and the beneficiary of your TIAA, IRA, or other retirement plan is not your spouse, he or she will own a special asset called an *Inherited IRA*. It could be an Inherited 403(b) plan that still may be invested in TIAA and/or CREF. The same basic tax rules apply for these other inherited retirement plans and IRAs. A non-spouse beneficiary may not roll an Inherited IRA or Inherited 403(b) into his or her own IRA or 403(b). Since the distributions from a Traditional Inherited IRA are taxable, our accounting office routinely, subject to rare exceptions, encourages IRA and TIAA-CREF beneficiaries to *"stretch"* or defer taxable distributions to the maximum allowed by law.

The old law allowed beneficiaries to *"stretch"* the Inherited IRA, at least to some extent, for their entire lives. The SECURE Act mandates that, subject to exception, the distributions of the Inherited IRA be fully distributed and taxed by December 31st of the year that includes the tenth anniversary of the IRA owner's date of death. From here on, we will simply just refer to this date as *"within ten years of the IRA owner's death."*

The SECURE Act was an attack on university faculty, TIAA investors, and other taxpayers who have the majority of their portfolio in IRAs and retirement plans. The impact of this legislation will be devastating for the children and grandchildren of anyone who has accumulated a significant amount of money in his or her retirement plans. In all fairness to President Trump who signed the bill, I strongly suspect he didn't understand the ramifications of what he was

> **The SECURE Act was an attack on university faculty and other taxpayers who have the majority of their portfolio in IRAs and retirement plans.**

signing. He may actually have thought it was helping wealthy IRA and retirement plan owners.

By passing this act, the government is essentially picking the pockets of children of retirement investors who played by the rules for years and diligently saved as much as they could in their retirement plan.

The deal all along was if you contribute money to your retirement plan, not only would you get tax benefits during your lifetime, but your heirs will enjoy the ability to defer taxes on your Inherited IRAs and retirement plans to some extent, for the rest of their lives.

Accordingly, you were prudent and made financial sacrifices and put in as much money as you could afford or were allowed to contribute into your retirement. You had good reason to believe you were being smart and prudent in planning for not only yourself, but also to pass money on to your family in a tax efficient manner after your death.

Then, late in the game for many older investors, President Trump and Congress changed the rules. The new rules will seriously jeopardize your legacy.

Quantifying the Difference Between the Past and the Current Law

Figure 12.1 shows the difference between inheriting $1 million from an IRA that could be *"stretched"* over a lifetime under the old law (solid line) *vs.* a child who inherits $1 million that is subject to the 10-year rule (dashed line). (The graphs show purchasing power, i.e. net assets, by taking into account the after-tax value of the retirement plan.) The only difference between these two scenarios is when the child pays taxes.

Do you think that's devastating? Wait until you see Figure 12.2 which shows what the ability to stretch the IRA could have meant to your grandchildren.

In Figure 12.2, the solid line depicts what would have happened if the IRA was left to a grandchild and the grandchild stretched the distributions over 55 years. The dashed line shows what happens now that the grandchild must withdraw the IRA and pay all the taxes within ten years.

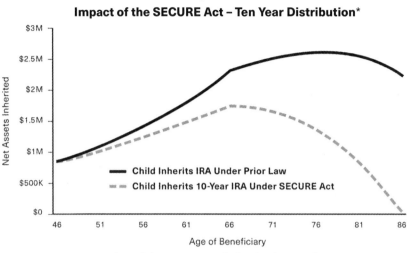

Figure 12.1
Impact of the SECURE Act – Ten Year Distribution*

* Detailed assumptions can be found in the Appendix.

In both cases, the grandchild immediately reinvests the withdrawals into a taxable brokerage account. The difference in wealth by the time they reach age 70 is an astonishing $16,245,105!

The old rules were a lot more fun for planners like me. I loved doing a series of Roth IRA conversions and then, through the use of disclaimers (please see

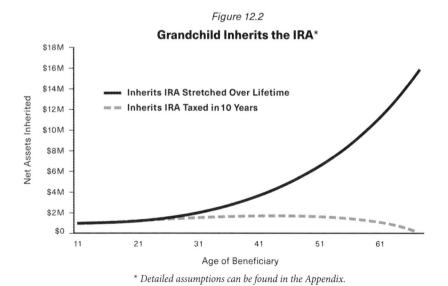

Figure 12.2
Grandchild Inherits the IRA*

* Detailed assumptions can be found in the Appendix.

Chapter 14), we protected the surviving spouse but left open the possibility of a tax-free dynasty to the next two and sometimes three generations.

But the more common result of the SECURE Act is (without the aggressive intervention that this book is advocating) it just hurts the children of hardworking professors, TIAA investors, and IRA and retirement plan owners who played by the rules and got burned.

Proposed Regulations from the IRS Released in February 2022

As I mentioned in last chapter, Proposed Regulations from the IRS released in February 2022 remove some of the flexibility that beneficiaries had for timing their distributions within that ten-year window to minimize taxes. As we go to press, the IRS has announced that these Proposed Regulations won't apply until they are finalized in 2023. I include them here because I strongly suspect they will become law, possibly by the time you are reading this book. I am repeating some of the information from the last chapter to make sure that if you only read this chapter, you are aware of how the IRS is currently interpreting the changes of the SECURE Act.

The Proposed Regulations split IRA beneficiaries who do not qualify for one of the exceptions detailed below into two groups, based on whether the original retirement plan owner had already begun taking distributions or was still under the age when their RMDs were to start.

If the decedent was under age 72 or their required beginning date for distributions had not begun, the beneficiary can take distributions from an Inherited Traditional IRA whenever they want, as long as the account is completely emptied in ten years. They can take zero distributions until year ten and take everything out at the end, or they can take regular distributions every year. They can take bigger distributions in years when they will be in lower tax brackets, and smaller distributions in higher tax bracket years.

But if the decedent was already taking distributions, for the first nine years, the beneficiary of the Inherited IRA will be required to take annual distributions that are at least as large as the decedent's annual distributions. Whatever is left will have to be withdrawn in year ten. These Proposed Regulations will force owners of Inherited Traditional IRAs to take taxable distributions every year, even if that leads to a tax bomb. However, if the original owner died in 2020 or 2021, the beneficiary won't need to start taking distributions until 2023.

These Proposed Regulations also reduce the games that I was planning on playing in timing the distributions of the Inherited IRA.

The good news is that these Proposed Regulations do not apply to an Inherited Roth IRA because the original Roth IRA owner didn't have to take a distribution. So, the beneficiary of an Inherited Roth IRA, assuming they have other funds to spend, can just let the Inherited Roth IRA grow for ten years and then withdraw it tax-free. If the investments earn 7% per year, the Inherited Roth will double by the time it has to be withdrawn. On the other hand, like the Inherited IRA, the Inherited Roth IRA must be distributed within ten years of the Roth IRA owner's death.

Now that you've seen a demonstration of the horrendous impact of the SECURE Act, let's look at the few exceptions that Congress included that will still allow advantageous tax treatment for inherited retirement plan assets.

Exceptions to the SECURE Act

The following section could be extremely critical to the protection of your nonspouse beneficiaries.

Unless the beneficiary of your IRA meets the new definition of an *Eligible Designated Beneficiary (EDB)*, the Inherited IRA will have to be fully distributed within ten years. Eligible Designated Beneficiaries include: a surviving spouse, an individual with a disability or chronic illness, an individual who is not more than ten years younger than the IRA owner, or a child of the IRA owner who has not reached the age of majority (age 21). Charities and charitable trusts are also exempt. Let's look into each of these categories in detail.

The Surviving Spouse

Thankfully, surviving spouses will still be able to do a spousal rollover or, preferably, a trustee-to-trustee transfer of your IRA or retirement plan. However, this doesn't necessarily mean that you should simply plan on having your surviving spouse inherit your retirement assets, and then at the second death, pass those assets on to your children.

Your surviving spouse will be required to take minimum distributions from the Traditional retirement plans they inherit from you as well as from their own IRAs and retirement plans. Remember, those minimum distributions will increase as the surviving spouse grows older, also increasing their taxable income.

And suppose you have accumulated a significant amount of wealth in Traditional retirement plans. In that case, the survivor (who now must file as single instead of jointly starting the year after you die) might move up to a significantly higher tax bracket. So, even though your spouse is exempt from the accelerated tax provision of the SECURE Act, it may make sense to plan on passing part of your Traditional retirement assets directly to your children at the time of your death either by leaving your IRA or other money directly to your children or more likely doing it by disclaimer.

Another option from the SECURE Act 2.0, passed in December 2022, allows spouses to elect to be treated as if they were the deceased spouse for puposes of the timing of RMDs from inherited IRAs. This provision is most useful when the decedent is younger than the surviving spouse because this allows the surviving spouse to postpone RMDs until the younger spouse would have started taking their RMDs.

The disclaimer solution to the difficult issue of predicting *"who should get what"* is to let the surviving spouse make the decision of who gets what within nine months after the death of the IRA or retirement plan owner.

We cover the details of this type of planning—which we call disclaimer planning—in Chapter 14, *The Best Estate Plan for Most University Faculty Members and TIAA Investors Before and After the Secure Act.*

Beneficiaries with Disabilities or Chronic Illness

In addition to surviving spouses, beneficiaries with disabilities or chronic illnesses are also exempt from the devastating rules of the SECURE Act. If you have a beneficiary with a chronic illness or disability, you are in a specialty area that offers both enormous opportunities and pitfalls.

If you do have such a beneficiary, it is critical to read Chapter 13, *Critical Information for Beneficiaries with Disabilities*. It is also critical that you consult with both an estate attorney* and a trusted financial advisor and/or CPA who is familiar with planning for beneficiaries with disabilities or chronic illnesses.

My daughter has a disability and this issue is close to my heart. In short, qualified beneficiaries with disabilities will meet the standards to use the old *"stretch IRA rules,"* which, as demonstrated above, are life changing. As readers will learn in Chapter 13, the rules for qualifying a beneficiary as disabled or chronically ill are rather narrow and may require substantial effort on your part before your death.

But favorable Proposed Regulations regarding beneficiaries with a disability

---

* There is no solicitation being made for legal services by the author nor by Lange Legal Services, LLC.

If you have a child with a disability who can use the old rules to "*stretch*" an Inherited IRA, getting your planning right is crucial.

could make that effort pay off by hundreds of thousands of dollars. In my personal situation, my wife and I have a daughter with a disability who will qualify as an EDB. In our estate planning, either our daughter or a trust for her benefit is the end beneficiary for our retirement accounts. Because of planning we have done for her in just two areas, she will be better off by $1.8 million dollars measured in today's dollars than if had we not taken just those two proactive measures. How we did it is explained in Chapter 13.

Even if your beneficiary does qualify as disabled or chronically ill, you will have to put in place additional measures to ensure their financial security. First, at least in the case of Supplemental Security Income, usually referred to as SSI, your beneficiary must meet income and asset limitations to qualify and ensure that your beneficiary remains eligible for government benefits.

In order to get around this income and asset limitation, the money will most likely need to be placed in a carefully drafted trust and/or a tax-advantaged savings account for individuals with disabilities known as a special needs trust (SNT trust), again, please see Chapter 13. Making sure that this trust meets all the qualifications to be treated as a SNT is a big deal, so I highly recommend you consult with at least one, if not two attorneys with expertise in this field.

One skill set is winning the case to be considered disabled or chronically ill. The second skill set is expertise in drafting the appropriate wills, trusts, beneficiary designations, etc. or advising other attorneys in this area.

Because many beneficiaries with disabilities or chronic illnesses face challenges with long-term gainful employment, they are typically more dependent on inherited funds to finance their basic living expenses than the average person who receives an Inherited IRA. Getting it right can make the difference between living in poverty—as many Americans with disabilities currently do—and having a secure financial future.

It's heartbreaking to know how much misery for these individuals could have been prevented with appropriate estate planning by parents, grandparents or other caring individuals had they had the right information and/or hired the right team to help them.

You can also understand why getting this right is crucial if you have a child with a disability who can use the old rules to *"stretch"* the Inherited IRA.

Fortunately, there are resources available for families of children with disabilities or chronic illnesses. Depending on your particular situation, there will be issues with what constitutes a disability or chronic illness. There will also be significant issues generating the proof of that disability or chronic illness. We address those issues in Chapter 13. It isn't difficult to predict a massive growth in the long-Covid patients who may qualify or certainly deserve to qualify for this special tax treatment.

I want your disabled child to get the same tax advantages that my daughter will get. But I want all professors and readers to be aware that planning for your child or beneficiary is critically important. The difference between the optimal plan and something that is just okay can have an enormous impact on the quality of life of your beneficiary after you are gone.

One potentially critical piece to the puzzle in the mess of the SECURE Act is that under the Proposed Regulations, if your beneficiary has already qualified as disabled for the purposes of the Social Security Administration, that beneficiary also meets the definition of disabled for the SECURE Act. This will allow your beneficiary to stretch out Inherited IRA distributions over his or her lifetime like the pre-2020 rules instead of being forced to empty the account within ten years.

This was big news in our household. Though we won our Social Security benefits case for our daughter, before this proposed change, we had no assurance that she would qualify for the exception allowing her to stretch her Inherited IRA after we die. Since we have a 7-figure Roth IRA, it will be even more valuable for her. Assuming the Proposed Regulations become law, and our daughter can maintain her status with the Social Security Administration, we know she will qualify for the inherited stretch IRA and inherited stretch Roth IRA after we are gone. That will be worth hundreds of thousands of additional dollars than if this provision doesn't pass or she failed to qualify for other reasons.

It also significantly lowers *"the number"* that we feel obligated to leave her at our death to feel secure that she will be fine financially for the rest of her life.

Minor Children as the Beneficiary of an IRA or Retirement Plan

Minor children of the IRA owner are also partially exempt from the SECURE Act's 10-year rule. The rules affecting children who have not yet reached the age of majority are complex. The SECURE Act potentially allows a minor child (who must be your child) beneficiary to stretch an Inherited IRA like the old rules until reaching their age of majority. While the age of majority varies from state to state, Proposed Regulations released by the IRS in February 2022, define this as age 21. A minor child will have to take distributions over their life expectancy until age 21.

Once reaching that age, however, the 10-year rule kicks in. So, you could theoretically leave an IRA to your newborn child, and the child would be able to *stretch* it like the old rules until they turn 21. Starting then, they will be required to withdraw the remaining balance within ten years of turning 21.

In certain instances, annuities can provide an exception to the onerous provisions of the SECURE Act. I cover some ideas for annuity owners in Chapter 9. Please note I am not a fan of commercial annuities and much of that information in Chapter 9 will be geared towards convincing you a commercial annuity is not in your best interest.

For most readers, however, the new law will have the most dramatic effect on your adult children and potentially your grandchildren. Let's look at why that is.

How the SECURE Act Affects Children Inheriting IRAs and Roth IRAs

As stated before, an IRA that passes to a *non-spouse* beneficiary becomes a special asset called an Inherited IRA. Subject to some exceptions listed previously (for minors, etc.), an Inherited IRA or retirement plan will have to be entirely disbursed within ten years following the death of the original IRA owner. Period.

If the Inherited IRA is a Traditional pre-tax account, all distributions are taxable. And if the Inherited IRA is large enough, the income from the accelerated distributions could force your non-spouse beneficiary into a significantly higher tax bracket even if the distributions are taken evenly over ten years. This tax acceleration can be devastating, as we saw above in Figure 12.1.

If the Inherited IRA is a Roth account, your child (or other non-spouse beneficiaries) will not have to pay taxes on the distributions because Roth account distributions are tax-free.

Assuming your beneficiary leaves the inherited Roth IRA account where it is, any distributions from the account and income received from interest, dividends, and capital gains will all be tax-free for ten years after the death of the Roth IRA owner. After the ten years, the principal would not be taxed, but any accruing income would be taxable because the principal is no longer under the tax-free Roth umbrella. That's a big change.

The idea that Roth accounts could compound over many years and distributions would be tax-free was a huge benefit for your heirs. So, in the case of an Inherited Roth account, there is an enormous incentive for your beneficiary to not take any withdrawals until they are absolutely required to—and there is no penalty for waiting until the very last minute, either.

The Ten Years Younger Exception

Another exception to the ten-year income acceleration on IRAs dictated by the SECURE Act is for a beneficiary who is no more than ten years younger than you. This would likely apply if you were leaving your IRA or a portion of your IRA or retirement plan to a sibling or an unmarried partner.

Please, please see Chapter 25 in the event you have an unmarried partner, gay or straight. I will present a strong case for the financial benefits of getting married. I previously wrote two books for same-sex couples. Today, when gay couples can legally get married in all 50 states, the main thrust of those books is moot. That said, the concept of the financial benefits of marriage is extremely relevant if you have an unmarried partner. I have even thought of writing a book titled *Get Married for the Money*. In the meantime, Chapter 25 will have to do.

Charities and Charitable Trusts

Charities and charitable trusts are a critical exception to the 10-year income acceleration rule for IRAs and retirement plans.

The charitable trust exception will create enormous opportunities for many readers, especially if you are charitably inclined. We include an entire section on charitable trusts in Chapter 18. The advantages to naming a charitable trust as the beneficiary of your IRA as opposed to naming your children directly is considerably enhanced by this exception to the SECURE Act. Along with two other strategies for charitable giving with IRAs and retirement plans also covered in this book, my goal is to move a billion dollars to charity and still have your children receive more money than they would have without your charitable donation.

The Disaster of the SECURE Act

Notwithstanding these fantastically helpful exceptions for some, the party for the rest of us is over. The SECURE Act is a horrible piece of legislation that is miserable for professors, TIAA investors, and their families. Losing the ability to stretch their Inherited IRA will be devastating for IRA and retirement plan owner's beneficiaries because the income tax on the inherited IRAs will be significantly accelerated.

Now that you understand the gravity of the situation and why I find it such a deplorable change for most professors and TIAA investors, please read on to see what you can do about it now.

KEY IDEAS

- An IRA that passes to a non-spouse beneficiary is a special asset called an Inherited IRA.

- The SECURE ACT mandates that an Inherited IRA must, subject to exceptions, be totally disbursed and taxed within ten years of the IRA owner's death.

- The Inherited Roth IRA must also, subject to exceptions, be distributed within ten years of death, but is tax-free.

- The new Proposed Regulations make things even worse for beneficiaries inheriting IRAs from an IRA owner who was 72 or older.

Key Ideas continue on the following page.

KEY IDEAS
(continued)

• Eligible Designated Beneficiaries (EDBs) are not subject to the ten-year rule. They include:

1. Surviving spouses;

2. Minor beneficiaries of a deceased parent;

3. Qualifying disabled or chronically ill beneficiaries:

    The new proposed regulations are very favorable for clarifying the terms of the exception to the ten-year rule for beneficiaries with disabilities or who are chronically ill;

4. Beneficiaries who are not more than ten years younger than the retirement account owner;

5. Charities and charitable trusts.

• Under the SECURE Act, if you do not take aggressive action, your IRA and retirement plan legacy will be decimated.

13

Critical Information for Parents of a Child with a Disability

by James Lange, *Certified Public Accountant, Attorney,*

Julieanne E. Steinbacher, *Esq., CELA, LLM in Estate and Elder Law,*

and Deborah McFadden,

Former US Commissioner, Administration of Developmental Disabilities

If you have a child with a disability, there is likely no better use of your time than to read this chapter and implement at least some of the recommendations.

This chapter contains both financial strategies that I strongly advocate as well as legal strategies that Julieanne and I advocate, and advice from our colleague, Deborah McFadden.

Julieanne Steinbacher is the founding shareholder of Steinbacher, Goodall & Yurchak, an elder care and special needs law firm. Deborah is an internationally known expert in the disability arena. She has special expertise in getting children approved for Supplemental Security Income (SSI) and Social Security Disability Insurance (SSDI) and helping individuals and families access valuable benefits that improve their lives.

To illustrate the life changing difference between pro-active and passive planning for your child with a disability, I am sharing my family's personal story. Our daughter, Erica, has a disability and will never be able to support herself. She is currently receiving Social Security Disability Insurance (SSDI). One of the most important things for me and my wife, as it is for most parents with a child with a disability, is to make sure we properly provide for our child both while we are alive and perhaps even more importantly, after we are gone.

Let's start at the end of the story.

Because of our actions on three critical fronts, our daughter will be $1,890,544 better off (measured in today's dollars) over the course of her life than she would have been had we not taken these proactive steps—and this is without factoring in any supplemental government benefits. A secondary consequence is that my wife and I will also be better off by $491,829 in today's dollars.

The three things we did were:

1. We won our SSDI appeal with the Social Security Administration formally establishing Erica's status as disabled. We are confident that Erica's disabled status with the SSA will fast track her status as an Eligible Designated Beneficiary (EDB) under the SECURE Act once she inherits our retirement accounts. Her EDB status will allow her to stretch distributions from her inherited IRAs and inherited Roth IRAs over her lifetime instead of the more common 10 years after date of death of the IRA owner.

2. We made a large Roth IRA conversion and a series of Roth IRA, backdoor Roth IRA, and Roth 401(k) contributions.

3. We drafted an optimized estate plan with appropriate wills, trusts, and IRA and 401(k) and Roth IRA beneficiary forms that, to a large extent, will allow Erica and/or a trust for her benefit to *"stretch"* or defer distributions of her inherited IRA and Roth IRA for her entire life. Erica not only needed her EDB status, but she also needed to have the appropriate documents in place. And we have planned for competent estate administration as well.

Figure 13.1, shown at the top of the following page, dramatically contrasts Erica's financial future as a consequence of our effective planning using Roth strategies as well as qualifying her as an EDB and optimizing our estate plan versus ineffective planning. It begins with our projected deaths when she is age 46 and continues to her projected death at age 86.

The bottom line is that rather than running out of money later in life, in a true *"apples to apples"* comparison, at age 86 Erica will still have a comfortable $1,890,544 measured in today's dollars. Or more to the point, she will be able to spend a lot more money over the course of her life, and still not worry about running out of money. She will be able to afford many more services and a much better lifestyle, both for her health and her comfort, in ways that would otherwise have been impossible. She will not have to worry about money, and now

> **Because of our actions on three critical fronts, our daughter will be $1,890,544 better off** *(measured in today's dollars)* **over the course of her life than she would have been had we not taken these proactive steps—and this is without factoring in any supplemental government benefits.**

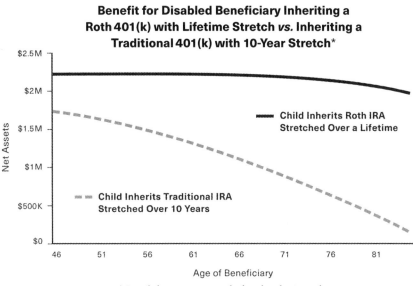

Figure 13.1

Benefit for Disabled Beneficiary Inheriting a Roth 401(k) with Lifetime Stretch *vs.* Inheriting a Traditional 401(k) with 10-Year Stretch*

* Detailed assumptions can be found in the Appendix.

neither Cindy nor I worry about her financial security after we are gone, or at least nowhere near the amount we worried before these plans were in place.

I realize not everyone reading this book will have as large an IRA as Cindy and I have accumulated over the years. In addition, we did our first Roth IRA conversion of $249,000 in 1998. It is possible you haven't made any Roth IRA conversions to date or at least not as big as the one Cindy and I made. But do not dismiss the strategies because you see a big difference between our circumstances and yours. There is still a tremendous value to your disabled child by taking the same steps Cindy and I took.

Scenario A:

Let's say you die at age 85 with a $500,000 Traditional IRA when your disabled child is age 54. Your child is receiving $25,000 per year in SSDI, and her annual expenses are $103,000, indexed for inflation (this is less than $4,650/month in today's dollars). Let's also assume your estate plan was not optimized to allow the *"stretch IRA."* Under this set of circumstances, your child would run out of money at age 88.

Scenario B:

Let's say your child is receiving the same $25,000 SSDI, and her annual expenses are the same $103,000 indexed for inflation. Her SSDI status confers her

EDB status under the SECURE Act so she will be able to take advantage of the lifetime stretch for distributions from inherited IRAs/Roth IRAs.

Let's also assume you completed a series of Roth conversions with your $500,000 Traditional IRA before you died, and you got the estate planning right. Under these circumstances, at age 88, your child will still have $239,068 in sharp contrast to Scenario A where he or she would have $0.

If your child lives a long time, he or she will have additional financial resources to live comfortably for another 12 years or longer. Alternately, your child could spend more money every year for needed care before reaching age 88.

Figure 13.2 plots the different outcomes from the two scenarios.

Figure 13.2

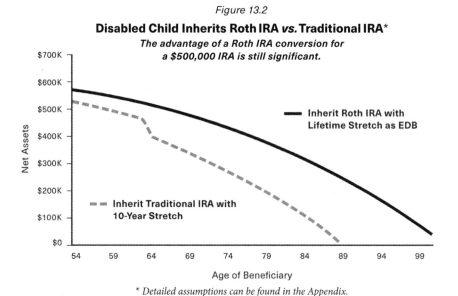

* Detailed assumptions can be found in the Appendix.

The Dread That Once Kept Us Up at Night is Now Gone!

Most parents care and fear for their children's well-being. But parents who care for a child with a disability often experience a much deeper dread when imagining their child's future.

Our daughter Erica is a very sweet and very smart 28-year-old who has a disability. Our concerns for her long-term security and safety kept us up at night. We could not rest easy until we were convinced that we had planned appropriately and substantively for Erica. I know that as the parent or grandparent of a child with a disability, you have these same fears.

It saddens me to think of children with disabilities who will end up in terrible shape simply because their parents failed to plan appropriately. Fortunately, as a Roth IRA conversion and SECURE Act expert, I had the technical knowledge to plan for our daughter's long-term financial security.

This chapter reflects my most heartfelt wishes that all parents and guardians of children with disabilities will learn about and use these strategies to dramatically improve the long-term financial security of their children.

Please note that the three co-authors of this chapter have also created a website with a free *Special Advisory Report for Parents of a Child with a Disability*. We have a one-page highlights report and a 55-page report, all available at no cost at **https://DisabledChildPlanning.com**.

A Brief Summary of Erica's Health History for Context

One day Erica was acing her SAT and two days later she got so sick that she had to quit school. To be fair, she had problems before this, but they were somewhat manageable. We consulted with gastroenterologists, neurologists, pain docs, cardiologists, psychiatrists, psychologists, acupuncturists, energy healers, chiropractors, Lyme disease specialists, and on and on.

We traveled to specialists in New York, Cleveland, Toledo, Minneapolis, Salt Lake City, San Francisco, and more. Spoiler alert: none of the doctors and therapists offered anything to significantly help Erica beyond partially managing her symptoms, which to be fair, was a lot better than nothing.

Finally, when she was age 17, we connected with a doctor who gave us what we are firmly convinced is an accurate diagnosis. Erica has dysautonomia, which means her autonomic nervous system doesn't function properly. The autonomic nervous system controls involuntary body functions like your heartbeat, breathing, and digestion. That explains why she has so many seemingly unrelated problems.

Unfortunately, there hasn't been much that the doctors have been able to do to improve her situation. It has been a heart-breaking journey for our family. We

Under the circumstances of Scenario B, at age 88, your child will still have $239,068 in sharp contrast to Scenario A where he or she would have $0.

attempt to control her symptoms—there are better days and worse days—but she has no real prospect of holding down a job.

I must mention that Erica, now age 28, is comfortable with sharing her/our story, and has given my wife and I her blessing to do so. She actually hopes that sharing our story will help provide financial security for other children with disabilities.

Acquiring Disability Status

After a grueling legal marathon with the Social Security Administration (SSA), we won our Social Security Disability Insurance (SSDI) case. That was a significant step in protecting her financial security.

Maintaining Disability Status

Navigating the definitions of a disabled and/or chronically ill beneficiary and qualifying for disability status with the SSA can be very difficult. Couple that with also having to prove disability status to qualify as an EDB under the SECURE Act (to allow for the lifetime stretch of the inherited retirement accounts), and you have a serious headache.

The IRS, however, is proposing regulations with a silver lining. And while they aren't officially the law of the land, we feel confident they will be adopted. In effect, they say that beneficiaries who have already been qualified as disabled by the Social Security Administration will also qualify as an EDB for the purposes of the SECURE Act.

So, if your child is already qualified to collect SSI or SSDI, you will not have to prove disability again beyond the required periodic updates.

This proposed regulation is a very big deal for us and if your beneficiary has already qualified as disabled for Social Security, it should be a big deal for you too. Though we won our SSDI case, we were not assured that this would be sufficient for our daughter to qualify as an EDB (allowing her to stretch the inher-

> **Beneficiaries with disabilities or chronic illnesses who have EDB status are one of the critical exceptions from the SECURE Act's mandatory 10-year disbursement rule for Inherited retirement accounts.**

ited IRA and Roth IRA that we will leave her) without having to jump through more hoops.

Now, with the IRS Proposed Regulations released in February 2022, we are quite confident that our daughter will be on the fast-track for the favorable EDB treatment once she inherits our retirement accounts.

Our Journey to Ensure Erica's Security:
SSDI, Roth IRA Conversions and Roth Contributions, and Appropriate Estate Planning and Administration Under the SECURE Act

The first proactive step was winning Erica's SSDI case, which will likely fast track her EDB status.

The second proactive thing we got right was optimizing our Roth IRA conversions and Roth contributions. Please note our accounting firm has four number-crunching CPAs who routinely do this optimization work as demonstrated in the detailed chapters on Roth IRA conversions in this book.

Our Roth IRA analysis is usually focused on optimizing conversions for the benefit of the client. For clients who have a child with a disability, the emphasis expands to optimizing Roth IRA conversions not only for the client, but also their disabled beneficiary.

Beneficiaries with disabilities or chronic illnesses who have EDB status are one of the critical exceptions from the SECURE Act's mandatory 10-year disbursement rule for Inherited retirement accounts. If the estate documents are also prepared optimally and if the estate is administered correctly, beneficiaries with a disability—or trusts for the benefit of a child with a disability—can treat an Inherited IRA or Roth IRA as any beneficiary could in 2019 (before the effective date of the SECURE Act), i.e., take advantage of *"stretching"* Inherited retirement assets over a lifetime.

Under the proposed regulations for the SECURE Act and assuming the appropriate planning and estate administration at our deaths, she will very likely qualify to enjoy a massive distribution deferral of our Inherited IRAs and Roth IRAs. This deferral, even without the Roth conversions would mean an extra $206,700 to her at age 86, again measured in today's dollars.

The Roth conversions will be worth $1,297,500 and the *'stretch'* feature by being considered an Eligible Designated Beneficiary (EDB) is worth approximately $600,000. The synergy of the Roth conversions and the inherited *"stretch status"* for our Inherited IRAs and Roth IRAs is where we got the approximately $1.9 million total savings in today's dollars with reasonable assumptions.

> **The Roth conversions will be worth $1,297,500 and the 'stretch' feature by being considered an Eligible Designated Beneficiary is worth approximately $600,000.**

The third proactive step was getting our estate planning right and putting in place measures to ensure optimal estate administration in response to the SECURE Act and the proposed IRS regulations.

While our projections for Erica do not include every variable of our financial life, the result is clear. Over the years we made a large Roth IRA conversion, have contributed to backdoor Roth IRAs, and since 2006, the assumptions for the calculation assumed I contributed all my 401(k) contributions to a Roth 401(k).

In fact, some years when my income was high, I contributed to a Traditional 401(k). But for the sake of the analysis, I am keeping it simple and assuming we only contributed to Roths and not Traditional retirement plans. The math used to make the projection can and has been reproduced by different number crunching CPAs in our office.

The most critical information to convey is the potential benefits for your child that result from getting the three things right—qualifying for SSI or SSDI and obtaining the formal status as disabled leading to EDB status, optimal Roth planning, and optimal estate planning and estate administration.

Your Gain, Uncle Sam's Loss

In this analysis, each dollar your child gains including interest and growth, is exactly equivalent to how much Uncle Sam loses. Basically, these strategies involve a massive wealth transfer from Uncle Sam to your beneficiary with a disability. To be fair, since I did include an investment rate of 6.5% and inflation of 3.5% on the IRAs and Roth IRAs, I assume the government would have earned

> Potential benefits for your child will result from getting three things right: qualifying for SSI or SSDI and obtaining the formal status as disabled leading to EDB status, optimal Roth planning, and optimal estate planning and estate administration.

the same amount to arrive at the total tax savings. Please note if we had used a higher investment rate, or if tax rates increase in the future, the benefits to the child would be much bigger.

Qualifying for SSI or SSDI: The Golden Ticket of SSI or SSDI Approval

Let's take a slight breather from the numbers and discuss qualifying for SSI or SSDI. Getting your child qualified as disabled by the Social Security Administration can be a crucial first step in ensuring they will be able to take full advantage of the *"stretch IRA"* as an EDB. Unfortunately, navigating that bureaucracy—as my wife and I discovered—is much harder than it should be.

My colleague, Deborah McFadden, is an internationally known expert in the disability arena. She has special expertise in getting children approved for SSI and SSDI and helping individuals and families access valuable benefits that improve their lives. She is also the mother of wheelchair racing champion, Tatyana McFadden, winner of 20 paralympic medals. *The following information is written by Debbie.*

As this chapter emphasizes, taking advantage of favorable payment options for Inherited IRAs is a huge benefit of winning approval through the Social Security Administration (SSA) for SSI or SSDI. But there are many other financial benefits that your child will also be eligible for once they get that Golden Ticket.

Besides monthly SSI or SSDI payments for life, your child will also be eligible for Vocational Rehab assistance, which can pay for college or even graduate school. They're eligible for Medicaid or Medicare and other medical benefits. Your kids can stay on your insurance after age 26 if they're disabled. Personal care attendants, SNAP benefits, and even respite care for parents are also available, among many other benefits that will help your child live their best life.

When your child is approved for SSI or SSDI, they get significant benefits in the short term and the long term. Your child doesn't need to use all these benefits, but isn't it reassuring that the benefits are available if he or she needs them?

> **Each dollar your child gains including interest and growth, is exactly equivalent to how much Uncle Sam loses. Basically, these strategies involve a massive wealth transfer from Uncle Sam to your beneficiary with a disability.**

Many (like Jim's daughter, Erica) get denied the first time. But this shouldn't happen if you know how to present your application. I've been helping families get approved for SSI or SSDI for years.

The McFaddens' Story

I have two disabled daughters who are also elite athletes. Tatyana was born with spina bifida and is one of the fastest wheelchair racers in the world. If she wins two more medals at the Paris Paralympic Games, she'll be the most decorated athlete ever. She's been winning medals in the Paralympic Games since she was 15. Hannah is an amputee who was born with a severe leg deformity. She's ranked third in the world in rock climbing. She also competed alongside her sister as a wheelchair racer at the London Paralympic Games in 2012.

I was able to get both of my daughters approved for SSI. Vocational Rehab funds paid for college for both, including master's degrees. For some families, this can be worth almost a quarter of a million dollars. I quit counting after I helped families secure $44 million in total benefits.

Distinctions Between SSI and SSDI

SSI: SSI is for people who don't have a sufficient work history to claim benefits on their own. It's a poverty program. For SSI, your child cannot have more than $2,000 in assets and their income is strictly limited. But if you apply after your child turns 18, SSA no longer counts your income or your assets when they evaluate his or her application.

SSDI: SSDI is for people who have worked at least 10 quarters (for the SSA a quarter equals 13 weeks) or who have a parent who has retired, is deceased, or is disabled and receiving disability benefits.

SSDI has no asset limits, but your child will still be subject to strict income limits if they work. In addition, if your child is claiming benefits on your work record, your child's disability must have begun before age 22. SSDI benefits are

> When your child is approved for SSI or SSDI, they can get significant benefits in the short term and the long term...But if you don't speak the right language, they won't get SSI and SSDI approval and they won't get benefits.

often higher than SSI. That's why I recommend getting your child on SSI while you are working, then switching to SSDI when you retire. The approval process for both programs is the same. The difference is which benefits your child qualifies for, based on your specific family situation.

The Three Keys to Cementing SSI and SSDI Eligibility: Initially and for the Long-Term

In my work with all kinds of families and disabled individuals, I've discovered three keys for qualifying for SSI or SSDI and for remaining eligible.

1. Pay Close Attention to Your Language:

The defining language of SSI and SSDI approval is *"I CAN'T."* If you don't speak the right language, you don't get the benefits. When applying for SSI, the emphasis must be on all the things your child can't do without some type of accommodation.

For example, if I asked Hannah if she could climb a flight of stairs, she'd say, *"Yes, of course, I can."* She can either hop up on one leg or use her prosthetic leg. But that is not the answer that will advance your application. You must be very cautious to not tout accomplishments.

You must describe your child's abilities in stark contrast to the abilities of someone living without a disability—what SSI and SSDI consider the norm. When applying for SSI or SSDI, remember to focus on what your child can't do, compared to the norm. You have to wear the *"I CAN'T"* hat.

It's true my daughters are both able to do what they want as long as they have the proper accommodations. They travel around the world and compete in elite athletic events. But compared to the norm, they can't.

SSI is for permanent disabilities. They will never get better. Tatyana's spine will never be normal. Hannah's leg is not growing back. This is not for someone who was in a car accident, but after six weeks or six months in a

The emphasis must be on all the things your child cannot do without some type of accommodation...You must describe your child's abilities in stark contrast to the abilities of someone living without a disability.

body cast and rehab, they will recover. This is also not for someone whose disability is so mild that no one at the child's school is even aware of any problems.

The bottom line is that your child is dependent. He or she cannot do things without help or accommodation.

I call SSI and SSDI *"the crippled, lame and infirm law."* This law was written back in the 1930s. Back then, if you were born with spina bifida, as Tatyana was, you would be in an institution for the rest of your life. Someone would need to take care of you.

Of course, that's not the way it is now. The original laws governing SSI and SSDI didn't anticipate the many advances in accommodations we have today, many of which came about as part of the 1990 Americans with Disabilities Act. I happen to know a bit about the 1990 ADA as I am one of the original 12 authors of the Act, and I was a United States Commissioner of Disabilities.

I am also disabled myself. In college, I was paralyzed after a Guillain-Barré syndrome infection. I have first-hand experience with the challenges of being disabled. Fortunately for me, with a lot of work over 12 years, I regained the ability to walk again.

2. *Support Your Application with Letters from Doctors—Language is Again Key:*

An essential part of your SSI application is letters from doctors. The mistake many doctors make is that these letters don't speak the right language (see above). They don't emphasize the *CAN'T* enough. These letters need to emphasize what your child can't do, not what they have been able to achieve through accommodations. And they need to emphasize that there is no hope for improvement from this disability.

If I use my daughter Tatyana as an example, she needs a shower with grab bars, a shower chair, and an accessible shower handle. If she has those things, she can manage quite well. But for SSI purposes, compared to the norm, she can't shower on her own.

Tatyana lives on her own and cooks for herself, but she needs a special kitchen to do that. If I asked Tatyana to help me with Thanksgiving dinner and asked her to carry the 25-pound turkey on my grandmother's antique China serving platter with hot gravy all around it, she can't do that.

Because she has spina bifida, for SSI purposes, she can't cook for herself compared to the norm.

As another example, what if I asked my daughter, Hannah, to help me with laundry? If I lived in a four-story townhouse and asked her to bring the laundry from the third floor to the basement, she wouldn't be able to do that.

For SSI, they're not asking about how your child manages to do things. They're asking if your child can do it based on the norm. Remember, SSI is the *"crippled, lame, and infirm law,"* which means that you can't function independently without accommodations compared to the norm. The definitions for eligibility were written a long time ago. It's the standard of the 1930s which meant your child would be in an institution and would need people to take care of him or her.

These letters from the doctors should always point out the activities of daily living that your child cannot do. Cooking, personal care, shopping, laundry, eating, paying bills—all the activities that most people do without even thinking about it. I give families the following outline to give to their doctors for their letters.

- The name of the disability.

- Age of onset.

- This is a permanent disability with no chance for improvement.

- Specifics on the impact of the disability on the Activities of Daily Living (ADL).

- Dates of first and most recent visits.

These letters can't brag about how your child is playing sports or how they're getting top grades in school or how they manage to help around the house. If your child's doctor focuses on how well your child is doing despite their disability, you run a high risk of your application being denied.

My goal with these letters is to make mom cry. Remember that the objective is to win that Golden Ticket, which will open doors for your child for the rest of his or her life.

This is a complete mindset shift for most parents because you have most likely encouraged your child to do as many things as they possibly can. You've probably told your child—as I did with Tatyana and Hannah—*you*

> **These letters can't brag about what your child can accomplish... If your child's doctor focuses on how well your child is doing despite their disability, you run a high risk of your application being denied.**

can do it. You've told them to get up if they fall down or to try again if they fail. And you've most likely found accommodations for your child that help them do as much as they can, and to stay comfortable. Like my daughter, Hannah, who sleeps with several different pillows to keep her little stump of a leg comfortable. But that's not normal for a person without a disability.

It can be emotionally difficult for parents to view their children through the *"I CAN'T"* lens that SSA uses. But you must make a conscious shift in how you represent your child's abilities if you want a successful application and get that Golden Ticket. You have to put on your emotional armor and do what it takes to get these letters.

Now I must mention that since my daughters are both working as professional athletes, they're not on SSI now. But that Golden Ticket helped them get where they are now.

Now, SSA will tell you that these letters are not needed because they will be contacting the doctors themselves. Don't take the easy way out. You want to paint a full picture of why your child deserves these benefits. You're also training the doctor about how they need to communicate about your child when they are contacted by SSA.

3. *Adhere to Asset Limits to Remain Eligible for SSI:*

Remember that SSI is a poverty program. It's not designed to make you or your child wealthy. There are income limits and limits on the assets your child has access to. Your child can't have more than $2,000 in assets. SSDI, on the other hand, has no such limits on assets.

Depending on your family situation, it might make sense to apply for SSI when your child is an infant. But most families make too much money or have too much money in the bank to qualify. That's why I recommend waiting until the month after they turn 18 to apply.

It can be emotionally difficult for parents to view their children through the *"I CAN'T"* lens SSA uses. But you must make a conscious shift in how you represent your child's abilities if you want a successful application and get that Golden Ticket.

Alternatively, your child might be eligible for SSDI, which doesn't have the limits on assets. If your child worked enough before they became disabled, your child will get SSDI based on their work history. However, if a parent has died or retired or is also disabled, your child will get SSDI based on the work history of the parent.

If your child is claiming SSDI benefits on a parent's work history, the onset of the disability must be prior to age 22. SSI and SSDI are the same program. That is how Jim's daughter, Erica, qualified for SSDI benefits. SSI and SSDI are still the Golden Ticket. It just depends on how your child qualifies.

Once your child is approved for SSI, your child gets everything, and he or she will stay on SSI for the rest of his or her life, until he or she has a change in qualifying circumstances. Those qualifying circumstances include:

• Getting married.

• Winning the lottery.

• Inheriting money (unless it's in a Special Needs Trust).

• Getting a job and earning money.

To be eligible and remain eligible for SSI, your child can't have ready access to more than $2,000 in assets. In practical terms, that means your child needs to spend almost all of their monthly benefit payment on living expenses.

Know The Rules and Work with Them Honestly

You always want to tell the truth to SSA, but that truth must be framed within the SSA's normative standards. This is why I apply the month after a kid turns age 18. By Social Security's definition, they're independent adults the month after they turn 18. Your income and assets no longer disqualify your child from eligibility for SSI. You can't start the process—not even requesting an appointment—until your child is 18 or they will treat the entire application as that of a dependent child, even if they're 18 when it's submitted.

No Joint Bank Accounts

Your child cannot have a joint bank account with a parent. If your child still has the joint bank account you opened with them as a minor, SSA will take your salary and your assets into account. You can't just ask the bank to take your name off the account when your child turns age 18. Social Security will look at the prior six months' history of any bank account they have when they apply. If they find a bank account with your name on it, it's an automatic disqualification. You must close your child's minor's bank account and open a new one when they turn age18.

The only exception to this rule is if your child has significant cognitive issues and cannot manage a bank account on their own. In that situation, a parent can be a representative payee on that bank account.

Keeping Your Child's Assets Under $2,000

Once your child is approved for SSI, he or she will start receiving benefits monthly. Your child can use those benefits to pay for their living expenses. If your child lives with you, you can charge your child up to $300 per month for rent and utilities. You can also charge your child for many other living expenses, such as their cell phone bill, transportation, or part of the grocery bill. I give my clients guidelines for calculating those monthly bills, so you don't run afoul of the SSA's picky rules.

When your child writes a check to you, and you cash it, it's now your money. You can do what you want with it. Your child can't ask you to buy her a car with *"her money."* It's your money. Remember, SSI is a poverty program.

You can also open an ABLE account for your child. As Jim and Julieanne explain below, ABLE accounts don't count against the $2,000 limit, provided the balance remains below $100,000.

What About Trusts?

The key with trusts is that your child cannot have ready access to the funds. A Special Needs Trust will allow you to accumulate funds for your child without counting against the $2,000 limit. Jim and Julieanne go into more detail below, but the key is that a Special Needs Trust must be set up and administered carefully so that it does not jeopardize eligibility for SSI.

What About Modified Vehicles, Special Wheelchairs, or Other Devices?

These don't count towards their assets. Technically, your child can have a car in his or her name, but in most cases, the vehicle is purchased by the parents. So, from the perspective of SSA, your child has the use of a vehicle that you purchased for them.

What Happens If Your Child Gets a Job?

If your child starts work and starts earning over the SSI income limit—as Tatyana and Hannah do as professional athletes—you are obligated to notify Social Security right away about the change in circumstances. It will take about four months for benefit payments to stop. When they do catch up with you, you must pay back the benefits you received, so make sure you don't spend it.

Your child's Medicaid or Medicare benefits will continue as long as your child has a disability that prevents him or her from working. If your child starts working, SSI has certain incentives to help him enter or re-enter the workforce. Monthly income plus Medicaid or Medicare benefits will continue for a finite period of time. If your child goes back to work but finds that it's really not feasible and that there is no good way to make the needed modifications so that they can earn a living, their full benefits can be reinstated if it's been less than five years. Your child will start receiving benefits right away while SSA reviews the case.

For example, I know a man with quadriplegia who went to law school. He has a brilliant mind, but he needs so much assistance to prevent pressure sores from his wheelchair and to use a bathroom that working in a law office is not possible.

What Is the Process for Applying for SSI/SSDI?

If you look on the Social Security Administration's website, they'll ask you to fill out a form online because they say it will be faster. In reality, it's not faster. It's just easier for them. Instead, I get on the phone with the young adult and call for an appointment. When the appointment comes up, I'm also on the phone with the young adult. I try to start the process on the first or second day of the month after the child turns age 18 so that benefits start as soon as possible.

During the second call, the SSA representative will collect basic information, including your child's name, date of birth and Social Security number. They will also ask about doctors, bank accounts, assets (including trusts, vehicles, property, and life insurance), and your child's work history. They'll also ask about household expenses like rent, food, and utilities and about other household members. SSA will send form letters to your child's doctors and medical facilities asking about the disability. In addition to those form letters, make sure your doctors also write those letters I described above. Those really are key to approval.

Once SSA has all the materials, they review your child's applications. It can take between eight and 13 months to approve. Many of the people I work with are approved in three months. My fastest approval was just three days, and my longest approval was eight months. Benefits will be calculated as starting with the date of the initial application. However, with the backlog from Covid, approval may take longer.

What Happens if Your Application is Denied?

If your application is even just a bit outside of SSA's parameters for acceptance, it will be denied. That means, if you make even a tiny mistake, you risk your child being denied. But you can appeal the decision. You can do this on your own, but your best bet is to hire an attorney, as Jim and his wife did. I don't help with the appeals process, but someone like Julieanne can help you out—bear in mind that can be expensive, perhaps $10,000 or more.

The least expensive—and fastest—option is to hire someone like me to help with the initial application. Because I've been doing this for years, I know how to get kids approved.

Now that we have covered the challenges and constraints for getting and maintaining SSI/SSDI status, we can bring our focus back to financial planning.

The Critical Role Roth IRAs and Roth Conversions Play in Our Story

We return now to numbers and to Jim: Our Roth story begins in 1997 when the mechanisms for Roth IRA conversions were just in the proposal stage. When the Roth was first introduced in 1998, I knew this would be huge for clients with IRAs and retirement plans. In May 1998, *The Tax Adviser*, the peer-reviewed journal of the tax division of the American Institute of CPAs published my article—the first on Roth IRA conversions—and it won article of the year.

But to go back a bit, on February 16, 1998, right at the beginning of tax season, my office suffered a devastating fire. At the time, my wife and I had combined Traditional IRAs and 401(k)s of $249,000. I wanted to convert all of it to a Roth IRA. My wife, Cindy, who has a master's degree in electrical engineering from Carnegie Mellon and excellent critical thinking skills, strongly resisted because she didn't want to pay the taxes on the conversion.

Then, we *"ran the numbers"*—my firm's specialty—using the same methodology that we used for the peer-reviewed article and to some extent we still use today. After seeing convincing proof that our family would be much better off by hundreds of thousands of dollars in the long run, we went ahead with the conversion. Also, to be fair, this was before we knew Erica had a disability. On the other hand, back then, children without disabilities were able to *"stretch"* Inherited IRAs and Roth IRAs over their lifetime, and we always intended the Roth to be for Erica unless we got desperate.

Figures 13.1 and 13.2 demonstrate the impact of making a series of Roth conversions, contributing the maximum to your Roth 401(k) account, making *"back door"* Roth conversions (while they are still permitted), and having your disabled child qualify as an EDB, and getting the rest of his or her estate planning right to qualify for the Inherited *"stretch IRA"* or *"stretch Roth IRA."*

Your Benefits from Getting the Roth Right

What do Figures 13.1 and 13.2 tell us and what does this mean for you and your child with a disability? First of all, it means you will be able to spend more money in your lifetime and still provide for your child with a disability. The benefits of the Roth conversion and contributions to you, not including the benefit to your child, at least consistent with my assumptions in my case, will be roughly $491,829 in today's dollars which was an intermediate step to the calculation to determine how much Erica would benefit.

To be fair, it is also easy to convert too much money to a Roth. Without the benefit of knowing how to make multi-generation projections, it is easy to get far less than optimal conversions. Jen Hall, one of our number crunching CPAs came into my office today after testing a million-dollar conversion in year one, two $500,000 conversions in years one and two, and ten $100,000 conversions in years one through ten.

In this client's case, the million-dollar conversion yielded reasonable results for the client, and enormous benefits for their disabled child. But, with different facts, multiple Roth conversions over a series of years often produces the best results for both the client and child. The other factor is some people do not want to write a huge check to the IRS. Even if the projections show that writing a big check is optimal, they prefer doing a series of conversions over time.

For the strategy to work, it has to pass the math test and the stomach test. One of the ideas of this type of planning is to not worry at night. If writing a whopper check for the conversion is going to keep you up worrying, that is a significant factor. Fortunately, in many cases, our recommendations are to do a series of conversions over time, again depending on the individual circumstances. Doing a series of Roth conversions tend to pass the stomach test much better than one huge conversion.

This chapter doesn't cover the important nuances of Roth conversions and Medicare Part B premiums and IRMAA calculations that are covered in Chapter 16. It also doesn't cover the peculiarities of accessing TIAA accumulations, which are covered in Chapters 8 and 9.

At a minimum, if you choose to annuitize your accumulations, you will most likely want to choose an option that will provide lifetime income for your child with a disability. Check the options available for your plan and consider working with an advisor who is familiar with both TIAA accounts and the special needs of children with disabilities. Depending on your plan, you may be able to convert a portion of your account to a Roth. In any case, choosing the best option for your situation may require working with someone who can *"run the numbers,"* as we do at our accounting firm.

The financial benefits from the conversion(s) will allow more money for caregivers for your child while you are alive, and that might provide you with more flexibility. For us, it has meant that we can afford certain services that allow Erica to live outside our home with her boyfriend. It also means we can afford to pay her other expenses so she can have a good life living outside of our home. Cindy still spends a lot of her day taking care of Erica's needs from a distance, and she visits Erica fairly frequently. Much of that time is care-related, not just family vacation time.

In addition to a lot more money that we can afford for her current care, we are taking advantage of the savings on taxes to enhance our life. We bought a place in Tucson to spend our winters and now, I am a working snowbird. You may be able to imagine things that would improve the quality of your life if you had to pay far less in taxes. Because we got the Roth IRA and Roth IRA conversions strategies right, we can enjoy additional spending and not worry that we will be jeopardizing Erica's future.

Perhaps you could enjoy some of these benefits too, all because of optimizing Roth conversions and if you are still working, investing in Roth 401(k)s instead of the Traditional 401(k)s.

Let me also mention the problem of whether to convert and how much and when to do a Roth conversion isn't really a matter of opinion. It is a matter of math. We believe in peer-reviewed science and math. One of the reasons we publish in peer-reviewed CPA and legal journals is to give readers the comfort that we did the math, and the peer-reviewers checked it and found it to be accurate. You can disagree with our assumptions. In addition, I will concede we are making projections with a lot of unknown variables, like future tax laws and future tax rates.

The stomach test—whether you can stand writing that big check to the IRS—is also important.

That said, our approach is to make reasonable conservative assumptions and do the math and show the client the result of the different options. We can also do the math using the client's assumptions. But again, the main point of this paragraph is that Roth analysis is a matter of math, not opinion.

The benefit that is hardest to quantify is the greater peace of mind you will experience from acting on the steps we advocate. Imagine letting go of the fear that your child will run out of money after you and your spouse are gone. These steps are a game changer! Truthfully, my wife and I still have worries about what will happen to Erica after we are gone—but running out of money is no longer one of them.

Benefits to Your Child

After you are gone, instead of running out of money, your child could enjoy enormous financial benefits just from the strategies mentioned here. Imagine your child being able to afford private social workers, nurses, a concierge medicine doctor, healthy organic meals specifically designed for her condition delivered to her door, out-of-network specialists, alternative treatments, medicines, and modalities that aren't covered by insurance, good housing, personal transportation services, mental health services that may not accept insurance, etc.

Depending on circumstances, your child or someone looking after your child will be able to prioritize what would serve them best. If your child already lives

> **Imagine letting go of the fear that your child will run out of money after you and your spouse are gone.**

or will eventually live in some type of group home, your child will be able to easily afford the most desirable housing, where he or she will be happiest.

If you know parents who have IRAs or other retirement plans and who have a child or grandchild with a disability, please let them know about this book, or better yet, buy it for them and tell them to read this chapter. You could also tell them they can download a report similar to this chapter at **https://Disabled ChildPlanning.com**. You would be doing them and their child an enormous service by recommending this report to them.

The Challenge of Coordinating All of the Moving Pieces for the Best Result

To make sure that all the pieces are correctly aligned, I think it is prudent to attempt to understand the important principles. *I advise you to do the following:*

- You will likely need a specialist expert to get your child formally qualified as disabled, and ultimately as an EDB.

- Work with pro-active CPAs or financial advisors who really understand and appreciate Roth IRA conversions and the benefits of the *"stretch IRA."* They should also be able to *"run the numbers"* to quantify the results of different Roth conversion amounts as well as integrating many other strategies for you and your child. There are wonderful software programs available today, but you still need a highly skilled *"number cruncher"* to do the kind of analysis I think should be done.

  I have had great success with training razor sharp CPAs to do this work, though it is a long training process. Trying to train a financial advisor or an attorney without a deep tax knowledge to do these calculations seems improbable. We also think the number cruncher should test their conclusions by preparing pro-forma tax returns comparing different conversion and other strategies.

- You will also need an estate attorney who knows how to draft and plan for a child with a disability to ensure your child doesn't lose their EDB status due to an improperly drafted estate plan.

  This attorney must have the specialized legal skills and knowledge that are required to get all the terms of the trust exactly right, assuming a trust is appropriate. You may need a Special Needs Trust and if so, the trust must be drafted to ensure that the beneficiary will receive all the tax benefits, and if necessary, that the proceeds will not jeopardize your beneficiary's

A Special Needs Trust must be drafted to ensure that a beneficiary will receive all possible tax benefits, and if necessary, that those proceeds will not jeopardize the beneficiary's eligibility for any kind of future government assistance.

eligibility for any kind of government assistance that the beneficiary may receive in the future.

- In addition, you must make sure the executor or person handling the estate either understands these concepts or at least plans to employ advisors and attorneys who understand these concepts and who understand how critical it is to get the estate administration right after your and your spouse's death.

If all the pieces come together correctly, qualified beneficiaries with disabilities will meet the standards to use the old *"stretch IRA rules,"* which, as shown above, are life changing.

The Burden of Proving Disability

The government administrative process puts a huge burden on the family to prove the need for SSI, SSDI, or Medicare. And if you haven't gone through the process of formally qualifying your beneficiary with a disability with the SSA, the law's definitions of who qualifies as an Eligible Designated Beneficiary (EDB) under the SECURE Act, is also quite narrow. Caring for individuals with a disability is already a financial and emotional burden and the medical system is already straining.

If you are the parent of a disabled child, please make sure you have appropriate experts working for your and your child's benefit.

Why Appropriate Estate Planning is So Critical

The contrast between the treatment of Inherited IRAs under the SECURE Act and the old law is bad enough for a beneficiary without a disability. Because their disabilities often preclude them from entering or remaining in the workforce, many beneficiaries with disabilities severe enough to qualify for the SECURE Act exemption are far more dependent upon inherited monies to finance their basic living expenses than the average recipient of an Inherited IRA might be. It is challenging enough to live with a disability, but to suffer that and be broke is tragic.

And it is particularly devastating to know that there will be potentially millions of Americans with disabilities who will live in poverty whose long-term financial security could have been insured if their parents/grandparents/loved ones had only known about and used the appropriate retirement and estate planning tools. Below we address some of the many technicalities involved in getting things right.

Our Challenges Gaining Social Security Disability Insurance (SSDI)

In our own case, our daughter was first turned down for benefits and she did not qualify for Medicare. With only weeks remaining for our appeal, our attorney fired us because she didn't think she could win the case. Upon a close examination of the record of the first case, my wife noticed glaring errors and omissions. Luckily, we got another attorney on short notice for the appeal.

My wife compiled a huge binder of accurate and detailed documentation and exhaustively reviewed the work of the first attorney. With the help of that second attorney, we did eventually win the case on appeal.

Because of this immense effort and our other steps, Erica is assured of a much better life with no money worries. She will have the funds to pay for high quality housing, concierge medical care, private nurses, social workers, specialists, treatment modalities not covered by insurance, and healthy food. In short, she will be financially cared for just as well after our deaths as she is while we are still alive.

Advice from Julieanne E. Steinbacher, Esq, CELA, LLM in Estate and Elder Law:

Families can apply for SSDI themselves. Attorneys only typically get involved in an appeal if someone is denied. The application will require the specific times and dates for appointments, discharge documents, and medical documents.

If you do not have it, medical information is available through patient portals. School records are often purged, so if you have a child with a disability, it is important to ask for a copy of every document provided to or by the school.

Social Security Means-Testing *(Back to Jim)*

A quick note about Social Security assistance for your child with a disability. Supplemental Security Income (SSI) is means-tested, but Social Security Disability Insurance (SSDI) is not means-tested. For example, to receive SSI, there are limits on both the child's income and their assets. To qualify for SSDI, the child could have both high income and high assets.

Once one of the parents of the child is receiving Social Security retirement (or disability) benefits, or for a deceased parent (if that parent had worked enough quarters to qualify for Social Security benefits), the *"adult child"* with a disability can claim SSDI based upon that parent's work history. In order to qualify, the adult child's disability must have begun before age 22. It does not matter that your child does not have any work history. Our daughter qualified under SSDI so she can have unlimited assets in her name and/or unlimited income in her name and/or in a trust for her benefit.

New Definitions Used to Qualify as an EDB

Frankly, I think the definitions that the IRS uses to determine who is disabled are far too limited and attorneys who work in this area will tell you benefits are often denied for deserving beneficiaries. Parents of a child with a disability have enough challenges in their lives that they should not have to worry about meeting the IRS's and the administrative judge's overly strict view of who qualifies as having a disability. Let's look at some of the definitions.

Disabled Beneficiary

A disabled beneficiary is defined in Code Section 72(m)(7):

"For purposes of this section, an individual shall be considered to be disabled if he is unable to engage in any substantial gainful activity by reason of any medically determinable physical or mental impairment which can be expected to result in death or to be of long continued and indefinite duration. An individual shall not be considered to be disabled unless he furnishes proof of the existence thereof in such form and manner as the Secretary may require."

This definition is quite limited. The intended beneficiary must have substantial health challenges which result in a limited capacity for earning a living. However, if the beneficiary can engage in *"any substantial gainful activity,"* even if very limited, that person will not qualify as an EDB and will not be eligible for the exception to the 10-year rule.

Partial disability doesn't count, nor does a disability that prevents the heir from working in a previous line of occupation but does not preclude some other type of gainful employment. We know of a parent whose son had low functioning Down Syndrome who was denied benefits because with substantial support, he could work bagging groceries.

> **If you have a beneficiary with a disability and you would like
> your child to enjoy the benefits of deferring your IRA over
> their lifetime, it would be prudent to establish proof of their
> disability while you are still alive and the sooner the better.**

The other issue IRA owners should worry about is that the beneficiary with a disability may not be inclined or able to prove their disability without your help. That is a frequent problem when it comes to proving disability for other benefits like SSDI. If you have a beneficiary with a disability and you would like your child to enjoy the benefits of deferring your IRA over their lifetime, it would be prudent to establish proof of their disability while you are still alive and the sooner the better.

In our case, our daughter, while bright, could never have assembled the exhaustive documentation her mother assembled to prove her disability—not to mention the grueling work it entailed. I believe that effort made the difference between winning and losing our case. My wife took on that Herculean task.

In the feedback we received from the judge, some of the most important information we presented were the personal stories from family and friends that described the real-life impact of her disability and the questionnaires completed by her medical providers.

This information provided the real-life evidence of her disability and ended up being most persuasive in helping win our case. It is important to mention that this sort of information gathering should continue, particularly from regular doctor visits, during the course of the disabled child's life so that disability can be confirmed during the periodic reviews by Social Security.

Chronically Ill Beneficiary

A chronically ill heir who will receive the same tax benefits as a disabled beneficiary is defined in Code Section 7702B(c)(2) with certain modifications. This Code Section provides:

"(A) In General—The term 'chronically ill individual' means any individual who has been certified by a licensed health care practitioner as—(i) being unable to perform (without substantial assistance from another individual) at least two activities of daily living for a period of at least 90 days due to a loss

of functional capacity, (ii) having a level of disability similar (as determined under regulations prescribed by the Secretary in consultation with the Secretary of Health and Human Services) to the level of disability described in clause (i), or (iii) requiring substantial supervision to protect such individual from threats to health and safety due to severe cognitive impairment.

Such term shall not include any individual otherwise meeting the requirements of the preceding sentence unless within the preceding 12-month period a licensed health care practitioner has certified that such individual meets such requirements. (B) Activities of daily living for purposes of subparagraph (A), each of the following is an activity of daily living: (i) Eating (ii) Toileting (iii) Transferring (iv) Bathing (v) Dressing (vi) Continence."

I would offer the same caution that I mentioned in the previous section on beneficiaries with disabilities. I think it is prudent for you to establish proof of your beneficiary's chronic illness while you are still alive. As Martin Shenkman wrote in *Forbes* (**https://www.forbes.com/sites/martinshenkman/2020/12/29/ secure-act**):

"The above definition suffers from the same overly restrictive terms as the definition of 'disabled' above. Many intended heirs are living with challenges that may limit or even prevent gainful employment, but they are not so severely incapacitated as to meet the requirements of chronically ill according to the above definition. Yet, these same people who need the protections of a trust, and who may desperately need the economic benefits from the plan assets to be bequeathed, will be forced to have the plan balance distributed in 10-years and lose the continued tax deferred growth, etc."

Any IRA owner planning on an heir meeting the requirements of being *"disabled"* or *"chronically ill"* to qualify as an EDB under the SECURE Act should carefully evaluate the stringent requirements involved.

The Three Critical Steps to Qualify for the EDB Ten-Year Exception

What must happen under the new law for a beneficiary with a disability or chronic illness to qualify for the exception to the 10-year acceleration of income taxes?

- First, you must have a favorable finding of the beneficiary being considered disabled or chronically ill.

- Second, you must have appropriate estate planning and more specifically, you must have the correct language for assigning the beneficiary of your

IRA and retirement plan. In addition, it may be prudent to have a Special Needs Trust, but even then, that trust must have the four conditions to qualify for the Inherited *"stretch IRA"* status.

- Third, you must have appropriate estate administration after your and your spouse's death.

A Critical Extra Step for Ensuring Qualification as EDB

There is pending legislation that requires documentation supporting the *"disabled"* or *"chronically ill"* diagnosis of the beneficiary be submitted to the IRA custodian by a certain date. Under the current proposal, the documentation supporting the diagnosis of a disability or chronic illness must be provided to the custodian of the account, no later than October 31 of the calendar year following the calendar year of the IRA owner's or employee's death.

This means if your disabled child or a trust for the benefit of your child is the beneficiary of your IRA and you die on July 1, 2022, the IRA custodian must be provided with documentation supporting the disability of your disabled beneficiary no later than October 31, 2023.

If this legislation passes and becomes law and you can do so, we recommend you provide the documentation for your disabled or chronically ill beneficiary to the custodian while you are still alive. If the custodian can notate your account file or minimally if you have a plan in place to obtain and produce this information after you pass away, you are making certain the important deadline is not missed.

The documentation and the timing of providing the documentation is very important and if not done properly, the lifetime stretch could be eliminated, and your disabled beneficiary would be limited to the 10-year rule. This means all of the painstaking efforts you took to provide for your child with a disability or chronic illness, could go up in smoke if the documentation is presented too late.

Additional Things to Consider When Planning for an Adult Child Who Has a Disability

Beyond the strategic IRA planning considerations for children with disabilities, it is important for parents to have an overall understanding for how best to guide their disabled child through the labyrinth of lifetime planning considerations. My colleague, Julie E. Steinbacher, provides both practical considerations for parents who are assisting their adult child with a disability, as well as recommendations for employing an attorney to help them successfully navigate these waters. *The following is from Julieanne E. Steinbacher, Esq, CELA, LLM in Estate and Elder Law:*

In most states, a child is considered an adult once they reach the age of 18. At this time, they are their own legal person. It doesn't matter if they have a severe disability or what type of disability it is. The law presumes they are competent/capacitated until proven in court that they are not.

If you as parents have not planned ahead, you will no longer have the right to make decisions for your child with a disability. This includes both medical and financial decisions. You cannot continue to sign documents or make banking decisions without the legal authority to do so, thus planning becomes very important. You also may not have access to health care information or be able to make decisions.

A few of the things to keep in mind when planning for your child with disabilities include:

1. Consider whether your child will have sufficient resources to financially support themselves in the future.

2. Evaluate the ability of any support services and the cost of those services or needed residential care.

3. Consider whether life insurance could be a valuable resource to pay for your child's financial needs when you are no longer around. See Chapter 26 for ideas on how to use life insurance as an estate planning tool.

4. Re-examine any trusts that you previously put in place to verify that the provisions are still appropriate for yourself and for your child.

5. Visit a special needs planning attorney to help you determine what your child's financial and legal needs will be when you are no longer with them.

6. Determine whether a guardianship will be necessary or whether alternatives to a guardianship are available.

Planning for the Care of Your Child After Your Death

One of the most important considerations as you age is preparing your child who has a disability for the fact that one day you will die. The following are important steps that should be considered at this time to protect your child in the future:

1. Name in appropriate documents who should be the successor trustee or guardian to avoid a time where there is no one to make decisions for your

child if you should suffer a sudden illness or die unexpectedly. Plan now for the possibility that you will have an unexpected change in your health. This will avoid anxiety for your child and will make sure that someone else has the authority to step in, if necessary.

2. Have a plan for succession in case those who have agreed to take over when you can no longer serve as the advocate for your loved one. Name these successor(s) in your legal documents.

3. Review and update your legal documents every three to five years or anytime there is a significant life or health change.

4. Determine a plan for your child's future, such as where he or she will live and whether he or she will be able to continue with his or her routine if you are not around.

5. Prepare a *"summary of our wishes"* document to guide the trustee, guardian, family, and caregivers. A template of the worksheet used by Steinbacher, Goodall and Yurchak can be found at **https://DisabledChildPlanning. com**. It covers such things as the family history, medical history, housing, education, religion, values, recreation, daily routine, likes, dislikes, and triggers for your child's various emotions or behaviors.

6. Come up with a plan to address how your assets will be distributed once you pass away. Determine whether your child with a disability will receive an inheritance and how it will affect their public benefits. Think about what share of your estate will be inherited by your child who has a disability and whether this could cause problems among your other children.

What You Need to Know Before Meeting with an Attorney

Here is the preparation I recommend for your meeting with a special needs attorney. Sit down and organize yourself and make a list of the following:

1. What type of government benefits is the child receiving or will the child receive and how much?

2. What other income is available to the child?

3. What is the family's current financial situation?

4. Is the child mentally competent/capacitated?

5. Is the child already under a guardianship/conservatorship and what are the details of this arrangement?

6. What is the child's condition? Is it stable or worsening? Are they more likely to need long-term care than the average person?

7. What type of accommodations need to be in place for the child?

8. What is the child's daily routine?

9. Is the child planning to receive SSI, SSDI, or long-term disability?

10. What are the current sources of support?

11. How is your health? Is long-term care imminent?

12. What are the family dynamics? Who is available for support in the long term?

13. What medicines is the child receiving? Who are their doctors?

14. Have you, the parent, completed your own specialized estate planning centered around your child with a disability?

A discussion about special needs planning is often about planning for multiple generations—you, the parent, the child with a disability, and other children or grandchildren. Any plan must also address the potential for being taken advantage of, especially since those with disabilities are a highly vulnerable population. Honest conversations about the availability and willingness of family members to provide support and/or provide oversight is essential.

Learning the Legal Language

Where do I start? What should I do? These are the questions for which you should seek advice and direction from professionals who are experienced in these types of situations. Your first steps in planning for your child who has a disability may be with a knowledgeable trusted financial advisor and with an attorney who practices in the area of special needs planning.

Special needs planning for an adult child with a disability is more than just putting a trust in place. It's not just about the documents. There is a lot of judgment involved in these situations.

In addition, the estate attorney must be prepared for considerable hand holding throughout this process. This legal engagement is much more consequential and critical than planning for children without a disability. This is why I do not think you can go to a general estate planning attorney and have a Special Needs Trust slapped together and get the same result as from a fully engaged specialist who has done hundreds of these cases. Also, the terms are confusing.

You may have heard about Special Needs Trusts or supplemental needs trusts. Is there any difference between them? No, the terms are interchangeable for the most part. Supplemental often refers to the special language found in the trust which refers to the trust assets being used to supplement the benefits provided by government programs such as Social Security, Social Security Income, and Medicaid.

The idea is to supplement but not replace the benefits that may be available to the beneficiary with a disability. Special needs often refers to the purpose of the trust, which is to provide for a person who has *"special needs."*

There are several types of trusts. A trust may be Self-Settled or Third-Party or a trust may be Testamentary or Living/Inter Vivos. These different trusts are detailed below.

Self-Settled Trust

A *Self-Settled Trust* holds the funds that belong to the individual who has the disability. These trusts may only be created by a parent, grandparent, legal guardian, or the court. In many states, the individual for whom the trust is established must be under the age of 65 when the trust is created. A Self-Settled Trust may hold assets that the individual accumulated through gifts from family and friends, or the individual could have earned the money through employment.

Frequently, a Self-Settled Trust can be funded from an inheritance when families have failed to plan ahead. This is unfortunate because of the pay-back provision needed. Self-Settled Trust could also be funded from the proceeds of a lawsuit.

Trust laws require that any assets remaining in the trust at the death of the individual with a disability be paid back to the state to reimburse Medicaid for paying benefits to the individual. Any funds remaining after Medicaid is paid back can be inherited by family or friends.

Third-Party Trust

A *Third-Party Trust* is established with the funds of someone other than the individual who has a disability, such as a parent, grandparent, or friend. The parents might create this type of trust to be funded upon their death with an inheritance in cash, IRAs, and retirement plans, including Roth IRAs, life insurance, or other assets. This trust can also accept gifts made by others for the benefit of the individual with a disability. This trust does not have an age restriction.

Whereas a Self-Settled trust requires a pay-back provision to Medicaid, a Third-Party Trust does not require a pay-back provision to Medicaid once the individual with a disability passes away. At the individual's death, the assets remaining in the trust can go wherever the person who created the trust directs. For this reason, a Third-Party Trust is usually a better option as compared to a Self-Settled Trust.

Inter Vivos Trust

An *Inter Vivos Trust* is one that is established during the life of the person creating the trust. An Inter Vivos Trust cannot be established without holding assets. Some assets will have to be transferred immediately to this type of trust, but a small amount of cash will usually suffice.

A good reason to have an Inter Vivos Trust for a disabled beneficiary is if you want to make a gift while you are alive, but you still want all the protections of a trust. An Inter Vivos Trust could be named in your will or in another person's will if he or she wanted to leave assets for the individual who has a disability.

Testamentary Trust

A *Testamentary Trust* is not technically created until someone dies; therefore, the terms are found in someone's will and the trust does not contain any assets until the person creating the trust passes away.

Irrevocable Trust

An *Irrevocable Trust* is a trust that tends to be difficult to amend or revoke without court intervention. Whereas a *Revocable Trust* can be changed or amended in many more circumstances. Self-Settled Trusts are typically irrevocable while Third-Party Trusts can be revocable or irrevocable.

Pooled Trust

A *Pooled Trust* is administered by a nonprofit organization that holds or *"pools"* the money from many enrolled individuals who have disabilities. The organization generally understands the eligibility rules for the various government programs and manages and disburses the funds in a way that will not disqualify the individual from public benefits.

Often a Pooled Trust is used when an appropriate individual cannot be found to serve as the trustee or if funds are too small for a bank to manage. This trust can be set up by the individual, parent, grandparent, guardian, or by the court.

Why a Special Needs Trust? *(Back to Jim)*

There is a very good chance that it would be most prudent to leave the money to the beneficiary in a *Special Needs Trust (SNT)* rather than leaving them the money outright. There are conflicting definitions in the literature about what an SNT is, so for the purposes of this chapter, I am talking about a very specific type of trust. A SNT can be drafted either as a Testamentary Trust or as an Inter Vivos Trust (defined above).

If the beneficiary has a disability or a chronic illness, whether they meet the IRS's restrictive definition or not, there is a reasonable chance that either now or at some point in the future, the beneficiary will qualify for some type of government aid that does place limits on the beneficiary's income and/or assets. It might be Supplemental Security Income (SSI), Medicaid, or another essential federal or state public benefits program like housing or a drug benefit.

The goal of the SNT is to make sure that the trust is not considered an *available asset* as defined by public benefit agencies. The attorney drafting the trust must be mindful of both income and principal when drafting the trust because too much of either, without the appropriate provisions, could result in loss of benefits or potentially the requirement to return benefits.

Over the years, competent attorneys who work in this area have found language that works for these purposes. Unfortunately, that isn't enough. It is critical that if the underlying asset of the trust is an IRA or a Roth IRA, then the trust must also meet four specific conditions in order to qualify for the "stretch" treatment. A detailed explanation of those conditions is beyond the scope of this book, but here they are in brief. Please work with a competent attorney to ensure your SNT qualifies.

1. The trust must be valid under state law.

2. The trust must be irrevocable, or by its terms become irrevocable upon the death of the original IRA owner.

3. The trust's underlying beneficiaries must be identifiable as being eligible to be designated beneficiaries themselves.

4. A copy of the trust documentation and the proof of disability must be provided to the IRA custodian by October 31 of the year following the year of the IRA owner's death.

We have reviewed hundreds of these types of trusts that other attorneys have prepared and by our estimate, 50% or more of the trusts where the IRA or re-

tirement plan is the underlying asset have significant flaws that if discovered could disqualify the beneficiary from being able to stretch the inherited IRA or Roth IRA.

The biggest and most expensive flaw we see is not having all the conditions in the trust to qualify for the stretch IRA, which allows able-bodied beneficiaries to stretch distributions out over ten years, and disabled beneficiaries to extend those distributions over their entire life. Without keeping score, we think at least half of these trusts are botched when the underlying asset is an IRA.

Ideally, the person drafting the trust to be named as the beneficiary of an IRA or retirement plan knows the rules to protect the beneficiary's government benefit and preserve the *"stretch"* of the Inherited IRA and the trusts they draft will not disqualify the beneficiary from receiving the *"stretch"* treatment. This provision is particularly important if the IRA and/or retirement plan is the primary asset in the estate.

Extreme Caution in Estate Planning is Warranted

Remember, in this and practically all cases when we are talking about an IRA or retirement plan asset, *the key document is not the will or Revocable Trust, but the beneficiary designation of the retirement plan.* One drafting technique is for the beneficiary designation of the IRA to refer to a testamentary trust inside your will or revocable trust that is specifically designed to receive IRAs and retirement plans. But, if that isn't done right (even if your will and the trust instrument have all the correct language), if the beneficiary designations for your IRA or other retirement plan assets are not correct, all that careful planning could go down the toilet, and your child with a disability may end up broke.

> When speaking about an IRA or retirement plan asset, the
> key document is not the will or Revocable Trust, but the
> beneficiary designation of the retirement plan.

Designation as Disabled or Chronically Ill Plus Special Needs Trust as IRA Beneficiary

The first strategy is to do everything you can to make sure your child receives the necessary designation as disabled or chronically ill. Then, if appropriate, work with a special needs attorney to draft a SNT with your child as beneficiary of the trust and make sure that trust is the beneficiary of your IRA and Roth IRA and other retirement assets. Most of the time, but not always, a SNT will be the best way to insure your child has access to the funds they need, that the funds are administered appropriately, and access to government benefits is not jeopardized.

Since a SNT will often be funded by someone other than the disabled beneficiary, it will typically be referred to as a Third-Party Special Needs Trust or a supplemental needs trust (there is also a First-Party Special Needs Trust funded with assets already owned by the disabled beneficiary or received from an outright inheritance). As I stated above, and Julieanne concurs, drafting this trust requires the expertise of an attorney who is experienced in these matters.

The Enormous Risks and Penalties of Not Doing Your Special Needs Trust Correctly

If not drafted correctly, the SNT will not stand up under the scrutiny of the IRS and the public benefits agencies. Two bad things can happen if the trust isn't drafted appropriately.

1. The trust will be considered an asset available to the child which could result in government benefits being terminated and potentially require that the government be reimbursed for past benefits the child received.

2. The ability to stretch IRA distributions will be lost, and massive taxes will be triggered at the very high trust income tax rates.

When planning for this trust, it may also be prudent to consider making a Roth IRA conversion and leaving at least a portion of your IRA as a Roth IRA.

In some situations, parents may choose not to leave their IRA to a trust but will leave it to the child directly.

Special Needs Trust Funded with Life Insurance

Another strategy is to buy life insurance and make a SNT the beneficiary of the life insurance policy. An advantage of this approach is that it may work well in the event your beneficiary will need special assistance but does not qualify as an EDB for the purpose of stretching the Inherited IRA. Also, the life insurance strategy is almost always just one part of the plan.

My wife and I have life insurance as one important part of our estate plan. The benefits of the life insurance are not included in our projection of saving $1,890,544 in taxes for Erica. One of the benefits of having the life insurance is it gives us *"permission"* to spend more money while we are still alive as we have comfort in knowing our daughter is provided for.

Before we had the insurance and had the Roth conversions and estate planning in place, my wife was more frugal because she wanted to leave more than enough money for our daughter. She is still far more frugal than I am, but less frugal than she was. *"Running the numbers"* also helped her feel more comfortable with spending more money. That said, I think she would only eat rice and beans before spending our Roth IRA.

Beware of High Trust Income Tax Rates for Accumulation Trusts

Even if the trust is drafted perfectly, having a lot of IRA or retirement plan money in this type of trust means that a good chunk of retirement plan money may go towards paying taxes at very steep rates, even with the smaller payouts of a stretch IRA. While this strategy is better than directing it to a beneficiary with a 10-year payout, retirement income retained in an accumulation trust will be subject to the steep tax rates for trusts.

Under current tax law, any income that stays in the trust will have a very high tax rate on the smaller payouts since retained income in the trust above $14,450 a year gets taxed at the 37% rate. To make matters worse, there are current proposals in Congress to tax all retained inco...me in trusts at 37%.

Because of the high-income tax rates for accumulation trusts, families with disabled beneficiaries should strongly consider Roth IRA conversions as part of their financial portfolio so that they can pass Roth IRAs tax-free to their disabled family members. Even if a Roth IRA is not directly payable to a disabled beneficiary, outright or through a trust, I have developed an estate plan which has become known as Lange's Cascading Beneficiary Plan (LCBP) to give the initial beneficiary named the opportunity within nine months after the Roth IRA owners' death to disclaim (or decline) the Roth IRA in favor of the disabled beneficiary. See Chapter 14 for more information about how to use LCBP as part of your estate plan.

Briefly, under LCBP, you set up a series of contingent beneficiaries who will inherit if the beneficiaries named as higher priority beneficiaries disclaim all or a part of the IRA or retirement plan. A disclaimer in favor of a disabled beneficiary will allow the Roth IRA to be stretched out for his or her lifetime rather than having the Roth IRA withdrawn within ten years. In addition to receiving the stretch Roth IRA, an accumulation trust for a disabled beneficiary avoids the high-income tax rates of the accumulation trust that would otherwise be applicable if the IRA was a Traditional IRA rather than a Roth IRA.

Like the majority of the retirement and estate planning strategies I discuss in this book, if you want to utilize the flexibility of LCBP, it is crucial to work with financial and legal professionals who possess the knowledge and experience to advise you and implement these strategies correctly.

Avoid Entrusting Siblings with Resources Intended for a Child with a Disability

I have seen IRA owners try to get around all these complications by naming a sibling as the beneficiary of the IRA or other funds. The tacit assumption is that the named sibling will use the money for their sibling with a disability and not themselves. This might work, but it could also be disastrous.

What if the named beneficiary falls victim to a lawsuit, bankruptcy, or a divorce and loses the money that was intended for their sibling with a disability? What if there is a dispute with the siblings? What if the greedy relative like

> Because of the high-income tax rates for accumulation trusts, families with disabled beneficiaries should strongly consider Roth IRA conversions as part of their financial portfolio so that they can pass Roth IRAs tax-free to their disabled family members.

Fanny Dashwood in Jane Austen's novel, *Sense and Sensibility*, interferes? The other problem with this approach is that only the beneficiary with the disability or chronic illness will qualify as an Eligible Designated Beneficiary that can *"stretch"* the inherited IRA or Roth IRA over his or her lifetime. So, this *"oral trust"* approach is a particularly bad idea under the SECURE Act when the underlying asset is an IRA or Roth IRA.

Critical Mechanical Issue if You Are Using a Special Needs Trust

You and/or your attorney will work together to decide whether a SNT is appropriate. If the goal is to protect government benefits, once a SNT is established or planned for a disabled beneficiary, it is particularly important to coordinate all anticipated future assets that the beneficiary might receive so that the terms of the SNT will control them all.

This often doesn't happen because of sloppy estate planning. For example, the beneficiary form of just one of the IRAs or 401(k)s names the child rather than the trust for the benefit of the child.

It is equivalent to establishing a revocable trust and not transferring all probate assets into the trust. Those assets that you fail to transfer to the trust will have to go through probate anyway. In the case of not directing assets to the SNT, that sloppy planning could cost a lot more than having to go through probate. In this case, that sloppy planning could be the cause of your child losing critical government benefits.

Tax-Free Savings Under the ABLE Act

There is also an easy (and cost effective) way for a beneficiary with a disability to save some funds (outside of an SNT) while still protecting eligibility for government benefits and providing a tax benefit.

Julieanne adds:

In 2014, the Achieving a Better Life Experience Act (ABLE Act) opened a door at the federal level to give each state the opportunity to set up programs for people with disabilities and their families to establish tax-advantaged savings accounts without impacting the disabled individual's public benefits.

An ABLE account (or a 529A account) is a tax-advantaged way to save for individuals with disabilities. The ABLE National Resource Center (ABLE NRC) website is a fantastic educational resource to learn more about state and federal ABLE programs: **www.ablenrc.org**.

At this time, regardless of whether or not your state has decided to establish an ABLE program, you are free to enroll in any state ABLE program provided that the program is accepting out-of-state residents and you meet the requirements for opening an account. The ABLE NRC website has comparison tools to make your decision easier as well as an interactive guide called *The Roadmap to Enrollment* to help you understand ABLE accounts better and navigate the enrollment process.

Although it makes sense to start by looking at ABLE programs within your state first, it's worth exploring other state's ABLE programs. There are a variety of reasons for taking this extra step. Some states provide residents with a state income tax deduction on contributions made to ABLE accounts opened in that state (although all contributions are made with after-tax dollars). Other states may offer debit card or checking account options that can make it easier to use ABLE account assets for qualified disability expenses. For helpful information and resources, visit the ABLE NRC website.

Back to Jim:

The primary purpose of the ABLE Act is to provide an alternative tax-free savings option similar to a traditional college savings 529 plan for parents of children with disabilities, though in this case the disabled person is the account owner. As of 2023, there is an annual contribution limit of $17,000 (higher if the disabled person is working) for the account and contributions can be made by any person using after-tax dollars.

The contribution limit is per beneficiary. This is different from contributions to a 529 plan where multiple family members can make annual contributions per year for the same beneficiary, though even with a regular 529 plan there are still limits.

There is only one ABLE account per disabled beneficiary. This means if there are multiple family members wanting to contribute to a disabled family member's ABLE account, the combined contributions cannot exceed the annual contribution limit.

Contributions to an individual's ABLE account may be made by an individual, trust, estate, partnership, association, company, or corporation. The contributions are not tax deductible on the federal level, but some states may provide a state income tax deduction.

In general, eligibility for an ABLE account is automatic if an individual is already receiving benefits under SSI or SSDI or has otherwise met the disability criteria under Social Security. In all cases, the onset of the disability must be prior to turning 46 years of age, though the ABLE account can be opened at any age even if after age 46. Prior to the 2022 SECURE Act 2.0, the onset of the disability had to be prior to age 26, so this extension to age 46 opens the door for many other people to take advantage of ABLE accounts.

ABLE account funds (whether cash or investments) grow income tax-free and are not subject to income tax when distributed so long as the funds are used for qualified disability expenses.

Most normal expenses would qualify so you probably don't have to worry that the distributions will be taxable. Qualified disability-related expenses include education, housing, transportation, employment training and support, assistive technology, personal support services, health, prevention and wellness, financial management and administrative services, legal fees, funeral and burial expenses, and basic living expenses. If you're interpreting this to mean that it covers basically everything, you are right!

The ABLE account does not impact the beneficiary's means-tested benefits, such as SSI and Medicaid, if the ABLE account balance is less than $100,000, though the balance can be higher, subject to state specific limits, if you are not concerned about means-tested benefits. A key difference between the ABLE account and the special needs trusts described earlier is that upon the death of the account beneficiary, the remaining funds in an ABLE account must be used to reimburse the state for Medicaid payments made on behalf of the beneficiary.

Accordingly, our plan for our daughter is to use this tax-free vehicle, the ABLE account, to accumulate more money for our daughter, but also to spend it at an appropriate time and not just let it sit there for the rest of her life.

Coordinate an ABLE Account with an SNT for Extra Benefits

If a disabled beneficiary qualifies for government benefits, coordinating an SNT with an ABLE account provides advantages to the disabled person. Generally, an SNT should not be used to pay for basic costs of living that would typically fall under government assistance (food and groceries, rent or mortgage, utilities, and basic medical care) or at least not be used without first consulting with an estate attorney, financial advisor, or other trusted professional who is familiar with planning for a disabled beneficiary.

Using the funds for a non-supplemental purpose could reduce the government benefit. ABLE accounts do not have this penalty and a trustee could contribute funds from the SNT to the ABLE account and those qualified disability expenses could be paid from the ABLE account without any negative impact to the disabled beneficiary's government benefits.

If you think about it, an ABLE account or even a college savings 529 plan is a lot like a Roth IRA. You contribute after-tax dollars. The fund grows tax-free assuming the eventual distribution is for a qualifying purpose. Even better, the accounts may not be taxed in your estate. Most states have their own college savings 529 plan and ABLE plans. You do not need to pay an advisor for the investments because you can use whatever the state has set up. Pennsylvania for example has a variety of asset allocation options, including Vanguard funds, and all the options have low fees.

Fund an ABLE Account with a Rollover from a 529 Plan

The Tax Cuts and Jobs Act allows tax-free rollovers up to the current gift tax exclusion amount (currently $17,000) from a 529 plan account to the ABLE account through the end of 2025. The $17,000 rollover limit replaces the $17,000 contribution limit.

This means, you cannot contribute $17,000 to an ABLE account in a given year and initiate a $17,000 rollover from a 529 plan in the same year. Funds distributed from the 529 plan must be contributed to the ABLE account within 60 days to count as a tax-free rollover. If the contribution limits are exceeded, there is a 10% penalty tax plus even worse, it could impact adversely the ABLE beneficiary's eligibility for certain public benefits.

To put the paragraphs above into perspective, if you or a family member, have several children with multiple 529 plans, and one of your children becomes disabled before age 46 and does not attend college, you could transfer any left-over monies from a 529 plan into the disabled child's ABLE account. That being said, you should discuss the matter with your advisor to make sure you receive the best advice for your particular situation.

What's more, there are some additional benefits that a 529 plan has over an ABLE account, and it may make more sense to retain funds in the 529 plan— higher contribution limits, higher total funding limit, additional ownership options, no state agency recapture, and a waiver of the IRS 10% penalty if used for care and support of a disabled beneficiary (though still liable for income tax on earnings). When transferring a 529 Plan to a disabled family member's ABLE account, the IRS rules consider a family member as a son, daughter, stepson or stepdaughter, brother, sister, stepbrother or stepsister, father or mother, son-in-

> **If you or a family member, have several children with multiple 529 plans, and one of your children becomes disabled before age 46 and does not attend college, you could transfer any leftover monies from a 529 plan into the disabled child's ABLE account.**

law, daughter-in-law, father-in-law, mother-in-law, brother-in-law, sister-in-law, spouse, first cousin, or adopted child.

Julieanne adds:

If the disabled beneficiary opts for continued education, ABLE accounts are not considered as a resource under the Free Application for Federal Student Aid (FAFSA) program.

An important consideration when looking into enrollment into an ABLE account is how your state handles the death of the individual with disabilities. In some states, when an individual dies, funds remaining in the ABLE account, after the payment of outstanding Qualified Disability Expenses (expenses such as funeral and burial costs), may be used to reimburse the state for Medicaid-related services.

Medicaid payback amounts can be calculated based on amounts paid by Medicaid after the creation of the ABLE account and excludes amounts paid by the beneficiary as premiums to a Medicaid buy-in program. This Medicaid payback provision has been prohibited by law in some states. Remaining ABLE funds are payable to the designated heir under the estate.

It is important to look at your specific state's rules about ABLE accounts. In some states, like Pennsylvania for example, the entire ABLE account (both savings and growth) is exempt from Pennsylvania inheritance tax. Also, in most cases, the ABLE account is protected from creditors. Since this is a complex area, we strongly recommend you consult with an advisor who has experience with disabled beneficiaries and Special Needs Trusts before making any decisions.

In terms of ease of set-up, most ABLE accounts are opened and managed online or can be set up with a paper application that can be mailed or faxed. The ABLE National Resource Center website offers an easy online comparison tool to compare state ABLE plans and their features.

The Under-Publicized Inherited 401(k) Strategy for IRA Owners in a High Tax Bracket with a Disabled Child *(Back to Jim)*

There is an entire discussion of the benefits of a one person 401(k) plan over an IRA discussed in Chapter 7, and that information would be a good background for this idea that some readers will absolutely love.

This fascinating strategy entails planning for your beneficiary to make a Roth conversion of an Inherited 401(k) or 403(b) after you die. This will not work with an Inherited IRA but will only work with non-IRA 401(k) and 403(b) retirement plans, provided it is allowed under that plan.

This strategy works really well if you are in a high income-tax bracket, but your beneficiary will be in a low income-tax bracket and your beneficiary will not need to qualify for any government assistance program that has an income and/or asset eligibility limit. That is, if it makes sense for the disabled beneficiary to receive means-based government benefits, then the income generated from the Roth IRA conversion will likely need to be recognized at the higher trust income tax rate rather than the individual level, reducing some of the strategic tax benefit (described in more detail later in this chapter).

The SECURE Act does allow accumulation trusts for chronically ill or disabled beneficiaries who also qualify for lifetime payout of IRA assets. With accumulation trusts, the trustee has discretion over how much of the annual IRA distribution will be paid directly to the beneficiary or used for the benefit of the beneficiary. The portion paid to the beneficiary will be taxed at the beneficiary's (usually lower) tax rate, and the trust pays tax on the portion retained at higher trust income tax rates.

Please note that we like to create our own one person 401(k) plans and specifically choose a plan that does allow this post-mortem conversion feature.

Converting Your Inherited 401(k) or 403(b) Retirement Plan to an Inherited Roth IRA After You Die

We had a client with a high RMD and a high tax bracket. He ran a small consulting practice as part of his post *"retirement"* activities. We recommended he roll his entire IRA into a new one person 401(k) which has practically the same rules as an IRA. But, when he dies, his disabled beneficiary (who is not receiving public benefits) will be able to make an Inherited Roth 401(k) conversion or even a series of Inherited Roth 401(k) conversions at their low tax rates. This plan could result in the savings of hundreds of thousands of dollars or even more for the beneficiary.

This fascinating strategy entails planning for your beneficiary to make a Roth conversion of an Inherited 401(k) or 403(b) after you die.

The big distinction between keeping the money in the IRA *vs.* a Solo 401(k) is that your beneficiary cannot do Roth conversions on an inherited IRA account, but assuming the plan allows it, your beneficiary could do Roth conversions on an Inherited 401(k) account.

This will likely work better for a beneficiary receiving SSDI who doesn't have an income cap to remain eligible for benefits. If this is not your situation, you will need to carefully evaluate the decision to do a Roth conversion and plan for the big jump in income for the beneficiary in the year of conversion so that the conversion does not jeopardize needs-based assistance.

Why we like the idea of moving the assets into a Solo 401(k) *vs.* an IRA is to have the *flexibility* to do a low-cost Roth conversion or a series of low-cost Roth conversions over a period of time, but only if it makes sense. The advantage of having this option is you can have the Roth account continue to grow tax-free, and your child will be able to take the stretched RMDs, providing you with the peace of mind that they will be cared for long after you and your spouse are gone.

The beauty of the Roth conversion either while you are alive or even after you are gone (which is only possible with an inherited 401(k) or 403(b) account and not an IRA) is your beneficiary can get all the benefits of 'tax-free' and 'stretched' RMDs of the Inherited Roth IRA for their entire life just like under the pre-2020 rules before the effective date of the SECURE Act.

Potential Downsides of the 401(k) *vs.* the IRA

One caveat to mention, a potential downside to having the Roth conversions done post-death is the inherent income tax liability on the conversion cannot be deducted on your federal estate tax return or possibly your state inheritance tax return (for example, Pennsylvania).

The biggest downside of a 401(k) plan designed to be used as an Inherited 401(k) is that it will be subject to the RMD rules while you are alive. You can get around the RMDs by converting that money to a Roth IRA, which has no

RMDs, but then the child will not be able to make an Inherited 401(k) conversion after your death. You might consider maintaining as much money in the 401(k) as you think your child should convert to a Roth. This means you would have both an IRA and a one person 401(k).

Be aware that not all plans allow money to stay in a 401(k) plan after the death of the plan owner, so your beneficiary may have to convert the entire balance as a 100% distribution and may not be permitted to perform a series of Inherited Roth 401(k) conversions.

Another possible downside to this plan is it is foreseeable they will change the rules on converting Inherited 401(k)s. Consequently, we still see doing the conversions yourself as the primary Roth strategy, not just relying on your beneficiary to perform the conversion after death.

This is one of the reasons why it is so important to do proper planning and *"run the numbers"* ahead of time to see what makes the most sense for your particular situation.

While this strategy could be extremely useful for a limited number of readers, it is usually secondary to making Roth IRA conversions while you are alive.

Another downside to this strategy that we learned from a column by Jeffrey Levine is that you cannot do a Qualified Charitable Distribution (QCD) with a one person 401(k) plan.

Flexibility In Planning with the Toggle Trust

As we have discussed, it is extremely important to plan for the future needs of a family member with a disability or chronic illness, particularly when that person is already receiving or qualifies for means-based government benefits.

That being said, you might be in a situation where your young child is diagnosed with a mild disability, and it is unclear whether the disability will prevent the child from working in the future or if the child would simply need some modest accommodations or assistance in order to work. Or a young person could have mental or emotional health concerns that may or may not get worse later on in life and perhaps the person will need someone else to oversee an inheritance.

Such circumstances create an uncertain future. It is possible to include a trigger or toggle within your will or trust that allows the disabled person's inheritance to be directed to an SNT based on the circumstances known at the time of distribution (generally the date of your passing). Alternately, the money could be directed to a different type of trust or even to the child directly depending on circumstances that would be determined after death.

This sort of planning is available for other scenarios where trust protections may also be necessary and is not only for disability planning. These are important considerations to discuss with your estate attorney and other trusted advisors.

Who Should be Trustee? *(Back to Julieanne)*

One of the most difficult discussions is trying to figure out who the trustee should be for the trust. There is a strong preference among professionals to appoint a corporate trustee because Special Needs Trusts can be complex to work with. Corporate trustees also have insurance which can cover any mistakes that are made which could affect government benefit eligibility.

A trust can be in place for 25 to 30 years, or even longer, so flexibility is important. A corporate trustee may be more permanent and provide consistency of administration for an individual who is expected to outlive their parents and likely many other loved ones.

Families will often want to name a family member, especially a sibling of the individual with a disability. Family members are also good choices for trustee because they have a more intimate understanding of the person with a disability, and they can make sure the person is receiving everything he or she needs.

However, if a family member makes a mistake because he or she didn't know the rules, the family member will likely not have the money to cover the mistake. Families are almost always concerned with the cost of a corporate trustee. However, the costs associated with mismanagement by a family trustee can be much more costly if mistakes occur.

Another option could be to appoint a corporate trustee and family member trustee to manage the trust together. The details of this relationship would have to be approved by the corporate trustee beforehand. The corporate trustee and family member trustee could be appointed as co-trustees, or the corporate trustee could be responsible for managing most of the trust while the family member trustee must be kept involved and has the power to change the corporate trustee to a different corporation.

If the corporate trustee agrees to the terms, there can be a considerable amount of flexibility in making this work with the corporate trustee and the family member trustee together.

> By granting guardianship to another person, the individual
> with a disability is deemed unable to make these decisions
> on their own.

Guardianship and Conservatorship

Seeking a guardianship should not be taken lightly. In some states, a guardianship will apply to both health and financial decisions. In other states the process is bifurcated, and a guardianship only applies to decisions about the person, which includes medical decision making. A conservatorship would be required if a person needed to make decisions about the estate, which includes financial decisions.

By granting guardianship to another person, the individual with a disability is deemed unable to make these decisions on their own. The person appointed as guardian will now step into the shoes of the individual with a disability and will make health and/or financial decisions on his or her behalf.

Guardianships are a legal process that require the involvement of a court to make a determination that a person is incompetent. Each state has its own laws and requirements for implementing guardianships. Many individuals who have developmental or intellectual disabilities can manage their own affairs with some assistance. They may only need a limited guardianship, if a guardianship is needed at all.

A guardianship needs to be implemented on an individual basis depending on the person's needs. Often, a guardianship may only be necessary when there are behavioral issues that will result in a person revoking more informal alternatives. Another reason for obtaining a conservatorship is to protect the person from those who would prey on the financial status of the person who has a disability. Other reasons for obtaining a guardianship or conservatorship could be:

1. When there is no clear understanding of the individual's ability to consent to treatment or services. Unfortunately, it is often a medical provider's concern over liability as to whether the person has the capacity to provide informed consent that is the issue.

2. If health providers are concerned over releasing records and information without a clear grant of authority under HIPAA, and if there is a concern of capacity to grant that consent.

Alternatives to Guardianship for an Adult Child with a Disability

There are several less restrictive options available as alternatives to seeking a guardianship or conservatorship. A representative payee may be appointed to deal with Social Security payments or government or military payments. By having a representative payee appointed, you can also limit the risk of financial exploitation when the individual with a disability is unable to manage his or her own money. The Social Security Administration will require regular accounting and the person appointed is liable if the money is mismanaged.

Joint ownership of property is another way to make sure that taxes, insurance, and other real estate ownership issues are taken care of. However, there is always a risk in joint ownership. For example, creditors of any of the joint owners could claim an interest in the property, including if the property is subject to divorce proceedings. Joint bank accounts can also be set up and can offer a simple way to pay bills automatically and prevent excessive spending of money. However, the risk is still present if any of the owners have creditors. A trust account could also be a good alternative to a guardianship.

Executing certain legal documents is another alternative to guardianship or conservatorship. A Health Care Proxy, also referred to as a Durable Power of Attorney for Health Care, Living Will, or Advanced Health Care Directive, addresses the medical treatment that an individual wants or does not want to receive if he or she is unable to speak with the medical professionals or is deemed incapacitated.

Some of these documents also address the life-sustaining measures that an individual wants or does not want if they are diagnosed with an end-stage medical condition or end up in an irreversible coma or vegetative state. The execution of one of these documents when a person is competent can avoid the necessity of obtaining a guardianship.

The Durable Power of Attorney or Financial Power of Attorney is a document that names someone else to handle a person's financial affairs. If validly executed, this document will avoid the necessity of obtaining a conservatorship or guardianship of the estate. Because it is durable, it will survive a person's subsequent incapacity.

Key Ideas for Chapter 13 can be found on the following four pages.

KEY IDEAS

My daughter, Erica, has a disability that will prevent her from providing for herself. My wife and I worried endlessly, as do most parents of a child with a disability, about ensuring her safety and prosperity after we are gone. Using just three strategies, we took care of that worry. Consequently, Erica will have close to an additional $1.9 million dollars measured in today's dollars to support her over her lifetime. Using the same strategies, someone with a $500,000 IRA can provide their child with an additional $239,000.

• The three strategies are:

1. Formally establish your child's status as disabled with the SSA. Remember, however, that the definitions are extremely narrow and may not cover your beneficiary who you consider disabled or chronically ill.

   We are confident that the SSA designation will fast track a child's status as an Eligible Designated Beneficiary (EDB) under the SECURE Act. The EDB status will allow the child to stretch distributions from retirement accounts over a lifetime. These qualifying beneficiaries are in effect deferring distributions on their tax-deferred Inherited IRA or their tax-free Inherited Roth IRA to some extent for their entire lives. The additional deferral of the Inherited Roth IRA and Traditional IRA was worth almost an extra $600,000 for our daughter.

2. Make a Roth IRA conversion (or several) and contribute to Roth IRAs, backdoor Roth IRAs, and Roth 401(k)s.

   $1.3 million of the $1.9 million dollar savings for Erica came from us doing a large Roth IRA conversion and contributing to Roth IRAs and Roth 401(k)s.

3. Draft an optimized estate plan with appropriate wills, trusts, and IRA and 401(k) and Roth IRA beneficiary forms that, to a large extent, will allow your child and/or a trust for your child's benefit to *"stretch"* or defer distributions of any Inherited IRAs and/or Roth IRA for life. And have plans in place for competent estate administration as well.

• Getting your beneficiary designated as disabled or chronically ill for the purpose of Social Security while you are still alive can not only provide an immediate income, but assuming they maintain their disabled or chronically ill status, allow them to qualify as an EDB and get the Inherited stretch IRA or Inherited Roth IRA distributions over their lifetimes.

KEY IDEAS
(continued)

- Qualifying your child for SSI or SSDI benefits is a Golden Ticket that opens doors to many financial and healthcare benefits. The three keys for successful applications with SSA are:

  1. Use the *"I CAN'T"* language to compare your child's abilities in contrast to the norm assumed by the SSA. If your child cannot fulfill the activities of daily living in the same ways that a non-disabled person does, your child most likely fits the legal definitions of disabled used by the SSA in evaluating applications.

  2. Letters from medical doctors that emphasize the ways your child *cannot take care of the activities of daily living* are extremely important for successful applications.

  3. To be eligible for SSI benefits, your child cannot have ready access to more than $2,000 in assets. ABLE accounts and special needs trusts are not counted in this limit. Starting at age 18, SSA does not count the assets and income of parents under their means testing.

- Keep in mind that most states consider a child an adult when they reach the age of 18. That means that after age 18, your ability to make decisions and get information about their health may be limited.

- Start planning now to protect your child with a disability after your death. Besides ensuring your child will have adequate financial resources, you may also need to name a successor guardian or advocate when you can no longer fulfill that role. Plan for where your child should live and provide a summary of your wishes to guide your successor.

- Working with an attorney who has expertise with special needs will help you make those plans. Before meeting with an attorney, gather information about your child's condition, current and future financial resources, daily routine, and other family sources of support, among other crucial details.

KEY IDEAS
(continued)

- Familiarize yourself with the differences between different types of trusts and how they are created and funded.

- In some situations, granting guardianship to another person for your disabled child may be appropriate. Granting a limited guardianship can help support your child in managing their own affairs. This is not a decision to be made lightly.

- Alternatives to guardianship include appointing a representative payee to deal with government payments, establishing joint ownership of assets, and executing legal documents such as a Durable Power of Attorney for Health Care.

- Be aware of the documentation requirements and the timing required by the custodian of your IRA or employer plan to support your disabled or chronically ill beneficiary. If possible, provide the required documentation to the custodian as soon as you have it, so nothing is compromised later after your death.

- Special needs trusts allow your child to inherit IRA funds without jeopardizing their eligibility for government aid. However, they must contain the four conditions to ensure they function as intended and to preserve the "stretch" of an Inherited IRA.

  A majority of the trusts we have seen fail to meet the four conditions meaning the stretch IRA is in jeopardy because of poor drafting.

- Naming a sibling of your disabled child as the beneficiary of your IRA with the understanding that the sibling will help to support their disabled brother or sister can backfire. This should only be done as a last resort.

- If your child needs to qualify for government assistance with income or asset eligibility limits, the financial benefit of Roth conversions may be reduced.

KEY IDEAS
(continued)

- Use an ABLE account to save and invest money for a disabled person in a tax-advantaged way and without affecting eligibility for government benefits, and if applicable, discuss with your advisor the option to transfer 529 plan funds to a disabled family member.

  In some states, ABLE account balances may be used to reimburse the state for Medicaid-related expenses after the death of the beneficiary.

14

Lange's Cascading Beneficiary Plan™
The Best Estate Plan for Most Married University Faculty Members and TIAA Investors After the SECURE Act

*"Planning is bringing the future into the present so that
you can do something about it now."*

— Alan Lakein

For the life of me, I can't understand why the plan I am recommending in this chapter is not the "standard" estate plan for many, if not most married couples who have IRAs and retirement plans. The other thing I do not understand is why the thousands of attorneys, including many estate attorneys, haven't incorporated the concepts of this chapter in estate plans that they draft.

I would read and if necessary, re-read this chapter as it could make an enormous difference for you and your family. It is also likely to make you want to make changes to your wills, trusts and beneficiary designations of your IRAs and retirement plans.

Choosing the Right Beneficiaries for Your Retirement Plan

What follows is an important concept that a surprising number of professors, and TIAA investors, and even estate attorneys get wrong. Your will (or your trust documents, if you have them) does not control the distribution of your retirement plans or IRAs after your death.

Any account with a specific beneficiary designation will be distributed to the individuals listed on the beneficiary designation form, regardless of what your will or trust says. In other words, the beneficiary designation of any retirement plan trumps your will (no pun intended, sorry about that).

In my practice, professors often came in with sophisticated wills or trusts, sometimes 20–30 pages or more, drafted with every possible contingency in mind. When I asked them where most of their money was, they usually replied *"in my TIAA"* or *"in my retirement plan."*

Then when I asked them about the beneficiaries of their TIAA, IRAs, and retirement plans, I found that, despite all of the time and money they had spent on these wills and trusts, the beneficiary designation form that controls the majority of their wealth which I often found out the client had filled out themselves had just two simple lines:

1. **Primary Beneficiary:** My surviving spouse
2. **Contingent Beneficiary:** My children equally

A little better is:

1. **Primary Beneficiary:** My surviving spouse
2. **Contingent Beneficiary:** My children equally, *per stirpes*

(The *per stirpes* protects the children of a deceased child so that the grandchild or grandchildren would receive what their predeceased parent would have received.)

This simple beneficiary designation, while better than nothing, is nowhere near optimal. Unfortunately, documents with those instructions are not likely to accomplish the family's goals because the beneficiary designations listed on their retirement accounts were not part of a coordinated and integrated estate plan. In situations such as this, the best option for the family is often to completely redraft, or at a minimum, make significant changes to their wills, trusts and beneficiary designations.*

Here's another scenario. The professor comes in with a basic *"I love you"* will and beneficiary designations. The *"I love you"* will says I leave everything to you (my spouse), and at the second death, everything goes to the children equally, *per stirpes*. Owners of *"I love you"* wills often have their beneficiary forms filled out like the above—and again, though much better than nothing, this is nowhere near optimal.

Unfortunately, the difference between effective and ineffective planning can mean the loss of hundreds of thousands, sometimes even millions, of dollars for your heirs. By the way, the problem with this simple beneficiary designation existed before the SECURE Act, but the passage of the SECURE Act compounds the problem.

The Elephant in the Room of Estate Planning

The problem with estate planning is uncertainty. One uncertainty is that you do not know when you are going to die. You do not know what the tax law on in-

Your will (or trust documents, if you have them) does not control the distribution of your retirement plans or IRAs after your death.

herited retirement plans will be at the time of your death. Or with respect to the SECURE Act and SECURE Act 2.0, you may know where the law stands now, or as is the case right now, whether the Proposed Regulations will ultimately be finalized.

The other uncertainty is the issue of both general tax rates and the specific tax rates of some of your different beneficiaries. Investment performance, future spending, and inflation rates are also unpredictable. Perhaps a terrible and expensive illness strikes one spouse, and most of the resources of the marriage pay that spouse's expenses, leaving the surviving spouse much worse off than previously projected.

In an alternative and more positive scenario, there is a lot of money left after the death of the first spouse. If so, it might make sense to have at least some of the money go to children or grandchildren after the first death instead of waiting for both spouses to die before anything goes to children or grandchildren.

We also do not know what the future tax laws are going to be. The SECURE Act was bad enough, but who is to say it won't be changed at least one more time before you die, or perhaps multiple times with multiple changes between now and the time of your and your spouse's death.

Whether it is a TIAA account, an IRA, a Roth IRA, a brokerage account, life insurance, an annuity, a house, or another asset, there might be compelling reasons for who should get what at the first and then at the second death. If you draft traditional estate planning documents that *"fix in stone"* the distribution of your assets to your heirs, they are not likely to get the full benefit of your legacy.

Better decisions regarding who should get which assets can be made after your spouse dies, when circumstances are current and clear. Furthermore, if your estate planning documents are drafted in the way I am going to propose, your surviving spouse will have nine months after your death to consider a myriad of options and discuss the best strategies with an advisor and other family members.

---

* There is no solicitation being made for legal services by the author nor by Lange Legal Services, LLC.

Similarly, for a *"traditional family"* after you both die, providing your heirs (usually your mutual children) with as much flexibility as possible is also optimal. So, what can you do to give yourself and your heirs maximum flexibility?

For most married professors and investors with traditional families, I assume that your primary goal in your estate plan is to first provide for your surviving spouse. Leaving money to children and grandchildren, while potentially beneficial in terms of tax savings and giving them money earlier in their lives when they are likely to need it more, is usually secondary. But perhaps you can potentially save hundreds of thousands or even millions of dollars for your family and get money to your children when they need it more, and still protect your surviving spouse. Doesn't that seem like a better solution that the traditional fixed in stone class approach?

Lange's Cascading Beneficiary Plan (LCBP)™

Lange's Cascading Beneficiary Plan (LCBP) is for professors, TIAA investors, and IRA owners who have traditional marriages with children from that union, and potentially grandchildren—what I like to call the *"Leave it to Beaver"* marriages. The plan outlined here is not for couples in second marriages who have children from the first marriage or other non-traditional families.

While some of the concepts of this chapter will apply to non-traditional families, those situations require additional strategic thinking that I do not address in this book except when I try to get unmarried committed couples to get married. Please see Chapter 25.

Starting in the mid-nineties, I began recommending additional flexibility to traditional wills and trusts and the beneficiary designations of IRAs and retirement plans.

In 1998, I described my plan in *The Tax Adviser*, the peer-reviewed journal of the American Institute of CPAs. An adaptation of that article is availa-ble by going to **https://PayTaxesLater.com/Reading/Roth-Iras-Accumulating-Tax-Free-Wealth**. Both the Roth IRA conversion and the flexible estate plan I recommended were extremely well received by the peer-reviewers and readers and that article won article of the year.

Then in 2001, immediately after a change in the law passed, I received explosive coverage for that same strategy that I called Lange's Cascading Beneficiary Plan (LCBP). The recommendations I made in the 1998 article, worked out even better after a new law was passed in 2001. I am still recommending that plan today.

At the time, the concept was groundbreaking. Since then, it has been covered many times in national publications with attribution to me in such journals as *The Wall Street Journal*, (twice) *Newsweek*, *Kiplinger's*, *Financial Planning*, *Trusts & Estates*, and many others. If you type in Google, there are hundreds of entries that mostly point back to me.

The concept takes complete advantage of delaying critical decisions until after someone dies and allowing the surviving spouse to make better decisions when more information is known. The idea is simple but is intended to preserve the maximum flexibility and provide the opportunity to get much more value from the assets you leave behind. My plan gives your spouse nine months after your death to make important decisions and the power to act on them.

If it's set up properly, LCBP can give your heirs an enormous amount of flexibility. Under my plan, your surviving spouse can make decisions based on his or her own needs, the needs of the family, and the tax laws in effect at the time of your death. And my plan is as simple as this: start by naming primary and contingent beneficiaries* to your IRAs and all retirement plans and for that matter potentially all your wills, trusts, etc. according to the following hierarchy:

1. Primary Beneficiary: Your spouse,
2. Your child (or children equally) as the contingent beneficiary or beneficiaries, per stirpes,
3. The grandchildren, though likely in a trust depending on their ages. There would be a separate trust for the children (your grandchildren) of each of your children.

Perhaps the best description of my plan from a noted source comes from *Kiplinger's* (with slight modifications for clarity).

> *"Lange paints this scene: You are married with children and grandchildren. You name your wife as the primary beneficiary. The first contingent beneficiaries are your children equally. The second contingent beneficiaries are trusts for your grandchildren. Each set of grandchildren has their own trust. At your death, your wife could roll over all or part of the IRA into her IRA. Your wife could also disclaim a portion, which would be distributed to your children. Your wife could also disclaim non-IRA assets. Finally, if neither your wife nor your children need all of the money, they could disclaim all or a portion to a trust for the grandchildren."*

---

* Please note that the beneficiaries you choose cannot be changed after you die, so your wishes will be respected. This can be an important consideration in cases of second marriages.

The key concept here is *disclaiming*. You cannot force anyone to accept a bequest—and if you do not lay out a contingency plan, a bequest that is refused might not end up where you would prefer it to go. My plan allows the beneficiary of the IRA (or of the TIAA, CREF, or other assets listed above) to accept the IRA for themselves or to say, "I don't want that IRA—give it to the next person on the list."

University faculty members frequently accumulate a significant amount of money in their retirement plans, and in many cases, it just doesn't make sense to have the surviving spouse inherit more money than they could possibly spend over his or her lifetime.

If the surviving spouse says, *"I only need this much money,"* we look to see who is next in line, or if we want to use the legal term, the contingent beneficiary. The primary beneficiary can accept all the money but can also make a *"partial disclaimer."* This means that they can accept part of the asset and let the contingent beneficiary or beneficiaries have the rest.

Laying the Groundwork Now for A Post-Mortem Tax Planning Strategy

We also recommend disclaimers because sometimes, when the surviving spouse is left a big IRA, the new tax brackets of single instead of married filing jointly will likely push the surviving spouse into a higher tax bracket. Even though the kids would have to withdraw the Inherited IRA in ten years, it often makes sense to disclaim a portion of the Inherited IRA to the children at the first death for income tax savings for the family.

You would think that a CPA thought of this idea, but it was actually but it was actually estate attorney Matt Schwartz. We call disclaiming to avoid the surviving spouse going into a higher bracket the *"Schwartz 24% Maximizer."*

Think about how disclaiming would work. If your surviving spouse needs all the money, that's fine. She can keep it—end of story. But if your spouse doesn't need the money, or more likely doesn't need all of the money, then she can disclaim either all or a portion of it in favor of the next beneficiary on your list—usually your children.

If you have two children with unique needs, one might accept the disclaimed inheritance while the other disclaims their inheritance or a portion of it to your second choice—which could be a trust for the benefit of their own children (the IRA owners' grandchildren). I know I said it earlier, but it deserves repeating: each beneficiary down the line can have a partial disclaimer if they want to retain some, but not all, of the Inherited IRA or other assets.

When drafting wills, trusts, and beneficiary designations of retirement plans, it is critical to make it crystal clear and specify that each beneficiary has the right to disclaim all or part of the Inherited IRA and other assets, and also what happens to the Inherited IRA or other assets if the beneficiary chooses to do so.

In addition to having specific disclaimer language in the will, revocable trust, and all the beneficiary designations, this plan anticipates the possibility of your grandchildren inheriting IRAs or other assets even if their parents are still alive.

With traditional planning and traditional estate administration, the children do not get anything until both parents are gone. The grandchildren do not get anything unless their parents are gone. The additional flexibility in the LCBP that allows children to receive money at the *first* death often not only has tax advantages but can also help them out when they are younger and need the money more than if they have to wait for the second death to get any money.

With traditional documents, the only way a grandchild typically receives an inheritance is if both of the grandchild's grandparents died and their parent died before the grandparents. With LCBP, we anticipate the possibility that a grandchild could inherit money even though there is a surviving grandparent or parent.

That gives us the ability to name your children as trustees for the grandchildren. As long as you trust your spouse to disclaim any part of the inheritance that he or she doesn't need, and if all of the parties involved understand the reasons for it, disclaiming can not only reduce taxes after your death but also increase the amount of wealth passed on to future generations.

It can also get money in the hands of adult children who need the money sooner rather than having to wait for both of their parents to die to spend any of the inheritance. In practice, clients love this plan both conceptually and after someone dies.

As a result of the advance planning, drafting an LCBP, and strategic planning after the first and second death, people with these plans save hundreds of thousands, sometimes millions, of dollars for their families. This can be accomplished all while fully protecting or even overprotecting the surviving spouse.

As a consequence of the SECURE Act, using the power of disclaimers will require more strategic thinking. Since your grown children and grandchildren will have to withdraw everything from the inherited IRA within ten years, it might no longer make sense for the surviving spouse to disclaim a large IRA to a child.

> As a result of the advance planning, drafting an LCBP, and strategic planning after the first and second death, people with these plans save hundreds of thousands, sometimes millions, of dollars for their families. This can be accomplished all while fully protecting or even overprotecting the surviving spouse.

So, let's assume you want the maximum flexibility possible for your heirs. You have established a LCBP for your estate planning documents. Now, let's look at how Lange's Cascading Beneficiary Plan (LCBP) can work to your advantage in conjunction with the SECURE Act.

Looking at LCBP in Conjunction with the SECURE Act

For this example, we will assume the husband dies first. He leaves a large IRA and the legal documents that give you, his surviving spouse, complete discretion. You have the option to keep the entire IRA, disclaim part of it to your children, or even have a portion of the IRA pass to a grandchild or grandchildren who your husband named as a second contingent beneficiary. Ideally, with the help of an attorney* or the appropriate advisor, or even a family member, you assess your financial position.

Let's assume you have more money than you will be able to spend over your lifetime and that your children do not have any need for their father's money either. Under the old law, more than likely, it would have made sense for you to disclaim a portion of your IRA to the beneficiaries with the longest life expectancies—specifically, your grandchildren.

Because of the SECURE Act, though, the better plan now might be for you to disclaim a smaller portion of the IRA. That is because we must now evaluate which generation will pay less tax under the new law—the surviving spouse, the child, or the grandchild (or, more than likely, a trust for the grandchild's benefit).

A second but equally important point is that it might make perfect sense to disclaim other assets, such as after-tax dollars. The surviving spouse will have a slower or longer payout period because his or her minimum required distribu-

---

* There is no solicitation being made for legal services by the author nor by Lange Legal Services, LLC.

tion will be much slower than ten years, which will likely be the payout period for a child or grandchild.

Here is another important consideration. Maybe minimizing taxes may not be your family's most pressing need. Perhaps your kids need some money after your death. Their financial situation is desperate due to a job loss because of Covid-19, they need money now, and your surviving spouse wants to provide that support. In that case, he or she could disclaim a portion of his/her IRA or other assets, and the kids could either cash in their Inherited IRA immediately or, better yet, do it gradually along a strategic timeline determined by financial need and a desire to incur minimal taxation.

Another scenario is that the person who receives the disclaimed asset could fall into one of the exceptions to the 10-year rule, such as a child or grandchild with a disability.

Furthermore, there may be changes to the SECURE Act or even the tax code that we can't anticipate. All these factors point to the value of decision-making flexibility. I don't know a better or more flexible plan than the LCBP. If I did, I would be writing about that plan. Of course, LCBP or even a variation of it isn't appropriate for everyone, but it is a great starting point for traditional families.

The Concept of Disclaimer, but Outside the Traditional Marriage

Suppose you are single and do not have any children. Let's assume you want to provide for your biological family. A reasonable plan would be to have your wills, trusts, and beneficiary designations leave money to your siblings equally.

Let's also assume if one of your siblings predeceases you, the share of the predeceased sibling would go to the children, if any, of the predeceased sibling. Further, if that niece or nephew also predeceased you, their share would go to your grandnieces or nephews of that predeceased nephew or niece, presumably in a trust if the grandnieces and nephews are still young.

You could still maintain that basic intent, of the above-mentioned plan, but add disclaimer provisions. In the event one of your siblings didn't want or need the inheritance or even part of the inheritance, you could have a clause that allows that sibling to *"disclaim,"* presumably to his or her children, your nieces, and nephews from that sibling.

Then, you could have each niece and nephew have the right to *"disclaim"* into a trust for the benefit of their children, your grandniece and/or nephew from that niece or nephew.

Do You Need Disclaimer Provisions in Your Documents to Disclaim?

Legally, there is no requirement that the wills, trusts, beneficiary designations have disclaimer language in order for the survivor to disclaim. I like to include the disclaimer language for several reasons:

1. Putting the language in there at least makes the issue of whether to disclaim or not be a part of the conversation after a death. Although all heirs have the right to disclaim even if the decedent's estate planning documents do not include disclaimer language, in practice, that right is rarely exercised when the language is not included.

2. I like to make it crystal clear what happens to the money and/or other assets if there is a disclaimer.

3. It is often the true intent of the parties to give the survivor choices and including these choices in the documents makes a lot of sense.

But let's say someone drafted a document that made you the beneficiary and for some reason you wanted to have the money go *"next in line."* You could disclaim and get the same result as if disclaimer language was included and you disclaimed. That said, it is rare to see a a an heir exercise that right to disclaim assets unless there is disclaimer language in the documents.

Forcing Ten-Year Payout for Successor Beneficiaries of Existing and Future Inherited IRAs

This is a technical point that could probably be skipped, but definitely read this section if you inherited an IRA and/or have an interest in the New York Yankees. In addition, it is part of the SECURE Act. The SECURE Act allows for the continued stretch of an Inherited IRA if the original owner died on or before December 31, 2019. However, it makes no accommodations for grandfathering those rules with respect to successor beneficiaries.

We had quite a few clients die in 2019 and earlier, leaving balances of more than a million dollars in their retirement plans. In many cases, we recommended significant disclaimers—saving heirs hundreds of thousands, perhaps millions of dollars over their lifetimes. We might look back on these days as the good old days in terms of when to die (not that there is ever a good time to die).

Some people do die at the right time in terms of tax law. George Steinbrenner, the former owner of the (for me) hated New York Yankees, died in 2010, the only year there was no estate tax. The timing of his death saved his family hundreds of millions of dollars in estate taxes.

For you long-time Yankee fans, all I have to say is 1960. That is the year the dark horse Pittsburgh Pirates won the seventh game in the ninth inning when Bill Mazeroski, known as a great fielder, but not a great hitter, hit the winning home run that clinched the World Series for the Pirates. Go Bucs! At the time, the capacity of Forbes Field, the site of the winning home run in Pittsburgh, was 41,000. There are at least 60,000 surviving Pittsburghers, including my brother, who claim to have been present for that game. You do the math.

The beneficiaries of IRAs in which the IRA owner died on or before December 31, 2019, are grandfathered. For example, if you inherited an IRA prior to or on December 31, 2019, you are still permitted to *"stretch"* that Inherited IRA over your own lifetime because the original IRA owner died before the effective date of the SECURE Act.

But let's say you inherited an IRA from your parent prior to or on December 31, 2019 and are appropriately taking an RMD from the Inherited IRA every year. Once you die and pass your Inherited IRA on to your own beneficiaries, they will be subject to the 10-year rule.

Under the old rules, your beneficiary could have *"stretched"* that Inherited IRA over what remained of your actuarial life expectancy, even though you were dead. If you pass when you are age 60, it means your beneficiaries will lose decades of tax-deferred (or, in the case of a Roth account, tax-free) growth compared to the old law. This entire *"Death of the Stretch IRA"* was a huge money grab by Trump and Congress, and this provision just rubs salt in the wound.

Unfortunately, even your heirs who initially qualified for exemptions from the accelerated IRA taxation rules will eventually fall victim to them. For example, once a minor beneficiary reaches 21, the 10-year rule kicks in. Furthermore, if your minor beneficiary dies before reaching the age of majority, then any subsequent beneficiaries are subject to the 10-year rule immediately—even if they are not of the age of majority themselves!

The same is true for the heirs of an individual with a disability who inherits an IRA. Any subsequent beneficiary must withdraw and pay taxes on the IRA within ten years.

So, while some accommodation is available for individuals with disabilities and for individuals who have already inherited IRAs under the old law, they will not extend the privilege to their beneficiaries.

Beyond what we have covered so far, is there anything else you can do to reduce the impact of the SECURE Act, as well as the looming specter of rising tax rates? The answer is yes.

The chapters that follow explore some options that can help minimize the bite of this tax bill, including naming trusts that you establish for the benefit of your heirs as the beneficiaries of your IRAs and retirement plans, Roth IRA conversions, and lots more. Read on!

KEY IDEAS

- A flexible estate plan offers multiple advantages to your surviving spouse and your heirs.

- Lange's Cascading Beneficiary Plan (LCBP) allows heirs to strategically disclaim to subsequent beneficiaries to take care of needs and minimize taxes.

- This plan provides or overprovides for the surviving spouse but also allows important options.

- The SECURE Act makes it even more urgent to plan for the long term.

- Though the LCBP is more popular with traditional families, the concept of disclaimers can be used in many situations.

15

Roth IRA Conversions Before and After the SECURE Act

"If there is one thing that marks families with money in the long term, it is this: delayed gratification."

— Bill Bonner

For many IRA owners, proactively developing a long-term Roth IRA conversion strategy is one of the best financial decisions you can make. This was true before recent tax-law changes, and it is still true.

You Can Trust this Information on Roth IRA Conversions

I wrote the first peer-reviewed article on Roth IRA conversions which was published in 1998 and won *The Tax Adviser's* article of the year award. We also wrote an entire book on the subject, ***The Roth Revolution, Pay Taxes Once and Never Again*** which you can download without cost by going to **https://PayTax esLater.com/Books/**. Some of the highly skilled number crunching CPAs on our team were involved in writing the Roth chapters in this book and creating some of the graphs and charts.

After the Tax Cuts and Jobs Act (TCJA) of 2017, the value of Roth IRA conversions surged. The TCJA reduced income tax rates effective 2018 through 2025. The TCJA includes a *"sunset"* date. Unless Congress takes action, many of its provisions, including the lowered tax rates, will expire at the end of 2025. At that point, without intervention, tax rates will go back up to 2017 levels plus inflation.

The lower tax rates of today often allow taxpayers to execute larger Roth IRA conversions at a lower tax cost. Forbes magazine featured my strategies on a front cover story in 2019 that emphasized the tax rates and the long-term value of a Roth IRA conversion. I also published several articles on the subject for Forbes.com, where I am a regular paid contributor. I don't mean to brag (ok, maybe a little), but I do not want you to disregard the information because you question my expertise or the expertise of the team contributing to these chapters. Roth IRA conversions are likely a good strategy for most TIAA and

IRA owners at some point in their lives even with steady income tax rates. With income tax rates likely to increase in the future, a series of Roth IRA conversions before 2026 could add significant wealth for both you and your family. In addition, Roth IRA conversions are an important defense to the dreaded SECURE Act that has occupied a major portion of this book because it is so devastating to professors and other IRA and retirement plan owners.

Roth IRA conversions usually make sense with steady income tax rates. But, with tax rates likely to rise in the future, they make even more sense now. Please see the following chart showing the difference in tax rates for 2017 and 2023. If the sunset provisions take effect in 2026, which will happen unless Congress intervenes, the income tax rates will revert to the higher rates from 2017 plus inflation.

Comparative Tax Rates for 2023 and 2017 (2026) for "Married Filing Jointly"

2023			2017 (2026)		
$ 0 – 22,000	x	10%	$ 0 – 18,650	x	10%
22,001 – 89,450	x	12%	18,651 – 75,900	x	15%
89,451 – 190,750	x	22%	75,901 – 153,100	x	25%
190,751 – 364,200	x	24%	153,101 – 233,350	x	28%
364,201 – 462,500	x	32%	233,351 – 416,700	x	33%
462,501 – 693,750	x	35%	416,701 – 470,700	x	35%
693,751 *and above*	x	37%	470,701 *and above*	x	39.6%

As I just mentioned, the TCJA temporarily reduced personal income tax brackets. For example, in 2023, your taxable income could be as high as $364,200 and you would still be in the 24% marginal tax bracket. That same income in 2017 would put you in the 33% bracket. Even if your income was closer to $100,000, that means in 2023 that you could potentially make a $260,000 Roth conversion and pay tax at the marginal rates of 22% and 24%.

Please note this is a simplified example that doesn't take into account some of the other taxes and costs that occur with increased income such as an increase in your Medicare Part B premium. That said, please keep in mind, these are still substantially reduced tax rates that even if they do not go up in 2026, they will likely go up in the long run. Right now Congress is struggling to find a way to fund the interest on the federal deficit, let alone the deficit itself, let alone the national debt, let alone paying for all the natural disasters, let alone the unrecognized debt that we have already incurred, etc. Congress has never cut expenses, so I don't see that as a way out. In conclusion, I think tax rates will increase in the future which strengthens the arguments and the math for Roth IRA conversions.

After the SECURE Act passed, we began recommending that many 72-year-old+ clients consider executing Roth conversions, even though they were taking RMDs and receiving Social Security benefits. Basically, it makes sense for many retirees to execute Roth conversions in the 24% tax bracket because we know that their future RMDs will be more heavily taxed when/if the current tax rates revert to their 2017 levels. Of course, every situation is unique, and the decision needs to be evaluated on an individual basis, but there are significant commonalities also.

Many investors are surprised to discover that their taxable income in retirement is often higher than when they were working. Take a simple example of a married retired professor who has $2,000,000 in his or her retirement plan or IRA. The RMD on that amount starts at roughly $80,000 and gets higher as he/she ages. If you add this RMD to the income from two Social Security checks and some interest and dividends, the couple's taxable income is often higher than when they were working.

Many people have their retirement plans outside of an IRA, perhaps in TIAA. Depending on the contract with your university or employer (please see Chapter 8), it might be possible to make a Roth 403(b) conversion, which would be almost identical, conceptually, to a Roth IRA conversion.

Hopefully, you already have part of your retirement assets in Roth accounts. I have been attempting to get many of my clients to be proactive about Roth strategies. These clients now have a lot of money in these tax-free accounts, and many of their families will be hundreds of thousands of dollars, perhaps even millions of dollars, better off because they did. Our family will be better off by $1,297,500 even measured in today's dollars because of the large Roth conversion we made in 1998 and additional Roth IRAs and Roth 401(k) contributions and Roth conversions since that time.

If you are reading this book, you likely have a significant amount of money in Traditional retirement accounts because your employer's matching contributions were deposited there and up until at least 1998 and likely much longer, that is where your contributions went also. If so, you should consider integrating a long-term Roth IRA conversion strategy into your retirement and estate plan.

A new provision in the SECURE Act 2.0 allows employer matching contributions to be deposited into a Roth account. If the plan at your workplace allows this, this could be an excellent way to kick-start your Roth retirement savings.

One of the things we like to do for our clients is to have our CPAs *"run the numbers"* as part of a Financial Masterplan. This is our affectionate term for detailed quantitative analysis comparing many different scenarios into the long-term future. Though we have several specialty software programs to help us test different conversion amounts and timing, it is more of a manual process than one might imagine.

One reason we do this is to determine an ideal long-term Roth IRA conversion plan. Of course, Roth IRA conversions are only one aspect of running the numbers; a well-integrated Financial Masterplan will include strategies for Social Security, spending, gifting, and estate planning.

A well-integrated financial plan is usually the *"after"* picture for most of our clients. The *"before"* picture tends to be far less integrated. Frequently, our clients arrive with an unintegrated *"financial plan"* that is the product of many independent financial decisions. Each individual decision probably made sense at the time, but they do not necessarily work together effectively.

Does the Following Scenario Seem Familiar?

Either on your own or with an advisor, potentially a TIAA employee, when you first started working you picked an asset allocation for your retirement plan that seemed quite appropriate at the time. Then, either on your own or with another advisor, you picked investments for your money outside your retirement plan. Later, perhaps you contributed to a Roth IRA or even made several Roth IRA conversions.

At some point, you may have switched your allocations in your retirement plan. At a different point in time, you may have seen an insurance agent and purchased some insurance. At another point, you saw an attorney and had wills, trusts and hopefully the beneficiary designations for your retirement assets drafted. Maybe you took Social Security before age 70 or maybe you read an article that made sense and held off taking Social Security until you turned 70.

In other words, what you likely have now is not part of an integrated Financial Masterplan that takes everything into account, including money, desires, family situation, taxes, etc. It is the end result of what seemed to be a lot of reasonable independent decisions made at different times, often without thought as to how that decision impacted the entire Financial Masterplan.

Frequently, our clients arrive with an unintegrated *"financial plan"*— **the product of many independent financial decisions. Each individual decision probably made sense at the time, but they do not necessarily work together effectively.**

We think you will get a much better result if you develop a Financial Masterplan that takes your entire financial and family situation into account. Though it sounds self-serving, few firms provide this type of planning.

It is even more rare to get integrated retirement plan and estate plan strategies. One of the advantages that we enjoy is the close association of number-crunching CPAs, with expertise in IRAs, investment experts, and wonderful money managers.*

Your Financial Masterplan should be updated at least every year, even if the original plan was a multi-year plan. We see many quantitative professors, especially engineers, who attempt some primitive version of *"running the numbers"* using Excel spreadsheets.

Sometimes they find a better solution than doing nothing. On the other hand, they aren't tax experts, and they often neglect to factor in critical considerations. But, of course, we have a significant advantage. We possess excellent software and highly skilled CPAs who know tax law inside out and have many years of experience *"running the numbers"* to develop Financial Masterplans.

We want all our clients to have a synergistic plan that accounts for all assets, income, goals, dreams, family situations, etc. But I digress.

Back to the subject: the basic premise of this chapter is to show you that at some point in your life, a partial Roth IRA conversion will likely be a good strategy for both you and your heirs.

Under the current law (lower income tax rates combined with accelerated income taxes on your Traditional IRAs when you die), making a series of Roth IRA conversions is likely to improve your and your spouse's financial position while you are alive. It is also more likely that it will significantly improve your children's financial situation after you and your spouse die.

---

* Please see restrictions and disclaimers at the end of the book in the section titled *Save More, Have More, Leave More! The Lange Edge! A Truly Integrated Long Term Financial Masterplan.*

Do the Math

One of the reasons we *"run the numbers"* is because I do not believe that decisions about Roth IRA conversions should be based on opinions: i.e., *"I like the idea of a Roth conversion, let's do it."* Whether you should make a Roth conversion and for how much and when is not just a matter of personal preference.

Maybe you like Celine Dion, and I like Whitney Houston. There isn't a way to objectively prove who is the better singer. Whether to make a Roth IRA conversion, on the other hand, is a matter of math, not opinions; it is possible and imperative to make objective projections.

We believe in peer-reviewed math, science, and following proven academic data-driven planning to enhance your finances. Yes, the results will depend on the assumptions used to make the projections. We address that by starting with assumptions that we think are reasonable.

But as the client is frequently present when we run our numbers, all assumptions can be modified or changed with the client's input. In addition, the goal of running the numbers is to arrive at the best solution given your personal values and your individual financial situation. But, given certain values and other parameters, the best results can be obtained by *"running the numbers"* rather than guessing.

Many factors should be considered when planning the ideal Roth IRA conversion strategy for your family. I will be the first to admit that Roth IRA conversions are not perfect or appropriate for everyone. But I believe that, with the help of projections of different amounts and timings of Roth conversions, coming up with the ideal Roth IRA conversion plan for you and your family can provide most professors and their families enormous financial rewards.

Critics of Roth IRA conversions will point out that the SECURE Act reduces the potential long-term benefits of Roth IRA conversions because the beneficiary will no longer benefit from the lifetime stretch of an Inherited Roth IRA. While this is true, in most cases, inheriting a Roth IRA is much better than inheriting a Traditional IRA. Of course, both types of Inherited accounts must be

We believe in peer-reviewed math, science, and following proven academic data-driven planning to enhance your finances.

distributed within ten years of the death of the IRA owner. That said, Traditional retirement accounts are taxable, leading to potentially massive acceleration of the income taxes for the beneficiary.

While the greatest benefit of Roth conversions is often assumed to be conferred on your beneficiaries, we have found surprising benefits for IRA owners who are willing to learn when and how much of a Roth IRA conversion to make. I have wealthy clients who either do not have children or aren't particularly interested in providing for the next generation who are still making substantial Roth IRA conversions.

The irony is even though these conversions will allow the clients to spend a lot more money over their lifetime, they probably will not. Chapter 24 addresses that frequent unwillingness to spend anywhere near what you can afford.

The math usually works even if tax rates are steady. If you believe like we do that the reduced tax rates established by the Tax Cuts and Jobs Act will not be in place permanently and tax rates will go up in the future, the Roth conversion is even more advantageous. *"Running the numbers"* will demonstrate that it is often beneficial for you to pay tax now on money that, at some point in your lifetime, you know you will be required to pay taxes on anyway—potentially at a much higher rate.

There have been times in history when Congress was not shy about taxing your hard-earned money. In 1944, the top tax rate peaked at 94%! We already have insurmountable financial problems as a country, and I think betting on future tax increases is a much better bet than future tax decreases.

Roth IRA conversions give you some control over your tax planning by reducing the balance in your Traditional IRA accounts, which then reduces your RMD—an advantage during times when future tax rates are likely to increase. Furthermore, Roth conversions reduce the amount of money held in Traditional IRAs that will be subject to the SECURE Act's accelerated income tax at your death. Inherited Roth IRA distributions are tax-free—which will seriously reduce the pain of accelerated taxes on Traditional IRAs.

Developing a long-term Roth IRA conversion strategy is most likely an extremely valuable use of your time and/or money if you chose to work with a Roth IRA conversion expert. Even if you go through the appropriate steps and determine a Roth conversion isn't for you, at least you will know and won't have a nagging feeling you should be doing something that you aren't doing. So, how do you move forward?

Know the General Principles First, *"Run the Numbers"* Next

Making changes to a retirement plan can be scary and overwhelming. You do not want to make a mistake, and it can seem safest just to stay put. I get it. I have a reputation for being a strong advocate for Roth IRA conversions for people of all ages. That reputation doesn't really reflect my beliefs.

I believe this is a more accurate statement—I am the owner of a firm that *"runs the numbers"* for our clients to make objective recommendations that often include making a series of Roth IRA conversions over several years.

The advice that follows comes from me having overseen our *"number running"* literally thousands of times. I have trained thousands of financial advisors, CPAs, attorneys, and consumers on the benefits of Roth IRA conversions. Our team of number crunching CPAs have also made major contributions to the Roth conversion chapters of this book.

I mention some of these things because Roth IRA conversions can be so valuable that I would hate readers to conclude *"Oh that's his opinion. My CPA or advisor said they weren't a good idea or at least not a good idea for me."* This isn't a matter of opinion. It is a matter of math. I cannot overemphasize the potential benefits of an objective math-oriented approach and coming up with the ideal long-term Roth IRA conversion plan.

If math indicates that not doing a conversion is best, then that is likely what you should do. That said, the math has to be done right and the biggest mistake that is actually adhered to more than the right answer is how to quantify the measurement tool for Roth IRA conversions.

The Secret: Quantifying the Benefit of Roth IRA Conversions Using the Concept of Purchasing Power

The following section could be a game changer for you. I would read this section carefully and you might have to read it more than once to fully absorb this critical concept.

Of course, if you have been following my work, you have heard me drone on and on about this point for over 20 years. I have been teaching this concept literally for 22 years to IRA and retirement plan owners, financial advisors, CPAs, and attorneys. The CPAs and engineers usually get it fairly quickly. You have to explain it multiple times to attorneys who have a harder time with it than even the IRA owners who attend our workshops. Despite having taught it to thousands, it is still a general secret that millions would benefit from understanding.

I am the owner of a firm that *"runs the numbers"* for our clients to make objective recommendations that often include making a series of Roth IRA conversions over several years.

"The Secret" involves determining the most accurate measurement tool for wealth. I am not interested in increasing your total dollars nearly as much as I am interested in increasing your purchasing power. Critical to evaluating the costs and benefits of Roth conversions as well as understanding your true wealth is thinking in terms of *"purchasing power"* vs. *"total dollars."*

For example, if I have $1 million in my IRA, and you have $900,000 in an after-tax account, then using a total dollar approach, I have more money than you. But what if we both want to make a large purchase? I must cash in my IRA and pay the taxes. Let's assume a flat income tax rate of 24%. I know that isn't realistic, but this is to demonstrate a concept. After paying the taxes, I'd end up with $760,000 in cash. (This ignores the tax on the money needed to pay the tax, but I want to keep this simple.)

Unless there are capital gains that need to be paid, there will be no tax consequence when you cash out your $900,000. Even if you have to pay some capital gains taxes, they will be much lower than my tax bill. That means you can purchase more goods and services with your $900,000 after-tax dollars than I can with my $1 million IRA. You have more purchasing power than I do, even though I have more *"total dollars."*

This is a critical concept, and I recommend rereading the prior paragraph until you understand it before moving on.

Now, let's look at Roth conversions in terms of purchasing power: Assume that both of us have $100,000 in our Traditional IRAs and $24,000 outside our IRAs. I will assume a flat income tax rate of 24%, as I did previously. If I don't make a Roth IRA conversion, I have $124,000 when measured in *"total dollars."* But, if I think of that amount in terms of *"purchasing power,"* I have $100,000.

Here's a breakdown of that purchasing power math:

$100,000 Traditional IRA dollars + $24,000 non-IRA dollars = **$124,000 *"Total Dollars"***

$124,000 *"Total Dollars"* - $24,000 non-IRA dollars* = **$100,000 *"Purchasing Power"***

The non-IRA dollars will be used to pay the tax due when the $100,000 IRA is cashed.

> *"The Secret"* involves determining the most accurate measure-
> ment tool for wealth. I am not interested in increasing your
> total dollars nearly as much as I am interested in increasing
> your *"purchasing power."*

Now let's assume that you start with the same $100,000 in your Traditional IRA and $24,000 outside your IRA, and you execute a Roth conversion of your entire IRA. Because you converted your Traditional IRA (which you haven't yet paid taxes on) to the Roth IRA, you will have to fork over $24,000 of after-tax dollars to Uncle Sam ($100,000 times 24% tax rate). But, after the conversion, you also have $100,000 measured in both total dollars and purchasing power because there will be no tax due when you cash in your Roth IRA.

The following shows that, when measured in terms of purchasing power and using simple assumptions, the breakeven point on Roth IRA conversions is Day 1, regardless of your age.

Roth IRA After Conversion		$ 100,000
Traditional IRA	$ 100,000	
Other Non-IRA Funds*	$ 24,000	0
Total Dollar Value of Accounts	***$ 124,000***	***$ 100,000***
Less Taxes Paid on IRA *(if distributed)*	$ 24,000	0
Purchasing Power	**$ 100,000**	**$ 100,000**

*$24,000 non-IRA Funds used to pay taxes on either cashing in the Traditional IRA or a Roth IRA conversion.

Again, I can't overemphasize the importance of this concept. The failure to understand this concept is one of the reasons why many so-called experts and advisors give clients advice regarding Roth IRA conversions that is completely wrong for them. And many of the free calculators available on the internet calculate the value of Roth conversions in terms of total dollars which, again, leads to underestimating the financial benefit that could be derived from a series of Roth IRA conversions.

If your measurement tool is total dollars, instead of the better measure of wealth which is purchasing power, then your inevitable conclusion will be that

Roth IRA conversions are only good for younger taxpayers who have many years for the tax-free growth to accumulate in their Roth IRA, which will outweigh the money they paid to convert their Traditional IRA to a Roth IRA. Using the same measurement tool of total dollars will also lead you to conclude that Roth IRA conversions are bad for older taxpayers.

Measuring value in total dollars instead of purchasing power is a very common but very costly mistake.

Let's look at this issue in a different way, but one that will lead to the same conclusion. If you were a farmer, would you rather deduct the cost of the seed but be required to pay tax on the harvest or pay tax on the seed and reap the harvest tax-free? A Roth IRA conversion is like paying tax on the seed—that is to say, paying tax on the amount of your Traditional IRA that you want to convert. Then, after you pay the tax, you plant the seed (open your new Roth IRA account with the money you have converted), and over many years, you watch it grow. Then when you or your heirs distribute or harvest the crop (the amount you converted plus all of the growth), *the entire harvest or distribution is income-tax free.*

If you're already retired, is the tax-free advantage of the Roth conversion great enough to write a big check, or perhaps a number of smaller annual checks over a period of several years, to Uncle Sam before necessary, let alone deal with all the paperwork? Paperwork can be quite time consuming. And most of my academic clients are as interested in saving time as well as money, which is one of the reasons why I appreciate you reading this book.

To address this question of whether the value of Roth conversions might outweigh the hassle and time required to execute the strategy, let's look at the comparison outlined in Figure 15.1 shown below. In this example, we *"ran the numbers"* for two professors whose circumstances (including financial history, annual income, annual spending, etc.) are identical in every way except that one professor did a series of Roth IRA conversions, and the other professor owner did not. Have a look at the figure below, which shows the outcome for the first professor owner who made a series of Roth IRA conversions of $175,000 over five years starting at age 65, compared to no Roth IRA conversions. Again, we measure in purchasing power, not total dollars.

Keep in mind that the current tax rates are set to *"sunset"* and return to 2017 rates at the end of 2025. For the couple in this example, it made sense to maximize annual conversions over five years before the tax rates are scheduled to increase even though their income will remain relatively low for an additonal two years.

Since 2025 and the potential of increased tax rates is rapidly approaching, time is of the essence. The sooner you are able to begin Roth conversions, the more years you have to maximize these current lower tax brackets. For those of you still employed and who do not have IRAs that you could convert to Roth IRAs, check with your retirement plan administrator and see if you are allowed to make Roth 403(b) or Roth 401(k) conversions inside your retirement plan. If you know you are going to be in a higher tax bracket in future years, it might be

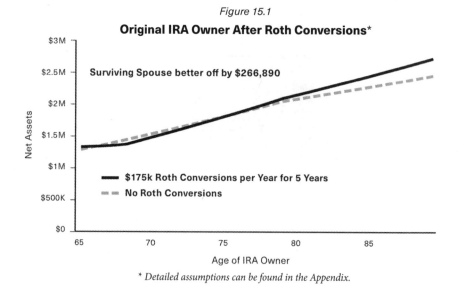

Figure 15.1

Original IRA Owner After Roth Conversions*

* Detailed assumptions can be found in the Appendix.

Measuring value in total dollars instead of purchasing power is a very common but very costly mistake.

profitable to start Roth conversions in your retirement plan at work, potentially either before or after you retire.

It is hard to see, but this shows that the IRA owner (that is you, not your kids) is better off measured in purchasing power by $266,890 if you make five $175,000 Roth conversions starting as late as age 65 and assuming you and/or your spouse survive until age 90. This assumes a 7.5% rate of return and 2.5% inflation, and we are measuring in today's dollars. If we measured without taking inflation into account, the advantage would be much higher.

This figure measures the accounts in terms of their purchasing power, which we believe is the only appropriate way to compare the value of a taxable IRA to that of an after-tax account. Of course, much depends on your personal circumstances. Still, you will likely benefit during your lifetime by making a Roth conversion or, more likely, a series of smaller Roth IRA conversions over a period of years. And the longer you and your spouse live, the more that benefit grows.

If you would like to learn more about why Roth IRA conversions are good for you and your heirs, please see our book, *The Roth Revolution, Pay Taxes Once and Never Again*, which you can download for free by going to **https://PayTaxesLater.com/Books/** or purchase on Amazon. Please note that while that book was written before the SECURE Act and is therefore dated, virtually all the concepts remain the same, and it can still be a valuable resource. We also have a video focusing on Roth IRA conversions before and after the SECURE Act. Please see **https://PayTaxesLater.com/Roth-Workshop/**.

Please note Shirl Trefelner, a number-crunching CPA in our office, did this analysis and when I reviewed it, I thought it was wrong. I would have guessed that doing Roth conversions up until age 72, not age 70 would have been optimal. I thought she made a mistake forgetting that RMDs didn't start until age 72 under the SECURE Act as the law stood when she made the calculations. When I questioned her on it, I saw she was a step ahead of me. She used the right year for the RMD calculation but in this case, the additional income from collecting Social Security made the optimal plan to stop converting at age 70, not age 72. I bring this up to point out that *"running the numbers"* is very fact specific and even experts can guess wrong with-out doing actual calculations.

Roth IRA Conversions are Definitely Good for Your Heirs

Let's continue with the previous example. Assume you begin making Roth IRA conversions of $175,000/year at age 65 and continue until you begin taking RMDs from what remains of your Traditional IRA, at age 72. You die at age 80 and your spouse dies at age 90, leaving the remaining estate to your son who is 56 when the second spouse dies. Let's also assume that both you and your spouse are dead and that your Roth IRA is now worth $800,000. Let's also assume you did not do any of the special planning regarding disclaimers covered in Chapter 14. Your only child is named as the beneficiary of the Roth IRA. Your child now owns a special asset called an Inherited Roth IRA. Under the SECURE Act, the entire Inherited Roth IRA account must be disbursed within ten years of your death.

Losing the long-term tax-free growth on the Roth IRA over their lifetimes as was possible under the pre-SECURE Act rules will be costly to your children but inheriting a Roth account is still way more advantageous than inheriting a Traditional IRA.

The following figure projects the difference between you completing the five $175,000 Roth IRA conversions versus doing nothing as measured in the lives of your child. Though we have more details for this figure in the Appendix, the most important detail is that this figure considers the taxes you had to pay to

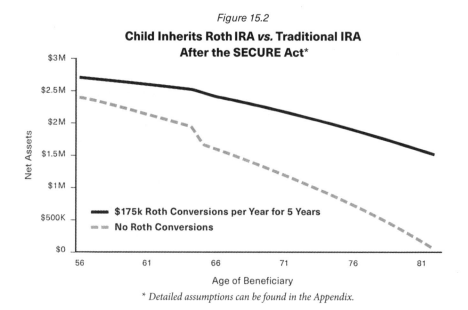

Figure 15.2

Child Inherits Roth IRA *vs.* Traditional IRA After the SECURE Act*

Detailed assumptions can be found in the Appendix.

make the Roth IRA conversions before you died and the taxes that would be paid by the beneficiary if no Roth IRA conversion had been done.

Figure 15.2 continues the scenario from Figure 15.1 and shows what would happen after your death. The bump at age 66 is when all assets from the Inherited IRA have been disbursed. The solid line shows what would happen if you completed the series of Roth IRA conversions by age 70, as depicted in Figure 15.1, and the dashed line shows where your child would be if no Roth IRA conversions had been done. As Figure 15.1 shows, with a Roth IRA conversion, your child will inherit a Roth IRA with a higher balance than if no conversion had taken place. During the first ten years after the death of the last surviving parent, this difference gets even bigger because the beneficiary of a Traditional IRA has to pay tax on the distributions while the inheritor of a Roth IRA can leave the assets in place to continue to appreciate tax-free until the tenth year.

Even though both of these IRAs are stretched for only ten years, inheriting the Roth (the solid line) gives your child well over an additional $1,000,000 over their lifetime. Again, please note that if you complete a Roth IRA conversion and if tax rates increase after the conversion, the value of the Roth IRA conversion to you and your children will be even higher because we do not assume increasing tax rates for this analysis. If you are leaving the Roth IRA to a beneficiary with a disability or chronic illness who can stretch the inherited Roth over their lifetime, the difference would really be enormous.

Our Process for *"Running the Numbers"*

You can skip to the next subhead if you have no interest in how our accounting firm *"runs the numbers"* and why we recommend running the numbers.

Are you considering Roth conversions? We recommend that unless you are an extremely skilled amateur number cruncher that you consider working with a firm that has great expertise in running the numbers on Roth IRA conversions to make objective recommendations.

We have a lot of clients, especially professors, who would rather have a root canal than pay an advisor. Often, they try doing some financial analysis and Roth IRA conversion analysis and don't come up with the right conclusion. They often make significant mistakes that lead them to far-from-optimal results. That being said, they may come up with a better conclusion than doing nothing.

Professors who measure in total dollars often come to the conclusion that a Roth IRA conversion is not appropriate for them. We might conclude that if they had used the more accurate measure of wealth that is purchasing power, they might have come to a completely different conclusion.

Please be wary of internet financial calculators. As I mentioned before, many, if not most, of the ones I see do not consider the concept of purchasing power and lead to the wrong conclusion.

If you measure in total dollars instead of purchasing power, you will often conclude that Roth IRA conversions are not good for older individuals. A young person will likely have a long enough time to make up for the fact that they had to write a check to the IRS to make the conversion. Seniors, on the other hand, will have less time, and they might not make up for the taxes they had to pay on the conversion.

However, both examples are based on total dollars instead of the more appropriate measurement of purchasing power. When you take purchasing power into account, Roth IRA conversions are often advantageous for seniors, as demonstrated in the analysis above.

Completing a Financial Masterplan, at least the way we do it, taking multiple variables into account, is a fairly complicated calculation that has to consider timing, taxes, and Social Security benefits. (I know this sounds self-serving, but there are very few firms that can thoroughly *"run the numbers"* and come up with the right answer, and we pride ourselves on our skillset.)

We also make it our practice to *"run the numbers"* with the client present, at least part of the time, either in the room or, in recent years when our practice has transformed from a basically local practice to a national practice, on Zoom. Of course, even with our long-time local clients many of our reviews are on Zoom to avoid Covid exposure. This allows the client to see how we arrive at our recommendations. And it allows them to evaluate the assumptions and choose the ones that best reflect their circumstances.

In practice, when we *"run the numbers,"* Roth IRA conversions are only one of many factors that we consider. For example, we often compare different Social Security strategies, gifting strategies, spending strategies, and lifestyle issues like buying or renting a second home in a warmer climate. We also work backwards to determine how much money a client can safely spend.

Evaluating the merits of Roth IRA conversions, though critical, is only one variable when we *"run the numbers."* Our goal is to develop a long-term Financial Masterplan for our clients. You might assume that in today's world, there would be killer software where all you need to do is enter a few numbers and *poof!*, the ideal Roth IRA conversion recommendation pops out. Unfortunately, that isn't even close to the truth.

Though we use the finest software available, *"running the numbers"* is much more hands-on than you would imagine, and the skill of the person running the numbers is more important than the quality of the software they are using.

Believe it or not, in addition to a variety of the excellent specialized software now on the market, for certain applications, we still use an Excel template that we developed years ago because we haven't found anything better. Other times the person running the numbers is using an Excel spreadsheet because no software can adequately handle certain situations, and we must make *"manual"* calculations.

It is also prudent to test your hypothetical results. Preparing mock tax returns will show the impact of alternative courses of action. For example, after arriving at a conclusion for the amount and timing of a Roth IRA conversion, we test that amount using all the facts and figures of a client's actual tax return in a mock tax return with different levels of Roth IRA conversion amounts included.

Even for veteran number crunchers, there are often surprises in this last step that cause us to change our recommendations, such as discovering we can reduce or eliminate the alternative minimum tax with a Roth IRA conversion. If you are curious about whether a Roth IRA conversion is something you should think about, here are some points to consider.

You may be able to minimize the sticker shock and stay in a lower tax bracket if you make a series of small conversions over several years rather than converting one large lump sum. One overly simplistic—though useful—idea would be to convert, each year, only enough to bring you to the top of your existing bracket, only moving into the next bracket if it made good long-term sense.

But that rule of thumb is overly simplistic. For example, right now, after running the numbers we often recommend that a taxpayer in the 22% bracket makes a large enough Roth IRA conversion to take them to the 24% bracket.

> **One overly simplistic—though useful—idea would be to convert, each year, only enough to bring you to the top of your existing bracket, only moving into the next bracket if it made good long-term sense.**

The Classic *"Window of Opportunity"* for Roth Conversions

The classic window of opportunity for Roth conversions has conventionally been after you retire but before your minimum distributions. You will not have the taxable income from your wages, nor the income from your RMDs. This will be even more critical for those of you who took advantage of the early retirement buyouts that happened at many universities and other organizations at the onset of the Covid-19 pandemic. Delaying your Social Security benefits until age 70 also widens this window of opportunity.

If you have accumulated after-tax savings that you can live on, or you can survive on your spouse's income, without applying for Social Security, you may have some years when you can convert more money to a Roth IRA while still staying in a lower tax bracket.

Related to this topic, one of my clients had a dilemma. He desperately wanted a low-income year to make more Roth IRA conversions. But he didn't want to retire, even though he was in his 80s. He asked the University of Pittsburgh if he could work but not get paid anything for the calendar year. They said no! He had to get paid whether he liked it or not. In his case, we partially made up for the fact that he had to accept his salary by making a sizable charitable contribution which he wanted to do anyway.

Charitable contributions, depending on if you itemize your deductions or qualified charitable distributions (QCDs) (please see Chapter 20) and Roth IRA conversions sometimes go together like peas and carrots. The reduced income from the charitable deduction or the QCD that reduces the minimum distribution often allows a bigger Roth IRA conversion at a lower tax rate.

If you plan, you can sometimes manipulate your income before or during retirement to ensure that the taxes you pay on a Roth conversion are as low as possible. Please note that we make similar calculations with regard to optimizing your Social Security strategy. Optimizing Social Security and Roth IRA conversions is often a synergistic calculation. For more about the various Social Security strategies, please download our best-selling Social Security book, ***The $214,000 Mistake: How to Double Your Social Security & Maximize Your IRAs***, for free by going to **https://PayTaxesLater.com/Books/**.

Finally, consider that tax rates are likely going to increase in the future. The value of paying taxes now at lower rates and making tax-free withdrawals at a later date will be even more favorable than indicated by the analysis presented here. Current tax regulations are set to *"sunset"* at the end of 2025. At that time, the federal tax brackets are scheduled to return to 2017 levels plus inflation.

For a married couple, the top of the 24% tax bracket currently ends at $364,200. After 2026, that same couple will be in the 33% tax bracket at that income level. It might make sense to maximize every penny of the 24% tax bracket now with Roth conversions in an effort to reduce future RMDs and paying 33% tax. As we approach 2025, the window to take advantage of the current favorable tax brackets is getting shorter and shorter. The sooner you start Roth conversions, the more years you have to take advantage of these reduced rates.

There are so many variables to consider when making Roth IRA conversions for retirement and estate planning. It has been our longstanding practice, when running the numbers, to determine the best long-term strategy for when and how much to convert to a Roth IRA. And while the advantages to your heirs can be impressive, our primary focus can be on the advantages of the conversion for our clients and not their heirs.

On the other hand, the truth is most clients are interested in the best conversion advice for both them and their heirs. We usually ask what income tax bracket your children are in, as well as which state they are living in, both of which are relevant for our calculations. We usually run our calculations through a reasonable projection for the life of your child or children.

It is also possible that after running the numbers, it becomes clear that you are not a good candidate for a Roth IRA conversion. For example, one group of people it might not be beneficial for are taxpayers who have no money to pay the income tax on the conversion except by invading their IRA. Paying for the conversion with IRA dollars isn't great, but there may be some long-term benefits in terms of reduced future RMDs and potential savings for your heirs. If that is your situation, please keep reading.

What you might need is a nontaxable source of funds to pay the taxes on the Roth conversion. But what if you do not have sufficient funds to live comfortably and pay taxes on your Roth IRA conversion because all your money is already in a retirement plan or even a Roth IRA? Should you just give up?

Let Your House Pay for Your Roth IRA Conversion

You could borrow the money to pay the taxes on a Roth IRA. The borrowed money would not be considered income. The most likely source of the borrowed money would be to borrow money from the bank, usually in the form of a home equity loan like a line of credit, a HELOC, a mortgage, or even a reverse mortgage. You can use the nontaxable money from that loan to finance your short-term living expenses and to pay the taxes on a series of Roth IRA conversions. Most people balk at this suggestion. I get it. It is a lot easier for our accounting firm to *"crunch the numbers"* than for you to go out and borrow against your house. I also recognize this advice goes against most everything you have read or heard and likely goes against your instincts.

Even Shakespeare said, *"Neither a borrower nor a lender be."* Dave Ramsey quotes Proverbs 22:7 *"the borrower is slave to the lender"* and wants you to pay off your mortgage early and not to go back into debt after retirement.

If there is any reasonable chance you will not be able to make the payments, obviously this would be a terrible strategy. On the other hand, the bank probably wouldn't lend you the money if they thought you could not make the payments. They don't want to foreclose.

I also always say for a tax strategy to work, it must pass the *"math test"* and the *"stomach test."* This strategy for more than half of the clients I have brought this up to fails the *"stomach test."*

But if you *are* interested in this strategy, I suggest you go to **Forbes.com**, type in my name, and download an article I published with them two years ago titled *Let Your House Pay for Your 2020 Roth IRA Conversion*. If you include projected gains from this strategy that our clients have implemented, we have saved a lot of family's tens if not hundreds of thousands of dollars with this strategy.

By the way, disclaimer, disclaimer, disclaimer. Do this strategy only after talking with a qualified financial expert who will likely try to talk you out of it.

Who Else Would Not Benefit from a Roth IRA Conversion?

Another example of someone who might not benefit from a Roth IRA conversion is someone who plans on leaving all their money to a charity. Again, this is because charities are tax-exempt, and the conversion would result in unnecessary taxes when the Traditional IRA and the money that would have been used to pay the tax on the Roth IRA conversion could have gone to the charity tax-free.

> I also always say for a tax strategy to work, it must pass the *"math test"* and the *"stomach test."* This strategy for more than half of the clients I have brought this up to fails the *"stomach test."*

There are certainly other IRA owners who would not benefit from a Roth conversion. That said, we find that most of the IRA owners that we see will benefit from developing and implementing a Roth IRA conversion strategy. Determining your best plan is a great use of your time, and if you find the right advisor to help you, a great use of your money.

Please keep an open mind when going into the process of determining how much and when to convert to a Roth IRA. It is okay to have preconceived notions, but please be data driven in this area.

One client was unhappy when the results of the projections of our best recommendations still left him with a significant IRA at the end of his lifetime. He was hoping for a plan that would have converted everything to a Roth. In his case, doing so would have pushed him into too high an income tax bracket. Then, when he hit age 72, since there would be so little Traditional IRA left, his income would be down. Both he and his family would have been worse off if we blindly followed his wishes of gradually converting everything to a Roth before he died. Remember, in God we trust; all others bring data.

Of course, this short chapter cannot tell you everything you need to know about Roth IRA conversions, which is why we have several more in-depth chapters. Also, I encourage you to download my book, *The Roth Revolution: Pay Taxes Once and Never Again* at **https://PayTaxesLater.com/Books/**.

After SECURE Act 2.0, the ages for starting RMDs was extended. Please see Chapter 6. This change gives many readers the benefit of additional years between retirement and taking RMDs meaning additional years where a Roth IRA conversion is even more desirable.

KEY IDEAS

- Most IRA owners should be proactive about at least considering and more likely developing a long-term Roth IRA conversion strategy.

- To better appreciate Roth IRA conversions, we recommend you measure wealth in purchasing power rather than total dollars.

Key Ideas continue on the following page.

KEY IDEAS
(continued)

- The current low tax brackets and inevitable tax increases add incentive to explore Roth IRA conversions.

- Act now, the window is getting shorter and shorter before tax rates are scheduled to increase.

- Your heirs will benefit more from inheriting Roth IRAs than Traditional IRAs.

- Running the numbers can result in much better decisions than winging it.

- An integrated retirement and estate plan that takes your assets, income, goals and dreams, family situation, etc., into account is decidedly advantageous. Roth IRA conversions are not for everyone, but the only way to really assess the situation is to *"run the numbers."*

16

Roth Conversions and the Effects of Medicare Income-Related Monthly Adjustment Amounts (IRMAA)

by Steven T. Kohman,
Certified Public Accountant*

We all would like to have more in Roth IRAs than Traditional IRAs since they grow tax-free and there are *no* Required Minimum Distributions (RMDs) for the owner. Additionally, if your children or grandchildren inherit your Roth IRA, the inherited Roth IRA can continue to grow income-tax free for ten years after the death of the IRA owner. In contrast, with an inherited Traditional IRA, RMDs over the ten years may cause higher income and higher tax rates for the beneficiary during those years. To get more in Roth IRAs and less in Traditional IRAs, a taxable Roth conversion is the only option for most retirees.

The costs of making a Roth conversion must be considered when deciding how much to convert in any given year. For people who are under age 63, higher income taxes are the primary cost of doing a conversion. Why age 63 and not age 65? This is not a typo. Please read on for more information.

For people who are older and who will be on Medicare in 2025, increasing income in 2023 with a Roth conversion may make their 2025 Medicare premiums higher. These Medicare Income-Related Monthly Adjustment Amounts (IRMAA costs) should also be considered as an extra cost of doing the conversion. In this chapter, we will look at how significant these additional IRMAA costs are in relation to the Roth conversions. All the costs discussed in this chapter are based on the Married-Filing-Joint (MFJ) costs for married couples.

Roth Conversions Can Increase Your Taxes in Multiple Ways

Without IRMAA costs, the current federal income tax bracket rates of 10%, 12%, 22%, 24%, 32%, 35%, and 37% are useful as a guide to quantify your con-

---

* Steve is our veteran number-crunching Roth IRA expert.

version costs. There are, however, additional costs beyond the income tax in these brackets. For example, the additional income from the Roth IRA conversion increases other taxes like net investment income tax when your AGI exceeds $250,000. For higher income taxpayers, the additional conversion income could trigger the higher 20% capital gains tax rate rather than the normal 15% capital gains tax rate on qualified dividends and long-term capital gains when your taxable income exceeds $553,850.

For lower income taxpayers receiving Social Security income, Social Security income may not be fully taxable up to 85% without a conversion, but with a Roth conversion, up to 85% of Social Security income may then be subject to federal income tax. The additional income from the Roth IRA conversion could also add to the tax cost of the conversion by changing tax-free qualified dividends and/or long-term capital gains to amounts taxable at 15% when ordinary taxable income is below $89,250 before the conversion. *Ordinary taxable income* is taxable income less the qualified dividends and long-term capital gains.

How Roth Conversions Impact Future Medicare Premium Costs

In November of each year, the Social Security Administration determines how much Medicare premiums including IRMAA costs you will have to pay for the coming year based on the most recently filed tax return. For 2023, Medicare premiums are based on your 2021 income because that was the most recently filed tax return as of November 2022. Similarly, the 2025 Medicare premiums will be based on your 2023 income which may include Roth conversion income. Because of this two-year lag between the time you file your income tax return and the effect it has on your Medicare premiums, tax planning during the year you turn age 63 impacts the amount of Medicare premiums you pay when you are age 65.

This means that taxpayers or their spouses who are age 63 and over must consider what the possible impact of additional income from a Roth conversion in the current year might be on their Medicare premiums two years in the future. Because the IRMAA cost increases and the income levels where the increases take effect are not known until well after the year of the conversion, calculating the impact of Roth conversions on future costs of Medicare premiums must be estimated.

IRMAA costs increase the Medicare premiums when your Modified Adjusted Gross Income (MAGI) exceeds certain amounts. MAGI is the AGI plus tax-exempt dividends and interest on your tax return plus some other less common income exclusions. For 2023 Medicare premiums, the IRMAA cost increases start when MAGI on a 2021 MFJ tax return exceeds $194,000. As MAGI increases, so do the additional costs for Medicare premiums.

These extra 2023 IRMAA Medicare premiums cost increases for a MFJ couple on Parts B and D of Medicare for a full year are as follows:

- $1,874 for 2021 MAGI over $194,000 but under $246,000
- $4,711 for 2021 MAGI over $246,000 but under $306,000
- $7,546 for 2021 MAGI over $306,000 but under $366,000
- $10,382 for 2021 MAGI over $366,000 but under $750,000
- $11,328 for 2021 MAGI over $750,000

It is important to know that if you are over the MAGI limits by any amount you will be charged the extra Medicare premiums. For example, if you convert $1 too much and make your MAGI $194,001, you will have the extra $1,874 of Medicare premium costs. This is different than how your income tax rates increase where the first dollars are taxed at a certain rate, say 10%, and then the next dollars are taxed at 12%, and so on. By earning only $1 more in income, a big difference in the effective cost of your Roth conversion could result. It makes sense to keep the conversion low enough to safely stay under the applicable income level in most cases.

It is also important to know that for the last few years, these MAGI levels have increased for inflation. By the time they calculate the IRMAA increase levels for 2025 Medicare premiums based on 2023 income, these levels will likely be higher since they are now indexed to inflation. For example, due to inflation in 2022, the first increase level changed from $182,000 to $194,000.

They also change the extra premium increase amounts from year to year so the extra IRMAA premiums could be higher by 2024. These extra charges are not based on normal inflation and from 2021 to 2022 the extra IRMAA costs increased by over 12% and in some of the lower income thresholds by 14.5%!

Avoiding IRMAA Costs Initially

What happens if your income drops between year 2021 (the year that Medicare uses to determine your premium costs) and in year 2023, when you pay those premiums? Fortunately, the Social Security Administration offers a way out—but it is fairly restricted. These IRMAA increases can potentially be avoided in the first year after you have a *"life-changing event"* that causes your income to decrease by filing Form SSA-44. A life-changing event includes retirement, death of a spouse, marriage or divorce, loss of pension, and a few other rare circumstances. Roth conversions are not counted as life-changing events. The most common reason to file Form SSA-44 is when you retire from a highly compensated position, and now that you have retired, your income will be less.

Using the 2021 tax return with high income before retirement may not be representative of the lower income you will have in 2023 after retirement. The SSA-44 is a way for you to get excused from the IRMAA Medicare premium increases in that situation, possibly saving you thousands of dollars.

Quantifying the Impact of Roth Conversions on Medicare

These extra IRMAA costs affect the overall cost of Roth conversions. As a basic example, let's assume that without the Roth conversion, the 2022 MAGI for a married couple filing jointly is $139,500 and taxable income is $110,800. For this example, we're ignoring the complications of investment income, state income tax, and other factors, so ordinary taxable income is also $110,800. This is in the 22% tax bracket for 2022. We are also assuming that the 2024 IRMAA cost increases will remain the same as they are for 2022.

- A Roth conversion of $42,000 can be done to keep the MAGI under the first Medicare premium increase level at a tax cost of 22% since the taxable income is still in the 22% tax bracket. *The IRMAA cost—which will affect Medicare premiums to be paid in 2024—is zero.*

- A Roth conversion of $88,000 can be done to keep the MAGI under the next Medicare premium increase level at an incremental tax cost of 22.47% above the $42,000 conversion, since this is partly in the 22% and partly in the 24% tax bracket. But the estimated extra Medicare premiums of $1,930 makes the incremental cost 27.09%. *The IRMAA cost is 4.62% of the extra conversion.*

- A Roth conversion of $144,000 can be done to keep the MAGI under the next Medicare premium increase level at an incremental tax cost of 24% above the $88,000 conversion, since this is in the 24% tax bracket. But the estimated extra Medicare premiums of $2,923 makes the incremental cost 29.22%. *The extra IRMAA cost is 5.22% of the extra conversion.*

- At this point, the couple may want to only convert $88,000 instead of $144,000 because this extra IRMAA cost is higher than the first level of IRMAA cost. In addition, if this couple has investment income, they may also be subject to the 3.8% net investment income tax because their AGI exceeds $250,000. Net investment income tax applies to the extent that AGI exceeds $250,000 MFJ ($200,000 if Single) and to the extent that you have investment income. In this example, AGI is $283,500 including the $144,000 Roth conversion. If the income included $33,500 of investment income, there is an extra $1,273 of tax cost to consider.

- A Roth conversion of $200,000 can be done to keep the MAGI under the next Medicare premium increase level at an incremental tax cost of 24% above the $144,000 conversion, since this is still in the 24% tax bracket. But the estimated extra Medicare premiums of $2,921 makes the incremental cost 29.22%. *The extra IRMAA cost is again 5.22% of the extra conversion.*

- If a larger conversion is done to the top of the 24% tax bracket, it would only be a $229,300 conversion or $29,300 more than the $200,000 conversion. The extra Medicare premiums result in an incremental cost of 33.96% which is the 24% tax cost plus an extra 9.96% for the IRMAA cost.

This is very high, so if the couple wanted to convert at least this much, it may make sense to convert $321,100 to the top of the 32% tax bracket at an incremental cost of only 32% because there would be *no additional IRMAA cost* over the $229,300 conversion. Similarly, if it makes sense to convert to the top of the 35% tax bracket with a $537,050 conversion, there is again *no additional IRMAA cost* over the $321,100 conversion.

As you can see, the IRMAA increases typically add about 4.62% or 5.22% to the cost of Roth conversions when you exceed the various MAGI levels unless you do a very large conversion or if you have high IRMAA costs even without a Roth conversion (MAGI over $340,000).

Recovering IRMAA Costs Paid on Larger or Multi-Year Conversions

On the other hand, doing larger Roth conversions all at once or over a period of years will lower your future taxable RMDs. For a 75-year-old person, reducing the balances in Traditional IRAs by $500,000 through Roth conversions will reduce the annual RMDs by about $21,000 initially, and likely by more in future years. By reducing your annual RMDs, your MAGI will be less, and thereby your IRMAA income level and Medicare premiums you pay will be less. Whereas without the conversions, you would be over certain IRMAA income levels due to the higher RMDs and pay more in Medicare premiums over a longer period of time.

In addition, if the $21,000 of extra income without the conversions is in a higher tax bracket (say 32%) than the tax bracket level with the conversions (say 24%), there could be additional income tax savings from the conversions to help offset extra IRMAA costs of the conversions done.

Determining the actual amount of Roth conversions optimal for your situation is beyond the scope of this chapter—too many factors are involved in the decision. If Roth conversions generally make sense in your situation, and if you are or will be covered by Medicare in two years, keeping conversions small enough to stay under the applicable IRMAA income level may help you determine the optimal amount to convert in any given year.

But in other situations, converting larger amounts to Roth may make sense despite these additional IRMAA costs. For example, if you are taking into consideration the benefit for your heirs of making Roth IRA conversions, the extra IRMAA costs might not weigh so heavily.

If you're wondering whether a Roth conversion makes sense, and would like some expert help in running the numbers, please read the letter in the back of this book titled *Save More, Have More, Leave More! The Lange Edge: A Truly Integrated Long-Term Financial Masterplan* to learn more about the services we offer and how you can take advantage of a free consultation with Jim.

Whichever method you use to calculate Roth IRA conversions, however, you should be taking the additional IRMAA costs created by the conversion into the calculation.

KEY IDEAS

- Determining how much and when you should make Roth conversions becomes trickier if you consider IRMMA costs.

- Many taxpayers will get the optimal result not by doing just one conversion in one year, but a series of smaller Roth IRA conversions over multiple years.

- One method you may consider is to develop a long-term Roth IRA conversion plan that may involve a partial Roth IRA conversion over a series of years. Then, update the calculations every year based on changes in investments, taxable income, tax rates, IRMAA rules, liquidity to pay the taxes, and any other factors which impact your family's financial situation.

17

Roth Conversions and Inflation

by Steven T. Kohman,
Certified Public Accountant*

Inflation erodes the value in terms of the spending power of all assets including after-tax savings and investments, Traditional IRAs, as well as Roth IRAs. A common measure of inflation is the All Urban Consumer Price Index or CPI-U. Inflation increased 8.58% from May 31, 2021 to May 31, 2022. It was up 4.99% from May 31, 2020 to May 31, 2021. These are very high inflation rates compared to the previous ten years or more when inflation was mostly less than 2-3%.

Inflation Reduces the Purchasing Power of All of Your Investments

Using our prior examples from Chapter 15 of the purchasing power of money with and without a Roth conversion, on Day One after the conversion they are equal as shown below:

Before Inflation	Without Roth Conversion	With a Roth Conversion
After-tax Investments	$ 24,000	0
Roth IRA	0	$ 100,000
Traditional IRA	100,000	0
24% Tax Allowance on IRA	(24,000)	0
Value Day One After Conversion	**$100,000**	**$100,000**

As you can see, immediately after the Roth conversion, purchasing power is identical. In both cases, $24,000 of cash outside the IRA, is used to pay tax, either on the conversion itself or when funds from the IRA are withdrawn as a distribution.

But what happens when inflation is taken into account after the conversion? Ignoring the effects of future investment returns and income taxes, and assuming a 20% inflation rate where the value of a dollar becomes 80 cents, the relative value of a Roth conversion is not changed just due to inflation as shown below. The inflation adjusted purchasing power of the money is lower, but still equal with and without the conversion is shown below:

After Inflation	Without Roth Conversion	With a Roth Conversion
After-tax Investments	$ 19,200	0
Roth IRA	0	$ 80,000
Traditional IRA	80,000	0
24% Tax Allowance on IRA	(19,200)	0
Purchasing Power After Inflation Only	**$ 80,000**	**$ 80,000**

So, inflation in isolation should not impact the decision of whether you do a Roth IRA conversion or not.

But the economic reality is that inflation does not occur in isolation. There are other factors related to inflation that will affect the future success of Roth conversions such as:

- Future tax rates on RMDs and distributions (from the IRA not converted) could be lower since the tax brackets are adjusted for inflation. If you drop to the 12% tax bracket after inflation from your prior 22% tax bracket, you paid higher taxes on the conversion than you will owe in the future on the incremental RMDs, so it may appear that the Roth conversion was not as effective as planned. In fact, you could potentially be worse off.

- An interesting quirk, however, is that for retirees with lower income in the 12% tax bracket, there are potential advantages from Roth conversions. After a Roth conversion, your RMDs from your Traditional IRA will be lower, which will increase the tax-free portion of capital gains and qualified dividends from your after-tax investments. This typically lowers the tax by 27% which is the 12% tax bracket on ordinary income plus the 15% tax on capital gains.

  Reducing taxable income may also mean that less than the full 85% of your Social Security income will be taxable. This factor alone typically makes the tax savings 22.2% for someone in the 12% tax bracket. These factors frequently result in an effective marginal tax rate of much more than 12% even though technically in the 12% tax bracket. If both of these factors apply together, the actual incremental tax savings rate could be even more than 27% for someone in the *"12%"* tax bracket.

- IRMAA cost levels are increased for inflation. As discussed in Chapter 16, Roth conversions may increase your IRMAA costs in the second year after the conversion year if the converted amount boosts your income to the next level of Medicare premium costs. Inflation could be an advantage for a Roth conversion if the IRMAA cost levels increase with inflation to the extent that even with the conversion, your future IRMAA costs do not increase.

  Conversely, additional IRMAA cost is a disadvantage for the conversion if your income in the conversion year pushes you into a higher Medicare premium cost bracket for the second year after the conversion. But in future years with less RMD income (from the IRA converted) the conversion has an advantage if you end up below the future threshold for an extra IRMAA cost. Higher inflation for future IRMAA increase levels help to make this happen.

- If there is a long-term advantage calculated for Roth conversions, in inflation adjusted dollars, that advantage becomes less due to higher inflation, although it would still be an advantage.

The real advantage or disadvantage of doing Roth conversions is not due to inflation directly, but due to the rate of returns on investments, the tax and IRMAA costs of the conversion, future income taxes including taxes on investment income, and to some extent future estate or inheritance taxes.

Advantages of Roth Conversions

In general, as converted Roth IRAs grow, you will have the advantage of paying less tax on investment income. This is because the tax paid to the IRS for the Roth conversion is normally taken out of other after-tax accounts, which reduces your taxable investment income, composed of interest, dividends and capital gains This tax creates a second layer of tax when a conversion is not done. In contrast, the assets converted to a Roth IRA have no such tax.

Also, starting at age 72 or age 75, depending on birth year, Traditional IRA owners must take RMDs, and the transfer of money from tax-deferred Traditional IRAs to after-tax investment accounts increases this second layer of tax. Roth IRAs have no such RMDs during the lifetimes of the owner and spouse, so more wealth can be protected from taxation.

If future tax rates increase, performing Roth conversions under today's relatively low tax rates offers the advantage of paying less tax overall. Of course, if the Roth IRA money is placed in investments with a higher rate of return than the pre-conversion IRA and after-tax accounts provided, that's another advantage of doing Roth conversions.

This would also be true if the value of the Roth IRA declines less than the IRA and other investments in a declining stock market. However, this is not usually the case unless market timing adjustments are made to the Roth IRA portfolio for protection.

Roth Conversions in Times of Market Declines

As of the time this is written in July 2022, the stock market has declined by more than 20% in the current year. The bond market has also declined due to rising interest rates. This follows several years of great returns as measured by the S&P 500 index: **https://www.upmyinterest.com/sp500/**.

Roth conversions done over the last decade have resulted in tremendous tax-free growth and have provided our clients and other IRA owners who made conversions greatly increased wealth compared to not doing the conversions. This holds true even if the rate of returns of the Roth IRA and other investments are the same. Many have benefited even more by having the Roth IRAs invested more aggressively than the other investments. Please see Chapter 22 for asset location of different types of tax environments.

However, market declines are not good for Roth IRAs after conversions. So far in 2022, the S&P 500 is down over 20%. If there is a negative rate of return on the Roth IRA at a future measurement date after the conversion, it initially may result in a disadvantage for the Roth conversion.

Suppose your tax bracket is 24% and you paid $24,000 in tax on a $100,000 Roth conversion, but the market later declines. If your Roth IRA is now worth only $80,000, then your tax cost of the conversion on the resulting Roth IRA would actually be 30% ($24,000 / $80,000). If you had done the conversion after the market decline, you would have paid much less tax. In the year 2022 with hindsight, a conversion done in July 2022 generally would have been much better than a conversion done in January 2022.

Many investors consider Roth IRAs to be long-term investments, perhaps for the benefit of children and grandchildren who inherit those assets much later. The stock market has recovered significantly from prior market declines in the past, so they hold course for the long term. Also, if conversions are done annually over many years, it is a form of dollar cost averaging, which makes the long-term result more favorable when there are swings in the stock market.

The disadvantages of Roth conversions caused by market declines can be offset, recovered, or turned into an advantage in the long run by the following:

- Obviously, if your Roth IRA increases in value over time, you will compensate for any temporary market declines.

- Your personal tax rate increases, due to your circumstances or a general tax rate increase, which we think is likely, will favor a Roth conversion.

- The lower RMDs in the future after the conversions reduce your additional Medicare premiums caused by IRMAA increases.

- In many cases, investors who are subject to the 3.8% net investment income tax could save this much in future tax from the reduced income that comes with lower RMDs.

- If your Roth IRA beneficiaries are your children who are in a high tax bracket, they will still enjoy a benefit from the conversion since they could easily be in the 32% or higher tax bracket in the future when they have not only their own income, but also income from inherited Traditional IRAs. This tax savings could well surpass the higher tax rate caused by a post conversion decline (30% rather than 24% in the previous example).

We do not claim to be market timers, but if we had a crystal ball, we would be more inclined to make Roth IRA conversions after a market decline.

KEY IDEAS

- Inflation in isolation neither increases the value of the Roth conversion, nor does it decrease it. But, in reality, inflation does alter other variables that will determine if a Roth strategy is for you, and if so, how much and when.

- Inflation reduces the purchasing power of all your investments, including Roth IRAs, Traditional IRAs, and other after-tax investments.

Key Ideas continue on the following page.

KEY IDEAS
(continued)

- Assets transferred to the Roth environment are protected from a second layer of tax on investment gains.

- Because Roth IRAs do not have RMDs while you and/or your beneficiary spouse are alive, you will not be forced to transfer wealth from a tax-free environment to a taxable environment.

- If tax rates increase in the future, making Roth conversions now will save you taxes over the long run.

- If the market declines after you make a Roth conversion, you will have paid more tax than you would if you had waited for the market or at least the particular investment to go down before the conversion and before going back up.

- Roth conversions can have the following advantages:

  1. Your lifetime and your heirs' tax burden may be lower, both over the lifetime of a married couple and for the surviving spouse as well as the end beneficiary.

  2. Medicare premiums may be lower.

  3. You may pay less of the additional 3.8% net investment income tax.

  4. Your children who are in higher tax brackets will pay less tax for inherited Roth IRAs than for inherited Traditional IRAs.

18

A Charitable Remainder Trust as a Beneficiary Deserves a Serious Look After the SECURE Act

"Wealth is not new. Neither is charity. But the idea of using private wealth imaginatively, constructively, and systematically to attack the fundamental problems of mankind is new."

— John Gardner

The Big Picture with Charitable Remainder Trusts (CRTs)

The scope of this chapter is limited to *Charitable Remainder Trusts (CRTs) as a beneficiary of your IRA or retirement plan*. There are other types of CRTs that certainly have merit, but that isn't what we are covering here.

The big picture is that for limited situations, naming a CRT as the beneficiary of your IRA or other retirement plan could be advantageous to your heirs and the charity of your or your child's choice. Your child, for instance, could get a steadier and sometimes even a greater income than they would if they inherited your retirement plan directly. And there is the additional benefit that the charitable trust would offer creditor protection. So, if you are charitably inclined and have a million dollars or more in your IRA, you should at least consider naming a CRT as the beneficiary of your IRA.

If you prefer to avoid CRTs and keep things simple but still intend to include charitable bequests in your estate plan, please read Chapter 20. In it you will learn a simple technique that can increase the amount of money your heirs receive at your death *without* reducing the size of any charitable bequests you intend to include in your estate plan.

What is a Charitable Remainder Trust?

First, when I say a charitable remainder trust, what am I talking about?

In this context, I am talking about naming a charitable remainder trust as a beneficiary or more likely as the contingent beneficiary of your IRA or retirement plan. In the vast majority of circumstances, if you are married, you would name your surviving spouse as the primary beneficiary.

This chapter compares naming your child as the contingent beneficiary after your spouse (or your child as the primary beneficiary if you don't have a spouse) as opposed to naming a charitable remainder trust with your child as the *"income"* beneficiary.

To oversimplify, the trust would provide your beneficiary (let's assume your adult child) with a distribution that has some but not a complete correlation to the trust's income. Then at the child's death, the amount remaining in the trust would go to a charity chosen by you or your child.

IRS rules require that CRTs are structured so that the charity receives at least 10% of the present value of the bequest at the date of death; that leaves up to 90% of the bequest for your children. Some people still reject this idea instinctively, believing that it will deprive their children of 10% of their inheritance. However, when you consider the enormous tax benefits of the charitable remainder trust and the draconian tax treatment of leaving your retirement plans to your children directly, your children may receive more money as the income beneficiary of a CRT than if they inherit the IRA directly—*sometimes hundreds of thousands of dollars more.*

To be fair, the benefits of the CRT vary widely depending on your unique facts, figures, desires, and goals and that of your child. If you have no charitable intent and do not see any benefit to your beneficiary receiving a regular income for their lifetime rather than a large distribution with a big tax bite, it is likely that a CRT isn't the right strategy for you.

CRTs After the SECURE Act

Designating CRTs as the beneficiary of IRAs was not popular or a great strategy before the SECURE Act. Did the SECURE Act make them more valuable? No. What changed is that the SECURE Act made the tax consequences of the likely alternative of naming your child or children as the beneficiary of your IRA extremely unfavorable. That is why they deserve a serious look. Even setting aside charitable intentions, in some situations, CRTs provide more income to the heirs.

In addition, the CRT makes even more sense in the light of likely income and estate tax increases.

The SECURE Act 2.0 introduced a new way to fund CRTs. Beginning in 2023, you have a one-time opportunity to fund a CRT by making a Qualified

Charitable Distribution (QCD) of IRA funds of up to $50,000. I'll discuss QCDs more in Chapter 20.

However, this provision comes with so many restrictions that it's unlikely to be appealing to most investors:

1. This will only count as a QCD if the CRT is funded only with QCDs. As I'll cover later, this contribution of $50,000 (or $100,000 if both spouses contribute to the same CRT) is not enough to make the administrative burden of a CRT worthwhile.

2. You can only do this if you are 70½ or older.

3. The only allowable income beneficiaries of such a CRT are the IRA owner and their spouse, not your children. So while this is an intriguing idea, I don't see this as something that I would recommend to anyone but include for completeness.

CRTs will not replace naming children as the beneficiaries of retirement plans for most IRA owners, but they will offer a great alternative to naming your children directly in five situations:

1. When there is true charitable intent.

2. In specific, perhaps limited circumstances, where calculations indicate that the beneficiary will be financially better off as the beneficiary of the CRT rather than directly inheriting the IRA.

3. You prefer the idea that your beneficiary will receive a regular income over his or her lifetime rather than a large distribution that will be subject to a large tax.

4. You prefer to have the creditor protection of a trust to protect your inheritance from a child's creditor. (The most likely creditor for your child is your child's future ex-husband/wife.)

5. You expect your child to live beyond a typical life expectancy.

We will present the arguments for and against CRTs, along with the math of charitable trusts as beneficiaries of IRAs versus directly naming your child as the beneficiary.

CRTs Require Strategic Planning

Leaving your IRA to someone other than your child or children directly requires strategic planning to get the best results. Remember, charities and charitable trusts are exempt from the 10-year tax acceleration rule established by the

SECURE Act. To benefit from this exemption, you could establish a charitable remainder unitrust (CRUT) or a charitable remainder annuity trust (CRAT) which is a similar type of charitable remainder trust and name it as the beneficiary of your IRA (after your spouse, if appropriate).

To be clear, this trust is a testamentary trust, meaning that it isn't funded before you or you and your spouse die. While you are alive, there is no tax return, no money goes into it, and it only exists in the form of some documents sitting in a fireproof drawer or safety deposit box. It is totally revocable, meaning you can change it as long as you and/or your spouse are alive.

How CRTs Work

Here's how a CRUT (or a CRAT with minor differences) works at the basic level. When you die or when both you and your spouse are dead, the amount in your IRA would be transferred to a CRUT, and the IRA could then be liquidated without paying taxes. The conventional approach would be to leave your IRA directly to your children or grandchildren, and all of it would be taxed within ten years following your death.

With a CRUT, however, your children will not get a lump sum of money when you die, but they also will not face a big tax bill immediately after you die, or as nearly as big of a tax bill even ten years after you die. They would receive a regular *"income"* from the CRUT for the rest of their lives.

The distribution from the CRUT to your child would be treated as ordinary income until the amount of the initial IRA and any interest and dividends earned in the CRUT have been paid to the beneficiary. After this ordinary income has been distributed, the distributions would be taxed as capital gains at a more favorable tax rate. Finally, when your child dies, whatever is left in the CRUT goes to the chosen charity.

Although you probably have some charity in your heart, you would most likely prefer that your child get the bulk of your estate rather than your favorite charity. Me, too. But, even if you feel that way, the CRUT is still worth considering. Please remember that the money (your IRA) that goes into the CRUT isn't subject to the new rules of the dreaded SECURE Act governing after-death IRA distributions.

Since it is an exempt beneficiary, a CRUT can mimic the benefits of the stretch IRA, providing your heir with a steady income potentially for the rest of their life. Distributions from a CRUT can be stretched and taxed over your child's life after the deaths of you (and your spouse)—mimicking a stretch IRA.

Disadvantages of a CRT

- Most clients want to simplify their lives and their estates. This trust complicates life for their children after they are gone.

- We like to look at everyone's unique situation, and we like to do the math. In most cases, without charitable intent, the CRUT will not be as good as leaving the IRA to your children outright.

- The child does not have access to the principle of the CRUT if more money is needed at a given time. On the other hand, if, in addition to the CRUT, you have after-tax or Roth dollars that you are leaving to a child directly, this will reduce this disadvantage.

- You need to have an attorney draft the CRUT.

- You can expect to pay an additional $500 to $2,000 (or sometimes more) every year for the remainder of the beneficiary's life to maintain the trust's legal and tax compliance. The additional complication of drafting and, more importantly, maintaining the charitable trust for the life of your child (or children—we will address naming multiple children later) should not be underestimated.

- You need to name a trustee.

- The trustee needs to file a special CRUT tax return which is not an easy return to prepare. Our CPAs routinely complain about the difficulty and time required to properly file the return.

- The trustee of the CRUT is required to report the income that the beneficiary receives to the IRS and must send a K-1 form to each beneficiary, complicating the beneficiaries tax return. If your beneficiary lives for 20 years, it's not unrealistic to think that the fees required to maintain the trust could exceed $20,000 or even $40,000.

- Ultimately, you could be creating significant complications for lower tax savings than you would have realized if you had just left the money to your child instead of the CRUT.

- If you leave your IRA to a CRUT, it could potentially hurt your family. If the income beneficiary of the trust (most likely, your child) dies prematurely, the remaining balance will go to the named charity and not to your grandchild as it would if you just left the IRA to your child. So, there is a very real risk with a CRUT, and it would likely not be an appropriate choice if you think that your beneficiary might have a reduced life expectancy.

Advantages of a CRT

- If you like the idea of maintaining a significant amount of money in the tax-deferred environment and having your beneficiary get regular distributions for the rest of their life, then you should consider charitable remainder trusts. The distribution rules of charitable trusts act like a *"stretch"* IRA, i.e., offering a longer period in the tax-deferred environment.

- The CRUT will protect your children from creditors.

- The CRUT will be more advantageous if your child will be in a high tax bracket from the time you die to ten years after your death.

- If your child lives a long life, the CRUT will hopefully provide benefits for their entire life.

Shirl Trefelner, a number-crunching CPA who did the quantitative analysis on CRUTs for this book, likes CRUTs for a lot of clients. She says, *"Look at the numbers under favorable circumstances for a CRUT. Including a CRUT as part of your estate plan may make an enormous difference for the long-term security of your children, and it may be the best way to maximize the number of dollars they receive. If you have charity in your heart as well as the desire to protect your family, this can be a wonderful thing."*

Steve Kohman, another number crunching CPA in the office, is far less enthusiastic about CRUTs and prefers to emphasize the disadvantages listed above. He doesn't like the assumptions used in her calculation as he says they are more typical of someone who chooses to use a CRUT and not a typical IRA owner.

Let's Run Some Numbers

Let's compare leaving your million-dollar IRA to a CRUT versus leaving it directly to your child. What is the best distribution option for the $1 million dollars if you leave the IRA to your child, and they will have to pay income taxes on the entire million (plus growth) within ten years of your death? Though we could do some post-mortem planning, it will be extremely difficult to protect that distribution from very high income and estate tax rates if you have an estate tax problem in addition to your almost certain income tax problem.

The Essence of the Simple Math

To oversimplify, the income tax on a $1 million Inherited IRA would have to be paid within ten years after the death of the original owner, plus taxes on appreciation, growth, capital gains, etc.

The CRUT pays no income taxes when you die. So, the income that your child will receive is based on the full $1 million, not an amount that will suffer dramatic taxation within ten years after your death. Let's assume for the moment, that you do not care about charity. Would you rather have your daughter get the net proceeds of the inherited IRA minus taxes within ten years or an *"income"* based on an amount not reduced by taxes for the rest of her life?

The answer that you likely expect from me by now is *"it depends."* It depends on a number of variables, but the most important variable is how long your child will live.

If your child survives you by one year and gets income for a year and then dies, the remainder of the trust will go to charity, which would be a terrible result for your family. If, on the other hand, your child survives into his/her nineties, the CRUT will likely be quite favorable compared to leaving him/her the Inherited IRA outright.

An Example by the Numbers of CRT vs. Naming Your Child Outright

What I show in Figure 18.1, on page 282, is that, given certain assumptions (please see the Appendix) your child could get more money over her lifetime as the beneficiary of a CRUT than if she receives your $1 million IRA outright.

Here's an example. Suppose Alice creates a CRUT that names her daughter, Roberta, as the income beneficiary and her favorite charity as the remainder beneficiary. Which inheritance will benefit Roberta the most—the money outright subject to accelerated taxes or the income from the CRUT?

The answer depends on what assumptions you make but the most important assumption is how long Roberta lives.

Given the assumptions in the Appendix for Figure 18.1 which include significant spending, Roberta would have $465,175 after taxes left at age 81 if her mom, Alice, left her IRA to a CRUT with Roberta as the income beneficiary. In addition, with the CRUT, if Roberta died at 81, Alice's or Roberta's favorite charity would receive $452,211. If Roberta lives past age 81, she will continue to receive an income, and the charity would likely end up getting less money.

If Alice had left Roberta the IRA outright, given all the same assumptions, Roberta would have no money at age 81, and the charity would get no money.

Please do not overlook the implications of this calculation. Given the assumptions in the Appendix, your child could have $465,175 after taxes at age 81 if you name your million-dollar IRA to a CRUT as the income beneficiary of your IRA, *and* your favorite charity would get $452,211. Given those same assumptions, if you named your child outright as the beneficiary of your IRA, at age 81, your child would be broke, and your charity would get nothing. The big loser with the CRUT is the IRS.

Again, to be fair, these assumptions include a potential estate and inheritance tax that would be reduced with a charitable remainder trust. Depending on how much money you have at your death and the residence of your state at your death and future changes in the federal estate laws might determine if there is a federal or state estate or inheritance tax and if so, how much would it be.

Given these assumptions, Roberta only must live past the age of 67 to receive more money from the CRUT than she would have received from inheriting the $1 million IRA stretched over ten years. (The breakeven point will change depending on your circumstances, assumptions, the Section 7520 rate when the CRUT is created, and how old your beneficiary is at your death.)

The other advantage of the CRUT is that she will have all the protections of a trust, including protection from creditors, protection from herself, and in some cases, financial protection from a husband if she were to divorce, or a husband who might have different ideas about how she should spend her money.

We include more specific details in the section titled *Nitty Gritty Details of the CRUTs and CRATs* later on in this chapter.

Figure 18.1
Income from a Trust *vs.* IRA Stretched 10 Years*

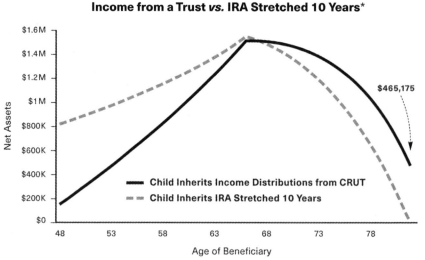

* *Detailed assumptions can be found in the Appendix.*

If we use a different set of assumptions or the family structure is different, the outcome will not be so favorable.

As mentioned earlier, a legitimate objection to the CRUT is that if the income beneficiary (presumably your child) dies young, his or her own family will get less money. This is because, after the beneficiary's death, the amount remaining in the trust will go to the charity rather than their own children. That is true.

An easy and inexpensive solution to that objection would be to purchase term life insurance on the income beneficiary. Then, if the income beneficiary dies prematurely, their children, i.e., your grandchildren, would be provided for by the insurance.

Without going into that scenario at length, suffice it to say we ran the numbers and found the insurance solution strong enough to overcome, or at least lessen, the *"leaving out the grandchildren in the event your child dies early"* objection to establishing a CRUT.

Hidden Benefit—Difficult to Quantify

Finally, there is another interesting benefit that is hard to quantify. One of the provisions of the charitable remainder trusts is that it allows either you or the beneficiary to choose the charity.

Assuming you trust the judgment of your child, who would be the lifetime income beneficiary, giving your child the ability to choose the end beneficiary has the advantage of getting your child interested in philanthropy earlier in their lifetime. Hopefully, the child would begin researching a variety of charities and not just look at the stated purpose of the charity, but also how much money was effectively spent on charitable works and how much was spent on administration and fundraising.

They might also become involved in the charity, maybe to the point of directing the funds to certain purposes within it. For example, you or your child may prefer that a charitable contribution to a university be used for scholarships rather than a new building.

Even if you aren't charitable, the potential benefits of the CRUT should certainly be considered if you like the idea of your child getting a regular income for the rest of their lives. If you are even somewhat charitable, the CRUT can make sense for faculty members who have accumulated a lot of money in IRAs and retirement plans. They will likely make even more sense if the estate tax exemption goes down because the calculations above were prepared using the 2023 exemption of $12.92 million.

Beneficiary Hierarchy

You can name your spouse as the primary beneficiary of your IRA and the CRUT as the contingent beneficiary. If your spouse doesn't need the money, she can disclaim all or part of it to the CRUT. Your child would have been named as the income beneficiary of the CRUT. The amount that the income beneficiary receives from the CRUT will be based on their own life expectancies, and at their deaths, the remainder will go to a charity that either you or the beneficiary designates.

What you can't do—which is an option I would like to have but don't—is to leave it to the child to determine if he prefers the outright inherited IRA or *"income"* from the CRUT. Of course, that conversation could happen before you die, but could not be changed after you die like in some of the other situations that allow disclaimers.

Is There a Dollar Value that Precludes Setting up a Trust?

The costs and aggravation of setting up and maintaining the trust are not inconsequential and need to be put into perspective. Though we do not have a hard and fast number, our rule of thumb is that if the value of the Inherited IRA is much less than $1 million per beneficiary, then the costs and aggravation of the trust may well exceed its value. In this case, funding a trust with $1 million for one lifetime-beneficiary meets our *"Is the amount going to the CRUT large enough to be worth the aggravation of setting up and maintaining a CRUT?"* rule of thumb.

For IRA owners who like the charitable aspects of a CRUT and the forced gradual distribution of the IRA proceeds, it might be reasonable to consider establishing a CRUT with less than a $1 million balance.

There are also some interesting methods of combining life insurance planning with CRUTs and CRATs. While this topic is beyond the scope of this book, you should be aware that opportunities not presented here also exist.

What If I Have More than One Child?

First, there is no law requiring that all children be treated exactly the same way. You could try to keep things relatively equal but still have different plans for different children. The charitable trust might be a good solution for one child, and a series of Roth IRA conversions and leaving the Roth IRAs to the child in the higher tax bracket with no charitable trust might be the right solution for another.

Treating Your Children Differently

Forgetting the world of charitable trusts for a moment, we frequently work with families with children of different dispositions. One child might be more of a spendthrift, another more fiscally responsible.

In such a case, we sometimes name a spendthrift trust in lieu of leaving money to the spendthrift and leave the other siblings' money to them free of trust. There is no reason to draft and plan on maintaining unnecessary trusts other than *"keeping things equal."* The specific plans for each sibling might be different, but the goal can still be equal treatment.

Let's assume you want to treat your children equally and similarly. Some IRA owners might assume that the solution would be to name two or more lifetime beneficiaries of one CRUT. Doing this is a good way to encourage fighting about money among siblings over the treatment of the trust after you're gone. It also reduces the amount the children get and increases the amount the charity gets because the life expectancy of two siblings is greater than one. This means that more money must be preserved for the charity, reducing the children's income.

I usually prefer having separate trusts, even considering the increased accounting and trust maintenance costs. If you have two children, you could name each of them as the trustee of the other one's trust. This might change my million-dollar minimum preference to, perhaps, $1,400,000 ($700,000 for each trust) because the work involved in maintaining two practically identical trusts is less than double the amount of maintaining one trust, and there is an easy and obvious choice of trustee.

Combining a Spendthrift Trust and the *"I Don't Want My No-Good Son-in-Law to Inherit One Red Cent of My Money"* Trust and a Charitable Trust

Before the SECURE Act, our law practice drafted quite a few trusts for adult beneficiaries. As mentioned previously, a common issue we had to address was how to protect a financially irresponsible adult, a child with a drug or alcohol problem, a child with a problematic spouse, a child with potential financial creditors etc.

In that case, leaving a lot of money to the child directly could be risky; rather than taking appropriate distributions and planning and investing wisely, there was the chance that the child would blow the money or have the money confiscated by creditors or as part of a divorce settlement. In such a situation, we typically left that money to a trust, with the adult child as the beneficiary. We also provided the trustee with some discretion with respect to distributions of both income and principal. Having to protect spendthrift adults from themselves is not a new problem; it was around a long time ago and will likely always be a problem.

Trusts are a great way to protect inherited money when there was a reasonable chance of the child developing or already having some type of liability. If your child has a judgment against them or was involved in a lawsuit, they could lose their inheritance to the judgment creditor (the person who sued your child and won). The same would be true if your child inherited your IRA or Roth IRA.

An Inherited IRA or Inherited Roth IRA does not enjoy the same creditor protection as an IRA or Roth IRA. Therefore, any money, whether it be after-tax dollars, IRA or retirement plan dollars, Roth IRAs, or any other funds that you want to leave to a child who has or potentially will have serious creditor issues should likely be left in a creditor protection trust for the benefit of that child.

On the other hand, if the IRA were left to a properly drafted trust, that money would be protected from the child's creditors while still providing income and support for the child. Trusts can also be used prophylactically. For example, suppose the adult child is a brain surgeon. Doctors get sued all the time, so money left to that child might be left in some type of creditor protection trust even if there is no pending lawsuit or even a threat of a lawsuit.

I am a big fan of a trust that we call the *"I Don't Want My No-Good Son-in-Law to Inherit One Red Cent of My Money"* trust. This trust protects your adult child from your future ex-daughter/son-in-law. Like it or not, if your child is married, there is the potential for a divorce after you die. In that case, the future ex-spouse of your child would likely go after at least a portion of the inheritance that you left to your child. At a minimum, they often go after a portion of the appreciation of that money between your death and when they get divorced.

An alternative to the *"I Don't Want My No-Good Son-in-Law to Inherit One Red Cent of My Money"* trust is a postnuptial agreement between your child and child-in-law that would protect your inheritance. While great in theory, as a practical matter, it is an excellent way to start a family fight. I prefer that wealthy parents discuss the value of prenuptial agreements with their children, preferably before an engagement and, better yet, before the child has even met their future spouse.

For all of these somewhat dire situations, a charitable remainder trust could be a great solution. It would have all the creditor protections listed in the trusts above and might be a much smarter choice for reduced income taxes. One downside is that it does not allow for distributions for health, maintenance, and support, so if there were years when the beneficiary needed more than the annual income, they could not get it. Depending on the amount of the total estate to be allocated to the problem beneficiary, if there were a more traditional trust for non-IRA assets, money could be set aside there that would allow principal distributions for health, maintenance, and support from the after-tax dollars. Alternately, you could just leave some money outright to your child and the rest in one or more types of trusts.

Please note this charitable trust idea only works as a great tax strategy if the underlying asset is an IRA or retirement plan, often making it a good solution for university and TIAA members.

But, while space doesn't permit, I will openly admit that most of the number crunching we have done on CRT as the beneficiary of the IRA versus outright distribution to the child, the outright distribution to the child is usually the better choice unless there is charitable intent.

The Relationship Between Charitable Remainder Trusts and Roth IRA Conversions

In Chapter 27, we discuss the benefits of combining different strategies, for example, holding off on Social Security, completing a series of Roth IRA conversions, and having the fundamentals of Lange's Cascading Beneficiary Plan for your estate. This is a good example of how combining different strategies produces a synergistic positive result. That *may not* be the case when combining Roth IRA conversions and charitable remainder trusts.

Let's take the simple situation in which you project your Traditional IRA will be about a million dollars or less at your death. You like the idea of a series of Roth IRA conversions, and you also like the idea of a charitable trust. So, you may think, *"Why not a little of each?"*

With those numbers, I do not like that combination. It doesn't make sense to name a charitable trust as the beneficiary of a Roth IRA. If you make a series of Roth IRA conversions, your Traditional IRA could be significantly lower than a million dollars at the time of your death. At that point, the cost of creating and maintaining the CRUT becomes too high relative to its value. So, for IRA owners who project that they will have about a million dollars in their Traditional IRA at their death, I would typically recommend either Roth IRA conversions or a CRUT, but not both.

Combining CRUTs and Roth conversions may be worth it if you have more than a million dollars in your Traditional IRA. Many university professors and TIAA account holders find themselves in this position at retirement because of generous employer matching contributions that prior to Secure Act 2.0 must, by law, go to a Traditional rather than Roth account. For many, it would make sense to execute a series of Roth IRA conversions, name individual family members as the beneficiaries of your Roth IRA, and still have a million dollars that you could allocate to the CRUT for the remaining Traditional IRA money.

The warning, however, is that if you intend to name a CRUT as the beneficiary of your Traditional IRA, do not make so many Roth IRA conversions that the value of the Traditional IRA is worth well less than a million dollars at your death. Remember, the CRUT doesn't pay taxes, but conversions will be taxed.

The main point is that a lot of IRA and retirement plan owners should pick either a Roth IRA conversion strategy or a CRUT strategy, but likely not both.

Nitty Gritty Details of the CRUTs and CRATs

To spare big picture readers some grief, I have simplified this chapter, but feel honor-bound to go into some details for those who are interested. If you are so inclined, please feel free to skip the following section and skip to the *Key Ideas* at the end of the chapter.

I will discuss two types of charitable remainder trusts as the beneficiary of an IRA or retirement plan:

1. Charitable remainder annuity trusts (CRATs)

2. Charitable remainder unitrusts (CRUTs)

The CRAT has nothing to do with the idea that you might name a trust as the beneficiary of your retirement plan (more on annuities in Chapter 9). Rather, it means that the CRAT pays a fixed income stream to your beneficiary from the time of your death until the time of their death. Like an annuity, it distributes a set amount of income that is guaranteed for the beneficiary's life. The CRUT, on the other hand, pays a fixed percentage to the beneficiary rather than a fixed amount.

For a CRAT, if the IRA were valued at $1,000,000 and the payout percentage was 6%, the distribution to the income beneficiary would be $60,000 per year.

CRUTs are trickier to calculate but often result in a higher distribution to your child. I have been using the term *"income,"* but that really isn't accurate. When determining the maximum payout rate to your beneficiary, you must project that what is left at their death will be at least 10% of the amount originally transferred to the charitable trust. Meeting this requirement allows the trust to maintain its tax-free status. To get even more technical, an individual can establish a CRUT to maximize the lifetime payout to the individual beneficiary provided that the payout does not exceed an amount that would cause an amount less than 10% of the present value of the amount used to fund the trust to be paid to charity.

For example, suppose you die with a CRUT as the beneficiary of your IRA, and the beneficiary of the CRUT is 45 years old. As we go to press, the current Section 7520 rate is 4.6%, which is higher than it's been for years.

The Section 7520 interest rate is used to calculate the percentage of the trust that can be distributed to your beneficiary. The higher the 7520 rate and the higher the beneficiary's age, the higher the percentage of the trust that can be distributed. With the current Section 7520 rates of 4.6%, a Trustee can make a maximum permitted annual distribution to the beneficiary of 7.9% of the annual value of the CRUT.

If the 7520 rate goes up, as it has been, and if your child is older than age 45, the amount going to your family could be even more favorable than the example above. Of course, if the market tanks, there is always the possibility that income distributions will decrease.

You also have the choice of distributing the CRUT over a fixed number of years. For example, your beneficiary's life expectancy may be 80, but you think they will only need distributions for the next 20 years. If you choose a fixed 20-year payout, the annual distribution would be 11.2% of the account balance. This provides a higher annual income for your beneficiary and still provides the 10% charitable distribution at the end of the 20-year income payout. I do not recommend making the distribution period too short; doing so defeats the purpose of keeping the annual distributions low in the effort to minimize the tax consequences for your beneficiary.

A CRUT can be a good choice when used for the benefit of a child who has a significantly reduced life expectancy. If you were to leave the IRA to the child outright, it would have all been taxed in the ten years following the IRA owner's death. Using the reduced life expectancy and naming a CRUT for a number of years rather than the life of the child is the perfect solution for that child.

While IRA owners who want the most for their children and the least for their charity want the highest payout rate for the trust, there is also a limitation on the lower interest range. The rules for CRUTs include an annual minimum payout rate of 5%. This means that any beneficiary 28 years old or younger will get the same 5% annual payout. The younger beneficiary would just get those payments for a longer period of time.

Finally, one more technical point. If you name a CRAT or a CRUT as the beneficiary of your IRA, when you die, your estate will receive a current charitable tax deduction for federal and state inheritance tax purposes of 10% of the account value (when it is transferred into the CRUT), even though the money may not be paid to the charity for years.

Although the vast majority of estates do not have federal estate tax liability under the current laws, this may change with the sunset of TCJA of 1997. In addition, the tax deduction for the charitable donation may reduce the state estate or inheritance tax liability if a state imposes these taxes.

KEY IDEAS

- In limited situations, it could make more sense to leave your IRA or a portion of it to a charitable remainder trust than to leave it directly to your child. It is possible, though not likely, that your child would end up with more money if you left the IRA to a charitable trust than if you left it to them outright.

- The charitable remainder trust has the same creditor protection benefits as other creditor protection trusts.

- Charitable Trusts have advantages and disadvantages that must be assessed on an individual basis.

- Depending on how much money you have in your IRA, it may be appropriate to either go the charitable remainder trust route or the Roth IRA conversion route, but not both.

19

Who Gets What?
A Guide to Tax-Savvy Charitable Bequests and Leaving Money to Children with Different Financial Needs

"A tax-advantageous way to give upon your death is by naming a qualified charitable organization as the beneficiary of your tax-deferred retirement plan."

— Nerd Wallet

The following content of this chapter is adapted (with some edits) with permission from **Forbes.com**. The content of this chapter was originally published in an article that I wrote that appeared in **Forbes.com** in January, 2021.

"Who Gets What?" is frequently an eagerly awaited question at someone's passing, especially when there is considerable wealth involved. How many movies have you seen with a dramatic *"reading of the will"* scene that introduced an unexpected plot twist? In reality, there is no *"reading of the will"* scene, but obviously beneficiaries want to not only know what they got, but what other beneficiaries got.

Most people seek an outcome that all beneficiaries will accept as fair and in character with the decedent's character. No one wants to set up a situation where the will is almost sure to be contested. If I predict a contentious outcome, I won't do the estate plan. Some attorneys might be attracted to the lure of additional billable hours. I can't stand conflict and would prefer spending my time helping people, not getting involved with siblings fighting over money.

But what is often forgotten in the quest for fairness and generosity is consideration of the tax implications of those bequests. In this chapter, I offer the suggestion that thinking ahead to the potential tax burden of the various assets in your estate can help you decide *Who Gets What*. This will allow you to fulfill your charitable inclinations while also making sure your children and any other beneficiaries of your estate are treated fairly, even if not exactly equally, while also minimizing the tax burden for your beneficiaries.

An Obvious but Frequently Missed Drafting Error

After reading this chapter, you are likely to think—that is so obvious. How could I and my estate attorney both have missed this? Don't feel bad. We have reviewed thousands of estate plans, and in our experience, hardly anyone gets this right. The mistake often costs families tens of thousands of dollars or more.

I'm referring to the decisions that you make when you are crafting your estate plan and are trying to figure out *Who Gets What.* In this chapter, I want to focus on the smartest solution for donations or inheritances that you leave to a charity after you and your spouse pass.

There are several critical ideas to cover, but the most fundamental is: what are the tax implications to each recipient if they inherit your money? By being very selective about who receives which type of money—whether Traditional or Roth IRAs, after-tax brokerage accounts, life insurance, etc.—you can dramatically cut the share that goes to the IRS and increase the amount going to your family.

In most cases, Traditional IRAs, subject to exception, are going to be fully taxable to your heirs. After the dreaded SECURE Act that effectively killed the stretch IRA, income taxes will be due on your IRA within ten years after your death. Inherited Roth IRAs have the advantage of being able to continue to grow for ten more years after your death and then can be withdrawn tax-free. After-tax dollars and life insurance proceeds are generally not subject to income taxes. All of these different types of inheritances have different tax implications for your beneficiary… unless your beneficiary is a tax-exempt charity.

First and foremost, a charity that is recognized by the IRS as being tax-exempt does not care in what form they receive an inheritance. They never have to pay taxes on the money they receive. To them, a dollar is a dollar. So, a charity will look at bequests of Traditional IRAs, Roth IRAs, after-tax dollars, or life insurance in the same light. In sharp contrast, your heirs will face substantially different tax implications depending on the type of asset they receive after your death. Please note in this chapter we are only addressing income taxes, not estate or transfer taxes.

Imagine this scenario. You want to leave $100,000 to charity after you and your spouse die. You have both Traditional IRAs and after-tax dollars. For the sake of simplicity, I am going to say that your child is in the 24% tax bracket. So, *Who Gets What?* In the vast majority of the estate plans that we review, we see instructions directing that the charitable bequest come from after-tax funds— usually found in the will or a revocable trust.

The problem is that your will (or revocable trust) does not control the disposition of your IRAs or retirement plans. By naming that charity as a beneficiary in your will or trust, you will likely be donating after-tax money to charity. The charity gets $100,000 so the *"cost"* of the bequest to your heirs is $100,000. Re-stated, the amount that your children inherit is reduced by $100,000 because you made that bequest to charity.

But what if you decide to leave $100,000 to XYZ charity through your Traditional IRA and/or retirement plan beneficiary designation?

It makes no difference for the charity because they get $100,000 tax-free. If your heirs receive $100,000 from your IRA, they will have to pay taxes on the money. Assuming that they are in a 24% tax bracket, that would be $24,000—leaving them with $76,000 after the government takes their share (though to be fair, they could stretch the Inherited IRA for ten years which would defer the tax hit). And the tax bite is even worse if your heirs are in a higher tax-bracket or live in a state that taxes Inherited IRAs.

So, if you were planning to leave $100,000 of your *after-tax dollars* to a charity but change the plan and instead leave $100,000 of your *Traditional IRA money* to that charity, you are in effect leaving your beneficiaries an extra $24,000 all at Uncle Sam's expense!

This is a simple tweak to your estate plan that can be very beneficial to your heirs. On a smaller bequest, smaller savings. On a bigger bequest, even larger savings.

Consider the purchasing power, after taxes, available to your beneficiary if you have $100,000 in a Traditional IRA, and $100,000 of after-tax dollars, and we switch *Who Gets What.*

Scenario 1:

Leave $100,000 to charity through your will or revocable trust and $100,000 to your heirs as the beneficiary of your Traditional IRA.

- Impact on the charity: They get $100,000 and pay no tax.
- Impact on your heirs: $100,000 IRA money – 24% taxes = $76,000.

Scenario 2:

Leave $100,000 to charity through your IRA beneficiary designations and $100,000 to your heirs in your will or revocable trust.

- Impact on the charity: They get $$100,000 and pay no tax.
- Impact on your heirs: $100,000 and pay no federal tax.

This simple switch of *Who Gets What* saved this family $24,000. The savings would be even greater with a larger bequest or if your beneficiary's tax bracket is higher.

Let's imagine another scenario. Suppose that your child is well off and, as a parent, you are totally comfortable with reducing the purchasing power of his or her IRA inheritance by $100,000. Does that mean you can leave even more IRA money to charity? Yes!

You could leave $131,579 to charity through your IRA or retirement plan beneficiary designation. The same tax implications apply. A $131,579 IRA bequest will only *"cost"* your child $100,000 ($131,579 x 24% = $31,579). If you left that $131,579 IRA to your children instead of charity, your children would have to pay $31,579 in taxes, leaving them $100,000.

By switching *Who Gets What*, you accomplish one of two things:

1. You save $31,579 in federal taxes for your child, or

2. If you increase your IRA bequest to the charity to $131,579, you still only remove $100,000 from the purchasing power of your heir's total inheritance, and charity gets the additional $31,579 that would have otherwise been paid in federal income taxes.

Who loses out with this strategy? You guessed it. The IRS. You are dramatically cutting the share that the IRS receives—giving the IRS a smaller piece of the pie. And I think that all of us can safely agree that we want more money to go to our kids and favorite charities, and less money to go to the IRS.

If you are only leaving a minimal amount to charity, it probably isn't worth the time and aggravation to change your documents. If you are leaving a substantial amount to charity, it probably is worth it. I recommend starting a list of the changes you would like to make to your estate plan and have all of them incorporated into new wills, trusts, and beneficiary designations at once.

What if My Children Have Different Needs?

Hardly anyone uses this strategy, but I like it in a lot of situations. Matt Schwartz, a veteran estate attorney has used this technique and even invented a method to establish approximate purchasing power equality in the right circumstances.

The application of the concept of *Who Gets What* can also sometimes save families hundreds of thousands of dollars in taxes even without any charitable bequest involved.

Many IRA owners have children for whom it can reasonably be predicted that they will be in significantly different tax brackets. The different income tax brackets of your beneficiaries may create an opportunity for tax savings by simply changing *Who Gets What*. For example, imagine you have two adult children, and one child is in the 12% tax bracket and the other in the 32% bracket. Let's also assume that though you might not know the details, you can reasonably predict one child will most likely always be in a higher tax bracket than the other child.

That said, let's also assume you want to divide the estate relatively equally between your two children. Situations such as this sound like an opportunity to reduce the total taxes your family may have to pay, but rarely do we see any attorney or advisor recommend the following strategy.

Consider increasing the *purchasing power* of both of your children after you die and reducing the share going to Uncle Sam by switching *Who Gets What*.

Let's keep it simple and assume that you have a $1,000,000 Roth IRA and a $1,400,000 regular IRA. The status quo is each of your children will receive 50% of both assets. If you forget growth, each child will get a $500,000 Roth and a $700,000 regular IRA. The IRS will get $308,000 which represents the taxes both kids will have to pay on the inherited Traditional IRA. ($700,000 x 12% = $84,000 and $700,000 x 32% = $224,000.)

Let's assume instead that you leave the $1,000,000 Roth to the child in the 32% bracket and the $1,400,000 in your regular IRA to the child in the 12% bracket. The IRS would only get $168,000 in taxes. This means your children would get an extra $140,000 worth of purchasing power, which is the difference between the amount paid to the IRS in the two scenarios. In addition, since hopefully, the child isn't planning on blowing their inheritance the year that you die, the extra $140,000 will continue to grow after you die.

Did I oversimplify this example, not taking into consideration many things that would cause this estimated tax savings to change? Yes. But I wanted to make the point clearly. By shifting *Who Gets What* there might be a significant tax savings that could then be divided between your children.

Ideally, this strategy would include some thinking about how to get a basically *"even division"* of purchasing power and have the family enjoy the tax savings. You might consider careful planning and/or an equalization clause to ensure that your estate is split roughly equally between them *measured in purchasing power*. Theoretically, all that is required to execute this strategy is a little expert *"tweaking"* of your estate plan to orchestrate it so that the majority of the higher-earning child's share of your estate is fulfilled using the Roth IRA and other after-tax dollars, and the majority of the lower-earning child's share is taken from Traditional IRAs and other tax-deferred vehicles. Sounds great, right?

I suspect most estate attorneys do not suggest this strategy because they never think about it. Other times, they don't use it even if it makes sense because it complicates the estate and many clients want to keep things simple, even if it does mean more taxes.

It can also potentially increase the chances of fighting between children because it is near impossible to make the bequests exactly even after taking taxes into consideration. One child might end up with 51% and the other 49% but both would be ahead by well over 10%.

Personally, I would prefer 49% of a much bigger number than 51% of a much smaller number, but some kids (or spouses) don't see it that way. But, as mentioned previously, for the right clients, Matt has figured out a way to potentially save the family a lot of money in taxes and approximate equality between children in different tax brackets.

Other Situations When You Might Consider Treating Your Children Differently

A similar situation where you might want to treat your children differently occurs if one of your children needs a trust as opposed to just leaving them money outright. They might need a trust because they are a spendthrift, have creditors, have a no-good spouse where they may lose money in a divorce, etc. The other child doesn't need a trust. My preference is to draft a trust for the child that needs it and to leave the child that doesn't need a trust their share outright.

Life gets tricky when the math or the legal situation shows treating your children differently is a great strategy. Naturally, I like the tax savings or added creditor protection if a trust is indicated for one child, but not the other. Then, the poor drafting attorney has to face the client's natural preference to treat their children not only equally, but identically.

As a result, in the real world, we often do not utilize *Who Gets What* when the math indicates it is a great strategy. We also sometimes end up with a trust for a child that doesn't need a trust because the other child does, and Mom and Dad want to treat the children identically (though I hate the thought of drafting unnecessary testamentary trusts which take effect after you die because of the continued cost and aggravation of maintaining trusts over the lives of the children).

There is an argument that it makes sense to treat sibling beneficiaries differently, only when there will be a large tax savings, a strong need for a trust for one child, understanding clients and hopefully understanding children.

I still like the tax savings and fewer trusts if they aren't needed. Unfortunately, it is often the financially weaker or less sophisticated child or the child who needs the trust that is most likely to object. That is true even though the plan I might prefer would put that child in a much better position.

Another circumstance to utilize *Who Gets What* could be if one beneficiary qualifies as an EBD (who can stretch the IRA over his lifetime) and the other doesn't qualify. In many cases it might make sense to leave the IRA to the beneficiary who qualifies for the stretch and other assets to the beneficiary that doesn't qualify for the stretch.

KEY IDEAS

- Thinking strategically about *Who Gets What*—specifically with regard to charitable bequests—can save the family 24% of the bequest if it comes from an IRA or retirement plan and not from the will or revocable trust controlling the non-qualified money.

- Considering your children's different financial situations offers an opportunity to divide your estate to leave all your children with more purchasing power and cut taxes.

- Family dynamics may indicate that a trust would be a prudent method of leaving wealth to one or more children, while leaving money outright to others would work best.

- Setting up trusts for all children, even if they are not necessary, may feel fair, but will result in additional expenses for maintaining those unneeded trusts.

- That said, sometimes *"threading the needle"* might not be appropriate even if there are tax savings and additional costs of having a trust for a child who doesn't need one.

20

Qualified Charitable Distribution (QCD) Rules Save Extra Money on Charitable Donations

by Steven T. Kohman,
*Certified Public Accountant**

*"As you grow older, you will discover that you have two hands:
one for helping yourself, the other for helping others."*

— Sam Levenson

Charitable giving and bequests are a broad topic, and mostly beyond the scope of this chapter. Before you make any substantial gifts, whether to charities or as gifts to people, you will need to first think about how much you want to give away while you are alive and how much you want to give to specific charities and individuals at your death. The focus of this chapter is on using Qualified Charitable Distributions (QCDs) as a tool to satisfy your charitable giving intentions while you are alive. Later in this chapter, I will provide a broad overview of the points to consider in gifts you make during your life and bequests you make at death.

Most university faculty members and TIAA members who are over age 70½ (not 72 as you might think is logical) will have money in a Traditional IRA, and many will make annual donations to charity. If this describes you, you should be glad to know that the Qualified Charitable Distribution rules are now permanent tax laws, and we can safely put them to use.

QCD Rules and Limitations

A QCD is a method for donating to charity directly from your IRA. It only applies to distributions from IRAs, not other retirement plans like 401(k)s or 403(b)s. So, if you are still working, you cannot make a QCD from your employer retirement plan, as QCDs can only be made from IRAs. If your plan permits

---

* Steve is our veteran number-crunching Roth IRA expert. Special thanks to Jen Hall, CPA, for her significant additions to this chapter.

in-service withdrawals, however, you could transfer funds from your employer retirement plan through a trustee-to-trustee transfer into an IRA account. You can then use QCDs using a *'back-door'* method by effectively using your work-related retirement plan money to take advantage of the favorable tax treatment by giving to charity through a QCD. Of course, you have to be charitably inclined to want to go through this extra step.

When the QCD laws were established, you had to begin taking RMDs by age 70½. Even though the SECURE Act raised the RMD age to 72, it didn't change the QCD laws. Before the SECURE Act, if you were making QCDs before you turned 72, your charitable contribution coming directly from your IRA counted as at least part of your RMD.

Now, however, if you are age 71, you may still make a QCD even though you aren't required to take an RMD. If you do not itemize deductions, the result does affect your taxes, because the QCD is not included in your taxable income. In addition, since you are using pre-tax IRA money instead of after-tax money to make the donations, you are inherently saving taxes.

The QCD rules allow you to make charitable donations directly from your IRA. The good news is that, even though you are taking a withdrawal from your Traditional IRA to make the donation, it is not taxable to you. On the other hand, you cannot claim a charitable contribution that was given via a QCD on your itemized deductions. People often think making a charitable donation through a QCD will not make any difference in their taxes, and, in some cases, it might not make a significant difference if you itemize your deductions, depending upon the amount of the contribution.

The Tax Cuts and Jobs Act of 2017, which cut tax rates but also restricted itemized deductions and increased the standard deduction, was a game-changer. Many taxpayers who used to itemize will no longer be able to do so. For the people who used to itemize but no longer can, QCDs provide a terrific way to save on taxes.

You get money out of your IRA without having to pay the taxes. In many cases, if you didn't have that option and you weren't itemizing your deductions, you would not get the benefit of the charitable deduction, with the exception of a lousy $300 per individual (maximum $600 deduction for a married couple) that was available as part of Covid relief for non-itemizers for 2020 and 2021. The $300 per individual deduction was not extended in 2022 or future years.

Rules limit the types of charities that can receive QCD donations. Donations to donor-advised funds, private foundations, or a supporting organiza-

For the people who used to itemize but no longer can, QCDs provide a terrific way to save on taxes.

tion under IRS Section 509(a)(3) are not permitted. Unfortunately, this means that donations to a Fidelity or Vanguard Charitable Giving account or any other donor-advised fund cannot be used for QCDs. However, most other 501(c)(3) charities qualify.

QCD rules limit direct IRA donations to charity to $100,000 per year per person. If you are married, you and your spouse can donate up to $100,000 each or $200,000 total. This amount has not changed since QCDs were first allowed in 2006, but starting in 2024, the maximum contribution limit will be indexed for inflation under the SECURE Act 2.0. If you are reading this book in 2024 or later, the QCD limit will be higher than the $100,000 figure we use here. For some clients, the best math solution for their goals was to aggressively use QCDs for the rest of their lives or at least to the point they wanted to continue making charitable deductions.

Even if you do itemize, the advantage of using QCDs is that you lower your taxable IRA income and thus lower the Adjusted Gross Income (AGI) shown on your tax return. If you only take the required distribution from your IRAs and you use a QCD, you will only be taxed on the remainder of your RMD above the charitable contribution. This provides many money-saving advantages in various tax situations, as discussed below.

For university professors and TIAA investors who have after-tax contributions in their IRAs, any charitable contributions made through a QCD will not use up any of the after-tax basis. The pro-rata rules do not apply to these types of distributions which is good news.

Watch Out for Limits on QCDs if You're Still Contributing to a Traditional IRA

One caveat I want to mention when making QCDs when you are over age 70½. As stated previously, with the passing of the SECURE Act, the age limit cap on making Traditional IRA contributions was removed. This means tax-deductible IRA contributions can be made for older employees up to their earned income to a maximum of $7,500 if their income is below the income thresholds. The SECURE Act also included an anti-abuse provision that disallows you from making a tax-deductible IRA contribution and taking a QCD in the same year for that amount.

Basically, the IRS is saying you cannot *'double-dip'* by taking a tax deduction for your IRA contribution and make a charitable contribution through a QCD. If you have earned income and contribute to an IRA after age 70½ and take a tax deduction, any future QCD will be reduced by the cumulative amount of deductible IRA contributions you make after age 70½.

For example, if you contribute $7,500 to an IRA in the year you turn 70½, then make a QCD of $10,000 the next year, you will only be allowed to make a QCD of $2,500. The remaining $7,500 will be a taxable distribution from your IRA, which you can also deduct as a charitable contribution if you are itemizing your deductions. If you are not itemizing, your taxable income will increase by the disallowed amount of your QCD with no offsetting deduction.

The purpose of the anti-abuse provision is to prevent individuals from deducting IRA contributions (above the line deduction, thereby reducing AGI) and then making a donation of the contributions on a pre-tax basis as a QCD— thereby, *'double-dipping.'*

A planning technique if you are married and making tax-deductible IRA contributions and using QCDs as your annual gifting strategy would be for one spouse to make a tax-deductible IRA contribution to their own account and the other spouse to make the QCD from their account.

Remember, notwithstanding the above, if you have post-tax contributions in your IRA, the QCD operates on a first-in-first-out basis, with the pre-tax contributions being distributed first.

Savings When the Standard Deduction is Used

The *"home run"* created by QCDs is for people who take the standard deduction rather than itemizing. The standard deduction for 2023 is $27,700 (for mar-

> **A planning technique if you are married and making tax-deductible IRA contributions and using QCDs as your annual gifting strategy would be for one spouse to make a tax-deductible IRA contribution to their own account and the other spouse to make the QCD from their account.**

ried, filing jointly) and an extra $1,500 each if over 65 or blind. Combining the higher standard deduction and the increased limitations on other itemized deductions like taxes paid, many more taxpayers will use the standard deduction than ever before.

Taking all or a part of your RMD as a QCD will reduce the AGI on your tax return because the QCD is not included in your AGI. While the standard deduction is not affected, your taxable income is reduced compared to not using a QCD, lowering your taxes. For example, if you use the standard deduction and are in the 24% tax bracket, you will save $2,400 in income tax if you donate $10,000 to charity using a QCD rather than taking your entire RMD and writing a check from your bank account.

Savings When Itemizing Deductions

Medical deductions are reduced by 7.5% of your AGI. If you have significant medical expenses and you itemize your deductions on your Schedule A, using QCDs to reduce your AGI and thereby increasing your medical deduction may be advantageous. By using QCDs, you reduce your AGI and taxable income.

It is important to *"run the numbers"* to see what is more beneficial, by either including your charitable deduction in your itemized expenses or using a QCD for charitable giving and reducing your AGI and increasing your medical expense deduction. Depending on the amount of medical expenses, usually you will pay less income taxes by using the QCD because the tax savings on the increased medical deduction outweigh the benefits of including the charitable deduction in itemized deductions.

Savings on the Taxation of Social Security

The *'Grand Slam Home Run'* created by QCDs is for people using the standard deduction and whose Social Security income is not fully 85% taxable when QCDs are used.

The taxable amount of Social Security is based on how much other taxable income you have to report on your tax return. Up to 85% of your Social Security may be taxable, but depending upon your other income sources, you may only have 50% of your Social Security taxed. If you employ a QCD to reduce your AGI to certain thresholds, you may reduce the amount of Social Security that is taxed.

Suppose a married couple, both over age 70½, had combined income in 2022 of $70,000 from their Social Security and $70,000 of RMDs from their Traditional pre-tax IRAs. In this case, their Social Security income was not fully taxable up to the 85% maximum.

If they had donated $5,000 to charity but did not have enough deductions to itemize over $28,700 ($25,900 MFJ standard deduction + $1,400/each for being over age 65), their federal income tax would have been approximately $13,000 without using a QCD. By using a QCD for their $5,000 charitable giving, their taxable RMD would have been reduced by $5,000, and now the taxes owed were approximately $11,000, a $2,000 tax savings comprising of over 40% of the donated amount!

Savings on Medicare Premiums

Nearly all people age 70½ are on Medicare, and the premiums for Part B and sometimes Part D are usually deducted from their Social Security payments. If your Modified AGI (MAGI, which is AGI plus tax-exempt interest) is over a certain amount, these Medicare premiums will be raised for the second following year.

For married couples, the first income threshold for 2023 Medicare premiums is $194,000 of the MAGI shown on the 2021 tax return. If the couple's MAGI was $196,000—only $2,000 over the threshold—in 2021, the 2023 Medicare premiums would be increased for each spouse by $65.90 per month for Part B and $12.40 per month for Part D. This is a $1,879.20 extra cost for both spouses in 2023. If your MAGI was approaching that threshold of $194,000, using QCDs to lower your MAGI below that amount by lowering the taxable RMDs would provide significant savings—at no real cost if you planned to donate to charity anyway.

There are additional 2023 thresholds of increased Medicare premiums at MAGI levels of $246,000; $306,000; $366,000, and $750,000. The increases in Medicare premiums B and D are larger at each of these thresholds—at $246,001, for example, the Part B premium increases to two times the standard rate, from $164.90 to $361.20 per month. Using QCDs to get under these thresholds can save a significant amount of money.

Since 2020 is history, and no RMDs were required in 2020, we should now be looking at using QCDs in 2023 to lower the taxable RMD incomes in 2023. This could have the effect of lowering the 2025 Medicare premiums if the QCDs result in income falling below the MAGI thresholds for 2025 Medicare premiums.

It is noted that the 2024 MAGI thresholds will not be determined until November 2023. In recent years, these MAGI thresholds have increased with inflation. Up to 2019, the first level was $170,000 of MAGI. Then for 2020 Medicare premiums, it was increased to $174,000. For 2021 it was increased less, to $176,000, based on lower inflation than the prior year. However, inflation in 2021 and 2022 pushed the thresholds all the way to $182,000 and $194,000, respectively, a jump of $6,000 and $12,000, respectively.

Of additional interest, while the MAGI thresholds overall have increased up to a maximum of 3.41% in 2022, for example from $176,000 up to $182,000, the Medicare premiums increased by 14.5% from $148.50 in 2021 up to $170.10 in 2022! Of course, all these rules could change by then, and the amounts of the premium increases could change (likely increasing), based on increased funding needs for the Medicare program.

Improved Roth IRA Strategy

QCDs can help in planning Roth conversions. Some people want to make Roth conversions but only up to the point that their Medicare premiums will not increase based on MAGI. Since MAGI is reduced by using QCDs, more can be converted to Roth IRAs. Others want to make Roth IRA conversions up to an amount that maintains a certain tax bracket, often 24%. Again, QCDs can lower your income, increasing the amount you can convert to a Roth IRA while staying within your desired tax bracket.

What if you are receiving earned income or self-employment income and are subject to the RMD rules and you would like to contribute more money to your Roth IRA, but you are slightly over the 2023 AGI income thresholds of $138,000 (single) and $218,000 (MFJ)? A good planning strategy would be to use a QCD for a portion of your RMD in order to reduce your AGI so you qualify to contribute to your Roth IRA.

Savings for Taxpayers Subject to Net Investment Income Tax or Alternative Minimum Tax

Higher income taxpayers with AGIs over $250,000 (married couple) or single taxpayers with AGIs over $200,000 incur additional taxes from the Net Invest-

> **Again, QCDs can lower your income, increasing the amount you can convert to a Roth IRA while staying within your desired tax bracket.**

ment Income (NII) tax. The NII tax is a 3.8% tax on investment income above the AGI limits cited. By using a QCD, your AGI is reduced, and you can reduce the amount of investment income subject to the NII tax.

While it is rare to be subject to the alternative minimum tax after the passing of the Tax Cut and Jobs Act, it is possible that QCDs can save on AMT for those subject to it.

Various Other Benefits of QCDs

Without getting too much more involved in the tax code, there are many other ways QCDs can benefit you by reducing your AGI. Higher AGI limits certain deductions and credits. A *tax credit example* is the lifetime learning credit for retirees taking college courses later in life. Using QCDs may help you qualify for that credit.

A *deduction example* is the rental loss deduction that can become limited if your income is over certain amounts. Using QCDs can lower your income, potentially allowing for a larger rental loss deduction.

Last but not least, if you plan to donate to charity anyway, it may make sense to do so using a QCD to reduce the balances in your Traditional IRAs. This can have the effect of reducing future RMDs and lowering your income taxes in an environment of rising tax rates.

A New Twist on QCDs from the SECURE Act 2.0: Fund a CRT with a QCD

As mentioned briefly in Chapter 18, the SECURE Act 2.0 allows investors to fund a CRT with a QCD. However, this provision comes with so many restrictions that I don't see it as a particularly valuable option.

- Funding is limited to just $50,000 per person, and this is currently a once-in-a-lifetime opportunity.

- This contribution will only count as a QCD if the only contributions to this CRT come from QCDs.

- Income beneficiaries are limited to the IRA owner and his or her spouse.

Even if both spouses contribute the maximum of $50,000, this would only result in a CRT funded with a maximum of $100,000. As I mentioned in Chapter 18, a good rule of thumb for the minimum contribution to a CRT is $1,000,000. The costs to administer a CRT don't make it likely worthwhile with smaller amounts.

No Downside or Costs of QCDs?

The downsides of using QCDs, which are minimal, are simply the procedures. There is no cost to using them. Usually, you only need to send your IRA investment manager or broker the name and address of the charity and tell them how much to donate. You will probably want to lower your other RMDs above the amount donated, so keep track of this.

You will still need to get the documentation letters from the charities as you would with any other charitable donation, and you will need to keep track of the QCDs and tell your tax preparer you made them. If you prepare your own tax return, you must follow the rules on presenting the QCDs on Form 1040.

Processing a QCD may add a slight burden on your IRA custodian. Because of the additional paperwork, you may want to use QCDs only for larger contribution amounts. You may even want to *"bunch up"* your charitable donations for the year, or even for two years at a time, to take advantage of the standard deduction and other advantages mentioned above.

I know of at least one brokerage firm that will give you a checkbook for your IRA, from which you can write a check directly to a charitable organization. I know some providers do not like this technique, and I am not certain all brokerages allow this, but it sure seems to simplify life for the IRA owner. One thing to remember is that the QCD checks need to clear before year end, so you should not wait until the last minute to send them out.

Are There Situations When Giving Highly Appreciated Stock is a Better Strategy than Using QCDs?

Because QCDs are limited to just $100,000, donating appreciated stocks to a charity will allow you to make more substantial donations during your lifetime. This can be a great way to reallocate your portfolio and to get rid of highly appreciated stock—before it goes down—without incurring capital gains taxes on the appreciation.

If you are already itemizing your deductions, you get a deduction for the fair market value of the stock; however, your deduction will be limited to 30% of your AGI as of this book writing. Any excess can be carried forward until used.

The downside of this is that if your itemized deductions are less than the 2023 standard deduction of $27,700 for joint filers, $13,850 for single filers, you will not receive any tax benefit from the portion that brings your total itemized deductions above those thresholds.

In other limited situations, it may be more advantageous to donate highly appreciated stocks to a charity rather than using a QCD.

On the other hand, if your planned annual charitable donation is less than $100,000, a QCD could be the best strategy. If you do not have enough other deductions to itemize, a QCD is generally the best strategy. QCDs, as mentioned above, can be a great way to minimize income tax when you are simultaneously performing a Roth conversion. QCDs also make sense if you want to reduce your RMDs and stay in a lower tax bracket or to keep your future Medicare premiums down. However, once all your Traditional IRA assets are converted to Roth IRAs, there are no more opportunities to make QCDs.

If you are planning a large charitable bequest, it is best to designate the charity as beneficiary of your Traditional IRA as the charity will not pay any taxes. But if the planned bequest is larger than your IRAs, donating a large amount of appreciated stock while you are alive may be a better strategy because the additional itemized deduction will save you on income tax. If you donate that stock by bequest after your death, you will not save on income tax, though you may save on estate taxes.

Use QCDs!

Assuming you do not want to give more than $100,000 or meet the less common exceptions where donating highly appreciated stock may be a better strategy than using QCDs, we like QCDs. Because there are no significant disadvantages and no costs for using QCDs, you should use them to make your charitable donations if you are over age 70½. If it is early in the tax year, you may not even be aware of how they will save you money for the current year.

I know this is a lot of technical information, and it is a shame the IRS makes you *"jump through hoops"* for QCDs instead of just allowing you to deduct all your charitable donations from IRA income. It certainly makes sense if you were going to make the charitable donations anyway.

Points to Ponder in Your Overall Giving Strategy

What follows is not an exhaustive treatise on gifting, but rather, broad points to consider when thinking about who gets what, both during your lifetime and at your death. As I mentioned above, using QCDs is simply one of many tools that can be used in your overall lifetime charitable giving strategy.

First, you need to think about how much money you will need to support your lifetime spending, and whether you want to gift money or other support to specific individuals. Next, you need to consider what form of gift or donation is available and most appropriate.

Let's say you have a portfolio of appreciated stocks and substantial retirement plan assets, and you want to give some of those assets to charities and some to individuals. You may want to use a combination of these gifting techniques by donating appreciated securities in addition to donating through QCDs. By doing so, you can reallocate your portfolio and save income taxes. This is especially important if you are already itemizing your deductions.

KEY IDEAS

- People often think making a charitable donation through a QCD will not make any difference in their taxes, and, in some cases, it might not make a significant difference if you itemize deductions. In many more cases, however, it will create significant savings.

- Because there are no significant disadvantages and no costs for using QCDs, you should, subject to limited exceptions where gifting highly appreciated stock to a charity might be a better strategy, use them to make your charitable donations if you are over age 70½.

- Depending on your financial circumstances and your overall gifting strategy, QCDs can be the best way to make planned donations to charitable organizations.

- The tax benefit of your QCD is diluted by the cumulative amount of any tax-deductible IRA contributions made to your IRA account after age 70½.

- Donating appreciated securities in addition to QCDs can be an effective way to reallocate your portfolio and save income tax, especially if you are already itemizing your deductions.

21

How You Should Respond to the Current High Inflation

As this book goes to press, the United States—*as well as the world at large* —is entering an extraordinary period of inflation. In June 2022, US inflation peaked at 9.1% before dropping to 6.5% for the 12 months ending December 2022. That June peak was the highest rate since 1981. With most economists predicting that inflation will remain elevated for at least the next three years, many people are worried about what that will do for their retirement plans.

This fear is fully justified—even with modest 3% inflation, purchasing power drops by a third over 20 years. At the same time, those inflationary pressures as well as other world-wide events are also bringing additional volatility to the stock market, so many investors are seeing their portfolios drop in value. Thus, we are suffering both from inflation and, at least for the short term, a down market.

When I interviewed Burton Malkiel he pointed out that historically the way the country paid its debts was by allowing inflation and paying in lower value dollars. With the huge debt and other problems that we have today, he believes inflation will continue to be a major problem for the foreseeable future

Don't Panic, But Don't Ignore Inflation

Just about any time the economy starts behaving in unpredictable ways, the natural instinct of many is to panic, so we batten down the hatches to prepare for the storm ahead. Today is no different, with some so-called experts ranging from Elon Musk to Jamie Dimon professing a *"bad feeling"* or predicting an economic hurricane.

If too many people follow the counsel of these influencers, then a recession may be the predictable outcome. Joe's Widgets will lay off employees, who happen to be customers of Lana's Diner, which will cause Lana's Diner to lay off employees, and so on in an endless chain of recession-driving panic.

Others, however, including Larry Kotlikoff, an economist whose opinion I respect, point out some of the positive things about today's economy. We've got low unemployment. Eighty percent of the working age population is employed, nearly a 70-year high. Job growth is slowing down because there aren't many people left to hire. The Bureau of Labor Statistics says there are currently about twice as many job openings as unemployed people.

So even though prices on many things are rising, Mr. Kotlikoff urges us not to panic, reminding us that *"[t]he three big concerns with inflation are whether wages will keep pace with prices, the impact of inflation on retirees on fixed nominal pensions and on other creditors, and hidden inflation-based tax hikes."*

We shouldn't be complacent about inflation, but as Mr. Kotlikoff also says, *"[w]hat can kill the economy is enough people, who should know better, talking it down."* Inflation by itself will not wreck the economy, but enough people panicking just might.

Inflation roughly follows from the law of supply and demand. As the population increases, demand for goods and services increases across the board. If the supply of those goods and services cannot keep up with demand, and we are experiencing enormous problems with our supply chain thus not being able to fulfill demand, then prices increase.

As shown in the chart below, average inflation in the U.S. from 1913 to 2020 has been 3.1%. Except for the Great Depression of the 1930s, we've had price increases in every decade, with the highest rates in the 1970s and 1980s.

Figure 21.1

Average Annual Inflation by Decade

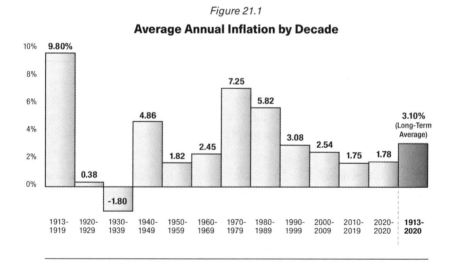

© 2020 InflationData.com · *Updated: December 15, 2020*

**Inflation by itself will not wreck the economy,
but enough people panicking just might.**

Inflation is The Enemy of Fixed Income

Inflation eats into purchasing power so the same dollars cannot buy as much. If the bulk of your income in retirement is from fixed income sources, such as fixed TIAA annuities, or a fixed pension from your employer, you may feel the pinch more than if you also have Roth accounts, Traditional IRAs and retirement plans, and after-tax investments to draw on to make up for any shortfall. Conversely, if you have a sound Financial Masterplan in place, you should have more than adequate financial resources to rely on to get you through most economic disturbances.

Inflation is generally uneven. It doesn't impact the prices of everything uniformly. The inflation percentage you see in headlines is measured by the U.S. Bureau of Labor Statistics on a broad *"basket of goods,"* which includes items you may or may not be purchasing. Gasoline and electricity are up by 48.7% and 12.0%, respectively, but medical care and housing show more reasonable increases of 4.0% and 5.5%. Yes, gas prices are high now. But they've been high before. In 1980, gas was $1.19 per gallon, which seems like a bargain. But measured in today's dollars, that's $4.33 per gallon, which isn't that much below what we're paying now.

While inflation is the enemy of fixed income, the benefit of annuitizing a portion of your TIAA or CREF accumulations is that you have a guaranteed stream of income for the period you elect, whether it's for a term of years, your life, your spouse's life, or for a certain period after your and your spouse's death. Just having that floor of guaranteed income to supplement your Social Security or other pensions can go a long way in ensuring that you and your spouse will never run out of money, no matter what the stock market does. If you want to learn more about the pros and cons of annuitizing your TIAA.

What's Indexed for Inflation?

The good news with inflation is that the federal government indexes many things for inflation. The bad news is that there are also things that are not indexed for inflation. Let's look at those things that change with inflation, which can be the silver lining for inflationary periods.

1. ***Social Security Benefits:*** For 2023, the Social Security Administration increased payments by 8.7%, the biggest cost of living adjustment (COLA) in four decades. If your monthly benefit for 2022 was $2,000, you got a raise of $174 per month, or $2,088 per year, without considering any changes to Medicare premiums.

   At least so far, benefits have never gone down after they've gone up, so this counts as a big win for those collecting—or soon to be collecting—Social Security. A provision in the law prevents those benefits from going down, even if the inflation adjustment or the Medicare Part B premium would cause them to decrease. In the case of the cost of living going down, benefit amounts stay the same as the previous year.

   I should also point out that in times of high inflation, income that is adjusted for inflation becomes much more valuable than income that is not. Social Security income is adjusted for inflation, but many pensions and Traditional TIAA annuities that are not adjusted for inflation are often fixed in amount and become less valuable in inflation adjusted dollars.

2. ***Social Security Wage Base:*** If your W-2 wages or self-employment income are greater than the current Social Security wage base, that income will not be subject to Social Security taxes. For 2022, that wage base was $147,000, and in 2023, the threshold increased to $160,200. However, be aware that among other fixes to Social Security that are under perennial consideration by Congress, that wage base limitation may be increased substantially or entirely removed.

3. ***Standard Deduction:*** In 2017, thanks to the Tax Cuts and Jobs Act (TCJA), the standard deduction for a married couple filing jointly was nearly doubled to $24,000. For 2023, that's now risen to $27,700. However, unless Congress acts to make the temporary provisions of the TCJA permanent, in 2026 the standard deduction will plummet to its 2017 level of $12,700

> **While inflation is the enemy of fixed income, the benefit of annuitizing a portion of your TIAA or CREF accumulations is that you have a guaranteed stream of income for the period you elect, whether it's for a term of years, your life, your spouse's life, or after your and your spouse's death.**

plus inflation since 2017. On the positive side, personal exemptions will come back if we would revert to the pre-TCJA law, so that will somewhat mitigate the drop in the standard deduction.

4. **Tax Rate Brackets:** Every year, the IRS adjusts the income ranges that a particular tax rate applies to. For example, in 2022, income for married joint filers between $178,151 and $340,100 was taxed at 24%. In 2023, that income range for the 24% rate increased to $190,750 to $364,200. Without these inflation-related increases, many people would see any gains in annual income devoured by bracket creep, which is a kind of stealth tax increase.

5. **Capital Gains Rate Thresholds:** For 2022, joint filers with taxable income up to $83,350 paid no tax on net long-term capital gains. The 2023 threshold for joint filers moved up to $89,250. Above that bottom rate, joint filers with taxable income of up to $517,200 for 2022 and up to $553,850 for 2023 pay 15% tax on net long-term capital gains, and 20% when taxable income is over those thresholds.

6. **AMT Exemption & Phaseout Thresholds:** Since 2012, the Alternative Minimum Tax exemptions and other parameters have been indexed for inflation, and temporary changes in the 2017 TCJA made this parallel tax assessment regime applicable to many fewer people.

   Prior to those changes, between four and five million taxpayers were impacted by AMT. Now only about 200,000 taxpayers per year pay AMT, but unless Congress extends those changes, as many as seven million taxpayers may be trapped in AMT-land in 2026. In 2022, the exemption amount for joint filers under the AMT system was $118,100 and for 2023, the exemption amount is $126,500.

7. **Contribution Limits for IRAs, 401(k)s, 403(b)s, & Other Retirement Plans:** By statute, these only go up when the calculated increases from inflation are big enough to increase by $500 or more. The IRA contribution limit remained at $6,000 for years 2019-2022. As a result of higher inflation in 2022, the 2023 IRA contribution limits have increased to $6,500, with catch-up contributions for those over 50 limited to only $1,000 (unchanged).

   In 2023, this threshold was met for most other retirement plans, including 403(b)s, which increased from $20,500 in 2022 to $22,500 with the catch-up contribution increasing to $7,500. With the passing of SECURE Act 2.0, beginning in year 2024, the catch-up contribution limit will be indexed to inflation. In addition, the income thresholds for making deductible and Roth IRA contributions goes up every year. Please see Figure 3.2 *(page 59)*.

8. *Medicare Income-Related Monthly Adjustment Amounts (IRMAA):* Due to ever-increasing costs for healthcare, Medicare Part B premiums go up every year. Premium amounts are based on income so that those with higher incomes pay more than those with lower incomes. Each November, the Social Security Administration determines the monthly premium amounts for Medicare beneficiaries based on their most recently filed tax return. This means that the premium amounts being charged in 2023 are based on 2021 income amounts. Please see Chapter 16 for more information about this and what steps you may be able to take if your income has decreased in the intervening years.

9. *Estate & Gift Tax Exclusion Amounts:* In 2017, the TCJA doubled the estate tax exemption. This exemption amount will be indexed for inflation until 2025. Unless the 2017 increase is extended by Congress, this will drop back to the 2017 level plus inflation in 2026. The 2022 exemption amount—*the size of an estate that can pass tax-free to beneficiaries*—was $12.06 million per individual. For 2023, the exemption increased to $12.92 million. The annual gift tax exemption also increases in increments of $1,000 according to inflation. From 2018 through 2020, this exemption was stuck at $15,000, but finally in 2022, it increased to $16,000 per person per recipient, and in 2023, it increased to $17,000.

What's Not Indexed for Inflation?

Many other provisions of tax law are set by statute so those provisions can only increase when Congress changes the law. *These include the following:*

1. *Exclusion of Capital Gain on the Sale of Your Primary Residence:* Even though home prices soared during 2022, the amount of capital gain from the sale of a primary residence that you can exclude from taxable income has remained fixed at $250,000 for single filers, $500,000 for joint filers since the law was passed in 1998. Back then, the average price of a home was $152,500. Today, the average home has more than tripled in value to $507,800 (*Source:* **https://fred.stlouisfed.org/series/ASPUS.**) If you sell your primary house at some point, you may be facing a substantial capital gain—and tax on that gain—when it comes time to sell the family home.

2. *Deductible Net Capital Loss:* Since 1978, investors with net capital losses can only deduct $3,000 per year and this has never been increased. Any

losses remaining must be carried forward until completely used up, or until your death, at which point they simply evaporate.

3. *Net Investment Income Tax:* This additional tax went into effect in 2013 for taxpayers with modified adjusted gross income exceeding certain thresholds, which have not changed since the law was passed. For a couple filing jointly, this threshold is just $250,000 ($200,000 for single taxpayers) and results in an additional 3.8% tax. This tax is imposed on the smaller of a taxpayer's net investment income or the amount that their MAGI exceed the threshold for their filing status.

4. *Amounts Used to Determine the Taxable Amount of Social Security Benefits:* Legislation passed in 1983 set the income limits for when Social Security benefits may be taxable, and those levels have not changed since then. Determining the taxable amount of Social Security starts by determining *"combined income"* which is essentially AGI adjusted by using only half of the gross Social Security income, plus tax-exempt income. If this *"combined income"* is $32,000 or less, none of the Social Security income is taxable. As *"combined income"* rises, more and more of the Social Security income becomes taxable up to a maximum of 85% of the Social Security being taxable. The amount of *"combined income"* needed to make the maximum 85% of Social Security taxable depends on the amounts of Social Security and other income.

5. *Trust Tax Return Exemptions:* Similar to individual tax returns, trust tax returns are allowed to deduct a certain amount from gross income to arrive at trust taxable income. But unlike the standard deduction and personal exemptions on individual returns, the exemption amounts for trust tax returns have not changed in decades. Depending on the kind of trust, this exemption may be $100, $300, or $4,300 (the biggest exemption is for qualified disability trusts). These stingy exemption amounts combined with the extremely narrow tax rate brackets for trusts mean that the highest rate of 37% kicks in with taxable income at just $14,451 for 2023.

Strategies to Mitigate the Impact of Inflation

Inflation will likely be around for the rest of our lives. When our CPAs *"run the numbers"* for a client, we always take inflation into account. Because inflation has been relatively low for the last 20 years, the recent sharp increases in prices have taken many by surprise and, as previously noted, have been putting many investors and retirees on edge. But as Mr. Kotlikoff and other advisors counsel, this is not the time to panic, but it is still prudent to consider the possible impact of inflation on your retirement plans. Here are some ideas on what you can do to mitigate the wealth-devouring impact of inflation.

Presumably, if you have a well-developed plan in place, that should have taken into account future inflation that is occurring now, and arguably you may not need to do anything. That said, there is a certain anxiety that comes with inflation and a down market. In addition, you may not have a plan that has taken inflation into account.

If that is the case, or if you just want to be a belt and suspenders investor, *here are a few potential action points:*

1. Keep working.
2. Delay applying for Social Security Benefits.
3. Seek out Low-Interest Debt.
4. Keep contributing to retirement accounts for Dollar-Cost Averaging
5. Convert to a Roth.
6. Rebalance your investments.

Keep Working

While the Covid pandemic and the combination of working remotely plus health challenges has driven many professors and other professionals to take early retirement, the recent downturn and threat of ongoing inflation is keeping many people in the workforce longer than they had originally planned. However, pay increases in some industries, including academia, generally do not keep up with inflation, as has been the case for the last several years.

Staying on the job also allows older employees to delay taking distributions from employer-sponsored 403(b) and 401(k) plans. At many universities, retired professors automatically receive the title of *"emeritus professor,"* which allows them to retain contact with their institution and perhaps teach only a few courses a year at a reduced salary. Some universities grant this status only on departmental approval.

Also, the biggest threat of a down market is not for young workers contributing to a retirement plan. Presumably, with a long-term recovery, they are in effect contributing money to their retirement while the market is down and will reap the rewards when the market recovers as it has historically done.

The threat of a down market is for recent retirees who are forced to liquidate investments at low prices to pay their living expenses at high prices. That is another good reason to keep working and when I say keep working, I am talking

The recent sharp increases in prices have taken many by surprise and have been putting many investors and retirees on edge. But if you had a well-developed plan in place, that took into account the inflation occurring now, arguably you may not need to do anything.

about not giving up your full-time job to teach a course or two or drop down to part-time work.

Teaching a course or two usually means a huge cut in pay compared to your existing salary. Dropping hours to part-time may also mean losing many of your workplace benefits. That is why, especially in the current environment of high inflation and the down market, it may be wise to continue working.

If you've already retired and feel the need for a bit of extra income, consider becoming a consultant in your field of expertise. You could also teach courses as an adjunct professor, even if you don't have a background in academia. While many universities are increasing the number of adjunct professors they hire, you are probably already aware that these professors are not generally paid very well. However, a bit of extra cash in the bank can be welcome, particularly if you're not yet taking Social Security.

Delay Applying for Social Security Benefits

Each year that you wait from your full retirement age until age 70 will give you a permanent raise of approximately 8% in your monthly benefit. This increase is a slam-dunk, as I detail in my book, *The $214,000 Mistake: How to Double Your Social Security and Maximize Your IRAs*, which you can download for free at **https://PayTaxesLater.com/Books/**. As the title of my book implies, back in 2018, this difference could amount to an extra $214,000 in benefits by age 95.

With the annual COLA increases to Social Security benefits since 2018, the financial windfall from delaying taking your benefits is even bigger today. So, before you apply for benefits, I encourage you to educate yourself on the topic to determine the best age for you to start receiving benefits based on your individual situation. There are various online calculators if you want to do this yourself, but you'll get a more accurate readout if your calculations look at your entire financial picture, as we do when we create a Financial Masterplan.

Seek Out Low-Interest Debt

If you do need to borrow, make sure your interest rate is lower than inflation. The difference between inflation and your interest rate is essentially a discount on the payments you need to make. You're paying off debt with money that's worth less than it was when you borrowed it. The key to leveraging this is to pay off only the minimum and invest any extra cash you would have used to pay this off with.

Keep Contributing to Retirement Accounts to Take Advantage of Dollar Cost Averaging

During inflationary periods, the stock market frequently drops in value as well. Companies struggle to turn a profit when their costs go up, so this is reflected in their market valuation. This means that if you continue to contribute to your retirement account, those same dollars will buy more shares when the price is low and fewer when the price is high. Over time, investors who do this generally come out ahead. This reduces the risk that you'll miss the low-cost windows or that you'll pay too much for those equities.

Convert to a Roth

Looked at in isolation, if you make a Roth conversion now, and the market goes back up, you will end up with more Roth dollars than if you had made that conversion when the market was holding steady or increasing. But if the market continues to drop after you make your Roth conversion, this will hurt you, not help you.

Let's say you had a $100,000 Traditional IRA at the beginning of the year. Now it's worth only $80,000. If you convert the entire IRA to a Roth, you'll only pay tax on $80,000 rather than $100,000. If the market recovers, you may end up with a $100,000 Roth for the price of an $80,000 conversion. But if the market continues to drop after your conversion, you will have paid too much in tax relative to the diminished value of your Roth.

> **Each year that you wait from your full retirement age until age 70 will give you a permanent raise of approximately 8% in your monthly benefit.**

However, the only thing that really matters with a Roth conversion is that the IRA grows in actual dollars. Inflation will reduce the purchasing power of your converted Roth, but it also reduces the purchasing power of your Traditional IRA and your after-tax investments as well. If you convert and pay taxes on $100,000, and the account value later drops to $80,000, you could have waited and paid less in tax.

Since I'm not a market timer nor an inflation timer, and I acknowledge I can't predict what will happen with the market, I usually do not take these factors into account. But if you consider the overall market, this may impact your thinking about whether this is a good time or a bad time to do a Roth conversion.

With a long enough investment horizon, performing a Roth conversion while the market is down can be a great strategy. Historically, down markets have been a good time to make Roth conversions. But over the short term, you'll only come out ahead if the Roth IRA investments outperform the IRA and after-tax investments. Otherwise, your purchasing power will be down until the market recovers sufficiently or the other advantages of Roth conversions occur. For a deeper look at the impact of inflation on Roth conversions, see Chapter 17.

That said, I still like Roth conversions. But the decision to perform one during a period when the market is also down may require additional courage.

Rebalance Your Investments

Traditional thinking has been that allocating your portfolio 60:40 between equities and bonds is one method to preserve wealth from the hazards of market declines. But according to researchers who looked at the historical performance of different types of investments during inflationary periods, this may not perform as well as you might think.

According to research published in 2022, as summarized by Larry Swedroe in an article on the **Advisor Perspectives** website:

> *"The best hedge against inflation—admittedly imperfect—has been a diversified portfolio of real assets including TIPS, real estate, commodities used sparingly, and certain equities selected for their ability to pass through cost increases to consumers. International equities and debt may also be a hedge against domestic inflation due to the currency effect."*

More details can be found at: **https://www.advisorperspectives.com/articles /2022/04/25/which-asset-classes-protect-against-inflation**.

Inflation Will Always be a Fact of Life

As I said at the beginning of this chapter, the best response to inflation is not to panic. But there's a substantial difference between inflation at the low levels of 2% or below that we experienced from 2000-2020 and the more than 8% we experienced in 2022. Depending on your financial situation, you may find it prudent to make some changes to ensure you make it through this inflationary period with little long-term harm to your finances. You may need to make some changes especially if your cash inflow isn't keeping up with the inflation-induced increases to your cash outflow.

Doing just one of the strategies I mention in this chapter will help you guard against inflation. Doing some or all of them will help more. But the best strategy of all to make sure that inflation is a non-issue during retirement is to start planning early for your retirement so that you will have way more money than you can spend for the rest of your life.

That means, during the accumulation stage, sock away as much as you can, and at least enough to max out your employer's match. Take advantage of any Roth options available to you. Then, during the distribution stage, make sure you're spending the right money first, as I outlined in Chapters 1 and 5.

Before you make any changes, be sure to *"run the numbers,"* either on your own or with a financial professional or possibly even our accounting firm. Please see the back of the book for more details about the possibility of working with us.

KEY IDEAS

- Don't panic about inflation. Too many people panicking can result in the self-fulfilling prophecy of a recession.

- Be aware of the tax attributes that are and are not indexed for inflation. Some increases to inflation may help you in the long run, while others can hurt you.

- Retirement income from Social Security and other sources that receive annual increases for inflation can help hedge against inflation.

KEY IDEAS

(continued)

- The best strategies to mitigate inflation will depend on where you are in your work-retirement journey:

  1. If you're still working, consider delaying retirement.

  2. Delay taking your Social Security until age 70 or at least as long as you can. Every year you wait will give you a permanent increase to your benefits.

  3. Keep contributing to your retirement accounts if you're still working.

  4. Consider the pros and cons of a Roth conversion.

  5. Rebalance your portfolio to make it more resistant to market declines.

22

Asset Location and How You Should Invest Different Assets in Different Tax Environments

Location, location, location...

Long-term tax, financial, and estate planning strategies (like Roth conversion analysis), are my area of expertise, so I don't usually write about investments and asset allocation.

I will spare you a basic discussion of asset allocation but would like to bring up a less familiar but extremely critical aspect of managing investments, especially after the passage of the SECURE Act—*asset location*. All of Lange Financial Group's strategic partners have used the concept of asset location in their investment advisory practices for years, but since the passage of the SECURE Act, it has become increasingly important.

Asset Location with Your Roth IRA

My wife and I incorporated the strategy that I am recommending here and the difference between what we did, as opposed to a more standard approach, will likely be hundreds of thousands of dollars over our lives and the life of our daughter.

We normally advocate that subject to exception, the last dollars you should spend are your Roth dollars—the tax-free growth of Roth IRAs is generally something you want to maintain for as long as legally possible. If you have Roth accounts, you likely have other investments and other retirement accounts that you will spend first and those accounts will probably take you through your retirement. That means you, and if you are married, your spouse, will likely die with your Roth IRA intact and likely it will grow substantially between now and the time of your and your spouse's death. Even if you spend part of your Roth to avoid higher tax brackets, you will still likely end up leaving Roth IRA funds to the next two generations.

Suppose you are 60 years old, and you have a Roth IRA. There is a good chance neither you nor your spouse will ever spend your Roth IRA. Let's say the survivor of the two of you lives 30 years. Then, the beneficiary, if they could afford it and assuming the laws are the same, can let the inherited Roth IRA grow tax-free for another ten years before they must start paying taxes on the dividends, interest and realized capital gains.

So, we are potentially talking about a 40-year plus investment time horizon. A tax-free investment with that kind of time horizon should be invested much differently than short-term investments or even large U.S. growth companies in either after-tax or even Traditional IRAs.

Our family used this technique to the extreme. To be fair, for us, our investment period is even longer because we made a roughly $250,000 Roth conversion in 1998 and we still have a 30-year plus life expectancy. In addition, our daughter will very likely be able to stretch the inherited Roth IRA over her lifetime because of her disability. We were able to put a plan in place to qualify to "stretch" our inherited IRAs and Roth IRAs over her lifetime. So the difference for our family of getting the asset location portion of the Roth is really enormous, that is hundreds of thousands of dollars.

Your beneficiaries, in keeping with the dreaded SECURE Act, will likely no longer be able to defer distributions from the inherited Roth over the course of their lives, but they will be able to defer distributions for ten years after you and your spouse die. That still confers a long-time horizon. Of course, if one of your beneficiaries qualifies as an exception to the ten-year rule, like our daughter will, that offers an even longer time horizon.

Under those circumstances it probably makes sense to alter your asset location strategy with a longer time frame in mind for the Roth investments. For instance, rather than focusing on a well-diversified portfolio or even a portfolio heavily weighted in large U.S. companies or an S&P Index fund, why not invest the Roth in asset classes that have historically done better in the long run?

For example, small cap or value company stocks have significantly outperformed large cap companies in the long run. Investopedia reports that over the same period, small-cap funds yielded an average annual return of 9.12%, and large-cap funds yielded a return of 7.12%.

Yes, they are more volatile, but with a 30-or-40 year or longer investment horizon, long-term performance will outweigh concerns over volatility. Burton Malkiel believes they may have hit their heyday already. That said, you want to invest your Roth in funds or sectors that you think will outperform in a long time horizon.

You can afford to have tax inefficient funds or stocks in the Roth because there will be no tax on the interest, dividends, or gains, even after the last withdrawal ten years after death.

There are arguments why small cap/value companies will do better or worse in the next year or even ten years. Again, I am not so interested in their short-term performance. A better question is which asset class will likely outperform in the long run? Whatever that answer is, a relatively disproportionate share should be invested in the Roth and perhaps have none of that asset class in the non-Roth portfolio.

In addition, since the Roth IRA grows tax-free, you can invest in assets that are tax-inefficient like an index fund that throws off phantom gains. Other index or our choice enhanced index funds can be designed to be at least somewhat tax efficient. A likely asset location for that type of asset would be an after-tax brokerage account. But the enhanced index funds that are not designed to be tax efficient belong in either IRAs or Roth IRAs. This is a prime example of asset location—that is to say where you place investments with different tax characteristics.

KEY IDEAS

- In conclusion, asset location represents a potential *"free lunch"* opportunity to maximize the growth of long-term wealth of the Roth IRA through investing in assets that tend to outperform over longer periods like small and value stocks.

- Likewise, you can afford to have tax inefficient funds or stocks in the Roth because there will be no tax on the interest, dividends, or gains, even after the last withdrawal ten years after death.

Key Ideas continue on the following page.

KEY IDEAS
(continued)

- Investors have two primary aversions: losing money and paying taxes. While we cannot control periodic market declines, we can assuage them through diversification and rebalancing.

- Although we cannot ensure that you will never pay taxes, you may be able to minimize them through asset location optimization, tax lot identification, tax-loss harvesting, capital gain harvesting, Roth IRA conversions, and income smoothing (tax bracket management).

- These are significant tax management strategies that have the potential to save you money and add significant value. Through education and quantification, we can get excited about saving money regarding taxes.

23

Family Gifting and Spending Strategies

"Life is Beautiful. It's about giving. It's about family."
— Walt Disney

Family Gifting: The Big Picture

Most of my current and prospective clients are looking for guidance on things like retirement plan distribution strategies, tax reduction, Roth IRA conversions, asset allocation, estate planning, saving and spending strategies so they never run out of money, appropriate trusts, and other things covered in this book. Of course, our offices try to do our best in these areas.* But sometimes, these areas incompletely reflect how we can provide the most value to clients and their families.

I can't tell you the number of people I consult with whose families could benefit from an aggressive gifting plan. Note, gifting and charitable donations are not the same things for tax purposes. You have likely heard stories of faculty members who have given what their university refers to as *"gifts."* From a tax standpoint, that's not accurate. What they gave was a charitable donation. The gifting I am referring to now is transferring money or property to a person (likely a family member) rather than a charity.

When I meet with clients, I genuinely try to listen two-thirds of the time and talk one-third of the time. As you can imagine, that isn't always easy for me. I also try to address what the client says is their biggest concern. But of course, I eventually bring up something I think most clients should have as part of their plan, that is a gifting plan.

---

* Lange Accounting Group offers guidance on retirement plan distribution strategies, tax reduction, Roth IRA conversions, saving and spending strategies, optimized Social Security strategies and gifting plans. Although we bring our knowledge and expertise in estate planning, it will be conducted in our capacity as a number crunching CPA. However, we will likely make recommendations that clients could have a licensed estate attorney implement. Life insurance can be offered by a CPA through Lange Life Care for those interested. It would be offered in their role as a CPA and not as an attorney. Asset location, asset allocation and low-cost enhanced index funds are provided by the investment firms with whom Lange Financial Group is affiliated. This would be offered in our role as an investment advisor representative. Please see the front of the book for disclaimers related to these services.

In our role for each of these instances, we will not be acting as the clients' attorney and there will not be an attorney/client relationship. There is no solicitation being made for legal services by the author nor by Lange Legal Services, LLC.

I met a single older woman who had a $35 million estate. She was spending roughly $10,000/month and had children and grandchildren with significant financial needs. She was facing a massive federal estate tax liability if she didn't make any gifts or even if she did, for that matter. Aggressive gifting could have reduced her estate tax liability by millions and would also have had the benefit of helping her family when they were younger and needed the money most— before she died, rather than after.

I brought up the idea of giving some money to her family members now. I had significant (multi millions) gifting in mind but was hoping (and even expecting) to convince her to make at least some smaller gifts. Her response: *"What if I get sick?"* Okay, so you are laughing. Are you sure you aren't at least a little bit guilty of the same type of thinking?

Of course, I will never advocate gifting to family members if it threatens your or your spouse's financial security. When estimating how much money you and your spouse will need, I always want to err on the high side. I also factor in provisions for long-term care and emergency buffers, as well as an unexpected market drop. I even add an optimistic if not realistic projection that I will convince you that you can start spending more than you currently spend and you actually do it.

But what if I do all that and there is *still a lot of excess money*. That's when I start thinking about gifting, even if it isn't on my client's radar. The goal of life, and even good financial planning, is not to die with the most money.

Obviously, our explicit goal is to optimize the things we have been talking about, including the best distribution plan for your IRAs and other retirement plan assets, Roth IRA conversions, wills and trusts, beneficiary designations, investments, asset allocation, etc.

I also understand being reluctant to gift in uncertain times. As we go into design, the market is down and inflation is rearing its ugly head. The natural tendency is to wait until later to make gifts even if gifting is on your mind.

The truth is all times are uncertain and I do not see them becoming more certain as time goes on. I know you are going to say with Covid, global warming,

> **The goal of life, and even good financial planning,
> is not to die with the most money.**

Without gifting, the children will not have benefited from the family money when they were younger and had greater financial needs. All of this makes a compelling case for gifting while you are still alive.

the invasion by Russia in Ukraine, problems with China and North Korea, the extreme political divisiveness, etc. these aren't *"normal times."*

But really, when were times *"normal"*? If you talk to some of my older engineering clients, they will describe their lives in the early 60s. Many of them went to work and came home and worked on their bomb shelter in their back yards because they feared a Russian nuclear attack. So, I don't think *"we aren't in normal times"* is a great excuse.

But what if, based on current assets and income, even using the most conservative assumptions, our projections show that you have way more money than you will ever need?

Consider the Impact of Your Gift—and the Potential to Reduce Taxes

In a typical will or trust, without any lifetime gifting, all assets will be left to the surviving spouse at the first death. Ultimately, when the second spouse dies—often in their 80s or 90s and when the children are in their 60s—particularly after the SECURE Act, there will frequently be a massive income and potential estate or inheritance tax on a sizable estate.

Furthermore, without gifting, the children will not have benefited from the family money when they were younger and had greater financial needs. All of this makes a compelling case for gifting while you are still alive.

Think about this. If you were given $100,000 today, would it make much of a difference in your life? Would you go on one more vacation or even go out to dinner one more time? What if you had inherited $50,000 thirty years ago (which is roughly $100,000 in today's dollars)? What kind of difference would it have made then?

I had another client with $3,000,000. He spent $7,500/month. It was reasonable to project that with his Social Security, he would die with a lot more money than he has now. He had never married and didn't have any kids. His sister, who he was close with, was too sick to work, had run up her credit cards, and was barely getting by with Social Security and a tiny pension. She lived in financial gloom. Her financial situation literally caused her to be sick. When he saw me for a review, and I learned of this situation, I suggested he give his sister $117,000. Much to my surprise, he did it.

That $117,000 gift truly did not have any significant impact on my client's finances. He didn't change his behavior one bit. The gift, however, made a life-changing difference for his sister. It was also life-changing for my client because he felt so good about the gift.

Gifting More than $17,000 (or $34,000, if Married) Per Year

You may wonder how my client made a $117,000 gift when the annual exclusion for 2023 is only $17,000 per beneficiary ($34,000 if you are married). Yes, theoretically, there would be a gift tax on the $100,000 remaining after the $17,000 exclusion. However, if you file the appropriate gift tax return, you can elect to have the $100,000 subtracted from your *lifetime gifting exemption*. (You should file a gift tax return, but you will not be taxed immediately if you do not.)

If you make a $117,000 gift, you simply subtract $17,000 that you are *"allowed"* to gift and deduct the $100,000 from your lifetime federal gifting exemption of $12.92 million (as of January 2023), leaving you with a federal gifting exemption of $12.82 million. As long as you don't die with more than $12,820,000, there will not be any federal estate tax or transfer tax at your death.

If the sunset provisions of the 2017 Tax Cut and Jobs Act take effect as scheduled on January 1, 2026, your estate would still have to exceed the $5,000,000 (plus inflation) lifetime federal gifting exemption. If you are married, double the exclusion to the current $25,840,000 exclusion or $10M (plus inflation) if the sunset provisions of the 2017 Tax Cut and Jobs Act kicks in in 2026.

A further benefit is that any of the appreciation that would have accrued on the gift from the time of the gift to your death is removed from your estate.

Don't get me wrong. The $17,000/year exclusion ($34,000/year if from a joint account or your spouse joins you in the gift) per beneficiary is a great starting point for a gifting program, especially if there are a lot of potential beneficiaries such as children and grandchildren.

Another way you might be able to provide substantial financial support to family members is to pay their education or medical expenses. If you make payments directly to an educational institution or a medical provider on behalf of a loved one, those payments are not considered gifts and do not count towards the $17,000 annual exclusion. This is different from sending your grandchild money with the expectation that they will use the funds for college tuition or medical bills. Those payments count as gifts while payments made directly to the university or hospital do not.

I met with a married couple in their 70s who had much more money than they would ever need. They had an adult child who was basically broke. I told them if they gave their child $2 million dollars, it could potentially save many millions in taxes.

Without the gift, in twenty years, the $2 million (assuming a 7% interest rate) would grow to $8 million which could trigger a federal estate tax of close to $3.2 million. True, by eating into their exclusion, they are only saving the estate tax on the growth, but that $6 million would be close to a $2.4 million savings for the family. Finally, even if there are no federal transfer tax savings, there could be substantial state inheritance tax savings with large gifts.

The fear of the child being inappropriate with the money or reducing the child's motivation to succeed still needed to be addressed. We partially, though not 100% solved that problem by making a gift to a trust with the child as the primary beneficiary. A good source of information to address that issue is a book called **Preparing Your Heirs** by Roy Williams. I did a radio show with him that can be accessed at **https://PayTaxesLater.com/Radio-Show/Episode-84-Transcript/**.

Two other professor families come to mind. They are both wealthy, have one child, and can afford to make substantial gifts to their child. In both cases, their children are financially responsible and do extremely meaningful and fulfilling work for charitable organizations for which their parents approve. But (surprise, surprise) their children do not make a lot of money.

One professor has been extremely generous to his child. His son was able to get married, he lives in a nice house, and the professor contributed generously to a 529 plan for his grandchild's college education. It didn't reduce the motivation of the adult child who continues to have an extremely productive career working for the charitable organization.

The other professor in a comparable financial position has a daughter doing meaningful—but not well-paid—work who is essentially living barely above the poverty level. Despite my pleading, he has never made a large gift to her. She is in her late fifties now. He will likely die owing massive taxes and she will inherit way more money than she will ever need when she is in her sixties or seventies. Which family do you think is making the best use of their roughly equal financial resources?

Another experience comes to mind about the challenges of persuading clients to spend more money and make gifts. I was always encouraging this professor to spend more money on himself and his wife and give more money to his children. After a while, I gave up on trying to get him to spend more money on himself and his wife. I did, however, keep trying to get him to give more money to his children—I was not successful.

On one of the last times I saw him before he died, he said *"I have considered what you have recommended about gifting money to family. Accordingly, I have decided I will happily accept any money my children wish to give to me."*

So, if, after running a series of long-term financial projections using a series of very conservative assumptions, there is sufficient money to make gifts, I firmly believe you should strongly consider a formal gifting program. The combination of getting your family money when they need it most and dramatically cutting the family tax burden should be a major consideration in many professors' Financial Masterplans.

How a Gift Can Continue Giving

Another way to counter the problem of accelerated taxes on retirement plans and IRAs in the wake of the SECURE Act is to bestow gifts on family members via regular taxed withdrawals. Not indiscriminately, but with *"leveraged gifting"* techniques that provide tax advantages for both you and your beneficiary.

This strategy will slowly reduce the amount in your Traditional IRA, leaving less to face the *"death tax"* burden. Plus, it can confer significant advantages to your children while they are still young.

Different Forms of Gifting

Of course, gifting can take on many flavors. It could be a straightforward gift of cash. It could be a contribution to a 529 plan (a tax-free college funding mechanism typically for grandchildren). For most older professors, this is one of my favorite ways to give away your money. I also like gifts that your beneficiary then uses to contribute to their own Roth IRAs or Roth 401(k)s. If you can afford to make gifts to your family, *I recommend five basic types of gifts:*

1. A plain old, no-strings-attached gift.

2. A gift for a specific purpose, such as a down payment on a house. Technically, there should be no *"strings"* on a qualifying gift, but a strong hint is a viable option!

3. Help fund a Roth IRA for a child or grandchild or assist a child in maximizing their Roth 401(k) account at work. The money could also be used to pay the taxes on a Roth IRA conversion of the child's IRA.

4. The gift of education for grandchildren in the form of Section 529 plans or even direct tuition payments or health care payments (which aren't technically considered a gift).

5. Permanent (not term) life insurance.

For some professors and TIAA investors, the source for the gift could be their retirement plan. The last three methods of gifting (assuming the source is the net proceeds after retirement plan withdrawals) are methods for transferring money from the taxable environment to the tax-free environment, all outside of your estate. All five gifting techniques could reduce the value of an Inherited Traditional IRA, thus reducing the tax liability on the inheritance.

Life insurance is free from income tax and, if set up properly, is also free from estate, inheritance, and transfer taxes. Because of the complexity of this type of gift, we discuss life insurance as a gifting option in Chapter 26.

The Exception to the Rule as it Relates to Gifting

Earlier I said, *"Don't Pay Taxes Now, Pay Taxes Later, Except the Roth."* Taking money from your IRA, paying the taxes, and then using that money to buy life insurance, a 529 plan, or even a Roth IRA for your children is conceptually similar to making a Roth IRA conversion. Taking money from your IRA and using the proceeds for these purposes is likely an excellent strategy. In all instances, you are paying income taxes now in return for tax-free growth in the future.

In the last three instances above, the added bonus is that, if handled correctly, they can avoid all transfer and estate taxes. That said, Roth IRA conversions, life insurance, 529 plans, and other gifting techniques should be complementary rather than competing strategies.

I have done a series of webinars for CPAs called **Transferring Money from the Taxable World to the Tax-Free World**. Of course, Roth IRA conversions was one focus. Withdrawing money from a retirement account, paying tax on it, and gifting it to family members who then use it for tax-free investments was the other focus.

> The combination of getting your family money when
> they need it most and dramatically cutting the family
> tax burden should be a major consideration in many
> professors' Financial Masterplans.

Annuities and Gifting

As I'm sure you can tell, I'm not a big fan of commercial annuities. I have never sold one nor recommended a client buy one. They typically have high internal hidden costs. In addition, assuming they were purchased with after-tax dollars, all the appreciation will eventually be subject to ordinary income, not capital gains tax treatment. There is no step up in basis with commercial annuities. But, even after all these disadvantages, I often recommend clients keep the commercial annuities they already have purchased.

Many of these contracts have penalties for cashing them in early. In addition, since many of these products have guarantees and owners have already incurred the high costs, it is often best to keep what you have. The other factor is if they were purchased many years ago when interest rates were higher than today, it might be a reasonable investment to hang on to.

But even though I don't recommend purchasing them, many professors, especially those who work for state schools, own them.

One thing to keep in mind is if they have a guaranteed return (and be careful because some of the guarantees that you may assume are a living benefit turn out to be only a death benefit.) If there is a true living guarantee, then consider investing in the riskiest asset class the annuity company offers. Notwithstanding you are investing in something aggressive, you can treat it as a fixed income investment for the purposes of asset allocation because of the guarantee.

But it can also be used as a source of income for you and/or your heirs. Most owners keep them until death, but then all the appreciation is subject to ordinary income taxes for the heirs. You might consider annuitizing early, and if you do not need the money, give the income to your children.

If you have come to the point where you will be required to annuitize (age 85 for many TIAA contract owners), it may make sense for you to elect an option that will provide a guaranteed income over your own lifetime as well as that of a younger survivor. The annuity income will stop as soon as your survivor dies.

On the other hand, if the survivor has a long life, it could work out quite well financially and your survivor will be reminded of your gift every year for the rest of their lives many years after you have passed. But, before you select this option, you should take into account not only your own life expectancy, but also the life expectancy of your heirs.

In addition to the types of gifts mentioned in this chapter, here is one more idea to protect yourself and your heirs from the death of the stretch IRA.

Spend More Money

Spend more money! To be honest, I have been only moderately successful in my efforts to convince clients to spend more money, even when they can easily afford it. Even if they intellectually understand the math and calculations behind the recommendations we make, few of my clients who are age 65 or older are great spenders relative to their income and net worth. I know it isn't easy to get a leopard to change its spots, but I aim for some change in the spending area.

One couple I worked with was drastically underspending. During our review, the man said that he had changed and he wanted recognition for changing his spending. He said he was spending money on things he would never have purchased in the past. He wanted me to congratulate him for paying $12/month for no ads or commercials on YouTube!

My suggestion had been to spend money of a different magnitude. Specifically, I suggested they rent or buy a place in the city where their daughter who is having a baby lives. Mom instantly liked that idea and to be fair, so did Dad.

I often ask clients if we talked to your children and asked if they would prefer you spend more money that would give you more pleasure or save that money for a larger inheritance, the clients without exception said their kids would encourage them to spend more money. Additionally, I have always encouraged my clients to spend more money *on taking care of themselves*. I believe all these things will bring you a higher return than the market, even in good times.

A Few More Thoughts About Spending

Please note that a discussion of the safe withdrawal rate, sequence of returns, and other issues regarding how much you can safely spend is beyond the scope of this book. Our CPAs like to calculate how much money clients can afford to spend without ever running out of money. Depending on your situation and how much you want or need to leave behind, chances are good that you can spend more than you are spending right now.

I am not suggesting you spend frivolously. You would not be where you are today if you did. As an example, though I am extravagant in many areas, I have never paid to fly first class. Until we gave one car to my daughter, my wife and I used to drive 11 and 13 -year-old Subarus. My wife, who has a master's degree in electrical engineering from Carnegie Mellon University, and my daughter, also a STEM kid, are both much thriftier than me.

True, I work long hours, and I am in the prime of my career in terms of productivity and earning capacity. One rationalization for some of our expenses is that I am buying time. I can make much more money per hour working than I spend paying for many of the things like shopping, cooking, or cleaning. That said, I am also buying health. To be fair, I have only spent like this in recent years and only after I thought I could afford it.

Finally, one more note; I gained a lot more personal satisfaction from having persuaded my client to give his sister $117,000 than I did from devising a perfect Roth IRA conversion plan that saved a family a million dollars. I like the personal touch.

The point of this chapter, however, is to show that additional spending and making gifts to your family can increase the quality of your and your family's lives and be a great hedge against future taxes. The next chapter extends this idea addressing the intersection of money, spending, and happiness. If that seems off-topic for a financial book, just keep an open mind!

KEY IDEAS

- Consider if you can afford more gifts for your family.

- Buying experiences, particularly with family and friends, is likely the best way to spend your money.

- There are many ways to spend your money to enhance the quality of your health and your life.

- Gifting is the most tax- and cost-efficient method of transferring wealth to your heirs.

24

Money Can Buy Happiness

"There is a puritanical streak that runs through all aspects of money in America…and most of the conversations about spending more money start with no."

— Ramit Sethi

Fortunately, for most of my readers, money does buy happiness in that it protects from hardship. Being able to count on access to good medical care, a general sense of well-being, a cadre of good friends and family, shelter, and food goes a long way to fostering happiness. But if we are in the position to be able to afford more, can we be happier spending more?

I am not advocating for spending carelessly. But, when the resources are there, are there ways to make your money *"work for you"* outside the investment realm?

The authors Elizabeth Dunn and Michael Norton published a book called **Happy Money: The Science of Smarter Spending**. They espouse five principles for ways to spend money to increase your happiness.

1. **Buy experiences.** I would add, buy things that allow you to do what you want to do. (For example, my e-bikes and house in Tucson allow me to significantly enhance my bicycling experience and that makes me happy.)

2. **Make it a treat.** Don't indulge in your favorite ice cream every day—it stops being a treat. (This is the hard one for me to get.)

3. **Buy time.** Pay people to do what you do not like doing. Or don't buy the cheapest airline ticket if it results in an endless layover where you do not want to be.

4. **Pay now, consume later.** That paid-for vacation seems *"free"* by the time you take it.

5. **Invest in others.**

Perhaps what gives the authors of this advice additional credibility is that they are both full time professors at the University of British Columbia and Harvard, respectively. Of course there is now a huge amount of happiness literature. But since I tend to favor peer-reviewed authors, I would say those five criteria, make a pretty good start.

Host a Family Vacation—*Two Birds with One Stone*—Experiences and Investing in Others

My favorite way to spend your money is for you to sponsor a family vacation. My 98-year-old father-in-law hosts a family vacation every year, picking up the tab for the entire family. He has been doing this for more than 25 years (though we obviously skipped during the worst years of the pandemic).

For a four-day weekend, the entire family drives, or flies into a resort called Woodloch in the Poconos (a recreational area in the mountains of Pennsylvania). All of the children, grandchildren, and now great-grandchildren come and hang out together to play games, swim in the pool, go to the *"beach,"* kayak in the lake, play golf and tennis, laugh at the Comedy Club, and enjoy family activities. We eat all of our meals together in the walled off semi-private dining room.

My daughter, Erica, our only child who is now 28 years old, knows all her cousins well, despite living in different states, and they are in frequent contact. She would not have this sense of being part of a bigger family were it not for these annual family gatherings. During the pandemic isolation, my daughter is having a blast chatting online with her cousins.

When my father-in-law passes, he will leave less money to his family, but he will have provided the priceless legacy of strengthened family bonds and a sense of *"clan,"* even though we live all over the country.

This advice, incidentally, is consistent with multiple other authors who say, *"buy experiences, not things."* Imagine how much your loved ones would appreciate such an experience after being unable to go anywhere or do anything during the pandemic. Better yet, make it an annual event.

A secondary benefit is that experiences tend to get better with memory. Remember that wonderful vacation you took…the minor inconveniences you experienced generally fade into the background and the good times grow even rosier. And then you can also relive the best parts with the people you shared the time with.

I have encouraged clients to spend more money for years and usually without a lot of success. Taking their family on a vacation, however, is one area that many clients have changed and now it is a regular event for many of my client's families.

Usually, the hardest part is working around everyone's busy schedule. My answer to that is to consider everyone's needs, and then pick a date. Mention that you are updating your wills and trusts and you sure hope that they will be able to make the annual family gathering.

Beware of False Economy—Treats are OK

Towards the end of her life, I took my mom on mini vacations to New York City, Washington D.C., and Cleveland. Can you think of a better way for me to spend my time and money?

She was in her mid-nineties when my wife, Cindy, my daughter, Erica, and I took her on the mini vacation to New York City. A retired professor, my mom was basically as sharp as ever. This mini vacation in New York City was a real treat for all of us, but one of the top attractions for my mom was to buy a silk scarf at Bloomingdales. She anticipated the purchase and spoke of it many times—we were very aware that it was a priority for her!

While there, we did the normal touristy things like going to museums, visiting Central Park, eating at wonderful restaurants, and seeing a Broadway show. On the last day, I misjudged the time it would take to get to Bloomingdales. We arrived before closing but without much time to spare.

Mom selected a beautiful silk scarf. I was so happy because this was the crown jewel of the trip for her. I told the salesclerk we would take it.

Then, Mom asked the salesclerk for the price. Frantically shaking my head, I tried to alert the salesperson that she shouldn't tell my mom the price. I would buy it as a gift, my mom didn't need to know the price, but my timing was too late. The salesperson told Mom the scarf cost $100. Instantly my mom said that that was much too expensive. They didn't have a less expensive alternative that she liked. I pleaded with my Mom to let me buy her the $100 scarf. She would have none of it.

As we were leaving, I tried to slip back and buy the scarf, but my mother knew me too well. She said, *"I know you're going back there to buy that scarf, and you may not buy that scarf for me."* She was my mother, I had to listen and be respectful, but it made me a little sad.

The $100 would have meant nothing to me. My mother could have had the pleasure of receiving a gift and owning the scarf and wearing it even if only a few times. After her death, it could have gone to my daughter, and that would have triggered a fond memory of that trip we all took to New York. But no, my mother could not accept me paying $100 for a scarf.

I see this type of thinking all the time with many of my clients.

Both my daughter and my wife are not great spenders. Erica made fun of me for buying a karaoke machine that adjusted the pitch of your voice, so you sang in tune. (I have a good ear and a bad voice.) It was featured on Shark Tank where I often buy the product the entrepreneurs are pitching. Erica accurately predicted I would spend hundreds of dollars on this machine, use it once, and it would accumulate dust in our basement, which is exactly what happened. So, I also suggest that you give yourself permission to forgive yourself if you make a mistake!

How do you balance desires with practicalities? On the scale of the trip, buying the scarf was inconsequential. But for my mother, the financial outlay for a personal indulgence crossed the line—too expensive. But, while I spend money on things that I think are important, I am a little bit the same way with things that I feel are just too expensive.

I was away from home recently and felt like watching television for a little while. (I needed a break from writing this book.) Like most of us in this *"cord-cutting"* era, I hate all the commercials on the regular channels, and, thanks to streaming service subscriptions, I've become accustomed to life without them. But the only alternative at this hotel for movies without commercials was to pay $19.95. I couldn't do it. So, I just watched the regular lousy television with the commercials!

So, how do you come to terms with what you can or cannot afford? When is an indulgence perfectly acceptable? When can you turn dreams into reality? The decisions are ultimately personal but thinking about your choices and knowing how much you can really afford (which, of course, is part of our Financial Masterplan service) is important.

Donate to Charity—Spend Money on Others

Dunn and Norton make some great observations about charity. In their research (you can listen to a short TED talk by Michael Norton on this topic at **https://www.ted.com/speakers/michael_norton**), they found that the amount of money you spend doesn't actually matter that much. What's most important is that you spend it on somebody else. They found a universal positive correlation between giving and happiness. So, focus a bit more on pro-social activities.

Purchasing and distributing 50,000 KN-95 masks to charities, family, friends, and clients was *"worth"* many times what I paid for them.

This increased happiness can be achieved by supporting your favorite charities on a large or small scale, but it can also mean investing in your friendships or building a camaraderie with your neighbors. Throw a party for your friends. Make a lunch date—your treat.

Donate Time

Sometimes, simply doing something to help others—no money involved—can really improve your sense of happiness and belonging. Volunteering is an obvious example, but there are other activities that you might not want to shy away from for fear of intruding.

Recently in my neighborhood, a natural disaster occurred. A strong summer storm severed a hundred-year-old oak tree (and more limbs from other trees), crushed several cars, and tore a hole in the roof of a neighbor's house. Fortunately, no one was physically hurt—though the riders in one car came pretty close.

Many of us had not spoken to each other, despite many years of living within shouting distance. This disaster gave us all permission to talk to each other, to

> **Sometimes, simply doing something to help others— no money involved—can really improve your sense of happiness and belonging.**

help each other where we could and fostered a sense of shared community. Our efforts to help—running electrical cords, helping to move obstructions, and simply being present to the disaster others were facing—increased our communal sense of happiness. Investing in others takes many shapes.

Buy Time

I belong to a business coaching group called Strategic Coach and we did an interesting exercise. Dan Sullivan, the coach, told everyone to write down what they would do if they had an extra 1,000 hours of time per year. Answers included spend more time with family, expand their business, play more golf, write a book, join a gym, eat better, etc.

Then, he said, OK, now figure out a way to free up those thousand hours. At least in my case the way I free up time is to pay others to do stuff that I don't want to do. Hint: delegating chores to your spouse is not what Dan or I have in mind.

Dan thinks we often ask ourselves the wrong question in attempting to solve a difficult, unpleasant time-consuming problem. Our natural inclination is to question *"how"* as in *"How can I deal with this problem?"* While many things cannot be appropriately delegated, many can. If so, the right question might be *"Who can do this for me?"* not *"How can I do this?"* Hence the name of his recommendation and the name of one of his books, Who, Not How.

A Personal Note On Avoiding Taxes

Your happiness is more important than your money.

I have a lot of snowbird clients who spend several months a year in the south every winter. I go to Tucson myself and think avoiding the Northeast winters is a fine idea. Neither Texas nor Florida have a state income tax or an inheritance tax so there is certainly tax-reduction motivation in having either state as your primary residence.

If you were planning on living in a tax-favored state five months and 29 days, (not that time spent in the state is the sole residency test), fine. Spend a few more days there, become a resident and save money on taxes while you are alive and after you are gone. What if you only want to spend three months a year there? Should you spend three more months in a state where you don't want to live just so you can save money in taxes?

I would say no.

Your happiness is more important than your money.

The same thing when it comes to saving inheritance taxes. Do you want to spend your last years in a state where you don't want to live so you can save taxes for your heirs?

The purpose of saving taxes, though it varies from reader to reader, is to have a more financially secure life, be able to do whatever it is that you want to do, and to optimally pass money to your family. If you were to ask any one of your kids point blank—*"What do you prefer, that I live in a place where I don't want to be so I can save taxes when I die so you can receive a bigger inheritance or would you prefer I live where I want?"*

If any of your children say they would prefer you try to save money on their taxes regardless of where you live, you have a bigger problem than a tax problem. In reality, I hope every child would say *"your happiness comes first."* In my experience, every client that I have would say that this is what their children would want for them.

Don't let the tail wag the dog. Live where you want to live.

KEY IDEAS

- Most discussions of spending start with *"No."* Please try to keep an open mind because the right type of spending can buy you happiness.

- Think about delegating things you do not want to do that someone else could do for you, even if you have to pay them.

- Happiness is more important than saving taxes. Even if an option such as living in a state with no state income tax or inheritance tax could save you a bundle on taxes, don't choose that option if it won't also make you happy.

25

Get Married for the Money

"I can handle being married for my money; it's being married
for my life insurance that gives me pause."

— Jacob M. Appel

This chapter is for people in a long-term committed relationship who aren't legally married. There are significant financial implications of getting married. With appropriate planning, getting married will likely be extremely beneficial for the couple as well as their heirs from a financial standpoint.

First, let me address a common objection. You were scarred at the financial and psychological devastation of your divorce and never want to go through that again. I get it. Though it isn't a perfect answer, the obvious answer is to have a prenuptial agreement, which I almost always recommend for even a first marriage.

The agreement can be as simple as what's mine is mine, what's yours is yours, what's ours is ours. If we ever split, I keep mine, you keep yours, and we split ours. We each retain the right to leave as much or as little as we want to anyone we want in our wills, trusts, beneficiary designations, etc. But having a solid prenuptial agreement is a great start.

In reality, especially as you are married for more years and your commitment and love grow and mature, you can be much more generous than the prenuptial agreement indicates. That is what my wife and I did. We got a prenuptial agreement when we married close to thirty years ago. At the time, she was a hotshot computer science engineer with a master's degree from CMU with a great job. I had a fledgling business. Now, thirty years later, our wills etc. are much more generous to each other than our prenuptial say is the minimum to provide for each other.

I have known many people in committed relationships when the partner with significant financial resources didn't want to get married, despite my best efforts at financial persuasion. Now if you do not want to get married because you don't want to get married for non-financial reasons, that is another story.

But, if you don't want to get married for financial reasons, the prenuptial agreement should be able to protect you. In addition, you could be adding enormous financial benefits for your partner, even if you do not leave your partner one red cent. (See the section on Social Security below.)

I have long known about the financial benefits of getting married. Back in 2014, I saw a "loophole" for same-sex couples to enjoy the financial advantages of marriage even if they lived in states that didn't recognize in-state marriages.

So, to help same-sex couples enjoy the same financial benefits as married couples, I wrote a book *Retire Secure! For Same-Sex Couples*, with testimonials from a lot of financial experts. The fun testimonials were from Billie Jean King and Martin Sheen. Evan Wolfson, founder of Freedom to Marry, wrote the foreword.

Anyway, the emphasis of that book was on the financial advantages and disadvantages of getting married, all of which are summarized in this chapter. At that time, for federal income tax, federal estate tax, and Social Security benefits, the federal government and the Social Security Administration recognized same-sex marriages that were performed in a state where same-sex marriage was legal (the state of celebration) even if the couple resided in a non-recognition state. So, the thrust of the book was that same-sex couples living in non-recognition states travel to recognition states and get married there so they could return and enjoy the tax and Social Security benefits of being married.

As an aside, though the book was favorably mentioned on wsj.com and Bloomberg and many other sources, I never got a lot of business from it. Potentially, the problem in hindsight was that I didn't have a personal affinity with the audience because I am not gay. I should have written *Retire Secure for Professors and TIAA Participants* first because I have affinity with professors through my mother, brother and 632 clients.

Now, of course, same-sex couples can be married in all 50 states, so that recommendation is no longer relevant, but the advantages of getting married for the money are even more relevant today than they were then.

When I was promoting *Retire Secure! For Same-Sex Couples*, it was natural for me to partner with somebody who was well known in the same-sex marriage world. And fortunately, I had a personal connection with Evan Wolfson, the founder of Freedom to Marry. Evan was the attorney in many of the cases, including the first case that allowed same-sex couples to be married in Hawaii. I went to high school with Evan, and he was nice enough to write a foreword to my book. He only agreed to write the foreword after his CPA read the book and said it was sound. I got a lot of testimonials for that book, but my favorite one was from my tennis idol, Billie Jean King.

Evan also appeared on my radio show. Evan is quick to admit that he doesn't have any special insights about finance, money, and taxes. That radio show with Evan was the only one I ever did that had nothing to do with money and everything to do with love.

That message of love is core to his book, *Why Marriage Matters: America, Equality, and Gay People's Right to Marry*. If you read Evan's book or listen to him speak, he doesn't sound like a Harvard lawyer, even though Evan is a Harvard lawyer. In that book and when he speaks, he discusses the advantages of lifelong partnership in marriage.

This is a money book. I'm not here to provide relationship advice, but I have encouraged couples to marry for financial reasons. Universally, the couples who followed my advice and got married said it did change things in their relationship, and that change was for the better. So in addition to the financial justifications for marriage, a better relationship is a definite plus for getting married. Of course, though, with any decision that has financial implications, it's essential to take precautions with iron-clad prenuptial agreements and to have open and candid discussions about all financial matters.

I understand that some couples, whether same-sex or not, feel that they do not need a piece of paper to validate their relationship. But I would be remiss in my desire to help professors and other retirement investors create a financially secure retirement if I omitted the financial benefits that come from marriage. So this chapter is about how unmarried couples can significantly increase their *financial security* by getting married and making specific decisions that are only available to them under the law if they are legally married. The difference can be so significant, in fact, that I will say that most committed but unmarried couples (where at least one member is age 60 or older) should, either on their own or with an advisor, evaluate whether it makes *financial sense* for them to marry.

Many of the strategies in *Retire Secure! For Same-Sex Couples* were based on finding ways to optimize dollars in retirement for couples who back then could not or did not want to get married.

For couples with a net worth of less than $1,000,000, the savings will not be as great measured in taxes saved. Getting married for couples with less than $1,000,000, however, could mean the difference between the surviving partner/

spouse being financially secure and living comfortably, versus the survivor living out his or her retirement years in relative poverty.

I want to make sure that, no matter what happens to the stock market, and no matter what happens to their partners or spouses—my clients and readers will always have food on the table, shelter over their heads, gas in the car, and a little bit of money for Saturday night. Getting married and taking the appropriate steps can, in many instances, make the difference between being the financially dependent partner/spouse secure and not having those basic necessities.

Let's assume you are in a committed relationship but not married. Let's further assume you are in a much stronger financial position than your partner. (Your partner likely doesn't read these types of books.) If you get married and if you predecease your partner and you leave your partner some of your assets, there will be substantial income tax advantages as well as estate and inheritance tax advantages. The advantages are even more profound if you have a large retirement plan because of the miserable SECURE Act, which is extremely unfavorable for unmarried couples, but extremely favorable for married couples. And, to give you the complete picture, I will also cover some of the financial downsides of getting married—or, at least, the downsides of getting married in the short term.

Stretch IRA for Unmarried Partners

Chapters 11 and 12 detail the changes to the timing of distributions from Inherited IRAs and retirement plans under the SECURE Act. If you inherit an IRA from your partner, you will only be able to take advantage of the ability to stretch or defer taxable payments over your life if you meet one of the exceptions to the ten-year rule. The most important exception related to this chapter is leaving your IRA or retirement plan to your spouse as opposed to your unmarried partner.

Another relevant exception is a beneficiary who is not more than ten years younger than the IRA owner. The two most likely beneficiaries that aren't more than ten years younger than you are unmarried partners and siblings. If your unmarried partner is more than ten years younger than you, there is an even stronger financial incentive to get married.

Let's assume you are planning to leave at least a portion of your IRA or retirement plan to your unmarried partner. The good news is that as long as your partner is no more than ten years younger than you, your partner will be able to use his or her life expectancy factor under the single life expectancy tables as the divisor to determine the RMD for the inherited IRA which is consistent with the old (pre-2020) law. But it is still much worse than leaving that IRA to a married partner who can use a far more favorable (lower) distribution rate. Plus, not all couples meet that "not more than ten years younger" exception.

If you marry and then die, your spouse could take a RMD not only based on their life expectancy, but also the joint life expectancy of themselves and someone deemed ten years younger than them. This would allow a much greater deferral or stretch IRA than if you died and left your IRA or even a portion of your IRA to your unmarried partner. If your spouse isn't 72 yet at your death, he/she could do a trustee-to-trustee transfer and not take any RMDs until they turn 72, or the age when RMDs need to start for them, which may be as late as 75 under current law.

A new provision in the SECURE Act 2.0 will allow surviving spouses to elect to be treated as if they were the deceased spouse for the purpose of the timing of RMDs from inherited IRAs. This is most beneficial if the surviving spouse is older because that means that RMDs can be postponed until the decedent would have been required to start taking them. RMDs will also be smaller in this case, because they will be based on the younger decedent's age and longer life expectancy.

Federal and State Gift, Estate, and Inheritance Taxes

For federal tax purposes, every legally married U.S. citizen is entitled to an unlimited marital deduction for receiving gifts or money transferred at the death of his or her spouse. That means you could give or leave your spouse a billion dollars, and there would not be one cent of gift or estate tax at your death.

Beyond that, there is a $12.92 million exemption from gift and/or estate taxes for individuals who die in 2023. With savvy planning, a married couple could gift and/or bequeath double that amount, or $25.84 million without paying any estate tax. However, unless Congress makes changes, in 2026 those generous levels could drop by nearly half to an estimated $7 million ($5 million plus inflation since 2017) under the sunset provisions of the Tax Cuts and Jobs Act.

But, even forgetting the exemption for married couples, very few professors will have federal gift or estate tax worries because most people will have less than $12.92 million, or even $7 million when the generous estate and gift tax exemption expires in 2026. But, for those of you who might have a federal estate and/or gift tax problem, getting married grants you and your partner an unlimited marital deduction.

At the state level, multiple states impose their own estate tax or inheritance tax which can inflict significant financial burdens on unmarried couples. However, married couples who leave or give their property and money to each other do not face similar problems because all states that assess a transfer tax also have an unlimited marital deduction. As of the writing of this book in 2023, seventeen states plus D.C., including Hawaii, Illinois, Massachusetts, New York, and Pennsylvania, still have either an estate tax or an inheritance tax or both but have unlimited marital deductions.

Social Security Benefits for Married Couples Can Be More Now, and Much More After the First Death

Even if you do not plan on leaving your partner any of your money, without any cost to you, you could significantly protect your partner's income with your Social Security benefits. So, even if you want to leave most or all of your money to your biological family or someone else or even your favorite charities, you would likely be able to get a prenuptial agreement that would protect your biological family and other heirs and help your partner out financially without costing you a nickel.

Social Security Survivor Benefits

One of the great advantages of getting married is the death benefits rules for married couples. Typically, the surviving spouse is going to receive benefits based on the higher of the two earnings records. So, by holding off until age 66/67 or 70, as opposed to collecting at age 62 or 65, you are not only creating a higher benefit for the rest of your life, but you're also protecting your lower-earning surviving spouse in the event you predecease him or her.

This is an extremely important area and may even be seen by some as so critical for protecting the lower-earning spouse, that this fact alone may justify getting married. If the objective is to have enough money to live comfortably for the rest of both of your lives, then the person with the stronger earnings record will usually be well advised to get married and wait to age 70 to collect.

Scenario 1: Married, Surviving Spouse Collects Survivor Benefit

Let's assume that the spouse with the stronger earnings record waits until age 70 to collect benefits, and his/her benefit grows to $4,000/month (close to the maximum in 2023). Let's assume the lower earning spouse has a benefit on their own lower earnings record of $1,000/month. The spouse with the stronger earnings record then dies. The surviving spouse, even though his/her benefit is only $1,000/month, can claim the full amount (which would be the $4,000/month), provided that the surviving spouse has reached full retirement age of 66 or 67, depending upon when they were born.

Calculating the survivor benefit can be more complicated if the survivor hasn't reached full retirement age. There is a phaseout from years 1955 through 1959 adding additional month(s) to reach your full retirement age. For those born in 1960 and later, the full retirement age is age 67. It is also more complicated if the deceased spouse claimed benefits before full retirement age.

The important thing to remember is that the spouse with the weaker earnings record, who is also likely the spouse that needs financial protection, will get their spouse's Social Security if their spouse predeceases them, *but not if they are not married.*

Scenario 2: Unmarried, No Survivor Benefit for Surviving Partner

Same fact pattern as *Scenario 1* but the couple in question is not married. Let's assume the same benefits: the lower-earner's benefit is $1,000/month and the higher-earning partner's is $4,000/month. Then the higher-earning partner dies. The surviving partner will continue to receive $1,000/month. The other partner's benefits stop when he or she dies. No survivor benefit is paid to the surviving unmarried partner.

The potential for the lower earner to take a survivor benefit if the stronger earner dies first could mean the difference between being broke and being marginally okay (the difference between $1,000/month and $4,000/month), assuming that there are no other resources. This is especially true if there is a big difference between the higher earner's benefit and the lower earner's benefit.

The issue of providing for the partner with the lower earnings record is critical. Providing for the lower-earning spouse, in my opinion, should weigh heavily in the decision of when the spouse with the stronger earnings record should begin collecting Social Security benefits. It is not just an individual issue—it is a family issue.

Living Spousal Benefits

A spousal benefit is a Social Security benefit paid to someone based upon their spouse's earning history. You can receive Social Security based upon your own earning history, or, if your spouse has a much higher earnings record than

Remember that the spouse with the weaker earnings record, who is also likely the spouse that needs financial protection, will get their spouse's Social Security if their spouse predeceases them, *but not if they are not married.*

you do, you can choose to receive a spousal benefit which is 50% of your spouse's Primary Insurance Amount divided by the amount they would be entitled to at full retirement age. For people born before 1954, full retirement age is 66. As previously stated, there is a phaseout from years 1955 through 1959 adding additional month(s) to reach your full retirement age. For those born in 1960 and later, the full retirement age is 67.

The lower wage earner can often collect a higher Social Security benefit based upon their spouse's benefit. The higher wage earner's monthly benefit is not affected in any way. The lower wage earner is eligible to collect more, simply because they are married. Generally, spousal benefits are available during a couple's joint lifetimes, and you have to have been married for at least one continuous year.

Consider an example. Sue and Mary are the same age (born before 1954) and they got married. Sue has a $4,000/month benefit at age 66 and she decides to take it then. Mary, her spouse, on her own earnings record, has a $1,500/month benefit at age 66. At age 66, Mary can collect her $2,000 spousal benefit, instead of the $1,500/month benefit due Mary based on her own earnings record.

I've mentioned elsewhere in this book, coordinating the timing of when you claim Social Security with Roth conversions can make a big difference in your long-term financial situation. For more about the various Social Security strategies, please download our best-selling Social Security book, *The $214,000 Mistake: How to Double Your Social Security & Maximize Your IRAs*, for free by going to **https://PayTaxesLater.com/Books/**.

Marriage May Be a Good Idea if You are Selling Your House

Another reason to get married and file jointly is if you are planning to sell your house for a significant gain. If you are married, you get a $500,000 exemption from your capital gain, but if you are single, the exemption is only $250,000. If you're going to sell your house and make a lot of money on the sale of the house, which would incur a higher capital gain, you are financially better off getting married. You must meet ownership and use tests and must not have excluded gain from another home in the past two years.

Tying the Knot or Not: Financial Considerations for Unmarried Couples

So, if financial considerations weigh into your decision to get married, does it make sense to get married? Now, don't get all excited about the federal estate tax because if you do not have more than seven million dollars, and are not likely to grow your estate to seven million dollars, the unlimited marital deduction for your estate may not be relevant for federal transfer tax purposes, but could be for state transfers tax or inheritance tax purposes.

For IRA and retirement plan owners, the financial implications of getting married are enormous. The ability to enjoy survivor and spousal benefits for Social Security can also make a big difference for couples where one member has a much higher monthly benefit than the other.

The Financial Downside of Getting Married

It sounds like I am pitching getting married for the money, and I am. But there are also financial reasons why you might NOT want to get married for financial purposes. The Tax Cuts and Jobs Act of 2017 attempted to adjust the tax brackets, deductions, and credits to eliminate any *'marriage penalty.'* They didn't fully eliminate the so-called marriage penalty.

If you and your spouse are both high-income earners, your income taxes could actually increase if you get married. The marriage penalty means that if you get married, you could end up paying more income taxes than you would have paid if both had filed single, which is bad. On the flip side, there is also a marriage bonus, which could mean that you will pay less in taxes, which is good. This is most often the case when one member has substantially higher income than the other one.

Besides the potential marriage penalty, there are potential financial disadvantages of getting married. I counseled one couple that is choosing not to get married now because the financially dependent partner can get cheap health insurance through the Affordable Health Care Act (Obamacare), but would lose that opportunity if they got married. Their plan is to wait until the financially weaker spouse qualifies for Medicare and then get married. That might work out well, or it could be disastrous if the financially stronger spouse dies before they get married. Only time will tell if it was a *"penny wise and pound foolish"* decision.

Finally, another potential downside is the potential liability if your spouse ends up needing long-term care. This area is fact dependent and far beyond the scope of this book. That said, it is potentially an extremely important factor to consider.

For the purposes of this book and for what we do in practice, our CPAs like to *"run the numbers"* to get a more accurate picture of the advantages and disadvantages of getting married.

After (or Before) You Say I Do, Do These Things

If you decide that the financial reasons—as well as the intangible relationship reasons—are on the side of marriage, here are some things you need to be sure to take care of:

1. Strongly consider getting a prenuptial agreement. Legal documents such as prenuptial agreements and other property agreements may be unpleasant, but are often necessary, particularly if you are marrying later in life. Besides setting out the division of property in the unhappy circumstance of a divorce, these agreements can also go a long way in easing fears for your children and grandchildren who may be concerned that the other spouse's family will inherit everything, leaving them high and dry.

   The psychological and financial misery of going through a drawn-out financial divorce settlement can make both of you miserable. Billy Crystal sums up the potential damage in the movie **When Harry Met Sally**:

   > *"But you gotta know that sooner or later you're gonna be screaming at each other about who's gonna get this dish. This eight-dollar dish will cost you a thousand dollars in phone calls to the legal firm of That's Mine, This is Yours."*

2. Update your wills, trusts, and beneficiary designations for IRAs and other retirement plans. Remember that the beneficiary designations on your IRAs and retirement plans will govern who and how those plan assets will be disbursed at your death, not the language of any trust or will. Also, keep in mind who gets what? Usually, it will make more sense to leave the IRA to the dependent spouse and the after-tax money to the heirs in a higher tax bracket.

3. Apply for spousal and survivor Social Security benefits when, after reviewing the entire picture, you and/or your trusted advisor feel it is appropriate to do.

We like to *"run the numbers"* to get a more accurate picture of the advantages and disadvantages of getting married.

Remember, because this is a book about money, this chapter has focused on the financial benefits of marriage. And these may be good enough reasons to tilt the scale in favor of marriage. But I also implore you to choose love above all as the real reason to marry.

KEY IDEAS

- Spouses have more favorable laws to defer payments from an inherited IRA or retirement plan than unmarried couples.

- Married couples can take advantage of the unlimited marital deduction for both federal and state estate, inheritance, and transfer taxes. Marriage also allows a couple to utilize both of their estate and gift tax exemptions.

- Spousal benefits for Social Security can be higher while both members are still living and for the survivor but only if the couple is married.

- Married couples can double the capital gains deduction on the sale of a house, from $250,000 to $500,000.

- That said, you should still check to see if there is a marriage penalty or marriage bonus for federal income tax purposes.

- Finally, it might not be prudent to get married if the dependent spouse is currently using Affordable Care Act (Obamacare) for their health insurance.

26

Life Insurance as an Estate Planning Tool

*"You can't put a value on a human life, but my wife's
life insurance company made a pretty fair offer."*

— Unknown Author

*In this context, I am not writing about life insurance for a surviving spouse or for
minor children who will need support should a wage earner die prematurely. In this
instance, we are talking about permanent life insurance that guarantees a death
benefit (whole life or universal life; not term insurance). If you need to protect the
income of one or two wage earners, the best way to do this is usually with laddered
term insurance, which I discuss in Chapter 2, The Accumulation Years: Fund Retirement Plans to the Maximum.*

Most of my clients would rather get a root canal than either talk about life
insurance or pay for life insurance premiums. I urge you to keep an open data
driven mind for this chapter.

Life insurance in the context of this chapter is about preserving and transferring wealth to the next two generations in the most tax-efficient manner possible. It is really a variation of a gift. If you cannot afford or are not willing to
make a gift to your children or grandchildren, you should skip this chapter.

If, on the other hand, there is sufficient money to make gifts, the gift of life
insurance should be considered for a portion of the total amount of gifts you
want to provide for your family.

Buying life insurance where you give up ownership of the policy is one of the
most tax- and cost-efficient methods of transferring wealth to your heirs.

Options for Buying Life Insurance

One way to buy a life insurance policy for you and your spouse is using a classic technique known as a *pension rescue*. With a pension rescue, you cash in a
portion of your IRA, often 1% or 2% of the balance of the IRA, pay the taxes on
the distribution, and use the remainder to buy a life insurance policy. Perhaps a
Second-to-Die policy, or a policy with a long-term care or chronic illness rider.

> **Buying life insurance where you give up ownership of the policy is one of the most tax- and cost-efficient methods of transferring wealth to your heirs.**

I'll discuss both of these options below. This is consistent with Chapter 5 where we covered transferring assets from the taxable to the tax-free world.

Many university faculty members and TIAA investors have a lot of money in Traditional rather than Roth retirement plans. If this is also true for you, adding life insurance to your estate plan can get your beneficiaries more money and provide them with additional liquidity. Because life insurance proceeds are tax-free, a policy can provide much-needed cash not only to settle the estate but also to pay income taxes that will be due on accelerated Inherited Traditional IRA withdrawals.

Without life insurance, your heirs may have to withdraw more money than required from the Inherited Traditional IRA just to pay the tax due on the transfer and withdrawals—leading to yet more taxes and forcing more and more money out of the tax-deferred environment. Life insurance could be a great solution. In addition, if you are paying the premiums from the proceeds of cashing in part of your IRA or retirement assets, you are reducing the amount of Inherited IRA that is subject to the accelerated income tax.

We recommend combining life insurance and other techniques, like Roth IRA conversions and a variety of charitable techniques, including giving IRA and retirement plan money to charity at your death in the strategy known as *Who Gets What?* which is discussed in Chapter 19.

For now, however, I am talking about life insurance as a type of gift to your children. As I said at the beginning, if you do not think that you can afford to give your heirs a gift of any kind, you should not give them gifts, and you should not consider buying life insurance to make their situation easier.

How the SECURE Act has Altered My Thinking on Life Insurance

Considering that several of the members of our accounting firm are licensed to sell life insurance*, you may find it surprising that we have sold an incredibly small number of life insurance policies over the years. One reason is that most clients, if they make gifts at all, prefer to take advantage of the first three gifting strategies mentioned in Chapter 23—an outright gift, a gift for a specific pur-

> **Now that the stretch IRA is mainly gone, life insurance is a great partial solution because dying with a large IRA is so unappealing.**

pose, and/or gift to fund an education. I was not opposed to life insurance, but I wasn't passionate about it. I did recognize the value when we *"ran the numbers"* under the old law, but it wasn't one of the first things I would think about when optimizing a client's estate plan.

Since the passage of the SECURE Act, however, my thinking has shifted significantly in favor of life insurance. It isn't because life insurance is a much better deal than before the SECURE Act. It is because the stretch IRA was a reasonable choice. Now that the stretch IRA is mainly gone, life insurance is a great partial solution because dying with a large IRA is so unappealing.

Be Conservative with the Amount of Insurance You Buy

If you decide an insurance solution should be part of your overall plan, I recommend that you be somewhat conservative in the amount of coverage you purchase so that you and your spouse will always be comfortable with the premium. As always, different situations require different solutions. In addition, life insurance isn't always a pure numbers decision.

Sometimes life insurance can be looked upon as a guaranteed investment that, given a normal or even long life, offers a great income-tax-free return on your investment. It is especially appropriate if you want your heirs to receive a certain amount of money no matter what happens to the stock market.

You Can Often Feel You Can Afford to Spend More Money if You Have Life Insurance

One interesting aspect of purchasing life insurance is that for some clients, it frees up what they can spend. If you want your children to receive a certain minimal amount of money at your and/or your spouse's death, and you get life insurance for at least part of that need, it frees you to spend more money now.

---

* Life insurance can be offered by a CPA through Lange Life Care for those interested. It would be offered in their role as a CPA and not as an attorney. There would be no attorney-client relationship. There is no solicitation being made for legal services by the author nor by Lange Legal Services, LLC.

Since we have a daughter with a disability, my wife and I want to leave her enough money so that upon our deaths, she can maintain her standard of living and afford to pay the high costs she is either incurring now or can reasonably be anticipated to need for the rest of her life. In terms of investments, if you do not count the value of my business, we haven't hit that number. With the life insurance we have purchased, we can come a lot closer. My daughter's future insurance proceeds after our deaths gives us *"permission"* to spend more now.

As you would expect, we have a lot of life insurance, which alleviates our worries about our daughter's financial future, and allows us to enjoy a better lifestyle ourselves.

Nitty Gritty of the Insurance Cindy and I Have

Personally, I have a term policy on my life because my wife and daughter would need to replace my income if I died prematurely. I also have a combination Life and Long-Term Care policy, as does my wife. I like that product and do not like traditional long-term care policies. Please see *An Alternative to Long-Term Care Insurance* later in this chapter where I discuss why.

We also have a Second-to-Die life insurance policy. We have also converted most of our Traditional retirement plans to Roth IRAs or Roth 401(k)s and have most of our money invested in Dimensional Fund Advisors (DFA) enhanced index funds.

We also have appropriate business, liability, car, and homeowner's insurance. Of course, we also have an umbrella policy.

Umbrella Policies

We have a $5,000,000 umbrella policy and I recommend you rethink your umbrella coverage. Assuming you have one, which you probably do, there is an excellent chance you are under insured. The higher your net worth, the more umbrella insurance coverage is needed. The reason for this is because the world we live in is much more litigious than the world in which our parents lived.

If you or a member of your household were to be involved in an at-fault automobile accident or if someone gets injured while on your property, the injured party could potentially see big dollar signs at your expense. The additional protection provided by a personal umbrella policy would cover not only the claim costs but any legal costs to defend the allegations, whether they are warranted or not. Purchasing your umbrella insurance coverage through either your automobile or homeowner's insurance company will often provide you with a policy discount. Even if you double the coverage—which I urge you to consider doing —the additional premiums will likely be just in the hundreds, not thousands of dollars per year.

Quick Get Enough Insurance Story

I met with an insurance guy regarding my business in 1995. He made a recommendation for fire, business interruption, flood, etc. Not giving it more than ten seconds thought, I said, *"Double it,"* meaning I wanted to double the coverage he was recommending.

On February 16, 1998, we had a fire at our business. Doubling the amount of coverage the insurance professionals recommended saved my you know what.

So, for what it is worth, *I practice what I preach!*

Life Insurance as Part of the Masterplan

Life insurance is no better now than it was before the SECURE Act. But if the alternative is leaving a lot of money in a Traditional IRA, only to suffer massive income tax acceleration under the SECURE Act, which of course will happen to most of us, incorporating a life insurance gift is an option to consider in your Financial Masterplan.

Another important thing to consider, even if the life insurance proceeds are identical, is that different policies work well in some situations, and others will work better in other situations. Personal preferences for how and when you want your money distributed will also come into play.

In most cases you are the owner of your life insurance policy. You can use Lange's Cascading Beneficiary Plan (LCBP) for the beneficiary of your life insurance policy, wherein you name a primary beneficiary of the life insurance, for example, your spouse, and then your children as the secondary beneficiaries. If your spouse does not need the insurance proceeds, they can 'disclaim' the life insurance proceeds to the contingent beneficiaries.

If you do not think that you can afford to give your heirs a gift of any kind, you should not give them gifts, and you should not consider buying life insurance to make their situation easier.

Depending upon the size of your estate, you may want to make an Irrevocable Life Insurance Trust (ILIT) the owner and beneficiary of the life insurance policy. This will remove the insurance proceeds from your estate for federal estate tax purposes. As always, we recommend consulting with a competent estate attorney* before completing the decision of who owns the policy as well as completing the appropriate beneficiary designation forms.

Second-to-Die Life Insurance

In the past, when recommending life insurance to help preserve an estate, we typically recommended a Second-to-Die policy for owners of large IRAs who could afford the premium.**

A Second-to-Die policy *"matures"* as the insurance people say, upon the death of the second spouse. The premiums are substantially lower than individual policies on one or both spouses because the life insurance company will not have to pay the proceeds until both spouses are deceased.

In the case of a married couple, the likelihood is that one spouse will outlive his or her life expectancy. Therefore, when determining the appropriate mortality cost assumptions, this likelihood is baked into the cost structure and reduces the overall premiums required versus individual coverage.

Also, with the advent of Covid and the prolonged lowered interest rate trends, the premiums have been increasing. Quite a few insurance companies have reduced the attractiveness of the 100% guaranteed product or reduced the product contractual guarantees. We will see where premiums will go now that interest rates, at least as we go to press, have risen considerably.

Most people who are considering this type of product are over age 55, and often age 70 or older. Obviously your and your spouse's overall health can affect how the policy is rated from a pricing standpoint. Having the ability to go to multiple insurance companies to obtain the best possible rates has the potential to save thousands of premium dollars.

Many life insurance agents are not fans of Second-to-Die policies and recommend other wealth transfer insurance policies such as a whole life insurance policy that you can borrow from. I won't say some of the other life insurance

---

* There is no solicitation being made for legal services by the author nor by Lange Legal Services, LLC.

** Life insurance can be offered by a CPA through Lange Life Care for those interested. It would be offered in their role as a CPA and not as an attorney. There would be no attorney-client relationship. There is no solicitation being made for legal services by the author nor by Lange Legal Services, LLC.

strategies aren't sound. I will say I prefer Second-to-Die permanent policies because it is often the best deal in terms of the amount of premium paid over time compared to the death benefit received, and they are pretty simple.

Another reason I like Second-to-Die is because it is a very common type of policy and virtually every major insurance carrier offers it, so it is easy to obtain meaningful competitive quotes. We will cover the best way to receive a competitive quote near the end of this chapter.

I usually like insurance for the death benefit, not to be used as your personal bank which I know is another popular insurance strategy. If you are going to use a policy for a death benefit and want to keep your premiums as low as possible and the death benefit as high as possible, a Second-to-Die policy is often the best solution.

If there is concern about the surviving spouse paying future premiums after one of the spouses die, a popular design has been to pay the premiums over a limited number of years, such as 15 or 20 years. By doing so, the future pressure of making premium payments in the latter years is eliminated. This is especially important if there is concern of mental deterioration of either of the spouses, as the premiums are paid up on the policy, and the policy remains in force.

The other advantage of using this paid-up premium strategy, is the total premiums paid in your lifetime are fixed, as ongoing premium payments are eliminated. With a traditional full-pay policy the longer you live, the more premiums you pay.

That said, I am generally a cheapskate and usually prefer the smallest premium with the biggest death benefit, even though that usually means paying a premium for the rest of your and your spouse's lives.

Quantifying the Benefits of Life Insurance

After objectively *"running the numbers"* using current tax laws, the results of buying a Second-to-Die policy are impressive. If income tax rates go up in the future, buying life insurance will work out even better for your children. The reason is the children will be getting a tax-free inheritance, rather than inheriting a bigger Traditional IRA, which will be subject to the ten-year rule for income tax acceleration and, potentially, inheritance taxes.

Another major advantage is the life insurance proceeds are guaranteed. They are not subject to market fluctuations or interest rates. On the other hand, to be fair, if inflation soars out of site or even continues at predictable levels, the death benefit will be reduced at least in terms of measuring in today's dollars. But that is also true if you don't buy the insurance and just invest the money and die and leave it to the same beneficiaries.

Here's an example. Let's say that you buy a $1 million Second-to-Die life insurance policy, and the premiums are $20,000 every year. Fifteen years later, both you and your spouse have passed. You've paid $300,000 in premiums, but your children are going to get a check from your insurance company for $1 million. That's a $700,000 difference that is income, inheritance, and capital gains tax-free.

Since the SECURE Act, we are also examining policies on the life of one spouse. In some cases, it can be beneficial to make a Roth IRA conversion with the insurance payout after the first spouse dies. Depending on the situation, this may be better than doing Roth IRA conversions now and buying a Second-to-Die life insurance policy.

A key consideration is that you may file a joint tax return for the year that the first spouse dies. So, you could take advantage of the lower married rates on just the year of death of the first spouse. Following that year, unless you qualify for another type of filing status, the survivor will have to file as a single taxpayer which have much higher tax rates. That said, a Second-to-Die policy is usually my starting point, assuming both spouses are insurable and want to pass tax-free money to their heirs.

Let's Look at an Example

Let's go back to our bread-and-butter example, Second-to-Die. In Figure 26.1, we compare two families with identical finances, interest rates, taxes, etc. The only difference is one buys a million dollar Second-to-Die policy, and the other does not. Using the reasonable assumptions detailed in the Appendix, the children of the couple with insurance will have $2,000,000 more over their lifetime than the children of the couple who didn't buy life insurance.

Why the big difference? One of the factors that was not a factor before the SECURE Act is you do not buy life insurance, your beneficiaries are forced to pay taxes on an Inherited Traditional IRA within ten years after the second death, a devastating effect. Figure 26.1 shows that buying life insurance can go a long way toward minimizing those effects and preserving your wealth for future generations.

When is the best time to buy? A Chinese proverb says the best time to plant a tree is twenty years ago. The second-best time is now.

Figure 26.1

Life Insurance Makes the Difference for This Beneficiary*

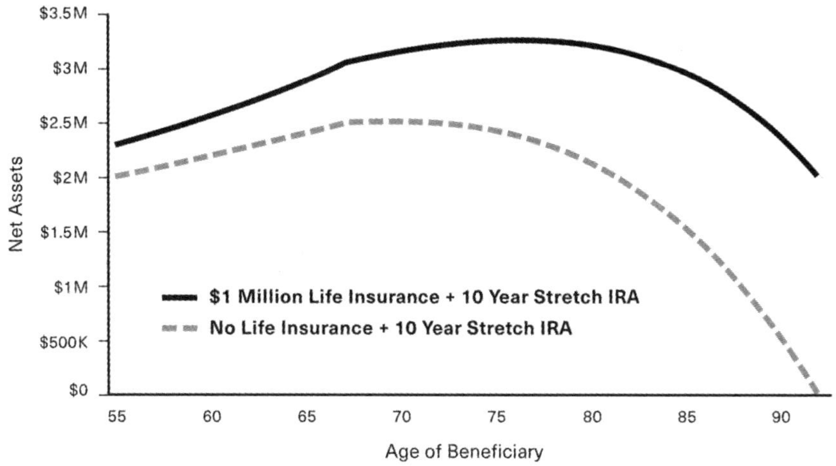

* *Detailed assumptions can be found in the Appendix.*

If you think buying life insurance might make sense for you, you should look into it sooner rather than later. The generally accepted rule for life insurance is to buy it while you are still insurable. Future health problems may cause insurance companies to reject you or rate your health so badly that the premium will be too expensive to consider. I had a client who really wanted to buy a second-to-die policy but decided to wait until he lost some weight to try to get a better rate. He never lost the weight and he developed cancer and became uninsurable.

An Alternative to Long-Term Care Insurance (LTC)

As long as we are talking about insurance, I would like to share my thoughts on long-term care (LTC) insurance. Simply put, I am not generally a fan of traditional LTC. I am licensed to sell LTC but haven't sold a traditional LTC insurance policy for probably 20 years or more.

A significant problem I see with LTC is that the premiums are not guaranteed, and buyers often suffer huge increases after the purchase. After the inevitable price increase, you face the option of dropping the policy in which case all the previous premiums paid go out the window. Or you agree to the higher rates and end up with a higher premium.

Another problem is that if you die in your boots without the need of long-term care, you have paid all those premiums and received no benefit other than peace of mind.

> **If you decide insurance should be part of your overall plan, I recommend that you be somewhat conservative in the amount of coverage you purchase so that you and your spouse will always be comfortable with the premium.**

An effective alternative to a traditional LTC policy is a combination LTC and life insurance policy. This type of product is typically called a *"linked benefit plan."* Technically, this is a life insurance policy with an LTC or Chronic Illness rider. Here's an example scenario subject to exclusions. Suppose you purchase a $500,000 combination LTC and life insurance policy.

If you are fortunate enough to not require long-term care, your heirs will receive the full $500,000 death benefit when you die. If, on the other hand, you need $250,000 of care, the policy will cover your care, and your heirs will be paid the remaining $250,000 upon your death. Finally, let's say you need $600,000 worth of care. In this case, the insurance company would pay the first $500,000, and you would be responsible for the other $100,000.

Another nice feature of this combination policy is that LTC disbursements are tax-free under current law. And since it is a life insurance policy with an LTC rider, it will likely be much easier for you to qualify for coverage at a more favorable rating than a traditional LTC policy.

Another important consideration is that many carriers offer complete waiver of premiums for all premiums due after an LTC claim is approved. This obviously will have a dramatic effect to the long-term cost of the product. I believe this is one of the most important product features required when choosing a product.

You may have specialized information that the insurance company doesn't consider. For example, let's say that Alzheimer runs in your family and you want to protect your family from those costs that you think is fairly likely. Your family history is not taken into account for the cost of the premium. It is a little bit like buying a stock with inside knowledge it is a bargain. But, in this case it is legal.

Getting the Best Deal on Life Insurance

Let's assume for discussion's sake you have decided on a Second-to-Die policy and the amount of insurance you want. The amount could vary depending on the premium but assume you have at least a range in mind.

Another important consideration is that many carriers offer complete waiver of premiums for all premiums due after an LTC claim is approved...This is one of the most important product features required when choosing a product.

Let's also assume that the primary goal is a low premium and a high death benefit. How can you get the best deal? Since this is a competitive and fluid marketplace, it is essential when looking to purchase this product that you use a broker who represents a wide variety of insurance companies and is unbiased about the selected product. The most efficient way to do this is to work with an ethical insurance broker who has access to many insurance company products.

Yes, there may be some differences in premiums with different companies at different times. The biggest difference in the premium is likely going to be determined by the insurance company's analysis of your life expectancy based on an application you must fill out, a paramedical examination, and their examination of your medical records. Since most people who are considering this type of product are over age 55, overall health can affect how the policy is rated from a pricing standpoint.

You would think in this day and age there would be whiz bang computer programs that all the big life insurance companies would use—pop in your stats and out comes their assessment of your life expectancy. That isn't the case at all. In reality, your information will be given to one of the underwriters who work for the company. The underwriter then consults with medical experts and actuaries. Obviously, opinions will vary greatly among insurance companies.

To oversimplify, you could be rated as uninsurable, standard, preferred, or super-preferred. Obviously, the better the rating, the lower the premium. In a Second-to-Die policy, it is usually the woman's health that is more important because she typically has a longer life expectancy simply because she is a woman.

But here is the kicker. Even with identical applications and health records, you could receive significantly different quotes from different companies. Since it is in effect a generic product, usually assuming the company is rated at least AA by Standard and Poor's or better, if you get one company that offers a substantially lower premium, and similar benefits and terms, that company is the obvious choice. Comparing multiple insurance companies to find the best pos-

> **If you think buying life insurance might make sense for you, you should look into it sooner rather than later. The generally accepted rule for life insurance is to buy it while you are still insurable.**

sible rates has the potential to save thousands of dollars on your premium payments. I have witnessed enormous disparities of quotes and the insurance broker we work with usually recommends the company with the lowest premium.

In one case a couple who both had health issues, the husband had a heart condition and the wife had several health problems, applied for a $1M Second-to-Die policy. The rating came back as standard for him and preferred for her. The premium was much lower than I expected.

After being presented the information, the client said let's get a $2M policy instead. I hesitated. I feared that if they didn't take the $1M and asked for $2M, the insurance company would take a closer look, realized they made a mistake, and give them a much higher premium per million. I recommended the client take the $1M policy and apply for another million. That is what they did, and the second quote came in much higher, so the client just kept the one policy.

The best way to buy life insurance is by using a knowledgeable and ethical broker who has the ability to shop the policy to a number of potential insurance companies. At this point, there is no such thing as *"no-load life insurance."* It would be extremely time consuming for you to try to do this on your own and in the end, you wouldn't save any money.

Finally, one more tip. The most important factor in the premiums is obviously the type of insurance and the age of the insured. But the medical records and the physical are also critical.

Here is what I would recommend for your physical. For most policies, a nurse will come to your house or office, ask some questions, draw blood, do a few other non-invasive tests and report back to the company. It is obviously in your interest to look as healthy as possible to the insurance company. I recommend you schedule your physical first thing in the morning. After your evening meal the night before the exam, don't eat anything or drink anything except for water. Without getting into the science behind this recommendation, it could potentially result in a lower quote.

Use Lange's Cascading Beneficiary Plan for the beneficiary of your life insurance policy...If your spouse does not need the insurance proceeds, they can *'disclaim'* the life insurance proceeds to the contingent beneficiaries.

Also, we have found many people automatically assume they cannot obtain life insurance because of a pre-existing medical condition. This may or may not be the case. We have found that often we can informally underwrite without an exam to determine your insurability on a confidential basis.

Since this is an *'informal'* process, any underwriting results will not become public record and will be held in strict confidence. This will keep your information from being reported to the Medical Information Bureau (MIB) which could possibly negatively impact your insurability in the future. MIB is a membership group owned by insurance companies designed to protect the insurance companies, policyholders, and applicants from attempts to conceal or omit information material to underwriting life and health insurance.

Once you receive an informal offer from an insurance company, the majority of the time the offer is honored even after you take the physical exam so long as there is not a material change in your health.

Policy Exit Strategies

In the event you cannot afford your life insurance coverage or decide your life insurance needs have changed, it is important to understand you have options to receive some value out of your policy versus just canceling your policy. *Below is a list of these options:*

- **Reduce the Face Amount of the Policy:** Depending upon the type of policy you purchased, you have the option to reduce the coverage and pay less premium.

- **Purchase Paid-Up Insurance:** If your policy has a cash surrender value, which some do and some do not, you may have the option of reducing the death benefit and using policy values to maintain a reduced amount of coverage for the rest of your life.

- **Sell the Policy to a Third-Party Institutional Investor** *(Life Settlement Viatical):* There are institutional investors willing to purchase your policy at older ages depending upon your determined life expectancy at the time of purchase. This has become an increasingly popular option and is deserving of exploration in the event you want to terminate your policy in the future. We recommend using an unbiased, ethical insurance broker to analyze this option for you.

- **Tax-Free Exchange for a Longevity Annuity:** This is often my favorite, but rarely used solution. You may be able to exchange the cash value of a life insurance policy you no longer want for a longevity annuity. I discussed this option in Chapter 10.

KEY IDEAS

- Life insurance offers a tax- and cost-efficient method of transferring wealth to your heirs.

- Depending upon the circumstances, you may want a term policy, and/or combination life and LTC policy, and/or a Second-to-Die life insurance policy.

- By using a guaranteed death-benefit policy, you will have a guaranteed rate of return and assets leverage versus equities which will fluctuate with the market.

- Using a linked benefit policy to pay for LTC and chronic care expenses on a tax-free basis is much more tax-efficient versus using other types of assets.

- Be conservative in the amount of life insurance that you buy so that you and your spouse will always be comfortable with the premium.

- Life insurance can be a great hedge against future tax increases on IRAs, especially in light of the elimination of the Stretch IRA under the SECURE Act.

- Informal underwriting process is worth pursuing when medical conditions exist.

- Consider policy exit strategies before cancelling your life insurance policy.

KEY IDEAS
(continued)

- You can do what you were planning to do anyway which is not get insurance because you don't like life insurance or the insurance industry. But in this case, you need to implement other tax-saving strategies so your heirs are not hit with huge—and largely avoidable—tax bills.

27

More is Better:
The Benefits of Combined Strategies

"The whole is greater than the sum of its parts."

— Aristotle

We have presented myriad strategies for savvy retirement and estate planning, tax savings, and investing. Rarely, probably never, will one strategy address all the issues. And despite what some advisors might tell you, there is no no-one-size-fits-all solution. We have found that the key to truly successful comprehensive planning only surfaces when we combine strategies that we customize to each client.

Our advantage is that we look at your personal financial situation from multiple standpoints: a strategic standpoint, an estate planning standpoint, an investment standpoint, and a tax standpoint.

We have CPAs and wealth advisors all working as a multi-disciplined unified team on the client's behalf.*

Our business model—coordinated fiduciary advice—relieves the client from the stress of parsing and evaluating conflicting advice from their independent CPA, wealth advisor, etc.

The United States has enacted laws that provide enormous rewards for implementing tax-savvy strategies. Let's look at one dramatic combination: Roth conversions and life insurance.

---

* Lange Accounting Group offers guidance on retirement plan distribution strategies, tax reduction, Roth IRA conversions, saving and spending strategies, optimized Social Security strategies and gifting plans.

Although we bring our knowledge and expertise in estate planning, it will be conducted in our capacity as a number crunching CPA. However, we will likely make recommendations that clients could have a licensed estate attorney implement.

Life insurance can be offered by a CPA through Lange Life Care for those interested. It would be offered in their role as a CPA and not as an attorney.

Asset location, asset allocation and low-cost enhanced index funds are provided by the investment firms with whom Lange Financial Group is affiliated. This would be offered in our role as an investment advisor representative. Please see the front of the book for disclaimers related to these services.

In our role for each of these instances, we will not be acting as the clients' attorney and there will not be an attorney/client relationship. There is no solicitation being made for legal services by the author nor by Lange Legal Services, LLC.

Combine Roth IRA Conversions and Life Insurance

Figure 27.1, below, compares two families with identical resources. One family makes a series of Roth IRA conversions and buys life insurance. The other family neither makes any Roth IRA conversions nor buys life insurance.

The figure shows the trajectory of wealth over the life of the child. The child of the family who made the optimal series of Roth IRA conversions and bought life insurance has $7 million when the child beneficiary is in his eighties and the child of the family that neither bought life insurance nor did Roth IRA conversions is broke at the same point in time.

When I first saw it, Figure 27.1 literally blew me away. It seemed too good to be true. It categorically quantifies the benefits of combining Roth IRA conversions (done over several years) and life insurance.

Figure 27.1

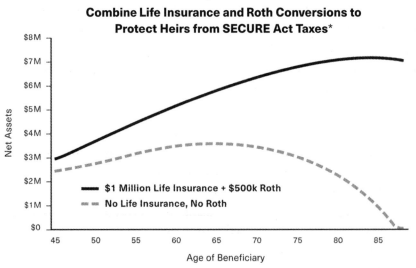

* *Detailed assumptions can be found in the Appendix.*

Combining multiple strategies allows you to create even greater wealth to enhance the financial security of your entire family. Roth IRA conversions, optimized Social Security strategies, life insurance, low-cost enhanced index funds, asset location, gifting, and of course, our favorite estate plan, Lange's Cascading Beneficiary Plan (LCBP) can be used in various combinations in your retirement and estate plan to benefit you and your heirs.*

---

* Please review the disclaimer on the preceding page.

The Challenge of Running the Numbers

In this example, we combined life insurance and Roth IRA conversions. We usually arrive at the best solution, however, by combining a number of different strategies after *"running the numbers."* One of the reasons that *"running the numbers"* is so hard is that the CPA doing the calculations must decide, in consultation with the client, which strategies to run and how to combine different strategies. Then even if you know which strategies you are going to combine, the next questions are, *"How much of each? How big of a Roth IRA conversion should you make and when?"*

How much life insurance, if any, should you buy? And many of these calculations are synergistic meaning that what you do with one variable will have an impact on a different variable, but potentially using both strategies in concert will confer more advantages than using both strategies separately. The matrix is very complicated.

That said, any examples are only meant to illustrate the potential value of combining multiple strategies.

We could present an array of successful strategy combination plans—but as mentioned earlier—each person's circumstances are unique, so we cannot say any one particular combination will work for everyone. But Figure 27.1 makes abundantly clear that there is an enormous difference between optimal and mediocre planning.

> **The overarching message of this book is that doing nothing—when you know there are so many great strategies to protect and secure your financial future and the future of your heirs—*shouldn't be an option.***

The overarching message of this book is that doing nothing—when you know there are so many great strategies to protect and secure your financial future and the future of your heirs—shouldn't be an option. Please consider combining strategies to have the biggest impact for yourself and your family. The Financial Masterplans we prepare offer these roadmaps to our clients, and many are hundreds of thousands of dollars better off because they listened, learned, and acted.

Please see *Save More, Have More, Leave More! The Lange Edge: A Truly Integrated Long-Term Financial Masterplan* at the end of the book to see how you could work with me and my team to get the most out of your TIAA-CREF and other retirement assets.

KEY IDEAS

- Roth IRA conversions, **Lange's Cascading Beneficiary Plan**, gifting, low-cost enhanced index funds and life insurance can be used individually in your estate plan to benefit you and your heirs. By combining two or more of these strategies, you can create even greater financial security that will benefit you and your heirs for generations to come.

- There is a phenomenal difference between optimal and mediocre planning. Strive for optimal planning.

Glossary

Professor: I recognize that there are many positions in academia that aren't *"professor."* And that there are tenured professors, associate professors, assistant professors, instructors, professor emeriti, administrators, etc., and retirees from any or all positions. I lump all these positions together for my purposes and refer to all these people as professors knowing it isn't accurate but that the advice and recommendations are suited to all.

Individual Retirement Accounts (IRAs): I recognize that IRAs are only one type of retirement account that generally consists of funds that have not yet been subject to income taxes but will eventually. Of course, there are many other types of retirement plans such as 403(b)s, 401(a), 457(b)s, etc. that in many ways are quite similar to IRAs, at least for tax purposes. For convenience, though I will sometimes distinguish between the different type of retirement plans, I will refer to all these plans as IRAs or IRAs and retirement plans.

401(k)/Roth 401(k) Plan: A tax-advantaged defined contribution retirement plan offered by many employers, typically in the private sector. Depending on the rules established by the employer, employees can add to their account by making Traditional or Roth contributions.

403(b)/Roth 403(b) Plan: Also called a tax-sheltered annuity or TSA plan, a 403(b) is a type of defined contribution plan offered by public schools and certain tax-exempt organizations. Depending on the rules established by the employer, employees can add to their account by making Traditional or Roth contributions.

After-Tax Contribution: Money paid into a retirement account after income tax has already been deducted.

Annuitization: The process of converting an annuity investment into a series of periodic income payments.

Annuitization, method: Annuity distribution structure that defines the periodic income payments that will be paid over the life of the annuitant (or annuitants), or for a specified period of time.

Annuity: A contract offered by a life insurance company that requires the insurer to make payments to you, either immediately or at some point in the future.

Annuity, fixed: A contract issued by a life insurance company that pays a guaranteed rate of interest on the owner's contributions.

Annuity, immediate: A contract between an individual and an insurance company that, in exchange for an up-front premium, pays the owner a guaranteed income immediately.

Annuity, joint life: An annuity payment agreement that guarantees an income for the life of the annuity owner and a survivor, generally their spouse.

Annuity, nonqualified: A contract issued by an insurance company that is purchased with contributions made on an after-tax and non-Roth basis. Nonqualified annuities can be used when a participant in a qualified retirement plan has contributed the maximum amount to the plan that is permitted by the IRS. Contributions are not tax-deductible, and annuitized payments are partially taxable.

Annuity, single life: An annuity payment agreement that guarantees an income for the life of the annuity owner only.

Annuity, variable: A type of annuity that can rise or fall in value depending on the performance of its underlying investment portfolio.

CREF: Common name for the College Retirement Equities Fund, a variable annuity established as an option for TIAA participants in many university retirement plans. Contributions to the CREF Annuity can be made on either a pre-tax or Roth basis.

Defined Benefit Plan: Commonly called a *"pension plan,"* this is a type of retirement plan in which the employer contributes money according to a formula described in the plan documents that will allow them to provide a promised monthly benefit to the employee at retirement. The amount of the benefit is determined by a formula that considers the number of years of service, salary and age, and the employer is responsible for paying the benefit regardless of the performance of the investments in the plan.

Defined Contribution Plan: A type of retirement plan that allows the employee or employer to contribute to an account on the employee's behalf. Depending on the plan rules, employee contributions can be made on a Traditional or Roth basis. As of this writing, all employer matching contributions must be made on a Traditional basis.

Direct Rollover: A method of transferring a retirement account from one custodian to another, during which the account owner takes possession of the money. The account owner is responsible for depositing the funds into a new retirement account within 60 days. In general, there is only one direct rollover permitted every 365 days from the same IRA and the IRA to which the distribution was rolled over regardless of the number of IRAs you own. The limit will apply by aggregating all of your individual IRAs, including SEP and SIMPLE IRAs as well as Traditional and Roth IRAs. This means all of your IRAs are treated as one IRA for purposes of the limit.

Guarantee Period: An annuitization option that allows the contract owner to receive income over a specific period of time, such as ten years or over a lifetime.

Mutual Fund: An investment vehicle that consists of a portfolio of stocks, bonds, or other securities. It allows small investors access to diversified, professionally managed portfolios at a low cost.

Non-qualified Retirement Plan: A retirement plan that falls outside of the Employee Retirement Income Security Act (ERISA) guidelines, such as a deferred-compensation plan offered to executives.

Qualified Retirement Plan: A retirement plan that meets the requirements of IRS Code Section 401(a) and is therefore eligible to receive certain tax benefits, such as a 403(b) or 401(k) plan.

Roth Contribution: A contribution made to a retirement plan that is not tax-deductible but is generally tax-free when withdrawn if certain conditions are met.

SERS (State Employees Retirement System): A defined benefit pension plan that covers employees of many state-owned universities.

Subaccounts: Investment options that are available within variable annuities, including CREF, that are similar to mutual funds, in that they have specific investment objectives and may result in a higher rate of return than fixed annuities.

TIAA: A non-profit organization also known as Teachers Insurance and Annuity Company of America, which was founded to provide guaranteed retirement income and life insurance to educators.

TIAA Traditional Annuity: Fixed (guaranteed) annuity offered by TIAA through many university retirement plans. Contributions to the TIAA Traditional Annuity can be made on either a pre-tax or Roth basis.

Traditional Contribution: A contribution that can be made to a retirement plan before federal and municipal taxes are deducted, assuming certain rules are met. Withdrawals are taxable, and plan owners are generally required to start withdrawing money at age 72, 73 or 75 depending upon your year of birth.

Transfer Payout Annuity: Also called a TPA, an option offered by TIAA that allows owners of the TIAA Traditional Annuity to transfer some or all of their account balances, either as a direct rollover or as a cash withdrawal.

Trustee-to-Trustee Transfer: Our preferred method for transferring a retirement account from one trustee to another. The financial institution holding your IRA makes the payment directly to another IRA or retirement plan. The account owner never takes possession of the money.

Vintages: A system of crediting interest payments to owners of the TIAA Traditional annuity, whereby older contributions made during periods of higher interest rates may be eligible for a higher than market rate on those contributions.

Appendix

The assumptions used in the Figures presented in this book are as follows:

Figure 1.1: Tax-Deferred Savings Build Wealth

1. 7% rate of return.
2. Annual salary to age 67 was $100,000.
3. Social Security at age 67 was $30,000 + spousal of $15,000.
4. Annual contributions to retirement plans were $12,000.
5. Annual spending was $80,000; $70,000 after retirement.

Figure 1.2: Spend the Right Money First

1. Investor retires at age 65 with $1.1 million in qualified retirement accounts.
2. Assumes annual Social Security income of $25,000 + spousal of $12,500.
3. 24% ordinary tax rates.
4. Beginning annual spending of $84,000; adjusted for inflation annually by 3.5%.
5. 6.5% rate of return.
6. Actual dollars.
7. No state or inheritance tax is factored into the analysis.

Figure 2.1: Retirement Assets, IRAs, etc. *vs.* After-Tax Accumulations

1. Investment rate of return is 6% including 30% ordinary income and 70% capital appreciation with a 15% portfolio turnover rate.
2. Professor Pay Taxes Later contributes $8,000 per year to his pre-tax retirement savings plan. Professor Pay Taxes Now invests $6,080 per year (24% less due to income taxes). Both amounts are indexed for 3% annual raises, starting at age 30 until age 70.
3. Starting at age 72, spending from both investors' accounts is equal to the RMDs from Professor Pay Taxes Later's retirement plan, less related income taxes.
4. Professor Pay Taxes Later withdraws only the RMD, pays the 24% income tax due on his distribution, and spends the rest. Professor Pay Taxes Now

spends the same amount plus he pays income taxes due on his interest, dividends, and realized capital gains.

5. The figure does not take into account the additional monies earned if Professor Pay Taxes Later invested the 24% tax savings into an investment account.

6. Ordinary income tax rates are 24%.

7. Capital gains tax rates are 15%.

8. Dividends are taxes as qualified dividends at the capital gains tax rate.

9. AGI is assumed to be less than $340,000 and there is no state income tax.

Figure 2.2: Retirement Assets Plus an Employer Match *vs.* After-Tax Accumulations

1. Investment rate of return is 6% including 30% ordinary income and 70% capital appreciation with 15% portfolio turnover rate.

2. Retirement savings of $8,000 per year.

3. After-tax savings is $7,000 per year.

4. Both amounts are indexed for 3% annual raises, starting at age 30 until age 70.

5. RMDs start at age 72 from retirement account.

6. After-tax funds fully depleted at age 84 when retirement accounts still have $5,446,284 remaining.

7. After-tax accumulation withdrawals reduced by tax = 74% of retirement distributions.

8. Ordinary income tax rates are 24%.

9. Capital gains tax rates are 15%.

10. Employer match is 100%.

Figure 3.5: Roth IRA Savings *vs.* Traditional IRA Savings

1. Contributions to a Roth IRA are made in the amount of $7,000 per year, beginning in 2022, for a 55-year-old investor, for 11 years until he reaches age 65.

2. Contributions to a regular deductible IRA are made in the amount of $7,000 per year by a different 55-year-old investor, for 11 years until he

reaches age 65. This investor's IRA contribution creates an income tax deduction for him of 24%, or $1,680.

I will give the best-case scenario and say that this investor did not spend his tax savings. Instead, he invested his tax savings into his after-tax investment account and did not spend it.

3. The investment rates of return on the Traditional IRA, the Roth IRA and the after-tax investment accounts are all 6% per year.

4. For the after-tax monies, the rate of return includes 70% capital appreciation, a 15% portfolio turnover rate (such that much of the appreciation is not immediately taxed), 15% dividends, and 15% ordinary interest income.

5. Ordinary income tax rates are 24% for all years.

6. Tax rates on realized capital gains are 15%.

7. Beginning at age 72, the RMDs from the Traditional IRA are reinvested into the after-tax savings account.

8. The balances reflected in the figures reflect spending power, which is net of an income tax allowance of 24% on the remaining Traditional IRA balance. If the full amount was actually withdrawn in one year, however, the tax bracket may be even higher and make the Roth IRA appear more favorable.

Figure 4.1: Roth 403(b) Savings *vs.* Traditional 403(b) Savings— RMD is Spent Annually-Lower Income Taxpayer

1. Contributions to a Roth 403(b) and Traditional 403(b) are $27,000 for 11 years from age 55 to age 65, until he retires at age 66. This investor's IRA contribution creates an income tax deduction for him of 24%, or $6,480.

   I will give the best-case scenario and say that this investor did not spend his tax savings. Instead, he invested his tax savings into his after-tax investment account and did not spend it.

2. The investment rates of return on the Traditional 403(b), the Roth 403(b) and the after-tax investment accounts are all 6% per year.

3. 24% ordinary incremental tax rate during his working years.

4. 24% ordinary incremental tax rate during his retirement years.

5. Capital gains tax rates are 18%.

Figure 4.2: **Roth 403(b) Savings *vs.* Traditional 403(b) Savings—RMD is Spent Annually-Higher Income Taxpayer**

1. Contributions to a Roth 403(b) and Traditional 403(b) are $27,000 for 11 years from age 55 to age 65, until he retires at age 66. This investor's IRA contribution creates an income tax deduction for him of 37%, or $9,990.

   I will give the best-case scenario and say that this investor did not spend his tax savings. Instead, he invested his tax savings into his after-tax investment account and did not spend it.

2. The investment rates of return on the Traditional 403(b), the Roth 403(b) and the after-tax investment accounts are all 6% per year.

3. 37% ordinary incremental tax rate during his working years.

4. 37% ordinary incremental tax rate during his retirement years.

5. Capital gains tax rates are 18.8%.

Figure 5.1: **Spend Your After-Tax Money First**

1. Both professors start from an identical position in 2022. They are both 65 years old and both have $300,000 in after-tax funds and $1,100,000 in pre-tax retirement funds.

2. Both professors receive $25,000 per year in Social Security income.

3. The investment rates of return on all investment accounts are 6.5% per year.

4. Spending is $86,000 annually, after paying income taxes.

5. Income tax assumptions include ordinary income and capital gains tax rates established by the Tax Cuts and Jobs Act of 2017 and subsequent tax laws. State income taxes are ignored.

6. Capital gains tax rates are 15%.

7. Actual dollars.

8. No state or inheritance tax is factored into the analysis.

Figure 10.1: **Buying a Longevity Annuity**

1. Professor at age 65 funds $100,000 of discretionary after-tax dollars into a deferred income annuity.

2. Monthly benefits received from the annuity are when the Professor is age 85.

3. Interest rates used in the analysis are from January 2022 rates.

4. Inflation rate = 2.5%.

5. Examples provided use a rate of return of 4%, 6%, and 8%.

6. The exclusion ratio is 28% with 72% being taxed at the ordinary income tax rate of 24%.

7. Professor does not spend any of his after-tax money.

Figure 11.1: Inherited IRA Distributed Over Lifetime of Beneficiary (Old Law)

1. $1,000,000 inherited at age 45.

2. 7% rate of return.

3. 3.5% rate of inflation.

Figure 11.2: Inherited IRA Distributed Under the SECURE Act Over 10 Years

1. $1,000,000 inherited at age 45.

2. 7% rate of return.

3. Annual distributions of $142,500 with balance fully distributed within 10 years.

Figure 12.1: Impact of the SECURE Act—10 Year Distribution

1. Child inherits $1 million IRA (adjusted to purchasing power) at age 45 and earns salary of $100,000 annually increasing at 3.5%.

2. Child retires at age 67 and receives $40,000 in Social Security income annually.

3. 7% rate of return.

4. Expenses are $90,000 and increase by 3.5% annually.

5. Inherited IRA annual distributions of $147,000.

Figure 12.2: Grandchild Inherits IRA

1. Grandchild inherits the IRA at age 11 and pays college tuition of $60,000 for 4 years from proceeds of IRA.

2. During his/her working years, he/she earns $80,000 increased annually at 3.5%.

3. The grandchild retires at age 67 and receives $40,000 in Social Security income annually.

4. Expenses are $80,000 and are adjusted by 3.5% annually.

5. Rate of return is 7%.

Figure 13.1: **Benefit for Disabled Beneficiary Inheriting a Roth IRA with Lifetime Stretch *vs.* Inheriting a Traditional IRA with 10-Year Stretch**

1. Starting balances: $65,000 after-tax investments; $250,000 Traditional IRA in 1998.

2. 28% income tax rate on distributions for parent; 15% for disabled child.

3. 28% Roth conversion tax rate (1998) – $250,000 Roth conversion done in 1998.

4. 15% tax on growth of after-tax investments.

5. Distributions are not spent by parent.

6. 6.5% rate of return (3.5% inflation).

7. Parent converts Traditional to Roth in 1998 – $250,000 (parent age 41; child age 2).

8. Parent dies at 85 in year 2041 when disabled child is age 46.

9. Figure shows child stretches retirement plan for 40 years when child is age 86.

10. Annual expenses for child after parent dies = $275,000, indexed by 3.5% annually for inflation.

11. Maximum 401(k) contributions by parent in years 1998 – 2026 (age 70).

12. Maximum IRA contributions by parent and spouse in years 1998 – 2026 (age 70).

13. We do not include any government benefits the child has received already or may receive in the future.

14. In year 2042, when the child is age 46, the child will pay their expenses with their inheritance.

15. Since this is 20 years from now, we used $275,000 in annual expenses for the disabled child which equates to $138,200 in today's dollars or $11,500/month.

16. Inheritance taxes, estate taxes, and any state income tax on a Roth con-

version have not been included in the analysis as Pennsylvania does not tax retirement distributions.

Figure 13.2: Disabled Child Inherits Roth *vs.* Traditional IRA

1. 6.5% rate of return.
2. Traditional IRA assets = $500,000 + $152,000 after-tax dollars at death.
3. Roth IRA assets = $557,000 + $0 in after-tax dollars at death.
4. Owner dies age 85.
5. Child inherits at age 54.
6. In *"inflation-adjusted"* dollars.
7. Tax rates = per AGI.
8. Child Social Security = $25,000 (plus 3% inflation).
9. Expenses = $103,000 [18 years from now (plus 3.5% inflation) which is less than $4,650/month in today's dollars].
10. Child with Traditional IRA runs out of money when he is age 88.
11. Child with Roth IRA has money through age 100.

Figure 15.1: Original IRA Owner after Roth Conversions

1. 7.5% rate of return.
2. 2.5% rate of inflation
3. Inflation-adjusted dollars.
4. At age 65, IRA value is $1 million.
5. At age 65, other assets are $500,000.
6. Roth Case: Annual $175,000 Roth Conversions for 5 years.
7. Each spouse earns Social Security income of $37,356.
8. Two-life pension of $50,000.
9. Annual living expenses are $125,000.
10. Professor dies at age 80.
11. Spouse dies at age 90.

Figure 15.2: Original IRA Owner After Roth Conversions

1. 7.5% rate of return.

2. 2.5% rate of inflation.

3. Inflation-adjusted dollars.

4. Child's Social Security income is $25000.

5. Child's annual living expenses are $150,000.

6. Bump is end of 10 years when Inherited IRA must be closed.

Figure 18.1: Income from a Trust *vs.* IRA Stretched 10 Years

1. 80-year-old parent dies with $1 million IRA and $100,000 after-tax investments.

2. 7% rate of return.

3. 3.5% inflation on income and expenses.

4. Child is age 48 when parent dies.

5. Annual distributions from Inherited IRA are $143,000 for 10 years— 32% tax bracket.

6. Total income distributed from IRA is $1,421,399.

7. Total income distributed from CRUT is $1,946,227.

8. Child's wages are $100,000 to age 65.

9. Child's Social Security at FRA is $27,000 annually.

10. Child's annual living expenses are $90,000.

Figure 26.1: Life Insurance Makes the Difference for This Beneficiary

1. 7% rate of return.

2. 3.5% rate of inflation.

3. $1 million life insurance policy.

4. Parents pay $22,000 annual premium on second-to-die policy at age 62 forward.

5. At age 66, parents have IRA balance of $1.5 million and after-tax savings of $500,000.

6. Parent's combined Social Security at FRA is $52,500.

7. Parent's annual living expenses are $90,000.

8. Parents die at age 85.

9. Child's wages are $60,000 annually.

10. Child retires at age 60.

11. Child's Social Security at age 62 is $15,000.

12. Child's spending is $120,000 annually.

13. Reported in actual dollars.

Figure 27.1: Combine Life Insurance and Roth Conversions to Protect Heirs from the SECURE Act Taxes

1. Planning parents do five $100,000 Roth conversions.

2. Both parents die at age 85.

3. Child inherits balance of all accounts at age 45.

4. Child lost his savings and retirement plan in divorce.

5. Unmarried child retires at age 60.

6. Unmarried child collects $15,000 in Social Security at age 62, COLAs at 3%.

7. Unmarried child spends $120,000 annually.

8. Numbers are in actual dollars.

9. 7% rate of return.

10. 3.5% rate of inflation.

Please note, rates of return are not representative of any particular investment or portfolio of investments and cannot be guaranteed. Portfolios holding securities are subject to risk, including the potential for loss of principal. Actual returns will fluctuate.

Table I: Single Life Expectancy

(For use by beneficiaries)

Age	Life Expectancy	Age	Life Expectancy
0	84.6	31	54.4
1	83.7	32	53.4
2	82.8	33	52.5
3	81.8	34	51.5
4	80.8	35	50.5
5	79.8	36	49.6
6	78.8	37	48.6
7	77.9	38	47.7
8	76.9	39	46.7
9	75.9	40	45.7
10	74.9	41	44.8
11	73.9	42	43.8
12	72.9	43	42.9
13	71.9	44	41.9
14	70.9	45	41.0
15	69.9	46	40.0
16	69.0	47	39.0
17	68.0	48	38.1
18	67.0	49	37.1
19	66.0	50	36.2
20	65.0	51	35.3
21	64.1	52	34.3
22	63.1	53	33.4
23	62.1	54	32.5
24	61.1	55	31.6
25	60.2	56	30.6
26	59.2	57	29.8
27	58.2	58	28.9
28	57.3	59	28.0
29	56.3	60	27.1
30	55.3	61	26.2

Table I: Single Life Expectancy

(For use by beneficiaries—continued)

Age	Life Expectancy	Age	Life Expectancy
62	25.4	92	4.9
63	24.5	93	4.6
64	23.7	94	4.3
65	22.9	95	4.0
66	22.0	96	3.7
67	21.2	97	3.4
68	20.4	98	3.2
69	19.6	99	3.0
70	18.8	100	2.8
71	18.0	101	2.6
72	17.2	102	2.5
73	16.4	103	2.3
74	15.6	104	2.2
75	14.8	105	2.1
76	14.1	106	2.1
77	13.3	107	2.1
78	12.6	108	2.0
79	11.9	109	2.0
80	11.2	110	2.0
81	10.5	111	2.0
82	9.9	112	2.0
83	9.3	113	1.9
84	8.7	114	1.9
85	8.1	115	1.8
86	7.6	116	1.8
87	7.1	117	1.6
88	6.6	118	1.4
89	6.1	119	1.1
90	5.7	120+	1.0
91	5.3		

Table III: Uniform Lifetime

Age	Distribution Period	Age	Distribution Period
72	27.4	97	7.8
73	26.5	98	7.3
74	25.5	99	6.8
75	24.6	100	6.4
76	23.7	101	6.0
77	22.9	102	5.6
78	22.0	103	5.2
79	21.1	104	4.9
80	20.2	105	4.6
81	19.4	106	4.3
82	18.5	107	4.1
83	17.7	108	3.9
84	16.8	109	3.7
85	16.0	110	3.5
86	15.2	111	3.4
87	14.4	112	3.3
88	13.7	113	3.1
89	12.9	114	3.0
90	12.2	115	2.9
91	11.5	116	2.8
92	10.8	117	2.7
93	10.1	118	2.5
94	9.5	119	2.3
95	8.9	120+	2.0
96	8.4		

Table III is for use by:

Unmarried owners.

Married owners whose spouses aren't more than 10 years younger.

Married owners whose spouses aren't the sole beneficiaries of their IRAs.

Save More, Have More, and Leave More!
The Lange Edge:
A Truly Integrated Long-Term Financial Masterplan

What if you could face the future with confidence knowing you were taking all the right steps to get the most out of what you've got with a manageable investment of time, effort, and money?

If you are like the vast majority of the 632 university professors and TIAA participants we work with, you didn't enter academia or the non-profit world for the money. Neither did my mom and brother when they entered academia. Yet, you have likely acquired significant retirement assets.

How can you get the most out of what you've got?

Haphazard Planning Undermines Your Future—This is No Time to Wing It

Unfortunately, most professors, TIAA participants, and indeed most IRA and retirement account owners, do not have a cohesive retirement plan. Instead, their *"plan"* has grown out of a series of individual, in-the-moment decisions that made sense at the time. But when analyzed, those unconnected decisions frequently threaten all the years of hard work and effort.

Consider two hypothetical professors: Professor Haphazard and Professor Planner.

Professor Haphazard's *"plan"* is the result of the in-the-moment-decisions made without a cohesive strategy. Professor Planner, on the other hand, has developed an integrated Financial Masterplan. The difference between their outcomes is significant, and it demonstrates the importance of having a comprehensive and coordinated financial retirement plan.

Professor Haphazard

When Professor Haphazard started working, he talked to someone in benefits to determine which retirement plan options were available and how and what to invest. When kids entered the picture, he and his spouse had an attorney draft wills and trusts and guardianship provisions for their children. They also met an insurance salesman and bought some life insurance to supplement what Professor Haphazard was receiving from his employer.

Down the line, they invested in stocks, bonds, and financial products outside of his retirement plan. They tried meeting with an investment advisor, but they never felt that the advisor gave them useful strategic advice or was always working in their best interest. They certainly never felt like they had a great plan in place.

At some point, the Haphazards hired a CPA. Though a competent tax preparer, their accountant did not offer proactive tax-saving strategies and advice.

They did invest in some Roth IRAs.

Each decision seemed to make sense at the time, but none of the decisions were part of an integrated plan. And so today, the sum of the parts does not add up to something greater than the whole. In fact, like a house built out of a heap of *Lego*™ *Bricks* and *Lincoln Logs*™, the parts don't fit together. The structure of the couple's retirement and estate plan is neither coherent nor solid.

Professor Haphazard's disconnected process fails to optimize his retirement and legacy plan. Worse, he has left their wealth vulnerable to massive tax liabilities both while they are alive and after they are gone in a post SECURE Act world. This is one of the risks of working with multiple providers who are not part of a team. Many providers and advisors are like a hammer and everyone they meet is a nail.

For instance, the life insurance agent wanted to sell them a large whole-life insurance product. The estate attorney tried to fit them into one of several standard pre-existing models for their estate planning, will, and trust. Their CPA was an excellent historian—accurately reporting their income and expenses from the prior year. But, like many CPAs, she did not provide them with meaningful tax strategies going forward. She certainly was not a tax strategist deeply familiar with retirement and estate planning for professors and TIAA participants.

One financial advisor tried to jam the Haphazards into one of several prefabricated portfolios. Another financial advisor was even worse: he tried to load them up with financial products that paid the advisor a fat commission.

They had multiple providers, multiple and often conflicting strategies, no integration, and no one with a deep knowledge of critical planning strategies when TIAA is one of the underlying assets. Adding insult to injury, some of the advisors *were not* fiduciaries—*fiduciaries must put your interests above their own*. Ultimately, they each talked to Professor Haphazard, but not to each other.

The consequences for Professor Haphazard and his spouse are confusion and stress about their financial security. Which retirement assets should they spend first—after-tax investments, pre-tax retirement plan money, or Roth investments? They are never sure how much money they can safely spend, so they don't travel to bucket-list destinations, and they end up depriving themselves of countless other small luxuries.

Furthermore, they don't really have a plan for the disposition of their money. What is the best estate plan for their situation? Worse, their estate is currently a sitting duck for a largely avoidable massive income tax acceleration due to the SECURE Act.

If this sounds familiar, join the crowd, but don't blame yourself. Up to now, you probably weren't aware that there was a better option. So, let's consider the alternative...

Professor Planner

Professor Planner and her husband took advantage of our *Retire Secure Consultation* and actually spoke with Jim Lange and one of his number-crunching CPAs who helped them devise a series of appropriate and advantageous financial strategies.

The couple assessed our full complement of services and became valued clients. They opted to work with Jim Lange, an investment advisor representative of a registered investment advisory firm, a licensed CPA, and an attorney (providing legal work, however, was not included or solicited). Although it was an option, they were not interested in becoming an assets-under-management (AUM) client, but they were interested in getting Jim's and his team's help in developing a personalized Financial Masterplan to get the most of their retirement assets.

Then, based on their priorities and long-term financial and life goals, they worked closely with the Lange team to develop their personalized Financial Masterplan. So, instead of a disorganized and scattered approach, every component of the Planners' wealth was integrated into a clear, strategic plan.

By implementing Lange Accounting Group's, customized retirement planning, tax strategies, and estate planning recommendations (no legal documents were drafted), she and her family were able to accomplish the following:

- She doubled her retirement contributions by taking advantage of a *"secret"* retirement plan available at her university that even the people in HR were unaware of (the 457 plan).

- She realized she had the option to retire at age 65 and be financially secure. Though she decided not to retire immediately, she did say *"I sure am not going to take any ___ from the chair anymore."* She knew she could happily walk away from university and departmental politics if they became extremely onerous in the post-COVID era.

- Now, every summer she and her husband take their children, their spouses, and all the grandchildren on an annual family vacation.

- Thanks to detailed financial projections, she knows how much she and her husband can spend annually, and which of her retirement assets she should tap into in sequence to minimize taxes.

- The projections gave them the confidence to purchase a second home to be near their daughter and grandchildren, knowing they could afford it.

- She has a plan for making a series of Roth IRA conversions, directly after she retires, that will save her family hundreds of thousands of dollars in taxes.

- Based on the family's situation, she decided to hold off taking Social Security until age 70.

- By developing a focused gifting plan, the couple can help their kids financially when they need it most. Timely financial help with housing, childrearing, and college planning for their grandchildren serves everyone better than living a frugal lifestyle without gifting and leaving a larger inheritance with a large tax bill after they die.

- Lange and his team's suggestions significantly improved their estate plan, and those recommendations were communicated to their estate attorney. Neither Lange nor his team drafted any estate planning documents like wills, trusts, or beneficiary designations.

So, how can YOU bridge the gap from haphazard planning to developing a personalized Financial Masterplan? Please read on.

An Easy Path to Financial Success for Professors: Get *The Lange Edge*

It All Starts with a Meeting with Me

The details of our consultation follow, but under current circumstances all qualified[1] prospective clients (professors, TIAA participants, or other IRA and retirement plan owners) will have an initial *Retire Secure Consultation* (without charge) with me, Jim Lange[2].

To be clear, you must qualify for an appointment with me. Our office will ask you to complete a questionnaire and provide a list of your assets. If you are married, subject to rare exceptions, both spouses must agree to attend the meeting.

After a preliminary review of your completed questionnaire and a review of your estate plan, if we don't think we can provide enormous value for you and your family, we will not meet. But we WILL send you some extremely useful resources free of charge.

If, however, I think we can help you and your family, I will bring to our meeting my expertise as a CPA and my knowledge of estate planning as a nearly 40-year veteran estate attorney[3] working with professors and TIAA participants.

I will also bring one of our number crunching CPAs to our meeting. I have held a countless number of these free consultations over the years, including people flying in from all over the country and no one has ever said or even hinted that it wasn't worth their time.

That said, as a courtesy to me and our team, if you know in advance of scheduling a meeting with me that you are not interested in working with us, we respectfully request that you do not sign up for a consultation.

At the end of our meeting, I will summarize our discussion and make valuable suggestions. If I don't think I can provide enormous value—certainly worth many times the investment in the Financial Masterplan—I will tell you and still provide you with the written summary. This summary in and of itself can provide enormous value.

If I think we would be a good fit to work together, and you would like to work with us, towards the end of the consultation, I will propose a plan of action.

I would like to emphasize that, at least at this point in time, your initial *Retire Secure Consultation* **is with me**—not a junior or even mid-level professional. You would literally be meeting with the guy who wrote the book on helping

---

1 Those interested in a one-time fee-for-services engagement to develop your family's Financial Masterplan (without adding an assets-under-management arrangement) should know that the fee for those engagements range from $12,500 to $22,500, depending on the complexity of the estate, but most engagements are running about $15,000.

2 We offer two meeting format options: in-person meetings at our offices located in Pittsburgh, Pennsylvania or virtual appointments via Zoom.

3 Although I will bring my knowledge and expertise in estate planning to this meeting, it will be conducted in my capacity as a financial planning professional and not as an attorney. There is no attorney/client relationship in this context. There is no solicitation for legal services being made by me, James Lange, nor by Lange Legal Group, LLC.

professors and TIAA participants maximize their retirement and estate plan (and eight other best-selling financial books for IRA owners). You would also be meeting with one of our experienced CPA number crunchers who also worked on the book. That number crunching CPA will be the person who does most of the work on your Financial Masterplan if we all agree this would be a valuable engagement for you and your family.

There are Two Paths to a Financial Masterplan

1. The first path is to engage Lange Accounting Group to develop your long-term Financial Masterplan on a one-time fee-for-service basis. Learn more about the Financial Masterplan in the Lange Accounting Group letter beginning on page 455.

2. The second path is to become an ongoing assets-under-management (AUM) client. If you choose to become an AUM client, a number crunching CPA at Lange Accounting Group will develop your long-term Financial Masterplan at no additional cost to you[4].

   You will also have the opportunity to have that plan reviewed and updated by our CPAs on an annual basis. The money management aspect of the AUM relationship is handled by one of our money management partners. Learn more about the AUM arrangement in the Lange Financial Group letter beginning on page 461.

   If you are interested in either service, the accompanying letters will provide you with the information to request a free initial consultation.

---

4 Financial Masterplans prepared by Lange Accounting Group, LLC for assets-under-management clients are completed in consideration for the portion of the client's account management fee that Lange Financial Group receives from the investment advisor and at no additional charge to the client.

Financial Security. For Life.

Working to Develop a Financial Masterplan Without Assets-Under-Management with Lange Accounting Group, LLC[5]

We offer a pure fee-for-service Financial Masterplan without the money management component. For a one-time professional services fee between $12,500 and $22,500 (most often $15,000) depending on the level of complexity (time dependent), I along with one of our number crunching CPAs can help you develop a Financial Masterplan without adding an AUM arrangement. In this model, you implement our recommendations and handle the investments without our ongoing support and continuing services.

We will likely make significant recommendations regarding your estate plan. Please note that if you engage Lange Accounting Group for our Financial Masterplan development services, you are not engaging us to be your attorney, nor do we act as your attorney, and there is no attorney/client relationship in this advisory context. If we make estate planning recommendations, we give you the option of sharing our recommendations with either your existing estate attorney, a different estate attorney, or one that we might recommend.

How We Work with You

First and foremost, we make sure your long-term financial, retirement, and legacy planning are totally on track. You will be working with a caring, smart, tax-savvy CPA, who will be very proactive in their advice; all our CPAs are fiduciaries who are required to act in your best interest. We will make sure you're not going to make costly tax mistakes. And we will provide you with tax-saving strategies and ideas you might never have considered.

---

5 Lange Accounting Group, LLC, offers guidance on retirement plan distribution strategies, tax reduction, Roth IRA conversions, saving and spending strategies, optimized Social Security strategies, and gifting plans. Although we bring our knowledge and expertise in estate planning into our recommendations, they are only offered in our capacity as financial planning professionals and not as attorneys. We will likely make recommendations, however, that clients could have a licensed estate attorney implement.

That's why it is crucial that you work with professionals who, like us, understand how to integrate traditional TIAA—with all TIAA's unique rules and investment characteristics—into the rest of your plan. We understand those needs.

Over the past three decades, we have developed and honed proven solutions to address the unique and particular needs of professors and TIAA participants with large retirement accumulations in TIAA and/or with other retirement plan providers. Serving those clients is what we do best.

"Running The Numbers" Provides Invaluable Information and Direction

One critical component of developing a Financial Masterplan is running the numbers. *"Running the numbers"* is our shorthand for testing a variety of strategies to see which will work best for you and your family.

Of course, we use a variety of specialized software programs, as well as our in-house tax preparation software, and even our special applications in Excel® to aid us in this analysis. But it is my expertise plus the expertise of our highly qualified number-crunching CPAs that really makes the difference.

My assessments and recommendations, based on your goals and circumstances, serve as the starting point, and then the ideas are tested and, frankly, challenged by our top-level CPAs who do the actual number-crunching. You are very much a part of the process, and you will give input, and get personalized guidance, from our CPAs who are analyzing and calculating the outcomes of different financial scenarios.

Together, we postulate multiple *"what if"* scenarios—involving tax projections, Roth IRA conversion planning (which more often than not involves a number of Roth conversions over a period of years), investment rates of return, Social Security, Medicare, and most importantly, your hopes and dreams for your retirement and your legacy planning.

We help you understand what you can afford to spend. It has been our experience that most professors end up accumulating more and more money, and then when they die, their children face massive tax consequences. This is especially true in the face of the SECURE Act and the potential for tax increases when and if the *"sunset provisions"* of the Tax Cut and Jobs Act of 2017 take effect in 2026, as well as other potential legislative tax increases in the future.

Our process is unique and performed by the Lange team of highly skilled CPAs, the same CPAs who helped with the quantitative analysis in this book. This process usually takes several meetings and much back and forth analysis.

While this may seem like a lot of information, be assured our initial discussion is followed by a summary memo from me to you, our number crunching CPA, and possibly your attorney.

"What If" Scenarios

When we run the numbers, a major component involves projecting scenarios for your financial future. During these sessions our experienced CPA, in conjunction with you and your spouse, quantify *what you have, what you and your family will have given the status quo using reasonable assumptions, and what you and your family could have* with different strategic steps that you could take under our guidance.

Since you are in the room—in person or virtually—when we do much of the work, you will know how and why we arrive at the recommendations we make for you. We typically start broadly, but eventually narrow the possibilities to a few choices. Typically, we identify our preferred solution, and provide you with our recommendations, calculations, and reasoning. Once we agree on a preferred course of action, we double check our work and recreate your tax return. By plugging in our best solutions, we can identify potential tax conflicts—perhaps due to Medicare Income-Related Monthly Adjustment (IRRMA) amounts—to give us additional information to make the wisest plan. Of course, the plan will reflect your goals and desires. Ultimately, the decision of what to do is yours.

How We Summarize Our Analysis for You

What we don't give you is 70 pages of computer-generated mumbo jumbo.

Our projections are clearly summarized. We outline which scenarios seem best for your situation and why. We also give you the spreadsheets to see how we arrived at our conclusions. Ultimately, you get to choose your path, but we are guiding you through the entire process and empower you to make great decisions.

As part of the Financial Masterplan development process, we will also review your estate plan and, when appropriate, make recommendations regarding updates or changes that could be made to optimize your plan[6]. Now we may find

---

6 Although we will bring our knowledge and expertise in estate planning to that review, it will be conducted in our capacity as your financial planning professionals. We will not be acting as your attorneys and there will not be an attorney/client relationship. However, we will likely make recommendations that you could have a licensed estate attorney implement. There is no solicitation for legal services being made by me, James Lange, nor by Lange Legal Group, LLC.

that the documents and plans you already have in place do the job. But frankly, that is rare. More often, they require vetting, changes, and updates—especially if your documents were prepared before January 1, 2020, the effective date of the SECURE Act. Our goal is to make sure your estate plan is continually optimized for your situation and consistent with the Financial Masterplan we develop and is appropriately executed.

To find out more, I urge you to respond now. The information is free. And there's no obligation.

Yes, Jim, I want to protect my TIAA, IRA, and other retirements accounts against the new SECURE Act and its accelerated taxation of my family's wealth.

In particular, I'm interested in a *Retire Secure for Professors and TIAA Participants* Initial Consultation for a Personalized Financial Masterplan that doesn't include assets-under-management.

Name _____

Address _____

City _____ State _____ Zip _____

Phone _____ Email _____

4 Easy Ways to Respond:

By Phone: Call toll-free **1-800-387-1129**.

By Fax: Fax this completed form to **412-521-2285**

Online: Visit **https://Faculty-Advisor.com/Consult**

By Mail: Erin Einwag
Lange Accounting Group, LLC
2200 Murray Avenue
Pittsburgh, PA 15217

LANGE FINANCIAL
GROUP LLC
Financial Security. For Life.

Put Your Financial Success on Autopilot as an Assets-Under-Management Client[7]

If, after our first meeting, you are interested in an assets-under-management (AUM) arrangement, you will have a second meeting with the number-crunching CPA who was in the first meeting, and our recommended money manager. Lange Financial Group does not manage money. We leave the money management to our strategic partners so they can do what they do best. But collectively, we need to agree that the working relationship is a good fit.

Becoming an assets-under-management client is often the best choice. Currently, the Financial Masterplan as described earlier in the Lange Accounting Group letter starting on page 455 is just one component of a package of services that recur annually[8]. The Financial Masterplan is included as part of the service our CPAs provide at no additional cost to you. You pay the money manager their normal fee and they pay us a portion of the fee you pay them.

With annual reviews, our CPAs can work with you to adjust your Financial

---

[7] Asset location, asset allocation and low-cost enhanced index funds are provided by the Lange Financial Group, LLC's investment firm partners. All services are offered in our role as an investment advisor representative and not as an attorney.

Lange Financial Group, LLC is a registered investment advisory firm registered with the Commonwealth of Pennsylvania Department of Banking, Harrisburg, Pennsylvania. In addition, the firm is registered as a registered investment advisory firm in the states of Arizona, Florida, New York, Ohio, Texas, and Virginia.

Lange Financial Group may not provide investment advisory services to any residents of states in which the firm does not maintain an investment advisory registration. This does not in any way imply that Lange Financial Group is failing to preserve its rights under the respective states' de minimis rule.

The presence of this book shall not in any direct or indirect fashion, be construed or interpreted to suggest that the firm is offering to sell or soliciting to provide investment advisory services to residents of any state or states in which the firm is not maintaining an investment advisory registration. Again, Lange Financial Group preserves all rights under each state's de minimis rule but wishes to emphasize that it is not directly or indirectly soliciting investment advisory clients in states where it has no legal right to do so.

All investing involves risk, including the potential for loss of principal. There is never any guarantee extended that any investment plan or strategy will be successful.

[8] Financial Masterplans prepared by Lange Accounting Group, LLC for assets-under-management clients are completed in consideration for the portion of the client's account management fee that Lange Financial Group receives from the investment advisor and at no additional charge to the client.

Masterplan to account for any of your financial and life changes as well as any tax law changes that may have an impact on your plan.

By becoming an AUM client, you get the Financial Masterplan described above as the starting point. Then, at a minimum, our office, typically the CPA who did the work on the Masterplan, provides an annual review; you will potentially have more frequent reviews with the money management firm.

We work closely with an elite group of top investment advisory firms that bring the same kind of dedication and concentration to their field as we do to ours. Our strategic partners follow a core investment philosophy rooted in the findings of Modern Portfolio Theory. That theory says that the best way to manage risk in an investment portfolio is through proper diversification within a broader asset allocation strategy.

Our partners follow an academic approach to money management that is rooted in the best academic thinking, and they will work closely with you to understand your financial goals and risk tolerance which will be used to develop an asset allocation designed to generate long-term returns that allow you to achieve your financial goals. As mentioned above, we leave the money management to our strategic partners so they can do what they do best.

As part of our AUM service, we help get the different components of your plan in order, and your assets are continually evaluated for asset allocation and asset location by the investment advisory firm.

You'll meet, usually virtually, with the money management firm's team, usually more often than once a year. At those meetings, you and your money manager will review portfolio asset allocation and investment strategies and track whether you are still on course to meet your financial goals.

Importantly, our investment partners do much more than simply manage the money. They have their own processes that support effective planning to help you reach your financial, retirement, and life goals. Yes, there is some redundancy between what they do and what we do, but, again, that is a good thing—a valuable *"second opinion."*

Please note that if you engage Lange Financial Group for our assets-under-management arrangement there is no attorney/client relationship in this advisory context.

To find out more, I urge you to respond now. The information is free. And there's no obligation.

Yes, **Jim**, I want to protect my TIAA, IRA, and other retirements accounts against the new SECURE Act and its accelerated taxation of my family's wealth.

In particular, I'm interested in a **Retire Secure for Professors and TIAA Participants** Initial Consultation that includes assets-under-management*.

Name _____

Address _____

City _____ State _____ Zip _____

Phone _____ Email _____

4 Easy Ways to Respond:

By Phone: Call toll-free **1-800-387-1129**.

By Fax: Fax this completed form to **412-521-2285**

Online: Visit **https://PayTaxesLater.com/Consult**

By Mail: Erin Einwag
Lange Financial Group, LLC
2200 Murray Avenue
Pittsburgh, PA 15217

* To qualify for this free consultation, which is now held by phone, through a virtual meeting, or in person, you must have $1 million or more in investible assets that you would consider placing under management with Lange Financial Group, LLC—assuming you like our retirement planning and tax-saving strategies as well as our money manager's process and investment options.

Although we will bring our knowledge and expertise in estate planning to this meeting, it will be conducted in our capacity as financial planning professionals and not as attorneys.

If you engage Lange Financial Group, LLC for our assets-under-management arrangement, there is no attorney/client relationship in this advisory context. There is no solicitation for legal services being made by me, James Lange, nor by Lange Financial Group, LLC.

For People Who Don't Want to Pack
Their Own Parachute...

What's the Advantage of Working with Us?

When you work with us, you benefit from the *integrated* experience of our world-class financial professionals—all of whom have different but complementary expertise.

You also benefit significantly, albeit indirectly, from the combined wisdom of all our clients, many of whom are colleagues of yours in the world of academia and TIAA. I think it is safe to say that we are privileged to provide services to some of the brightest minds in the country. They ask good questions and push us to provide the most comprehensive answers.

Please note, as we go to press, the services described in this section are currently available and I personally lead all initial consultations. That said, we are optimistic we will experience significant growth in the future, and we are still a small firm, so this is all subject to change should circumstances change.

If You Choose the Assets-Under-Management (AUM) Partnership

CPAs at Lange Accounting Group develop the Financial Masterplans. Our asset management affiliates manage the money. And with the right hand knowing what the left hand is doing, the Lange team develops a comprehensive retirement and estate plan[9]. Together we help you implement your customized Financial Masterplan.

But all good plans need to be modified and adjusted due to changing circumstances. Each annual Financial Masterplan re-evaluation gives you the opportunity to make accommodations for financial or life changes—portfolios increase and decrease because markets turn bullish or bearish, tax laws change, companies you own in your portfolio take a downturn, children marry, grandchildren are born, divorces happen, inheritances, marriages, deaths, etc.

When you choose an AUM partnership with Lange Financial Group and our premiere money management services, you get the benefit of our peer reviewed

---

[9] Please note that if you engage Lange Accounting Group, LLC for our Financial Masterplan service or receive Financial Masterplan services as part of our assets-under-management arrangement, there is no attorney/client relationship in this advisory context. These services are provided by Lange Accounting Group employees in their capacity as CPAs. There is no solicitation for legal services being made by me, James Lange, nor by Lange Financial Group, LLC.

retirement and estate planning strategies on an ongoing basis all for *one* rea-sonable fee—a fee comparable to what you would pay elsewhere for money man-agement services alone.

All you need to do is show up for the annual reviews—we take care of the de-tails, and then bring you totally up to date. One of my current clients remarked, *"I can't even calculate how many hours of anxiety and frustration I haven't expe-rienced because of Lange."*

In essence, you are getting what we think are the best retirement, estate, tax planning, and money management strategies available anywhere. It's all about helping you save more, have more, and leave more. That doesn't even include what for some is the biggest benefit of working with us—saving time and gain-ing peace of mind.

I should mention that there are professors and TIAA participants who we are not interested in working with. Granted there are financial and fee minimums and/or potential clients for whom we don't think we could provide enormous value. But there are also non-financial factors that are deal breakers. If you are abrasive and difficult with financial professionals, please look elsewhere. If you are in the middle of a nasty divorce, we aren't a good fit for you. If you anticipate a big fight about money among your children either while you are alive or after you are gone, we are also not the right fit for you.

The Next Step: Take Action Now

We have put our hearts, souls, and decades of accumulated financial and re-tirement planning knowledge into this book. I trust you will find it an informa-tive and valuable resource.

Most importantly, I hope reading the book will motivate you to take action. I embrace an active definition of learning: *learning leads to a change in behavior* through experience, instruction, or study.

So, by that definition, if you find the information in this book interesting, but don't take any action, then you don't get full value from the ideas and concepts. It's only when you implement these retirement strategies *and* take action—especially when it comes to your family's long-term security—that you will have accomplished what you need to be financially secure for life.

So, what's the next step? If you think we would be a good fit to work together, I urge you to take advantage of the initial *Retire Secure Consultation*—which at this point is still with me, James Lange, personally—by responding in one of the ways indicated on the forms within the letters above. You will be glad you did.

For contact information, if you are interested in:[10]

- Assets-under-management *(including a personalized Financial Master-plan)*, refer to the Lange Financial Group letter above.

- The Financial Masterplan without assets-under-management, refer to the Lange Accounting Group letter above no matter where you live.

Finally, let me end by repeating a quote from John Bogle, founder and former CEO of Vanguard. He was on my former radio show twice before he passed away. At the end of the first show, I asked him if he had any other advice that he didn't cover during the radio show. Here is part of his response:

"The financial advisor is very valuable for the things that we don't much think about—like asset allocation, Roth IRAs, and Roth conversions. The system is loaded with nuances. Estate planning is a whole other complexity. So, with this complex world, I think most people need some kind of help."

Sincerely,

James Lange
CPA/Attorney

---

[10] Lange Accounting Group offers guidance on retirement plan distribution strategies, tax reduction, Roth IRA conversions, saving and spending strategies, optimized Social Security strategies, and gifting plans. Although we bring our knowledge and expertise in estate planning to our recommendations, all recommendations are offered in our capacity as financial planning professionals and not as attorneys. We will, however, potentially make recommendations that clients could have a licensed estate attorney implement.

Asset location, asset allocation, and low-cost enhanced index funds are provided by the Lange Financial Group, LLC's investment firm partners. This referral is offered in our role as an investment advisor representative and not as an attorney.

In our role for each of these instances, we will not be acting as the clients' attorney and there will not be an attorney/client relationship. There is no solicitation being made for legal services by me, James Lange, nor by Lange Legal Group, LLC.

Lange Financial Group, LLC is a registered investment advisory firm registered with the Commonwealth of Pennsylvania Department of Banking, Harrisburg, Pennsylvania. In addition, the firm is registered as a registered investment advisory firm in the states of Arizona, Florida, New York, Ohio, Texas, and Virginia.

Lange Financial Group may not provide investment advisory services to any residents of states in which the firm does not maintain an investment advisory registration. This does not in any way imply that Lange Financial Group is failing to preserve its rights under the respective states' de minimis rule.

The presence of this book shall not in any direct or indirect fashion, be construed or interpreted to suggest that the firm is offering to sell or soliciting to provide investment advisory services to residents of any state or states in which the firm is not maintaining an investment advisory registration. Again, Lange Financial Group preserves all rights under each state's de minimis rule, but wishes to emphasize that it is not directly or indirectly soliciting investment advisory clients in states where it has no legal right to do so.

All investing involves risk, including the potential for loss of principal. There is never any guarantee extended that any investment plan or strategy will be successful.

About the Author

James Lange, CPA, Attorney, and registered investment advisor is the author of eight best-selling financial books that help protect IRA and retirement plan owners and their families.

Jim has been quoted 36 times in *The Wall Street Journal*.

Jim's mother and brother were college professors. He has 632 college professors as clients. Many have been with Jim since he started working with professors more than 35 years ago.

Jim is passionate about protecting the financial security of his professor clients and readers and their families. This book is a result of that passion.

Jim is a well known Roth IRA expert, having written the first peer-reviewed article on Roth IRAs, as well as a dedicated book on Roth IRA conversions. Jim also developed Lange's Cascading Beneficiary Plan (LCBP)™*, an estate plan that provides the maximum flexibility for most married IRA, TIAA participants and other retirement plan owners. His office has administered hundreds of estates whose families have benefitted from these plans.

Jim is truly passionate about helping people. For example, he purchased and distributed 50,000 KN-95 masks to charity and non-profits, family, friends, clients, and employees.

Jim lives in Pittsburgh, in the home he grew up in, with his wife of 29 years, Cindy, who has a master's degree in electrical engineering from Carnegie Mellon University. When Jim is not devising strategies for clients and readers to save taxes and preserve wealth (which is most of the time), he enjoys bicycling, hiking, and traveling with his family and friends. He also plays chess and bridge both online and with friends.

* Lange's Cascading Beneficiary Plan™ is a proprietary trademark of James Lange.

Notes:

Notes: